THE KROTONA SERIES, VOLUME VI
1932—1940

Krishnamurti's Departure from
the Theosophical Society

Joseph E. Ross

The Krotona Series, Volume 6, 1932-1940: Krishnamurti's Departure from the Theosophical Society.

© 2012 Joseph E. Ross
All rights reserved. No part of this book may be reproduced or transmitted in any form or by any means, electronic or mechanical, including photocopying, recording, or by any information storage and retrieval system, except brief quotations in reviews, without permission in writing from the copyright owner.

Unless otherwise credited, illustrations or photos are from the author's archives, and are under copyright protection.

First Edition, 2012

Library of Congress Catalogue in publication data
Ross, Joseph E., 1943-
Krotona, Theosophy, & Krishnamurti, 1932-1940: Archival Documents of the Theosophical Society's Esoteric Center, Krotona, in Ojai, California.
Volume VI of the Krotona Series.

ISBN: 978-0-925943-01-9

1. Ojai Region (Califo.)-History. 2. Theosophical Society-History

Cover photo by Sherrill Schell: Author's collection
KFA © release for post 1933 talks used

www.krotonaarchives.com

Table of Contents

Author's Preface i

Acknowledgements v

Foreword vii

Introduction ix

Chapter 1: 1932 1

Chapter 2: 1933 65

Chapter 3: 1934 157

Chapter 4: 1935 203

Chapter 5: 1936 237

Chapter 6: 1937 271

Chapter 7: 1938 279

Chapter 8: 1939 295

Chapter 9: 1940 311

Author's Preface

This is the last book on the history of the Krotona Institute and its relationship to the Theosophical Society. The author wants to say though that he is no longer a member of the Theosophical Society, nor a member of the Esoteric School. The eight volumes written on the activities within the Krotona Institute and the Theosophical Society are published because Shrimati Rukmini Devi suggested it was the author's duty to write the books for all those interested in the Theosophical Movement. The books are not a publication of propaganda, but a means of protecting new members from inaccuracies which they have not the wherewithal to gauge. It is not fair even to the members of any organization that they should be flooded with inaccurate statements calculated to prejudice the history of the Krotona Institute or the Theosophical Society. Radha Burnier wrote the author in September 1966 that, "Those who have put private material in the public domain have broken obligations, but it is their Karma." It is the first requisite of the historian to heal ignorance. Let each reader think for themselves, and use their own intuition if what is written here should be for privileged members only. Each individual should make up his or her own mind. The documents provided the author not only with much indispensable information, but with something even more precious—a mirror. How many lessons are to be learnt from them! Whether right or wrong, wise or otherwise, one day all the facts will come out.

We quote the Outer Head, C. Jinarajadasa of the Esoteric Section during the 1930's: "*Furthermore, The Society's work does not now require the secrecy concerning its teachings which was considered advisable in its early years.*" It is very interesting, if one would really read the Three Objects of the Theosophical Society to discover that it does not mention "teachings" in the Objects, but does mention study and investigation.

Readers who have followed this chronicle of the Krotona Institute with sidelines on the history of the Theosophical Society will have noted that we have concerned ourselves with the records left by the writers as tangible proof; and as with many other subjects mentioned, which may, at first sight, seem out of place in this volume, these records are necessary in truth to promote interest and to provoke enquiry. Incidents here and there are given, which, though of little seeming significance at the moment, can, when followed, be found to lead to important results.

The most delicate and human of all the branches of the art of writing has been relegated to the journeymen of letters; we do not reflect that it is perhaps as difficult to write a good life as to live one.

The spirit of dispassion and impartiality has in all cases been striven for, and the pros and cons of any major event given as fairly as may be without ulterior intentions. Here and there details have been allowed, which, more truly than any comment or argument, showed the value of a situation. History is made up solely of persons, their ideas, their actions, and how these impress others and influence and direct their lives. Therefore the actors, as they come and go—or stay, finding their life's work in the Theosophical Society—have been allowed to express themselves, and the results are shown in the activities and development of The Society, and the reaction of the world to The Society.

It was necessary to give some attention from the historical point of view that human beings are too important to be treated as mere symptoms of the past. They have a value which is independent of any temporal processes—which is eternal, and must be felt for its own sake. Let us observe and watch the temperaments and outlooks of the characters on the stage as they make the history of the Krotona Institute.

It is with confidence, therefore, that this history is presented, in the hope that it will give insight into a great movement which cannot be measured by statistics, which has profoundly affected thought for the past 146 years, and will evidently go on doing so in the years to come. The Krotona Institute is a living tree, putting forth new branches and new leaves.

The history of the Krotona Institute is unknown to the masses. It is a veiled mystery even to the learned—because they have never had the key to a right understanding of the abundant hints thrown out by the Esoteric School or the ancient classics.

To accomplish the proposed task, the writer has had to resort to the rather unusual means of dividing and jumping into different parts of it, even though the material is written in chronological order. This may, at first sight, seem out of place in this volume, but although fragmentary, it is the consecutive history of the Krotona Institute. This is necessary in truth. The public, even its own members, have heard but one side of the history. Whether the rest of its history will ever be written or published will depend on the interest of a future scholar.

We could hardly end on a more resounding note than that struck by Josephine Ransom herself. "I would recommend the reader of this history not to be too concerned with success and failure as they come and go, but to watch the steady fulfilment of a purpose no matter what the obstacles."

Acknowledgements

The author extends his deepest gratitude to all the many writers of the letters, documents and diaries left as a record of the history of the Krotona Institute and the Theosophical Society. My special thanks to the staff of the Krishnamurti Foundation of America Archives for being exceedingly helpful in giving me access to their archives, and permission to reproduce documents for this volume. I wish to repeat my thanks to the many helpful and tolerant friends of the Theosophical Society, especially in the headquarters at Wheaton, Illinois, and people all over the world who have helped me, through the contribution of information, interviews, letters, documents, photographs and criticism, to arrive at as complete a portrayal of this organization, who did not know the characters personally.

Special mention must also be made of R. E. Mark Lee's remarkable patience, his counsel and valuable expertise in suggestions for structural changes, and especially for the Foreword. This project would not have proceeded without his friendship, and his enduring encouragement towards the completion of the final version. Words will never convey the debt of the author's gratitude.

Appreciation to Robert Boyd who carefully pointed out numerous mistakes and made excellent suggestions getting facts straight regarding the history of the Theosophical Society.

It's quite extraordinary to have a dear friend, who is not only skillful in speaking Spanish, but who in the spirit of an enduring friendship took her busy time to translate many of the 1935 letters: my deep appreciation to Linda Lambert.

On a personal note I would like to thank Michael Lommel, to whom I owe thanks for responding so sensitively to the task of designing the last two volumes, and assisting me in the final preparation of the photos.

Throughout the documentation, please be advised that the letters and memos form a narrative, broken by "transitions bars" which are really inserted miscellanea!

Pencil sketch by B.A. Ross
A.P. Warrington

Foreword

As a whole, the Biblical gospels are no more than the contents, as a whole, of *The Krotona Series, Volume 6, 1932-1940: Krishnamurti's Departure from the Theosophical Society*. The writings and facsimiles in this volume are of a religious nature because they are dedicated to and inspired by the truths of the Theosophical movement. They show no artifice and, particularly those of the principals of the Society, speak of Truth-seeking and devotion to the highest principles of life.

A more certain way to ensure that historians do not eschew facts when a chronicle of events is told or written is to preserve and protect by publication the second tier of eyewitness accounts, original documents, and personal letters of the era and particularly those that originate by the hand of intimates and associates of the principals.

The fact that Krishnamurti disavowed the very community that gave him his first voice points to a high natural law he espoused: namely, that truth is not personified, it is impersonal. Truth is blind; it is both absolute and relative, and most importantly, truth is essentially what is religious. This volume gives full and ample testimony of this.

Krishnamurti's great act of leaving the Theosophical Society was seriously misunderstood. It engendered myths alive today and that will likely engage scholars for a thousand years. In fact he began to question and challenge with courage established Society beliefs as early as 1918. What started as doubt and questioning the Society quickly expanded and included all of humankind's organized and established beliefs. This continued to the end of his life in 1986. What documents in this book prove is that questioning and doubt were encouraged by the Society itself to some extent, and that some of Krishnamurti's mature teachings can trace their origin to living insights he had from his discovery in 1910 to the formal end of his association with the Society in the late 1930s.

It is undeniable that the Theosophical Society saved Krishnamurti's life, that it prepared and nurtured his religious mind, and that it conditioned him as a modern man for a mission to serve humanity. What is deniable, and is the subject of this book, is that Krishnamurti destroyed the Society; that Krishnamurti was the World-Teacher as the Society defined the role; and that Krishnamurti was a "biological freak."

The documents are arranged chronologically and encompass the esoteric to the mundane. There are inevitable gaps in the chronology as it unfolds because the documents came from so many diverse and disconnected sources. As there is no oeuvre of Theosophical Society history world-wide or in America except for the several volumes that comprise the Krotona history in California by Joseph Ross, the reader has no other source to refer to that could provide the larger framework that would make sense of the history of the Society, of Krotona as the Esoteric center, and of Krishnamurti's association with the Society.[1]

Ross does not even suggest his sixth and last volume is a definitive history of Krotona. But readers and scholars will feel a deep connection with the Society and Krotona as the true back story of Krishnamurti's disconnect with the Society simply and humanly unfolds. The story itself dissolves blame, with the plain unadorned truth.

R.E.Mark Lee
Trustee, Krishnamurti Foundation India, Krishnamurti Foundation of America

---

[1]Ross, Joseph, *Krotona of Old Hollywood 1866-1913 Volume I. Krotona of Old Hollywood 1914-1920 Volume II. Krotona: The New Krotona from Hollywood to Ojai 1921-1922 Volume III. Krotona: Krotona in the Ojai Valley 1923-1926 Volume IV.*

Introduction: J. Krishnamurti's Relationship to The Thesosophical Society and his Departure

It is important to remember that the Krotona Institute is an Esoteric Center, and that it has no official connection with the Theosophical Society. When the Esoteric Section was first organized by H.P. Blavatsky, it was known as a section of the Theosophical Society, but Blavatsky saw that the perfect freedom and public character of the Society might be interfered with it, she broke the connection with The Society. What is written within the following pages should be read with care as the written words may contain several meanings.

There is no such thing as occult obedience as it is usually taught by the current occult schools. In the early days of the E.S., and the E.R., the Master or Teacher exacted from His disciple that implicit obedience which actually made the Teacher responsible and placed upon His shoulders the destiny of the disciple. The intellectual principle in the individual is now too much developed to warrant this type of expectancy. This condition no longer holds good today. Therefore, there is no teacher, and no disciple, the individual is the teacher and disciple. The Teacher is responsible for the offering of opportunity and for the right enunciation of the truth but for no more than that. In these more enlightened days, no such position is assumed by the Teacher as in the past. It is necessary to change the old ways of habit and conditioning, dropping the old methods in a new experiment. Today, knowledge is widespread and many people are already thinking for themselves.

It was back in February, 11, 1931, while C. Jinarajadasa was absent at Ootacamund in the hills of India, that the O.H. Dr. Besant called Bishop Leadbeater and Bishop Arundale to her and spoke about the E.S. The following is only a paragraph from the letter written to C. Jinarajadasa from Bishop Leadbeater on what she had to say regarding the E.S.

"She says that the Inner Head (Master M.) finds it inefficient in its present condition, and wants it made far more real and living, restored, in fact, to something like what it was before the suspension, though perhaps simplified. She reiterates that it is the heart of the Society, and says that unless that heart beats forcefully and regularly, the outer Society cannot function properly. It needs reconstruction, and people who are too fossilized to adopt the wider outlook must be put aside. She does not care how few the members are, but they must be in real earnest, devoted to the service of the Masters, and willing to work cordially with their brethren for Him. She spoke of you in connection with it, saying that we four—she, you, I and George—would make a nucleus and set an example, and so by degrees vivify the whole body again."

C. Jinarajadasa certainly felt that they still have in the E.S. many whose place is not yet in an occult body pledged to the uttermost to the service of the Masters. Since the O.H. has spoken so definitely in the above paragraph, he would now narrow the entrance gateway, so that only real workers come into the E.S. The rule as to the opportunity to join the E.S. after two years' membership in the Society is henceforth changed to three years' membership. In conclusion, C. Jinarajadasa wants more than a mere idealist wanting to do good work to join the E.S., but is in fact one who seeks to tread the Path of Holiness to serve the world as a disciple of the Great Ones.

We have to take into account the statement made by Krishnamurti back in 1928:

I could not have said last year, as I can say now, that I am the Teacher; for had I said it then it would have been insincere, it would have been untrue. Because I had not then united the Source and the Goal, I was not able to say that I was the Teacher. But now I can say it. I have become one with the Beloved, I have been made simple, I have become glorified because of Him, and because of Him I can help. My purpose is not to create discussions on authority, on manifestations in the personality of Krishnamurti, but to give the waters that shall wash away your sorrows, your petty tyrannies, your limitations, so that you will eventually join that ocean where there is no limitation, where there is the Beloved.[2]

C. Jinarajadasa makes a comment that it has appeared to him that the E.S., and through it the Theosophical Society, has to now take up the work which the Star dropped back in 1930. He mentioned that the idea of the Lord Vaivasvata[3] some years ago was that the Star should emphasize citizenship, in the widest sense of the term, and stand for the ideals of the Sixth Subrace. Since Krishnamurti closed the Star, one can see how complicated it can get when only sentences or paragraphs are given referring to another aspect of the work. Such as the one above. One would have to have access to all of the E.S. material to discover what was meant by the idea of the Lord Vaivasvata. There were so many pamphlets, single sheets, and small booklets written during the early years for E.S. members regarding the inner workings of the Esoteric School.

It is also the primary intent of this book to show Krishnamurti's relationship to the Theosophical Society, and his departure. It will contain unpublished thoughts of his we thought would be of interest to include, and those that are published found in the answers he gave to several questions posed to him while he was in Adyar in 1933, and 1934, since we believe that they still apply today.

In order to leave the field clear for Krishnamurti in his priceless work, Dr. Besant suspended the E.S. for a short period. But the Theosophical Society suffered from that, so she reopened it in the 1930's with a revived form of the Raja Yoga Discipline. C. Jinarajadasa writes his point of view of the various aspects of Krishnamurti as the World-Teacher for the students of the Esoteric School.

---

[2]Krishnamurti, J., *The Star*, "Selections from Krishnaji's Writings", Vol.I., n7, July 1928, p.23.
[3]According to the *Theosophical Glossary* He is the present Manu, literally Father of the Aryan Race.

Krishnaji

With the reopening of the E.S., a certain number of old members have not cared to reenter it, as they have considered that an acceptance of Krishnaji's teaching is incompatible with membership in the E.S. Exactly the reverse; others have not reentered (though these are only a few) because they cannot subscribe to the clause that Krishnaji is "the vehicle of the World-Teacher." One of the Corresponding Secretaries in India has reported to me as follows: "Some people remained out because they could not conscientiously accept Krishnaji as the World-Teacher. They cannot understand why the World-Teacher should denounce the T.S. and E.S. so much, since they have been established in accordance with His wishes, They could not therefore accept the new conditions and remained out."

Since Krishnaji himself is also averse to any occult claim concerning himself, and particularly emphasises that no one must quote him as an authority, some have wondered why a recognition of him as the vehicle of the World-Teacher should be made a requisite for entry into the E.S.

It is not for me to solve the difficulties of members on this matter. All I can do is to *state* the problem in its various aspects, begging members to think clearly and not confusedly. To any one really in earnest about truth, the existence of contradictions is not a sign that the problem is hopeless and not worth further attention. Nearly every step forward into the domain of truth has been by the clash of contrasted views.

1. The O.H. knows that Krishnaji bears a very special relation to the Lord Maitreya, the Head of the Second Ray. She states this relation in the phrase, "the vehicle of the World-Teacher." As the E.S. is an instrument in the hands of the Great Hierarchy, the E.S. must be in no doubt concerning the work which the World-Teacher has done through Krishnaji.

2. The relation between the vehicle and the World-Teacher is one that we cannot understand. The Lord has not revealed to us how He proposes to do His work; nor has He revealed to us *all* the parts of His plans. He has revealed *some*, in the instructions already given through the O.H. in the past. But it is obvious that to Him, as He

is carrying out His plans, there are no conflicting purposes. We must therefore, however confusing it all appears to us, go upon the working hypothesis that all the seeming contradictions are parts of one harmonious whole. Therefore, because the problem is difficult for us to understand, the O.H. while asking assent to the statement that Krishnaji is the vehicle of the World-Teacher, is emphatically against any enquiry as to how much or how little an E.S. member accepts Krishnaji as the mouthpiece of the Lord. Whether on some occasions it is the Lord speaking, on other occasions it is only Krishnaji, all such problems are not problems for the E.S. as a whole. Each member is given perfect freedom what to think on this matter, with the proviso obviously that he must not try to impose his convictions on others.

3. All E.S. members must make a point of *trying* to understand the drift of the message given through Krishnaji. Any great message intended to help the world must surely have some illumination for every soul. As Bro. C.W. Leadbeater has said again and again: "Do not, particularly when listening to Krishnaji speaking, allow the response of your mind to be arrested by something which you cannot understand, which you cannot fit into what you already know. Put aside for the time what confuses you. Accept what you can, and leave the rest aside. Do not allow the objections of your mind to be a barrier to the *outpouring of the Life* which the World-Teacher is pouring through Krishnaji."

4. To all of us who have accepted Theosophy, no one teaching at any given epoch is the whole truth. Hinduism gives truth, proclaiming Samskâras or sacraments, with rituals and priest, and bases itself on the existence of God; Buddhism completely ignores a Creator and is consistently against all ceremonies. Are these two teachings contradictions? Obviously they are, if contrasted. But the Theosophist does not contrast them; he tries to see them as *Complementaries*. The lofty "non-dual" teachings of Advaita Vedânta of Shri Shankaràchàrya, with their tendency to starve out all love towards a Creator, are repellent to the devout Bhakta follower of the "modified dual" teachings of Vishishtàdvaita Vedânta of Shri Râmânujàchàrya, with his teaching of devotion to God. How far rituals are helpful, or necessary, or the reverse, is one of the problems which Hindu philosophers have long discussed. There could be no greater contradiction than between some of the teachings of the Lord Buddha, the World-Teacher of the last Dispensation, and the

teachings of Shri Krishna and the Christ, the World-Teacher of this Dispensation. Yet in the light of the truths which Occultism reveals, the student learns to harmonise them. This attitude of ours in the past should be our attitude today. We shall not deny that contradictions exist; but we shall know that they can be harmonised when we shall possess a larger knowledge.

5. In the meantime, the E.S. is not a group of seekers of truth who are to think alike, but a group of workers to lessen the misery of the world, under the leadership of the Masters,. Intellectual problems, however confusing or painful, should not be allowed to make our hands idle in the doing of good work. If a member thinks he can do better work outside the E.S. than within it, he should leave at once, and go on his way rejoicing. And all E.S. members who for various reasons feel that the E.S. is their best channel of service to the world should listen to Krishnaji in order to learn if perchance there may not be ways of making their service more fruitful still of good to the world.

6. Krishnaji has spoken no more against the E.S. and the T.S. as organizations than against any other bodies. He is impersonally pointing out the dangers in all organizations towards subservience and towards the crushing out of individual judgment and effort. One need only glance at rigid and crystallized organizations like the Roman Catholic Church and the Brahmanical priesthood in India to realise how they do terrorize the individual, crushing his freedom of thought and action, molding him to a pattern. There are advantages and disadvantages in organizations. Krishnaji is emphasising the latter. Those of us who have decided to remain in the E.S. and in the outer Society must protect ourselves against any defects in them as organizations while utilizing to the full their advantages in living our lives of service.

7. In the first pamphlet given to the candidate in the E.S., *Order of Hearers*, the O.H. stated long ago: "The methods of seeking differ in each [Discipline], but the end and object of each is the same—the realisation of the INNER GOD. This is the true Wisdom, the true Gnosis; it is the direct knowledge of the ETERNAL, by the unveiling of our own eternal nature, and that man can thus know is the essence of Theosophy."

Has anything which Krishnaji has so far said been contrary to this proclamation by the O.H. of what is the nature of the E.S. or what is meant by Theosophy? Is not all that he has said an amplification of what every E.S. member is supposed to realise for himself? C.J.[4]

Published in June 1932 for use in the Esoteric School only, we publish these private papers called *Shishya*[5], (this address, which exists in a French manuscript, has not been revised or corrected by Krishnaji. In the stenographic copy there are certain gaps which have not been filled in, and certain phrases are not clear in the report.) —C.J.

Mr. Krishnamurti rose and said:

I beg you to listen to me with patience because I shall attempt to speak in French; but if I do not succeed I shall ask Monsieur Demarquette to be kind enough to translate me. I shall tell you in the beginning that Mrs. Besant and Mr. Leadbeater have often said and in forcible terms that the School is the soul and the heart of the Theosophical Society.

Now I am so convinced of that idea that I should like you to analyse and examine it in order to understand it profoundly and seriously. This is the place for self-preparation; it is here that we should prepare ourselves for the mature work in the outer world and in the inner world.

It is here that we must attain to the goal whence we are able to see the little things that are around us which make us suffer, or in order to understand them it is necessary to have an objective attitude.

Now, in order to acquire this objective attitude, it is not necessary, to my way of thinking, to always remain or think in the same order of ideas; it is necessary to get away from them. We have created religious and Theosophical grooves of every kind; it is necessary to get away from such narrowness, to rise, if you can do it—but it is very difficult—to rise as on to a high mountain whence you can see

---

[4]Jinarajadasa, C., *Shishya*,"Krishnaji" Vol.I, n2, September 1931, pp.27-31.
[5]A Sanskrit word meaning "disciple".

what is passing below you. You will then see that they are altogether insignificant.

Now we are like children. We place our hands on our eyes and ask where is the sun. The sun exists on all sides; it is necessary to feel the sun with our souls, not with our words. It is easy to feel it—this goal—with our words, but it is difficult to attain it. I should therefore like that the School should be completely different, altogether worthy, if I may so say, so to be an instrument of spirituality.

For this School is a spiritual instrument. It is here that the Masters—if we believe in the Masters—can work. Firstly, it is necessary to believe profoundly in the Masters—not in sentimental Masters, not in imaginary Masters, for such Masters do not exist; but the real Masters exist, who can help the world which is suffering and which is in misery under the weight of . . . .

Consecrate yourself to the Master. For that, it is necessary to be a man in the physical sense . . . It is for this reason, I think, that this School was founded by Mme. Blavatsky. That was some 40 years ago nearly. Naturally we have created a road for Theosophists along which only Theosophists have gone. It is we who have created this way. We think that only we can walk along this way. I believe that you are wrong in making this School very narrow. It ought to be at once broad, it should have high views, and put our ideals so high that the whole world can come. That is the way in which we can help the world. It is for us to relieve a little the suffering. . . .

But to do that—please believe that I am very serious—it is necessary to prepare oneself—not by courses of lectures, not by books, not by words, that is quite easy and that is what the politicians do, but at bottom they are selfish, or they do not possess ideas great enough to help the world, no matter what nation, race or religion it may be.

It is for us to be this instrument. To become that, we must have the sacred fire, enthusiasm; we must have clear vision. Each one of us has something of it, I see that, I am quite sure of it, but we are afraid of being . . . The goal is so strong and powerful that it becomes somewhat blinding, and so we put as our goal other things in order to understand it better. So we create wants, we forget the true God Who is in the whole world. It is there that God exists. He does not exist in Tibet, that is to say, He exists there but He exists in the whole world, in you and in the worst person who may be in the world. For this God there is no race, there is no religion, no class.

We must become this God. We must become this Lord Who will soon give hope to the world. Above all, we must be full of compassion for the world, even for the Germans, I mean, I beg you not to accuse me of being too German, Hindu or French. For myself I desire to be very international. Do not charge me with being a Bolshevik. It is the fault of the whole world to say: "If you are not fully ... you are a black soul."

I beg you to believe very seriously that this School ought to become something towards which the whole world will come; something that can mitigate the sufferings which the whole world has. You have that suffering, and the whole world has that suffering. It is for you to relieve it. From the beginning you must have the attitude of a God. You can be a God, the whole world can be a God, and once you have aquired this attitude all evil is unreal. Also I ask you to create a School such that a God can be proud of it. I shall say very frankly and very kindly that this School is not what the Masters wish—the Masters in you. You can see, if you examine it, all that in yourself, perhaps: "for yourself" is the meaning and for that once again it is necessary to attain the goal.

I should like you today to go from here with the sacred fire lit in you, in order that tomorrow you can be men and women of such a sort that the whole world will come towards you, so that you will awaken in the the same sacred fire.

It is for that that I want you to leave here with this enthusiasm, which you will have in you, if you are eager to help.[6]

After reading the above statements by Krishnamurti, we can understand why others to whom the thought of the Master, the personality of the Master is not real. They are still undecided, the Masters are to them still pictures, what Krishnamurti called "turbaned Masters". To many, the Masters are just thought-forms and they feel that unless the Master's picture is there before them

---

[6] Jinarajadasa, C., *Shishya*, "Address by Krishnaji to the E.S.", Vol. I, n3., June 1932, pp. 6-9.

they cannot come near to Him. To these also there is the opportunity of linking up with the great forces, and that is through Theosophy. If the teachings are to you something which is not only just laws, but a great scheme of the operation of the Divine Mind, it will bring you into communion with the great rates of vibration. As you bring in that quality, you will be able to give out to the world your own truths, your own realizations. You are the cup but the drink is not yours. Not because it has been presented to you by Krishnamurti, or Besant, but because out of your own inner strivings you have seen for yourselves.

The following is said to be extracted from a letter dated January, 1924 from J. Krishnamurti printed in *The Disciple*, August, 1934, n3, (New Series), p.92. This is published to show how material was edited when reprinted over the years. The first half of the first paragraph below, does not appear in the later issues.

Adyar as a Spiritual Centre

It is essential for the individual member and for The Society that Adyar, as a great spiritual centre, should be maintained worthy and dignified. The importance of this is so obvious that few can doubt it.

In this later issue published in *The American Theosophist*, February, 1943, Vol. XXXI, n2, on the inside cover it reads:

Adyar

Adyar is, and always has been, a spiritual oasis to which the weary traveler looks for comfort and repose. Though it may not be the privilege for each member in the Society to go there from the world of wilderness, yet the mere existence of such a center gives one an encouragement.

I have visited many a wonderful land and seen many a famous sight, but there is none to equal the extraordinary tangible something of our Adyar. There is an atmosphere there that does not exist in many a church and temple, and there is a Presence there that we expect a perceive in a sacred shrine. One can become either a God or a pitiful sinner at Adyar. It is a wondrous spot, and it must be maintained as though it were a holy temple.

Adyar Day exists to remind the members of the glorious place and to urge them to do their best to make Adyar a worthy and dignified shrine for the Masters.

Publications today show that it is printed with an additional paragraph:

Adyar Day exists to remind the members of the glorious place and to urge them to do their best to make Adyar a worthy and dignified shrine for the Masters.

Printed at the bottom of the inside cover: J. Krishnamurti, *Adyar Notes and News*, April, 1928.

At the special request of the officials of the Theosophical Society, Krishnamurti gave a talk to the New York Theosophical Federation in 1930. He put forward his general attitude of the futility of spiritual organizations, and declared that he was not a member of the Theosophical Society and that evidently most leaders of the Society were out of sympathy with his attitude to life. That is why the following address is important as the unfolding chapters will show the conflict between the Theosophical Society and the point of view given by Krishnamurti.

I hope that I may speak frankly, and if I do, that none of you will be hurt. It sometimes happens that one man dominates a number of individuals and leaves his imprint on them. That is not at all my desire. As most theosophists in the world accept a great deal of authority—perhaps you may be the exceptions—please do not class me among your leaders, because I am not a leader, and it is the last wish of mine that I should become a leader.

From my point of view, a man who desires to seek truth cannot leave his mark on another. Neither can a man who has attained truth because truth, liberation, or happiness, is purely an individual matter approached by no path whatsoever. Therefore I do not wish you to accept anything that I say, and I mean this.

The majority of theosophists throughout the world—and probably here, too, because it is in the nature of human beings—when they get discontented, leave one particular cage of an institution and join another n which they are, equally, caught. I am not saying that you are in a cage—you must investigate that for yourselves—but that is what happens throughout the world. You became members of the Theosophical Society because you were dissatisfied with the things around you. You did not approve of your religion, of a certain way of thought, a certain crystallization, and you left those and joined this Theosophical Society to find truth, understanding of life, or with some similar aim.

If you would find anything in life, you must be continually discontented until the moment of attainment. Discontentment is joyous. It is the only thing that is creative in man, because by continually discarding and eliminating he finds what he desires to seek. The moment you become crystallized in thought, in emotion, it is death. The individual will never find that which he is seeking, through crystallization. Crystallization comes into being the moment you accept the authority of anyone, and it generally happens that in societies, in religions, in institutions, one or two individuals dominate the whole by their personality, by their knowledge, by their strength, by their oratory, and so on.

I am not insinuating anything, I am just stating facts as they happen in the world. The moment you bear the stamp of authority or the mark of another, or allow your heart and your mind to be moulded by the hand of another, you are incapable of finding truth. From my point of view, no religion, no institution, no society can ever lead man to truth nor does any society, institution or religion hold the truth, because truth is purely an individual affair and has nothing to do with any organization whatsoever. That is my point of view, please. Do not all resign from the Society because I say it.

As you know, I have dissolved the Order of the Star and I do not belong to any Society, but do not think that I am working on my own. I am not. It does not interest me to create an organization. I say that for me the truth is the perfect poise of mind and reason and affection and, to attain that, organization is wholly unnecessary. I am not working or talking to imprint what I think on another, because that would be creating another cage instead of setting man free. I have dissolved the Order, and it is my last wish that any of you here who listen to me should follow anyone, including myself, because no one has the truth except yourself. No one can give you truth. No Master, no guide, no teacher, no messages can give it to you.

I am sorry if I speak strongly. It is my point of view. Please examine it as you would examine anything else, quite impersonally, without any antagonism. I do not want anything from anyone—your money or your buildings or your possessions or your organization. If you care to listen to me, you must do what you think is right. That is the only way to attain, the only way to arrive, and not through the reaction of a crowd around you, of your society, religions, sects, and classes.

Truth for me, that which every man is seeking, can only be achieved, arrived at through self-perfection, through the constant readjustment between reason, conscious thought, and fluttering, fluctuating emotion. That perfect balance, harmony, poise, can only be arrived at through experience—*your* experience, not the experience of another. That to me is the truth, which is unconditional because it is the incorruptibility of the self, and when once you have made that self incorruptible, it becomes the whole, and not the part. Then there is no separation. When the self is incorruptible it is omniscient because it includes the whole. There cannot be omniscience, perfect knowledge, in the world of phenomena, which is relative, because there is constant change, multiplication of manifestations, whereas the perfect incorruptible self is omniscient, because in it is no separation. And that lies entirely and wholly within oneself, not outside, however much you may examine the planes at different levels. Such truth, such perfect harmony, such happiness, such ecstasy of purpose and delight, does not lie in any organization, does not lie at the door or at the altar of churches, or within the folds of religions or priests, nor can force radiating from any place give it to you. That is my point of view.

Who can tell you if you are corruptible or incorruptible except yourself? Who can make you happy except yourself? What is the use of surrounding yourself with innumerable gods to find the eternal? You must tear yourself away from all gods to find life. If you must worship, worship; the man that is next to you, the man in the field, the man in the street. That is my point of view. And when once you have that vision of the perfect man, the liberated man, then your vision is your yoga, and all the problems that confront you are no longer problems. It is because you do not know what you want, because you are uncertain of your desires that you seek the innumerable channels which you think are essential.

The idea of discipleship, mystery, occultism—which is only the examination of phenomena on another plane—from my point of view will not lead to truth. I repeat, from my point of view; do not quote it tomorrow and say it is your point of view. Think it over. Either accept or reject, but do not be indifferent to things. If what I say is false, and what you say is right, then go after it with vehemence, with an open mind, with eagerness; but if what I say is true, practise it with the same interest—not enthusiasm because enthusiasm fails, whereas interest never disappears.

You have divided life into many temperaments, many systems, many paths, mystic and occult, and all that paraphernalia, and in this way you think you understand truth. From my point of view truth has no path. it is a pathless land through which you must thrust your own way, and that way is not the way of another, and that way cannot be laid down for another.

This is a serious matter, and I am fully aware of the confusion in the Theosophical Society with regard to my attitude, and naturally so, because I will not compromise in my attitude with your leaders, and your leaders are not with me. I do not mind it in the least, because to me, truth is a thing that cannot be stepped down or altered for the convenience of societies, organizations and religious bodies. Because you have leaders, because you follow your leaders, there is confusion.

Do not say that because I am 'disloyal', I am asking you to be disloyal. I am not talking about loyalty, I am talking about truth; and once you are loyal to truth, you are loyal to everyone, to every man, every human being, every thing that is animate or inanimate. Your leaders have said that I am going to be something, and when that something contradicts what they have said, naturally there is confusion. It is very simple. They are not in agreement with me, nor I with them. It is a very simple matter so why hedge about it?

And it must always be so if you are following someone, if you are always sitting down under authority and worshipping the shade of authority. I do not know why you have leaders at all, of any kind—especially spiritual leaders. How can you have spiritual leaders? How can you follow anyone except yourselves, when you are a body of seekers after truth? You are not seeking truth the moment you follow anyone. You are seeking to satisfy your frightened desires. You are afraid.

Please do not look at all this from the point of view of an organization, because I have no organization. I do not want you to leave one organization and come into mine. I do not want you to be followers of Krishnamurti, that does not interest me. Personality is nothing, but to you personalities are the chief thing. Naturally, therefore, there is confusion.

You are quarrelling over how much of the consciousness of the Lord Maitreya is working through Krishnamurti, and so are your leaders. This is not personal, and I hope you will not take it in a personal way. Of what value is it to know who is speaking? They can never know who I am. No man can know except the man who is made perfect in himself, and then he will understand. I am not doing any propaganda here. I am talking very seriously, because you started out to seek truth, and you are caught up in dogmas, creeds beliefs, ceremonies, forming new religions and new creeds, and it is a sorrowful thing to watch people caught up in cages, and thinking that they are breaking down cages when they are only decorating the bars and becoming brilliant in their skilful decoration in the world of phenomena.

Please believe me when I say that I do not want any following, that I have no organization, and that I am not working on my own in opposition to someone else. I am just stating what I know to be the truth for me, what to me is the highest reality, what to me is the uncompromising attitude between the essential and the unessential. Naturally there is an immense difference between your leaders and myself, and it is no good going about concealing these things. You cannot be politic with regard to spiritual things. Then you put organization before the real. Then you hedge about the real with your artificialities of organization. Then a sect becomes greater than the whole.

There cannot be crystallization of thought, solidifying of your emotions, if there is the continual, conscious, active, intense interest in what you are seeking, and to find out what you are seeking you must discover the secret pursuit of your thought. If your thought is pursuing comfort, you will have shelters, *gurus*, Masters. You will at once say, "Do not Masters exist?" I say to that, Masters, apparitions, devas, angels, have nothing to do with the realization of spirituality. They are of no use for your realization. That is my point of view, please. Therefore, examine your secret pursuits of desire, because once you have your desires open, then you can walk cleanly and freshly without the burden of unnecessary things.

From my point of view, when there is that intense desire to find out and to become—not merely to live in theories—then you do not live in a world of a different phenomenon, however high that be. What is the good of all your theories, your immense organizations, your churches and your religious worships, when there is sorrow? Who cares for all of these things? I know you look at it all very intellectually and say one must have knowledge. Yes, but what is your knowledge worth when there is not this burning thing behind it?

You may go down any street and see churches where vast sums of money are being spent in adoration and worship born of fear, and walking beside them you see a man or a woman in tears. What is the good of such things?

Sorrow gives understanding, not knowledge. Sorrow gives you the energy, the vitality to fight all this, not your comfortable, secluded spots of specialized sects, worships, religions, the competition of degrees of spirituality.

Please do not get emotional over this. To understand anything you must look at it quite detachedly and, when there is that understanding of detachment, there is action, the real kind of action that does not leave a mark on the life of another.

From my point of view, there is no path to truth, nor will the cultivation of innumerable paths lead you to truth. Truth can only be approached through experience, through constant growth, through sorrow, strife, ecstasy. Through that growth you become, and in that full conscious being lies balance and hence truth. If a man would find such a truth, if he would become that whole, he must not have any compromise. Compromise is the result of fear, of uncertainty, is destructive, negative; whereas certainty gives that dynamic quality which will enable you always to choose the essential and put aside the unessential. When you perceive the vision of life, then the manner of attaining it is to make the end the means, by always keeping that vision in full clarity and by walking in that clarity.

I know—please do not think I am speaking out of harshness or out of narrow fanaticism—that Theosophists all over the world have done great things, sacrificed immensely, and it were a pity if they merely became followers instead of using their capacity to develop themselves, and hence, everyone around them.

The quality of a bourgeois, to me, is that of fear which incapacitates the mind and the heart from free function and spontaneous activity. If you would attain truth, let no man leave an imprint of his hand on your mind and heart, and do not leave your imprint on another's.[7]

On October 30th, 1930, Rajagopal announces that since the dissolution of the Order of the Star, and that since there is danger that its readers will become a sect, the present name of the *International Star Bulletin* has lost its significance, and a new one has become necessary. From January 1st of 1931, the *International Star Bulletin* will therefore be published under a name that will more accurately describe its nature and contents. But a change of name has proved impracticable. Therefore they decided to keep the name *Star Bulletin* for another year, omitting the word *International* as unnecessarily long and cumbersome. Another reason for the change, was that Krishnamurti's travels prevented his total attention to the necessary corrections of manuscripts, so not giving enough reasonable time for publication.

Since the dissolving of the Order of the Star in 1929, Krishnamurti felt that the word Star should no longer be used in connection with his writings or activities. As a symbol it has lost its meaning; and they had no further use for symbols. To change the

---

[7]Krishnamurti, J., *International Star Bulletin*, "An Address", n5, May 1930, pp. 18-24.

name would cause considerable difficulty and expense. No perfect name could be found to make it worth while.

It is reported that the Order of the Star has been revived since 1982 by a group in England, and is now a small international organization hoping to invoke the presence of Christ on earth by meditation. The new Order of the Star sees itself as continuing Besant's work and draws heavily on the Alice Bailey writings. It is believed by this group that when Krishnamurti dissolved the Order of the Star, the World-Teacher withdrew His influence from Krishnamurti, and that Krishnamurti failed. More information can be located in a book by Catherine Wessinger, *Annie Besant and Progressive Messianism:* 1847-1933 (Studies in Women & Religion).

Alice Bailey (1880-1949), who broke away from the Theosophical Society in the 1920's is probably the first to coin the term "the Age of Aquarius." The hope for the coming of the World-Teacher designed the "The Great Invocation," a prayer to invoke the presence of the Christ on earth.

The Theosophical Society itself is no longer a progressive messianic movement due to the disappointment and confusion caused by Krishnamurti.

Dr. Besant returned to America for the last time in 1929, it was then that some of her staff noticed a fragment, as it were, of her old self shinning through. She made a large decision at this time regarding Krishnamurti and his teachings, that maybe she may have come to regret. Her forces were feeble then, and there was not that grand completeness in her which many were so accustomed to see.

It was in 1931 that she reminded her followers to go deep within themselves and give their trust there. "Learn to trust the divine in you," she said, "There lies your real strength. You are divine." Warrington looked upon this utterance as the summing up of her life's philosophy, and coming as it did, as the last she ever made in public after a lifetime giving selfless devotion to the welfare of humanity.

What The Society has achieved, what it is today, and most of all what we can make of it if we take hold of our trusteeship rightly, are matters evaluated less by our words than by our lives.

Sidney A. Cook was born in England, and after living quietly in retirement in England, died on August 5, 1965, after fifty-one years of unbroken membership in the Theosophical Society.

Sidney A. Cook had been elected to the National Presidency in 1931 to 1945, as successor to Mr. L.W. Rogers, who was resigning as National president in order to turn his full attention to lecturing and writing on Theosophy. He spoke of the responsibility he felt to carry on "the work of the Society that it may be truly Their work, conducted in deep humility in a manner acceptable to Them." He was International Vice-President of the Society from 1946 to 1960.

He brought to the work a business acumen and administrative genius that enabled the Section to achieve a debt free Headquarters by 1938, when a "Burn-the-Bonds" campaign cleared the final liabilities.

In 1932, a year after he became National President, the then twenty-acre estate was given the name of "Olcott," thus memorializing the President-Founder of the Society on the 100th anniversary of Olcott's birth.

Chapter I
1932

On December 18, 1931, due to the uncertainty of Dr. Besant's health, it was thought advisable that the Vice-President, A.P. Warrington should take up his residence, along with Mrs. Warrington at Adyar, and assist in the administration and guidance of The Society with Ernest Wood, Recording Secretary, and A. Schwarz, Treasurer. Subsequently, Mr. Wood accepted the nomination for President and resigned his post. Mr. Frei would replace him as the Recording Secretary.

Warrington wrote from Hong Kong in December en route to India that they had been having a great trip and enjoying it immensely. Thanksgiving dinner was in Shanghai with Dorothy Arnold and Mrs. Kay Campbell, both of whom had friends in Ojai.

Still leading the Society was Dr. Besant as ever powerful and compassionate. She was now at her last hour, gradually losing her strength. She stressed the work of the Elder Brethren which always lay so dear to her heart—the Future of the Theosophical Society. Her message for the year 1932 was on the question—"What are we doing to turn our claim into a reality—being a nucleus of Universal Brotherhood?"

Beginning the new year, C.W. Leadbeater gave a talk in the Shrine Room to the E.S. members regarding a lot of discussion about liberation and freedom. This was due to the fact that Krishnamurti had been emphasizing liberation very much during his talks. Leadbeater felt that liberation for most of the E.S. members is a thing that they can attain only by degrees. He knew that Krishnamurti spoke of leaping to the ultimate liberation, but Leadbeater reminded the students that it is hardly a possibility as yet for most of them to have reached that point when they can escape from the round of births and deaths. Leadbeater told them that Krishnamurti had lived many lives to earn the true Liberation of all, from Samsâra. (Sam-sâra,

Sans., wandering.); the passage through the three worlds; the "wheel" of birth and death.

Leadbeater reminded the students, that each of them must not be entangled in Krishnamurti's use of words, because the very words liberation and freedom is sometimes misused by him. Remembering one lecture that Krishnamurti gave about Theosophy to an audience during the early years at Adyar. Krishnamurti said, "God has a plan and that plan is evolution." By 1932, Krishnamurti took the meaning quite differently when he said there was not a plan. Of course, Leadbeater did not understand that, because it seemed very obvious that there certainly is a plan to all this chaos.

Adyar Theosophical Society Headquarters, 1905

—⋞⋟—

Dr. G. de Purucker, successor to Mrs. K.A. Tingley, of the Universal Brotherhood and Theosophical Society, with Headquarters at Point Loma (now Covina) California wrote to Dr. Besant.

The American newspapers had given exaggerated accounts of the unrest in India, and Dr. de Purucker thought if a violent outburst did occur, work at Adyar might have to be moved, and he offered 200 of their 330 acres at a very modest price.

January 25 1932
Point Loma, California

Dr. Annie Besant
President, the Theosophical Society
Adyar, Madras, India

My Dear Dr. Besant,

I am writing to you by request of our Leader, Dr. de Purucker, and also on behalf of all the members of our Headquarters' Staff here at Point Loma, to express to you the concern that we have felt in regard to the reports of your health; and also the pleasure at the most recent report that you were better, and were able again to attend and to speak at meetings of the Society at Adyar.

We feel indeed that there is still work for you to do, and it is our hope that this improvement of your health may continue.

We have felt much concern also over the general unsettled condition in India; and indeed, we hope that a peaceful solution may be found, and that there may be no resorting to violence, still all this is in the balance. We know the deep interest that you have in India, and that the present time must be quite an anxious one for you.

It is our hope, as just said, that there may be no outbreak of violence which may sweep over the whole country, but if this should be imminent, and the political conditions in India should become so unsettled as to make it impossible or inadvisable for your Headquarters Adyar to continue to carry on its work, we here, and I write, as said above, on behalf of our Chief, Dr. de Purucker, and the Headquarters' Staff—would be glad to offer you personally a peaceful and more central home for your activities, here at Point Loma. Furthermore, in the event that the General Council of the Adyar Society might deem it advisable, on account of conditions in India, to remove your Theosophical Headquarters from India, and if they would agree to transfer your Headquarters' activities here also to Point Loma, we would be most happy to offer to your General Council two hundred acres of our present estate of some three hundred and thirty acres at a very modest price.

We hope, of course, as said above, that a peaceful solution may be found for the difficulties which at the present time are so acute in India, and indeed all over the world; but in case of serious eventualities that may make a change appear inevitable, we should be very happy to have you yourself personally, and also the General Council of the Society, give consideration to this letter.

Indeed, dear Dr. Besant, in this connection I am strongly reminded of something that I heard several years ago; namely, that on more than one occasion you yourself had said something to the effect that you looked forward to the time when our Point Loma Headquarters and your own work would be closely associated. The remarkable thing about this, my dear Dr. Besant, is that Katherine Tingley many times during past years stated that it was her conviction that Point Loma—not necessarily our own Headquarters—would some day likewise be the seat of your Society, as well as our own. Truly would not this contiguity or juxtaposition of the two Headquarters, if it can be brought about, be one of the noblest efforts towards unification of the two main bodies in the Theosophical Movement?

With fraternal and affectionate greetings,
Most sincerely yours,
Joseph H. Fussell,
Secretary-General

There had been some fraternization between Lodges of the various twenty or more different kinds of Theosophical Societies. By the 27th of June, at the invitation of Dr. de Purucker, Dr. and Rukmini Arundale, with a number of members from other countries, met and in speeches throughout the day expressed their feelings of good will to all theosophists, and to all other Theosophical Societies outside their own, uniting in loyalty to their envoy Mme. Blavatsky.

> March 7 1932
> the Theosophical Society, Vice-President's Office
> Adyar, Madras, India
>
> Dr. Joseph H. Fussell, Secretary-General, the Theosophical Society
> Point Loma, California
>
> Dear Doctor,
>
> I have pleasure in acknowledging your most fraternal communication of January 25th, addressed to the President, Dr. Annie Besant.

It has been many months since Dr. Besant has been able to attend to business of any character except at rare intervals, and then only for a few minutes when she appeared to be least in a state of fatigue. Even her correspondence has had to be answered by others authorized to do so. Hence the present reply by myself to your letter.

I am sure Dr. Besant would wish me to express her sincere appreciation to Dr. de Purucker and all the members of your Headquarters' Staff at Point Loma for their sympathetic feelings of concern in regard to the reports of her health. At the same time we, her co-workers here, regret we cannot confirm "the most recent report" that she is "able again to attend and to speak at meetings of the Society at Adyar," although one incident of the most unexpected nature occurring at the late Convention, as published in *The Theosophist*, does tend to give coloring to that view. Since then she has kept closely to her room, save for an occasional drive.

The concern you feel "over the general unsettled condition in India" is no doubt being felt by all the friends of India throughout the world. But to us here on the spot, so to say, the outlook does not seem so very dark. There are no signs to me of anything akin to such an upheaval in the country as will put the life of the ordinary citizen in jeopardy. Moreover, the Theosophical Society has from the beginning eschewed all politics as a Society, and we here do not see any danger at all to its routine activities.

Nevertheless your thoughtful and generous offer to provide our Headquarters with asylum in case of trouble is met with a hearty and understanding appreciation. Moreover your willingness to sell to us a portion of your beautiful estate at Point Loma in the unlikely event that conditions in India should become permanently forbidden, is deemed here to be a gesture of great brotherliness such as our Foundress, H.P.B., would have rejoiced to see expressed by any of her faithful followers. That our membership may be informed of all this, we shall take the liberty of publishing both your letter and this my reply in an early number of *The Theosophist*.

But, as to Adyar, there is to my mind no more favored spot in all the world for the headquarters of a spiritual society. It was to Adyar that H.P.B. and Colonel Olcott were sent by the Masters to found the centre for Their outer use. It is Adyar that bears the powerful imprint of Their sacred influence. It is Adyar that is near to Them, geographically considered, and to that august spiritual capitol of the world, Shamballa, whose primary channel of influence it long since came to be.

And it is India, Adyar's home, that embodies the most uplifting and dynamically spiritual atmosphere of any land; for it is here that great Rishis, Avatars, Buddhas, Masters and Adepts, have lived and labored as no where else, and the power They exerted and impressed upon this land can never be erased, even by the distracted conditions that have existed on lower planes during centuries of decadence, and from which, like another Phoenix, India is rising once more to take the lead in the world's spiritual regeneration.

With fraternal greetings to all, I am,
most sincerely yours,
A.P. Warrington, Vice-President[1]

Written in *The Theosophical Messenger* for January 1932, Vol. XX, the Editor of the magazine reports that he received the following corrections from Joseph H. Fussell that the newspaper report referred to by L.W. Rogers in the December *Theosophical Messenger* misquotes Dr. de Purucker and that the statement as reported, that 'The Adyar Theosophist Society of India was formed late in the last century, after the death of H.P. Blavatsky,' was not made by Dr. de Purucker, nor did he say that he believed 'that this faction would soon return to the mother-organization.'

It was believed that Krishnamurti would not get back to Ojai again until 1934, so letters went out to Mr. & Mrs. Staggs, Miss Mequillet being told they had better not miss the June 1 to 8 Ojai Camp, even if they have to walk, but they were not able to attend, but hoped to see Krishnamurti's visit to Cleveland in September.

February 29 1932

Dear Mr. Warrington,

I have a little news item for you that I think will please you, and this is my excuse for bothering you with a letter. I enclose a copy of the minutes of the annual meting of the Krotona Trustees which was held last Tuesday in Hollywood.

---

[1] Single pamphlet of 6 pages "Point Loma's offer to Adyar".

The resolution referring to the exchange of real estate or the note owed by the Order of the Star in the East should perhaps have a little explanation. You will remember that we took an option on the Madge Mercer Tract before Krishnaji ever had any idea of coming to that end of the valley with his Camp, our purpose being to purchase the land and then re-sell it as a subdivision in order that Krotona might have a chance to buy the rest of the hilltop directly south of Mr. Munson's house. However, before Mr. Zalk or I had concluded the transaction, the option was turned over to the Order of the Star in the East, and the arrangements I had made with Mrs. Mercer for absorbing two of our Sutter Basin bonds at par was continued by the Order of the Star and Krotona took a note for $2000.

As the Ojai Star Institute Trustees have arranged this year for the refunding of all the old loans, I took advantage of the opportunity to secure this hilltop, which they seemed quite willing to let go to Krotona in order to retire the $2000 note. Thus after many years our original purpose is accomplished, and I thought you would be pleased to hear about it.

I assume that you and Mrs. Warrington are intending to stay at Adyar indefinitely, as I have heard no rumors to the contrary. We would be pleased to get a little note from you if you have time, telling us the news about Adyar and particularly about Dr. Besant. The last word I had, which was by letter today, was that she is just about the same. I should certainly appreciate it, if you have opportunity, if you will convey to her my love and best wishes.

With kindest regards to both yourself and Mrs. Warrington,
I remain ever,
Very sincerely yours,
G. H. Hall

To which came the reply:—

April 6 1932

My dear George,

I am very glad indeed to learn that we are to have the north-east corner of the Mercer Tract, giving us that fine site with the western outlook over Santa Ana Valley, which has been so much admired. The next time you write, I should be glad to have a little pencil drawing of the piece we shall get, in its exact relation to our west line, and how far the intersection of our line with the north line of the piece lies from the gate leading into the Star lands near the Nursery. How close does the piece come to that Carnes Boulevard we built down the side of the hill? It would be interesting to learn what is to become of that part of the Star property which lies immediately north of the Mercer piece and co-extensive with it as far north as our north-west corner. For a long time I have felt that our hill acreage will never be properly protected until by acquisition it is extended westward as far as that Carnes road. The acquisition of the piece you mention goes a long ways towards this. Some day I hope it may be completed. You know, that balance due to us by the President was borrowed, not for herself, but to help in the purchase of some part of the lands held by the Star people. I suppose there is no way to bring this into a settlement by having them deed to us that remaining piece we need if we will cancel the balance due to us on the President's note. When these people realize how much the President has done for them, having sacrificed in many ways, I cannot but see that they will want to do this act of grateful service to her before she passes. Talk it over with Louis, but please don't quote me anymore than you absolutely have to do. I am sure you will see my point in all this. When I say, don't quote, I mean to others than Louis. When you write, tell me also how last year's budget came out.

The President continues about the same. She is very weak and thin. She told Betty the other day, she did not know why she was staying, for she was so very old and weak. When she talks, it is in a piping, childlike voice, so different from the deep, round tones we have admired so in her. It is reported here that she is waiting for a body in one of the few remaining pure Aryan families now in India. But I have not yet had the rumor confirmed by CWL who is quoted as authority. After she passes, there will be about nine months in which I suppose I shall have to carry on until the new President is elected. Then—well, God bless the new President; I shall not want his job, but shall wish to return to Krotona and see what can be done there.

I hear very good reports of your restored health, and hope you have heard similar reports of mine. I am really feeling better than I have felt for many years, with not a pain in sight any longer.

We shall be glad to hear from you whenever you may wish to write. With the most cordial greetings to you both. From us both,
Sincerely always,
A.P. Warrington

———❦———

March 10 1932

My dear Miss Poutz,

I have not really broken out in the above letter-head. It is just the first proof, which I have rejected.

I am enclosing this week, for the edification of the Krotonians ALONE, some correspondence that will highly interest every member there. It had been my purpose to send off today, which is mail day, a regular Krotona letter to be shared by a few others. But the enclosures, I thought, were too rich to be shelved for any kind of cause. So here they go to you. I should like to be there to hear some of the remarks. But ask them not to say anything about it until there is some announcement of it made in some publication. Sooner or later *The Theosophist* will publish the letters, perhaps in the next issue. Meantime we must not say anything, but just chuckle to ourselves. *The enclosed were the first draft of Warrington's reply to Fussell with the remarks that the cancellations etc., were made for policy's sake.*

I have at last taken up the same kind of evening work here as that I did on Friday evenings at Krotona, using the very same evening in fact. And I have done this in spite of the sorry fact, that I have been suffering from a bad cold and an obstinate case of diarrhea, two ailments I never have in California. If I don't catch anything worse, I guess I can survive, though such troubles to do take it out of one.

Anyway, I have lost every vestige of my arthritis, and that is something, let me tell you.

Much love to you all,

A.P. Warrington

———❦———

From George Hall to Louis Zalk:—

May 10 1932

Dear Louis:

Regarding my reply to A.P.'s letter, there are two difficulties which I overlooked and which I am sure you also did not think of. A.P. is very clever in putting forward a very logical and compelling argument based on a false premise, and if you overlook this false premise you are in difficulty. For instance, his entire proposal about the Camp paying Dr. Besant's note to Krotona with land is based on an assumption which we should not under any circumstances admit; namely, that Krotona loaned money to the Camp through Dr. Besant.

Now the facts are these: In 1927 Dr. Besant received money from many sources, three of which I know personally. Over $40,000 came in for Happy Valley. She transferred funds of her own from England to this country, and she borrowed from Krotona $25,000. These were the sources of supply.

She spent money for Happy Valley; to buy an orange grove for Arya Vihara; to build two Pacific Ready Cut cottages at Arya Vihara; to take over the Ojai Publishing Company and otherwise fix up the whole of the affairs in which Fritz Kunz was involved, many of which transactions no one knows anything about. She also loaned $6000 to the Order of the Star. Obviously it is impossible for anyone, and probably for Dr. Besant herself, to say what was the source of any specific money she spent for any special thing. All the receipts went into her hands and all of the expenditures came out.

Therefore in replying to Mr. Warrington I must first deny emphatically his premises that the loan from Krotona to her had anything whatever to do with any special expenditure which she might have made. I can then go ahead and make the remark you suggested, and that disposes of that.

Now regarding your letter written on the train, I fear that Union Pacific is a very sporty road, and I am surprised that you should indulge in any of their so-called soft drinks and then write me such a letter. To propose that I should suggest to A.P. that it is up to him to decide any matter connected with Krotona in any way that he sees fit, as though he were the whole works, is forgetting completely any knowledge you may have of my last twelve years experience in connection with Krotona. I deny emphatically that any trustee of Krotona can accept a proposition from the Ojai Star Institute or anyone else to buy as much land as they wish. Briefly, your idea is most brilliant coming from a trustee of the Ojai Star Institute, but when we remember that you are also a trustee of the Krotona Institute it is a complete flop. Much as I should like to fall in with any suggestion you may make, and much as I regret having to injure your tender feelings, I positively refuse to suggest to A.P. that he can buy anything for Krotona without my consent, even if it is only a soft drink furnished by the Union Pacific.

Hoping you will forgive me for all my naughty words, I remain as ever,
With much love, strange as that may sound,
G.H. Hall

From Louis Zalk to George Hall:—

May 16 1932
Louis Zalk
300 East Michigan Street
Duluth, Minn.

Dear George:

Reference to the land on top of the hill and Mr. A.P.W.'s suggestions, etc.

Referring to your letter of the 10th, I am quite sure that the Union Pacific has not joined the aeroplane service and I was really on the ground and not up in the air when I wrote my letter. We can forget that suggestion.

Regarding the rest of it, it is certainly satisfactory to me that you put the matter in your own way, as to why the Ojai Star Institute feels it has no debts other than those at present on its records.
As ever,
Louis

Around June 18, C.W. Leadbeater returned to Adyar from Australia to continue his work on occult chemistry. After seeing Dr. Besant, she told him that her work on the physical plane was finished, and that she was now only a "pipe" through which the Hierarchy was sending force to the world for Their purposes. She was content to be that, so long as They wished it, but she wanted a Theosophical School on the Estate before her life was over.

C. Jinarajadasa was in London, April 5, when he wrote to Miss Poutz at Krotona stating his point of view regarding if an E.S. Warden can address the Group discussing Krishnamurti's teachings.

Krishnamurti

A reply to a worker, who has the privilege of addressing E.S.T. Groups, and asks if he can discuss in them Krishnaji's teachings. C. Jinarajadasa

The E.S.T. stands for a certain infinite attitude to life which must be kept constantly before its members. The School is a body of organized WORKERS for the service of Humanity. There are necessarily many requirements for those who desire to serve. The particular requirements which the E.S. emphasizes may be summed up in the phrase, "The world problem is the individual problem." For, the individual is expected to discover his possibilities of highest service by expanding his mind and making it a mirror of the Divine Mind. Therefore, the knowledge gathered by the Masters through millennia of discovery, and stated today in the Theosophical scheme of evolution, must be carefully and urgently studied by him, if he is to be successful in service. Through such intellectual and institutional grasp of the great scheme, the individual is inspired to see for himself how to work at his personal reorganization and purification. In order to assist him, the Great Teachers offer Themselves as ideals of the work which is to be done. For, each Adept is fundamentally a mirror of an ideal of service. In addition, and under certain conditions, a Master is willing to train as apprentices these who show, by life and by pledge, that to them "the world problem is the individual problem."

There is, however, another angle to this great problem of service. It is the reflex of what I have stated, and is summed up in Krishnaji's phrase, "The individual problem is the world problem." That, too, is a correct statement of the relation between the two problems, but seen from an angle opposite to that which is represented by the E.S. Yet, if a person honestly and with true purity of heart works at his individual problem, having no resentment or criticism of others at the way they work at their problems, such an individual will presently discover his unity with all who suffer, and he will then dedicate himself to the helping of the world. It is with this thought that Krishnaji concludes his ***KINGDOM OF HAPPINESS***:

"There you will find the Eternal Refuge, the Eternal Truth; and there you will lose the identity for your separate self; and there you will create new worlds, new kingdoms, new abodes for others."

So long as the "goal" is that vision of "for others", it does not matter in which way the idealist states the solution of the two problems—the individual and the world.

The chief duty of the E.S. member is—if he has any belief in the Masters as the Directors of evolution, and if the idea of working under Them attracts him, and there is no other reason why he should be in the E.S.—to understand the work which the Masters are doing, and to train himself to give his contribution to that work. This does not mean that there are no other possibilities of spiritual growth, outside of this particular career within the E.S. For instance, there are thousands of Gurus or teachers in India who gather disciples round them, offering to conduct them to Moksha or Liberation. They all stress in various terms the urgency of the individual problem as the key to Liberation. The E.S. has no quarrel with them, but it concentrates its energies to help a selected band ALONG ITS OWN SPECIAL LINE, which is to lead them to the presence of the Masters.

E.S. members are aware of my attitude to Krishnaji's teachings, how I have advised such as feel drawn to them to study them and gain what help they can from them. But I do not desire in any way that there should be an imposition on any to study his teachings. The teachings of the Lord Buddha also emphasize the individual problem, and the individual is warned of the pitfalls of ceremonies—there were no organizations in those days—and how he must rely on no one, not even his Guru. But I do not think that E.S. members will gain in the work, which they need to do for the growth of their character, by my insisting that they should study Buddhism rather than the teachings of Bhakti of the Gita. On these matters I want to leave members alone. But while they are within the E.S., their chief task is to assist in certain ACTIVITIES; and since character is essential as an instrument of action, the E.S. gives a certain training. This training, however, does not exclude every possible help which they can get from the teachings of the Lord Buddha, Sri Krishna, Jesus Christ, or any other Teacher, and today from Krishnaji himself.

It is because I have recognized the value of Krishnaji's teachings to all sincere idealists that I advise a person interested in Krishnaji NOT TO ATTEMPT TO UNDERSTAND HIM THROUGH THE MIND OF ANOTHER. There is an Italian proverb that "traduttore e traditore"—"translator is traitor", which to my mind applies to Krishnaji's teachings. For he has a very lofty standpoint which must be understood primarily by the intuition; if that standpoint is filtered through the medium of another's mind, it is difficult for the seeker to contact Krishnaji's ideas through the mind of another, there is necessarily misunderstanding. That unfortunately is what has happened in various countries, where enthusiastic followers of Krishnaji, taking up what he has said about not being entangled in organizations, have definitely set to work to smash the Theosophical Lodge of the place in the name of Krishnaji's teachings.

I do not want members in the E.S. AS GROUPS to study his teachings, though I do advise those drawn to him to read and study them, each for himself. I have consistently in India urged Krishnaji's band of workers to flood the country with his literature, translating his teachings in to the Indian vernaculars, so that the minds of hundreds of thousands of men and women who cannot read English can directly contact his thought.

I know fully how greatly his standpoint is required to supplement the other standpoints, and how thousands will be awakened to a new vision by Krishnaji. There is plenty of room within our Theosophical studies for Krishnaji's standpoint, for there is only one Wisdom of the Ages and not two. But unfortunately, as you know, he, and more particularly his followers, will not allow any room whatsoever for the Theosophical standpoint.

I think that such an exclusion of Theosophy from a new presentation of Truth is inevitable. The Buddha as He emphasized His message, excluded Hinduism, though He did it in a gentle way which gave offence to none; Christ had no place in His outlook for the discovery of Reality characteristic of Greece. Each new presentation meets a definite need of the age; it is intended to push the millions a few steps onwards to the higher life. But Theosophy is not the presentation for one particular age; it embodies what is needed for all ages. While there are truths in Theosophy for all, even children, yet its full inspiration is for the few, whose hearts and minds long, not for any personal fulfilment, but to know Truth IN ITS ENTIRETY and to live by that Truth for the fulfilment not of the individual alone, but of all. Theosophy is a science, philosophy and ethic of the universe as one whole; the teaching given by a great Teacher at any one time is a religion, philosophy and ethic of the individual and for the individual. There really is no contradiction to "one who knows", as is the Upanishad phrase.

It is true that no statement has been made by Krishnaji to the effect that the Masters do not exist. But what he has said concerning Them, when questions were asked, have clearly given the impression that, if They exist, They can have no value at all for an individual who is seeking true understanding. Furthermore, I think it is not incorrect to say that he has clearly given his listeners to understand, that those who pin their faith on the existence of Masters, and on the guidance to be received from Them, are utterly deluded and are going on a wrong path. And his representatives particularly—for though he states that he has no disciples, there are those who have taken upon themselves to be his mouthpiece—have pointed the finger of scorn at us, members of the E.S., because we do believe in the Masters.

To sum up, I do not want the teachings of Krishnaji to be made the point of discussion or even study within E.S. Groups. For there will inevitably be disputes, with the result first of misunderstanding his thought, and second, of creating unnecessary feeling among the students. For it is a strange fact that those who accept Krishnaji's ideas with enthusiasm are very impatient of any other standpoint.

I give my sincere wishes always to anyone who will study Krishnaji's teachings; and if the study makes him leave the E.S. I have no criticism. But as said before, it is the private and personal study, aiming directly to contact Krishnaji's thought with the intuition, which will be more fruitful, than listening to another's exposition of what Krishnaji means. In that sense it is indeed true that Krishnaji can never have any "followers".

Krishnamurti has to remind his audience at the Camps over and over again, that words can become but a cage and, one must look through the illusion of words. We can observe that ourselves by watching whatever we say can be easily misunderstood, therefore we seem to contradict ourselves. One has to pass through the illusion of words in order to discover the thought that another wishes to convey.

Geoffrey Hodson took a larger interest in the Summer School at Olcott, making a statement on June 26, 1932, on what should be the attitude of the theosophists towards Krishnamurti. It may sound like he is talking down to his audience as if they were children, which he may be, for he was acclaimed to be an Arhat[2].

> The problem is one of ego and personality. The ego is perfected in a technical sense, the personality is not. The ego is fully illuminated, the personality but partly yet. Time will solve all problems. Dwell in your thoughts up in the illuminated ego and its light. Wait patiently upon the personality which will also be illuminated in its day. Your thoughts of illumination help, of limitation hinder. Help therefore by dwelling on the light. Of what use your knowledge of the mechanism of consciousness if in spite of it your understanding fails?
>
> Such a Light requires an appropriate mechanism for its projection. Not in ten years or even twenty can the mechanism be perfected. Be patient therefore, dwell upon the light and insist that all who are pledged should follow your example.
>
> In spite of seeming differences of method you are all one band, one chalice. Learn to live and work as one. Intuition not mind will provide the key. The difficulty is admitted, yet minimize it. The harm known; work to undo it; be loyal now as never before even in the face of apparent disloyalty.
>
> Karma is not outworn by far. The brain is very limited. The attackers ceaseless in their attacks; the personality their target; the results of boyhood unhappiness upon the present personal consciousness permits an entry for their shafts.
>
> Yet still the Lord broods over him. Still the Lord pours through his illumined ego, His greater light, though with

---

[2]This word is used in a general sense for "the spiritual Intelligence that has conquered, subdued, and trained matter until his body is but the materialized expression of himself". (*Pâli*, the worthy).

the personal self He may not interfere. That light is reaching the world despite the barriers. The spiritual link remains, despite an apparent denial. In consciousness the twain are one.

Help therefore by your thoughts of unity in the face of apparent separateness; tolerance in the face of intolerance, patience in the face of apparent failure. Help thus the light to shine.

This problem is your problem too for you also are one with the Lord of Light. See therefore that through you that light shines perfectly, for the perfection of the few helps forward the perfection of all, and he is one of you despite all denial. Let these considerations weigh with you when studying and especially when discussing the problem of Krishnaji. The full perfection of his work demands a measure of the mellowness of age. Therefore be patient. Even the difficulties caused will be turned to good purpose.

We must know in these days upon whom we can depend. Whether they be many or few matters less than that we known them through their conduct rather than their words for what they are. Now is a time of winnowing, that the chaff may be divided from the corn which we require for seed. Look to yourselves that you be steadfast in the winnowing, firm in the strong wind.

Think you that when hundreds are called all will be chosen? Know you not the ancient Law? We seek the few. Those who are Ours and know themselves as such, show themselves as such by their works not only by their words. The ancient rules of Chelaship still stand despite their seeming abrogation. From the many who have been called we shall gain the few to whom those rules apply and who will subscribe to them.

The path of discipleship is a passage through fire. He who trends it faithfully emerges occultly clean. Most western pupils need greatly to deepen their realization of what that path can mean, its inner occult significance, the ancient rules and the real nature of the relationship between disciple and Guru; occult and governed by occult laws.

There is a lightness and a shallowness in the western attitude towards that Path and that relationship. Most of the failures are due to the lack of depth, of stability of penetrative and intuitive reasoning and in America to lack of leadership and unreadiness to follow. Look for and help the few, be not downcast for the many. Their karma gave all the opportunity, blessed are those who rightly perceive and grasp their karmic fruits.

The days of the Mysteries are here again and as of old, to all who knock the outer door is opened, the inner is for ever closed save to the few who themselves can open it.[3]

It was reported that Dr. Besant was mostly confined to bed, and could not attend the annual Convention for 1932, but all delegates went past her giving greetings. July 6th completed her 25th year as President of the Theosophical Society. She is quoted as to a definition of Theosophy, "There is no authoritative, dogmatic Theosophy. Theosophy is the living of the highest ideal that one is capable of doing with the greatest nobility."[4]

Due to the fact that Dr. Besant is on her death bed, C. Jinarajadasa sent out to all the Wardens of the E.S. the following letter to be read to the members giving them a view of the greatness of Dr. Besant's life for India and its many achievements, for her faith in mankind and knowledge that the present is worth working in for a future far but sure.

The following letter contains information regarding the Regent of India. There are many books on India, and theosophical literature abounds with the activities of the Rishis, those mighty Guardians who move majestically against the background of India's eternal greatness. Dr. Besant came into direct conscious touch with the Rishi Agastya, in 1913, known to theosophists as the Regent of India in the Inner Government. To list only a few articles if you are interested, referring to Rishi Agastya, can be found in *The Theosophists*, for March 1930, pp.523-524, *The Hindu Colony of Cambodia*, By Prof. Phanindra Nath Bose, T.P.H., Adyar, 1927, and *The Adyar Bulletin*, for August, 1918.

---

[3]Two single sheets of typed paper by Geoffrey Hodson.
[4]*The Theosophical Messenger*, May 1932, Vol.XX, n5, pg.103.

July 4 1932
Adyar, Madras, India

Dear Brother,

It is necessary that you should understand the role which the O.H. has played in the regeneration of India. That was planned long ago by the Great Hierarchy; even in 1881 the Mahachohan said: "Oh! for the noble and unselfish man to help us effectively in India in that divine task. All our knowledge, past and present, would not be sufficient to repay him." As events proved, it was a woman and not a man who came as Their wonderful Messenger.

In all which the O.H. has done in this department of her work, she has tried to carry out the instructions received by her. it made her first popular and then unpopular with the India which she loves so dearly. But she has not swerved. The following are briefly the facts.

It was at the end of 1913 that the O.H., under instructions from the Rishi Agastya, who is known as the "Regent of India" among the Masters began her definite political work for India. Under His instructions she delivered a series of eight lectures in Madras on general Reconstruction of India, religious, social and political. These lectures were published by her in the book *Wake Up, India*. (A few years later, following a suggestion from Him, this book was widely distributed to all libraries in India.)

Then on January 2nd, 1914, she started her weekly magazine called *The Commonweal*, and on July 14th she purchased a daily newspaper of Madras, *The Madras Standard*. The name of this paper was changed to *New India* from August 1st.

As all know, the Great War broke out on August 4th. It was evident by the latter part of 1915 that it would be a very prolonged struggle, and great efforts were made throughout the whole of the British Empire to concentrate on winning the War. But the O.H. did not in any way slacken her energies towards making India a Dominion within the British Empire. She did not suspend her political activities, for a reason which can now be stated, though she was then bitterly denounced by most British people as "helping the Germans to win the War."

I well remember how after tea on a certain Sunday—it was August 15, 1915—Dr. Besant told me that that very afternoon, between two and three o'clock, our two Masters M. and K. H., C.

W. Leadbeater and herself had been called to Shamballa, and how on receiving the call she had gone and lain down at once. (C.W.L. had left for Australia in February, 1914, and was then living in Sydney.) She told me that the Ruler of our world, Sanat Kumara, had given certain instructions regarding the future, showing by means of pictures certain of the great changes which would take place in the world's affairs for many centuries ahead. Because these changes affected the work of the Sixth Root Race, its Manu and its Bodhisattva were bidden to be present, and she and C.W.L. also as Their successors. As a part of these changes, pictures were shown of the outcome of the War and that the Allies would be victorious. Dr. Besant specially asked me at the time to say nothing on this point. The result of the naval battle, the air raids, the peace dictated by the Allies were a few among the pictures shown, but she did not mention these to me. They are however in the memorandum which she wrote on awakening, and in C.W.L.'s letter on the subject written by him from Sydney with his recollection of the instructions. At the conclusion of the interview, the Lord of the World gave definite instructions to her with regard to her Indian work.

The moment she returned to her body she woke up instantly and wrote them down. She sent to C.W.L. in Australia a statement of her recollection of the interview, which he corroborated as representing in the main what he recollected also. Those instructions, written down on a piece of paper, were carried by her in her handbag all the time thereafter. For several years they were not revealed except to a few trusted workers, but a few years ago she published them. They are as follows:

You will have a time of trouble and danger. I need not say 'Have no fear', but have no anxiety. Do not let opposition become angry. Be firm, but not provocative. Press steadily the preparation for the coming changes, and claim India's place in the Empire. The end will be a great triumph. Do not let it be strained by excess. Remember that you represent in the outer world the Regent, who is My Agent. My hand will be over you, and My Peace with you.

With these instructions received, she went straight ahead with her work for the reconstruction of India. Though she used the influence of her paper in every possible way to help the Allies, and also did a certain amount for recruiting, yet she refused in any way to slacken her work for India's freedom. Now that we know that she has been shown the outcome of the War, we can understand why she refused to suspend her political work to devote her energies to winning a war which, it had been decreed, should be won.

Soon after her political activities began, she found that the pressure on her physical brain was such that it was necessary to renounce the exercise of her psychic faculties. She had developed remarkable faculties of clairvoyance, and through Yoga she used to arrange to "bring through" to the physical brain important recollections at the moment of awakening. But as her political work proceeded, her mind became so absorbed in the strenuous and anxious work on the physical plane, that she asked her colleague C.W.L. to help her in informing her on any matter that she might not "bring through". She felt that, with the terrific pressure on the brain from her political activities, if any additional pressure from the occult side were to be put upon it, the brain would be damaged. Thus it was that in July, 1916, he was asked by the Regent to give her the following message:

I have already told Annie that my people must show that they deserve this Home Rule which they desire before they can expect to have it. I definitely desire the upholding of the Empire, and, unsatisfactory as is the present position in many ways. I would far rather that it should continue indefinitely than that there should be any cleavage or even any appearance of disloyalty. Every protest against existing conditions should begin and end with the strongest affirmations of absolute and unchangeable loyalty and devotion to the Emperor, and should include generous recognition of the frequent and most noble self-sacrifice of individual officials of the English administration in the execution of their duty towards my people—a self-sacrifice for which I wish personally to thank them. I strongly disapprove all exaggerated and inflammatory statements, even when they have a basis of fact, and I have specially asked Annie to act on my behalf in watching for such statements, and emphatically repudiating and discountenancing them.

On June 16, 1917, the Government served on her an order of internment. Seven days were allowed before it was necessary to obey; she left for Ootacamund on June 21. When leaving she said: "We shall be back in three months." (Two others, G.S. Arundale and B.P. Wadia, were also interned with her.) But so definitely was she by then the mouthpiece of Indian aspirations that, throughout the length and breadth of India, resentment steadily grew at Britain's action. She was released on September 17th. That same year in December, she was elected the President of the Indian National Congress.

All, particularly in India, well know how the O.H. utterly refused to endorse in any way the policies of Gandhiji with regard to the "non-co-operation" movement which he started in 1920. She has further condemned his subsequent campaigns to rouse the masses as a means of bringing pressure to bear on the Government to hasten political changes. Her refusal was guided by the instructions given to her in 1915 in the words: *Do not let it be stained by excess*. She saw clearly the dangers ahead in any kind of a mass movement, and she felt instinctively, when Gandhji began his Non-co-operation, that a situation would be created that would in the long run be detrimental to India's welfare. It was then that she called on E.S. members who went into the Non-co-operation movement to leave the E.S.

It was her opposition to Gandhiji's policies which cost her the wonderful position which she had gained in three years as one of the most brilliant leaders of the Indian National Movement. She has never swerved from her opposition to his politics, while warmly admiring him as a saintly man with a great sense of the Oneness of all life. But even as late as May, 1930, she dared to say publicly in *New India*: "I regard him as the most mischievous man in India, since he undermines respect for laws, the foundation of civilized society. But he is sincere, however wrong-headed, and is ready to suffer for that which he believes to be true."

These few facts will make E.S. members realise why she has insisted that the link between India and Britain must never be broken, as each is needed for the other's future, and why, though she is the most fiery of Indian patriots, she has fearlessly denounced the excesses of the Indian masses.

Yours sincerely,

C. Jinarajadasa

Records in *The Theosophical Messenger* for July 1932, gave brief duties for members of the Staff at the American Headquarters that later came to live at Krotona such as: Sarah C. Mayes, Eva Minnich, Mignon Reed, Blanche Krauss, Donald Greenwood, and Fred Menzenwerth

Former Ojai resident Fritz Kunz returned on visit with his family July 14. He was the former manager of the newspaper *The Ojai*, his wife Dora van Gelder Kunz and their small son John were guests of Mr. Kunz's brother-in-law and sisters, Mr. and Mrs. Hervey Gulick and Miss Minna Kunz. Fritz Kunz was a Theosophical lecturer of international note and is primarily an educator in India and America. He was in touch with such notables as Mahatma Gandhi; the scientiest J.C. Bose and P.C. Ray; the poets, Tagore and Sarojini Naidu. A very close friend of Edward Carpenter. While in Ojai, he was associated with J. Krishnamurti, Frank Gerard and Dr. Ernest Stone in the management of *The Ojai*.

By August of 1932, *The Beacon*, issued by Foster Bailey announces: "The New Group of World Workers" dictated by The Tibetan. The information tells of two groups of people. The first group, that is committed to the work of crystallization which will result in the complete destruction of the old forms of thought. The second group, embodying that which is essential and rejecting the non-essential. They will be knowers of reality, belonging to no religion or organization, but laying of a true emphasis upon the fundamentals of the Ageless Wisdom, the manifestation of a true understanding. Many are influenced by the Bailey writings which were not available in the Krotona Library when the author arrived in Ojai in the late 60's. The history of the Bailey writings can be found in Volume II, *Krotona of Old Hollywood*.

The Ojai Valley Oaks Lodge presented a group of their friends in a musical and dance program on the lawn at Krotona Hill, the proceeds of which helped to defray expenses of furnishing the lodge room.

Annie Besant sent her personal Message to all the members of the American Section. It was written on her writing pad, and the original is preserved at Olcott along with the letter written by C. Jinarajadasa.

> *My love to the American members: I pray to our Masters for Their blessing on all members who are faithful to Theosophy, and who work to spread it in the world.*
>
> *Annie Besant*

18th August, 1932

Dear Mr. Cook:

    I presume you duly received the President's Message and the cable from Bishop Leadbeater and myself. Regarding the former, I went in to her and informed her of your Convention that was to open in two days' time and asked her if she had any message. She promptly wrote the message which I despatched. Feeling sure that you would like to preserve it among the records of your Section, I send it under separate cover. It is written in pencil, as you will note, and as she wrote it in bed on the pad, naturally the writing is not what she would approve were she stronger than she is now.
Yours sincerely,
C. Jinarajadasa

    Olcott is truly a place of natural beauty, but its real power lies in its consecrated workers and its permanent community life. The author had the privilege to visit Olcott at the invitation of Tim Boyd, President of the Theosophical Society in America—National Headquarters, to spend seven days. Olcott is where there is beauty, joy, harmony, mutual tolerance and creative labor for a common end. Yes, it is a training ground for action, an experimental laboratory of life, and an art exhibition of life studies.

    Mr. L. W. Rogers' elder son, Stanley Rogers, as he has been known to many, took up a career of human service. For many years he was a social worker and advocate of labor reform years before Theosophy claimed him for his great life work. In 1932 he was secretary of a progressive political movement in Los Angeles, and later appointed to a professorship of sociology at the American University, Los Angeles.

July 16, 1932

Dear Mr. Cook:

    Due to my various connections with the T.S., I thought that it might be of interest to a number, at least, of the members to know that your predecessor's elder son has been appointed Professor of Sociology at the American University.

This university is a small, very progressive institution which is keenly interested in giving its students a practical education and in promoting international understanding. The faculty is selected on a basis of competence and background which harmonizes with the university's purposes. It should be gratifying to note that a member of the T.S. was chosen to give instruction in sociology. I am especially happy to serve as one of its professors because it grants its faculty complete academic freedom—a rare thing in an age in which money no longer talks but shouts.

American University is located in the heart of down-town Los Angeles. Its organization is very similar to that of the University of Southern California, but, having no football team, it isnot so well known!

Fraternally yours,
Stanley Rogers

August 24 1932

My dear George,

I hear Mrs. Hall is ill. We are very sorry. It was enough to have one bad illness in the family. Now you are getting the lion's share. We both hope by now it may be all over and forgotten.

We are still held here by the uncertainly of Dr. Besant's condition. A final change may come at any moment, or not for months, no one can tell. Meanwhile we must stand by.

I hope conditions are not as bad as the papers represent. Not much difference here. At the bottom any way. With all good wishes for you both from us both.
Sincerely A. P. Warrington

A small note, that I do not want to be the one to even suggest to the Trustees of the Ojai Star Institute that they regard as a debt to be returned, a personal gift made by Dr. Besant to Krishnaji so many years ago.

The following are translations of shorthand notes sent to Sarah C. Mayes by A.P. Warrington from Adyar during the Roof-Talks by C. W. Leadbeater for distribution among the special group at Krotona. She reported that reading another person's shorthand is difficult, but it was easy for Warrington to send them in this format.

Notes from a Roof-Talk given by C.W. Leadbeater in answers to questions put to him.

C.W.L.: Said he was not sure that any mistake had been made by America in eliminating immigration. He said it might be necessary to mix races to some extent but not too general. Some mixings had already taken place in America. He said the new Sixth Sub-Race would come into being very gradually. You would see a type here and another there. He had seen the new type in Australia, New Zealand and England, as well as in America. No one of these types had all the characteristics of the new race. Some would have one, another would have other characteristics. The whole would be developed very gradually. When there were sufficient new types drawn together to make it possible for the Manu to use them, He would incarnate in one of the families and start a family of His own. His children would be the real new race type. This would take place in America. He said He would not live to see it come about, but many others present would.

Questions were asked about the elemental which C.J. writes about in *The Theosophist* for October-September (soon to come out). It is the elemental worship by the Panchamas just across the walk from our compound. This elemental is a fierce old hag of terrible appearance, according to C.W.L. It was made 200 years ago out of feelings of hatred. It lives on blood sacrifices but we are waging war against it, and such a thing will never happen upon this compound again. They have come here for their sacrifices because of a certain tree that is here, a neem or margosa tree which is sacred for that purpose. But they will never do it again. The old hag will have to look for her sustenance somewhere else. Well, he said it would be proper to destroy a man-made elemental like that because it had no soul. The only point would be injustice to the worshipers who honestly believe in the thing. He said the Jehovah was the same kind of elemental made in the days of Atlantis. Since the Jews have stopped animal sacrifices to this God, he has to go and live in Africa for his sustenance. The principal thing about this elemental here in the nearby village is she has always obsessed a little boy at a certain part of the sacrifice and he would speak for her. When this took place the crowds would rejoice and go into a wild dance. If I had $50,000 to give away, I would buy up that whole village of the Panchamas and turn it into our compound. It would square up our property and protect us forever from such savage performances right at our very gate.

C.W.L. has recently spoken of Krishnaji a number of times in answer to questions. He is always very kind in his viewpoint. He says Krishnaji is giving one aspect of the truth just as all the rest of the Teachers have respectively done. There will be some who will grasp it but many who will not. He asked that when Krishnaji comes everyone shall think most kindly and lovingly of him and not be engaged in arguments as to what he may say. The thing that matters is not so much what he says but the great power that flows through him, that wonderful Second Ray power. I am pleased to see that this is the viewpoint that I have taken for some years. He again said that Krishnaji's way was the straight upward way, not the road that leads around the mountain. He does not think it will be easier to attain, now that He is here, than at any other time. It will be always an individual matter. He says that Krishnaji is doing his work at a very great cost to his body and is doing it well. He thinks that Krishnaji's message ought to be more for the masses. He does not really say that there are no Masters or Path. He merely means do not bother about them but go straight toward your goal. C.W.L. had nothing to say but what was kind and helpful. He said if Krishnaji should say that Masters or the idea of the Path were not necessary, he must mean that they are not necessary for him, for he may have transcended them. When Krishnaji says that his teaching is the most important teaching, he means it is the most important teaching that could be given at this particular time. All the rest of the Teachers have said the same thing, for each time it is important that the particular teaching in hand should be given at the particular time. Therefore it is the most important for that time.

The question was asked about the Mars and Mercury controversy, but there was not time to answer it. He said, however, that H.P.B. had admitted that A.P.S. was right. If this be so, I do not remember that she ever published such a statement. Certainly it would do the H.P.B. writers a world of good if they could see it. Anyway, it is not important enough to divide brother from brother. But Betty says there was an old article published by H.P.B. back in an early *Theosophist* saying Sinnett was right. Some one might interest himself in looking it up.

There is nothing new here. The President remains about the same and C.W.L. is flourishing. We both are very well and happy. The daily dip in the sea continues to be our chief delight.

Love to everybody from us both.

A.P.W.

For more information regarding the elemental worship by the Panchamas, there is an article "The Purification of a Tree at Adyar", August 16, 1932, by C. Jinarajadasa in *The Theosophist*, October, 1932, Vol.LIV, n1, pp. 68-79.

To A.P. Warrington from George Hall:—

November 16 1932

Dear Mr. Warrington:

As you will not be able to attend the annual board meeting this year, I am sure that the trustees would appreciate having the benefit of any advice you wish to give regarding two matters that will have to come up for consideration at that time. Aside from this the meeting will be entirely routine, as far as I know.

When Mrs. Gardner married Mr. Mayes and moved to Krotona, she suggested that she might be willing to help financially if we could get gas lines installed. As you know, I have taken this matter up with the gas company a number of times, and the cost was always prohibitive. A further difficulty was that many of the tenants were not enthusiastic over the change for fear it would increase their heating and cooking costs. However, I feel that Krotona will never be a modernized place to live as long as the heating and cooking arrangements are as primitive as at present. Therefore if it is ever possible to install gas, it seems to me we should take advantage of the opportunity. I have, therefore, spent considerable time in negotiations with the gas company, and they finally submitted a proposition that seems to me very favorable. They offer to put in the main line from the street to the garage at a cost of approximately $3000 without any charge to Krotona or deposit by Krotona provided that Krotona will use the gas universally for heating and cooking. I had Mr. Munson go into the matter very thoroughly with all of the tenants, and they all finally agreed to the change if Krotona should wish to do it. The expense involved for Krotona is as follows: About $500 for service lines to the different houses and plumbing the houses themselves to the gas fixtures and the installation of gas water heaters and the conversion from distillate to gas, at a cost of $775 for the hot water heaters, $315 for furnaces and $190 for meters, or a total outlay for Krotona of about $1780. The tenants will, of course, have to provide themselves with gas ranges or gas plates as they prefer, and this is all agreed to by them.

I have personally gone over this entire matter with Miss Poutz twice to be sure it had her approval, and you are the only resident at Krotona whom we have not been able to consult. It would not be necessary for you to throw out your electric range and buy a gas range, as I particularly excepted this one electric range from the agreement with the gas company. However, if this change should be made, we would like to know that it has your approval, and that you would be willing to use gas for your water heater and furnace.

At the time these negotiations started we were depending upon Mrs. Mayes for a substantial donation towards Krotona's cost, but just as they were completed she informed me that a change in financial circumstances would make it impossible for her to do as she had anticipated. However, I feel that this is only a temporary embarrassment on her part, and since the arrangements for gas have, for the first time after many attempts, reached a feasible possibility, I wish to place it before the board of trustees for their consideration. They will then be able to decide under what conditions and at what time they may wish to put it into execution.

The other matter I wish to mention is that for the first time the income at Krotona is not sufficient to meet the upkeep expense, and the books will probably show a deficit at the end of the year of several hundred dollars. I see no way that this can be avoided under present business conditions, but if you have any suggestions to make, they will be most welcome. As soon as the books have been balanced for 1932, I will forward you a copy of the financial statement. Also I will send you a copy of the minutes of the annual meeting as soon as it has been held.

It was very kind of you to write when you heard that Mrs. Hall was ill. She had quite a bad time of it during June and July, and just as she was able to be about again her sister, Mrs. Davis, died very suddenly. She left quite a hole in our lives, and we miss her very much. Mrs. Hall is now feeling quite her old self again and keeps very busy with her club and Masonic duties. You probably heard that the Masonic ladies in Ojai organized an Eastern Star Lodge here, and Mrs. Hall is, of course, a member.

Louis has been in Duluth all summer and has just now started to drive back to California. Also my father was at this summer home on the Brule from March to November, just getting back here in time to vote, although his vote did not do him any good. He and his wife are coming up tomorrow to stay with us until after Thanksgiving.

We watch *The Messenger* and *The Theosophist* for news about you and Mrs. Warrington and hear more about you that way than we do from the folks at Krotona. I wish I could be at Adyar for the Convention this year and the Camp that follows.

With cordial good wishes to you and Mrs. Warrington from us both, I remain,
Very sincerely yours,
G.H. Hall

We do not know for sure why Catharine Mayes was not able to give Krotona the donation she promised to help out with the gas line, but it could have been due to the fact that she had been given back her property in New Hampshire after she gave it to Meher Baba as a gift in 1931. Since the mortgage was held by the bank, and the buildings were in very bad condition, Meher Baba was asked by the bank to repair them or ask Catharine Mayes to take care of it. Meher Baba decided to deed the property back to Catharine, so she had to do the repairs, and then try to sell the property at a loss.

The announcement of Catharine Gardner's marriage in the Boston papers reported that the man she married was a person of a totally different background, but a perfectly fine person. The family have not yet discovered that Mrs. Gardner's husband is the man whom they met a couple of years back as the husband of Sarah Mayes. As a matter of fact, it was one of those rearrangements which eliminated useless friction and established a really happy situation for Catharine and Billy.

December 3 1932
Ojai Fire Department
Mr. Fred Linder, Chief

Dear Mr. Linder:

This is to thank the boys of your department for their prompt and efficient services in connection with the fire at Krotona on November 26.
I realize that there is nothing we can do to pay for such service, but I feel that our appreciation should be expressed in some manner more substantial than mere words of thanks, and so I enclose a small check, which I hope you will use to buy the boys some cigars or in any other way that you think best.
Very sincerely yours,
Krotona Institute
G.H. Hall, Secretary Treasurer

The small fire at Krotona on November 26th was good news, for the nursery was not entirely destroyed, and it was their intention to rebuild it anyway. Because of the fire, all the dwellings had to have the tile roofs; this was to include the old ranch house, which was partly shingles and partly composition brought up to code.

The last meeting between Krishnamurti and Dr. Besant took place in November 1932, when Krishnamurti went to see her on her deathbed. We do not know what actually transpired between them, only from what was published by C. Jinarajadasa in the E.S. pamphlets, and E.S. journals do we get some ideas of their relationship. Radha Burnier, President of the Adyar Theosophical Society, and Outer Head of the Esoteric Section has not allowed anybody to see the actual written reports by Miss A.J. Willson, nor the diaries of Dr. Besant and those of C. Jinarajadasa to verify what actually took place. Until then, it is best not to speculate, judge or attribute motives to what took place, but record from the E.S. papers left by C. Jinarajadasa. The room in which Dr. Besant was lying was the same which H.P. Blavatsky had occupied at Adyar during her Presidency.

The following records were all published in the *Shishya* and read in the Shrine Room at Adyar to the E.S. members, and Pupils who signed the December 1932 New Pledge or Promise ONLY. Where "Message" is typed in the following, it was changed sometime in the 1950's and reprinted as "Communication" and sent out as individual E.S. papers. They are no longer given to E.S. members today.

For use in the Esoteric School only

E.S. meeting at the Theosophical Convention, Adyar, December 27, 1932,

A Message from the O.H.

C. Jinarajadasa said:

My Brothers,

I have a very important communication from the Outer Head to give you, For many months past she has told us that she is very little in the body, that she is not able to control her memory; and many times she has said to her devoted friend and medical adviser, Dr. G. Srinivasamurti: "Do not mind all these things." So there has not been very much of her real self, of our President, in the body, except now and then in flashes, in wonderfully beautiful flashes.

However, on the afternoon of the 22nd, there took place a very striking event, and I want first of all to describe to you what happened, as recorded by one in attendance on Dr. Besant. For over two years Miss A.J. Willson has attended upon her night and day, and the strain is very great. I have therefore been most glad that a friend who has been working for many months for us, Miss Nettie Ockenden, of New Zealand, was able to help. And the President, who is rather particular about anyone trying to help her, has tolerated Miss Ockenden.

I am near the President night and day, and when wanted I am by her side in a few seconds, as my rooms are next to hers. I go and see her several times each day, but I go "on duty" only in the afternoon, to relieve Miss Willson while she gets out for an hour and a half's change, from 4 to 5:30. On the afternoon of the 22nd I arranged for Miss Willson to be away from 3 o'clock, and for Miss Ockenden to be in the President's sitting room, in case there was a call for Bishop Arundale or for me. About 3:45 I came on duty; but as it was mail day, I sat in the anteroom signing letters. Our brother Arundale was with the President by her bed-side. What then happened is narrated by Miss Ockenden.

Statement by Miss Nettie Ockenden

On Thursday, December 22nd, things seemed much as usual. About 3 p.m. Miss Willson went out for a walk and I sat in a chair in the President's sitting-room near the open door leading to her bedroom where she lay in bed, so that I might be "on guard" without obtruding my presence upon her. Soon after I had taken up my "honourable duties," Bishop Arundale went to talk to the President about the future of Adyar and of the T.S. and about a hope that a school might be founded at Adyar. She asked some questions about the project and he answered them, and he said if she approved the scheme of the school it would help if she wrote or dictated a few thoughts regarding it.

After a short talk in this way, he left the room (I think to get his notebook) and before he came back, I heard a low steady voice speak. I took a pencil and paper from a desk beside me and crept noiselessly into the bedroom and sat where I was not observed and tried to take down what was said, but the voice went steadily on quicker than I could write long-hand; but I got parts, and the sense of what was said. At a certain point she said "this day" and asked the date, no doubt thinking Bishop Arundale was present; I then quietly walked forward to a place where she could see me and told her the date, but she regarded me as a stranger—hardly welcome, and was glad when in a minute Bishop Arundale came back.

When the President saw him, she said she would like to dictate and he immediately commenced to write down what she said. The first part was similar to what she had said while he was absent; she again came to the point where she desired to know the date—but this time of course it was not a "stranger" who supplied the information. I had retired to the chair where I was unseen, but I still tried to write down what was said, in case she spoke too fast for Bishop Arundale to get all down.

After the dictation seemed finished, Bishop Arundale went away to type out what he had taken down, and I remained in my seat unobserved. Then a further sentence was spoken and I took it down, after which the President wanted "George". I again went forward and said he had gone to type out her message. She looked at me very sternly and said, with some severity in her voice, that she required exactly what she had dictated. Fortunately Mr. Jinarajadasa came in at this moment, and I ran off to deliver the additional sentence to Bishop Arundale.
Nettie Ockenden (Signed)

C. Jinarajadasa resumed:

I will read you her message later. Yesterday morning she wanted Brother George. We have now a bell from this building to his rooms in the Western Octagonal and Guest House. So it was rung and when he came at 4:30 am she dictated these words.

The President's Message, dictated on the early morning of the 26th

"I send my blessing to you all. I am very old now, for 86 years is old for a woman who has worked as hard as I have throughout my life. And in this outer world I shall not be able to work much more. But I can give you my blessing, and I know that through it comes the Blessing of my Master, for Whom I have been most happy to work for nearly half a century, and to Whom I have tried to be faithful. This is my greatest privilege, and I have always tried to pass on to Their Society any words that They may speak or send. While this can be done let the Society hear, for there might come a time when the direct words of the Masters will no longer be heard."

C. Jinarajadasa resumed:

In the same way, Brother George was called at 4:30 on the morning of the first day of Convention, and she dictated the following message glowing with the warmth of her realization of Adyar as the home of the Masters.

The President's Message dictated on the early morning of the 24th

(The message that follows was read to the Convention by the Vice-President, Mr. A.P. Warrington.)

"Dear friends and brothers, sons and daughters:

I welcome you here today with all my heart. Each one of you is dear to me as though my own son or daughter, and there is nothing could make me so happy as to have you gathered round me in the Master's home. To Their home indeed I welcome you.

May His blessing rest on the head of each one of His children.

May you all rest in His presence.

May His love remain with you.

I now declare this Convention open, for the service of the Masters and the helping of Their children."

C. Jinarajadasa resumed:

There was however one part of the above message which was not read to Convention, because I was sure she would desire it to be read to the members of the School only. The O.H. has been most particular not to impose her knowledge of the plans of the Masters upon the Society, though she has never said she did not know what those plans were. But in her capacity as President, she has striven not to impose on the Society any kind of a dogma as to the relation today of the Masters to the Society. The omitted part is as follows, and it refers to the event of the 22nd afternoon.

The O.H. to E.S. Members:

"It is the greatest privilege of my life that One of Them should at any time use me as His mouthpiece, as did One of Them a day or two ago. This makes me more happy than I can tell you, for everything is precious to us that comes from Their gracious lips. I am rather ill, and cannot speak to you, but He has spoken, and I know you will all be glad to have that which He said through me, which was taken down. He spoke through me in His own beautiful voice—a voice, of course, far more beautiful than my own, and I was so glad to hear it. It will make this the happiest Convention we have known."

C. Jinarajadasa resumed:

And now, my Brothers, I shall read to you her Message regarding our Work in the future, which she dictated to Brother Arundale on the afternoon of the 22nd. I was not present by her bedside when she dictated it. But I was there when Bro. Arundale came back with the Message after he had typed it. I had ready her favorite writing-pad to put upon her knee so that she could sign; I held up the electric table lamp so that it would illuminate the paper better. She sat up in bed, put the pad on her knee, and the paper on the pad. Then she read it very slowly, and then said: "There is nothing to change," and signed it. I saw her sign the Message, and also the statement about the Theosophical School.

The Message of the O.H.

"It is necessary to build on the past so that the foundations may be laid strongly and true, but the building on the past must be with the view to the raising of a still greater future.

We have still with us some of the greater of our older workers who link the old and the new together. All that is good in the old we must carry on, but all the fresh impetus of the future must come from the spirit of youth. It is not enough to dream in this work, we must also work, and the work must be done by young hands for the generations yet to come. But to work without a dream to inspire us would be futile and useless. You, dear Indian brethren, know well that Benares is great from her past, but on it she must build a greater future, for the life of India is a young life and not a life of outworn energies.

Today, the 22nd December, we lay the foundation of the future life. We who are old will gather round to keep alive the great traditions. You who are young must gather round us, so that youth and the strength of youth may be with us for the splendid work of the future.

George is with us to lead for us in the vanguard. Annie Besant, our oldest worker, is ready to take the burden when the new life comes to raise itself on the foundations of the old which is behind us. But the new which is in front of us shall be full of the newness of life. We begin the building today with the splendour of the future before our eyes. Let the elders bring their wisdom. Let the youngers bring their energy and their strength. Then shall the world arise in her strength, and India shall arise in *her* might and lead the world of the future.

Let age and youth together plan out and build the better days to come.

Annie Besant, *Warrior*."

Another message which she gave two days earlier contains the idea of what has since become the Besant Memorial School.

It was reported that the Elder Brethren have indicated Their desire that at no distant date an Educational Institution shall be established in connection with Adyar. Dr. Besant was hoping that perhaps that Educational Institution may come into existence before she passes away. Adyar is undergoing to a certain extent a little weakening in power, it is only temporary, for by June 27, 1934, the Educational Institution is founded.

The Message about the Theosophical School:

"To help to make Adyar a Flaming Centre I should very much like to have a Theosophical School near our Headquarters, and I earnestly hope the necessary funds may be forthcoming.

I will do all I can to help as I think a school is necessary for Adyar's future.

December 22nd, 1932
Annie Besant,
President,
Theosophical Society"

C. Jinarajadasa resumed:

That night (of this Message) about ten o'clock, I went to her; she was lying in bed and still in that exaltation which had come to her in the afternoon. I was alone with her, and she is always glad to see me. As I was holding her hand she said these words, which I wrote down: "Out of His great kindness the Master spoke through me this afternoon." And she also said: "You might tell Charles this; it will please him." (Charles, however, knew already.) Then she spoke again; she is very humble and she seemed to think that if I told everyone she would be put upon a pedestal; and so this is what she said: "Do not tell anyone except Charles; I do not want people to think a lot of me."[5]

C. Jinarajadasa reported that her last published motto for 1933 was "Work For Adyar." which hung in her own room. The following addresses were also read in the Shrine Room to E.S. members during the Convention in Adyar, and published in the *Shishya*.

Address by C. Jinarajadasa

Now, brothers, the Masters want us to build once again, and more gloriously still. And what shall each of you do? What but build on

---

[5] C. Jinarajadasa, *Shishya*, "A Message from the O.H.", January 1933, Vol.I, n4, pp.1-9.

the Great Plan laid down in 1880 by the then Mahachohan, when He said that the work of the Theosophical Society was not only to give occult information but to build a Universal Brotherhood of Humanity. The work of each one of us surely faces us all the time. It is to diminish the suffering of the world in all practical ways that our throbbing hearts feel are necessary. Who wants guidance from above in this practical work? Look around, open your eyes and see the misery of the world, the oppression, the suppression, the degradation; sometimes those sufferings never show in any sign on the face, but you can sense them if you look into a person's eyes. Our work is with the world.

We have the Wisdom to guide us, and the help of the great Elder Brothers always with us. They are always ready; They are looking through our eyes, if we will allow them, and They will suggest what to do. It is not always certain that any piece of work will succeed; They are always experimenting, but They are not dashed in courage if Their schemes fail, for They are the channel for the Will of the Logos. They have become one with that Will, and They know that there is no greater outpouring of Life than to work for Him above who is also Him here below.

To work to minimise suffering is one part; the other is to spread the Wisdom. That we have done, for fifty seven years now. We have given to the world a Wisdom which inspires men to feel that there is a light which guides wanderers in the dark, which floods the heart with illumination; it is that Wisdom that is Theosophy. In a thousand and one ways we must create new modes of giving the Wisdom. This work—to teach Theosophical truths—is needed for the building. You and I are supremely blessed that we have become, each in his measure, a guardian of the Wisdom.

As we go and do our work we shall not impose our knowledge on others; we have not done it in the past. We must speak forcefully and from conviction, but we offer it to others for examination. But remember this mystery: if you have discovered Theosophy *for yourself*, then, even though your lips do not speak, you will rouse the flame of Theosophy in others. I have said: if you know for yourself. Do not think of "yourself" as only this little brain; your consciousness in the brain on the physical plane is not necessarily all of "yourself." One way of knowing is through this brain, but another is through the purified heart. There are things which you can know with the intuition which are far more the truth for you than anything which anyone can ever say. You *can* know certain things for yourself. Do not think: "I have only heard, I do not know." If that is all you have made of your opportunities, you have accomplished but a small part.

You are in this School to discover for yourself, and if you have not discovered, gather now your energies, purify your character, so that the Godhead within you will flash out His intuitions, and you will know for yourselves. That is what Krishnaji is wanting the whole world to do—to flame in intuition. That is what the Masters ever want. Do you think that when They speak, They want us merely to believe? They appeal to our ordinary judgment. If we go to Them for advice, not a single one of Them ever impose His judgment. The Master meets our troubles as one who has had troubles himself. He sympathises with us, even though He cannot lessen the pressure of our Karma; He reverences the Divinity in us, and causes our own wisdom to shine forth. Krishnaji said long ago that when in the presence of the Master you feel you can achieve all things. In the presence of the Master all seems clear, because it is your own Light which for the time He is evoking, and so you see for yourself.

If you have worked for the Society, in your Lodge, in any way of consecration which you have chosen, you will know that all the great truths are true; and as you speak about them, people also will know, they will see for themselves. You will not be merely quoting others, you will be speaking out of the recesses of your heart, and you will carry conviction to some one person at least. If you have lessened the burden of one brother-man who is suffering, be glad.

To sum up, I can only quote those words of the Master K.H. which He spoke to my brother, Bishop Leadbeater, long ago in 1883. Our brother asked: "What can I do to come nearer to you?", and then it was that the Master Koot Hoomi said: "*Force* any one of the Masters' you may happen to choose; do good works in his name and for the love of mankind; be pure and resolute in the path of righteousness (as laid down in *our* rules); be honest and unselfish; forget yourself but to remember the good of other people and you will have *forced* that 'Master' to accept you."

To some of you the Master is near, mankind not so near; to others the Master is farther away, and mankind is near. It does not matter from which end you begin to work. Do good works for the love of mankind and in His name, or do good works in His name and for the love of mankind. if you will remember this great thought, that we are the Master's workers in order to help the world, the light will come, the inspiration will always be with you.

For the Masters founded this Society to be the channel of Their love and benediction to the world, a precious vessel through which They might pour out Their light on mankind in darkness. As as we work for Their Society, we come near to Them. This work is now just 57 years old, just one cipher in the centuries during which the building will continue. And now, my brothers, They have called upon us once again to associate ourselves with Them in Their building. Let us see that we understand our privilege, and that in the name of mankind, or of the Master, or of the God whom we worship, we think and think again how to build more nobly.

Address by Bishop Leadbeater

Well, brothers, you have heard the message. Now it is for us to carry it out. It is for us to obey the command that is given. We are very singularly privileged in that it should be delivered to us in this direct way, from the channel through which for all these years we have been accustomed to receive our directions. It is true, as you are aware, that for some time past our Outer Head has been less active. The tremendous work which she has been doing unceasingly, and we might say mercilessly, has told in the end. It is sad, but all machinery must wear out in time, you know; and I should think that she probably never thought of sparing that machinery in any way, but only of the work that she could do through it. Many and many a time the body must have been tired, must have felt worn out and incapable, but she forced it on, drove it through, and so she has helped the world perhaps more than any single person now living on the physical plane. And so she sinks now into a period of comparative quiet, but she roused herself from that, or has been roused by her Master, in order to give you at your Convention this particular message.

Is it not fortunate for us who are here that we should be so close to the fountain-head? Therefore, I say, like other privileges it brings with it responsibilities. You to whom this came so directly, you must be the first people to carry it out, the first people to set in motion, to express this new energy which has been poured out so wonderfully and so freely.

I do think that this has been a very harmonious and very beautiful Convention. I have always felt myself that that was the real function of a Convention. It is necessary to do certain business and that business must be done, but surely that necessary business should be subsidiary to the wonderful things which the Convention brings down upon itself. If you send out a strong feeling of devotion, if you feel strong affection or brotherhood, you are sending out from yourself great force. You do not think of it that way, but that is what you are doing; and that force always evokes a greater force from above. I am putting that perhaps a little wrongly; let me say it in this way: the tremendous power of the Divine Life is always hovering over us, and it comes through and touches us just as much as we will allow it to come. Every time you feel a rush of great devotion, every time you feel a rush of strong affection, you are laying yourself open to a high and wonderful wave of Divine Influence. If you were always at that level of devotion or affection, then the additional downpouring would be taking place through you all the time. But we are very human, we are only at the foot of the great ladder, and so we cannot always keep the same level of feeling and the same strength of outpouring, whether of devotion or of love. When we can do so, the reply is certain.

In one way you might say that it is automatic, for that great Divine Love is, as it were, to use a very low simile, like the water in some great cistern; the moment you turn the tap and open the way, down comes the water. It is exactly the same; you turn the tap when you have a feeling of uplift, devotion, affection, and down it comes.

When we all gather together like this, we to a certain extent magnetize one another. The vibrations of affection which are radiating from each one acts upon his neighbour and stirs up the same affection and devotion in him. And so it comes that when a thousand come together, you open not a little tap, but a great one for a mighty deluge of Divine Influence, of Love and power; and even Wisdom comes when you are full of earnest desire—you see more widely, you are less likely to make mistakes, you understand one another better, and therefore are of more use to the world because you understand a little more.

And so this is to me always the great feature of a Convention. Sometimes it happens unfortunately that at some given Convention there is some point about which people argue and become quite bitter. Now every man has a right to his own opinion, and it is his duty to state his convictions, but always with kindness and courtesy. Sometimes in the heat of argument people forget that, and they then mar the higher effect of their Convention. Argue by all means, if you have to. I do not believe that any good has ever come from argument, but still it is well enough if you keep it in bounds; but the feeling of Brotherhood must never be affected by any difference of opinion. It seems to me ridiculous. I differ in opinion from large members of my old friends, but it has never made one bit of difference in the affection I feel for them. Surely you may all do that. You differ, but you need not all the time talk about that difference; remember the points on which you agree.

So the great point of a Convention is the splendid outpouring of Love. I think we have laid it at this time in very full measure. In going away from this Convention I think all will take with them added strength and a greater power of love, and a more earnest resolution to help. You can practise these resolutions in daily life in all sorts of small things, to do a kindly deed, a friendly act. A small thing, but many small things make up a great thing; and if you are in the habit of watching to help all the time in small things, then when the great opportunity comes you will seize it; otherwise you may not even see it.

So. brothers, she has called upon us, and the Inner Head through her, to make a new start in many ways, not along new lines but intensifying our energies along the old lines. The great truths are always true. There may be many aspects, and it may seem a little different; never mind, the work remains to be done and the work is to help humanity. Our Masters live for the work of evolution which is the Will of the Logos; They live to serve Him, and in so far as we come into that glorious army of Theirs, we also must be permeated with that same idea—always ready to help, always anxious to help. I know you are all anxious to be hopeful here and at this moment, but, when you go out into the world with its tremendous mixture of magnetism and its different aims and objects so far apart from your own, it is difficult to maintain that attitude in its perfection; but we must try.

You must live that inner life which shall not waste itself in contemplation but shows itself in action; you must be doing something definite for your great Master who exists to help the world. Anything whatever that you, being members of this Society, of this School, can do to promote the work of the Society, that is of course the first duty; but you have all of you livings to earn outside the Society. Let your lives be permeated with the same idea, so that always you have at the back of your minds: how can I help? What can I do to forward the great work of the Master? So many things, you know, have been put before you over and over again; only now we must do them. It is very fine to hear, but the man who hears and is not thereby stirred to do something is after all absorbing selfishly and not sharing with his brethren.

So, brothers, work for our Masters, cling to our Masters, remember always the glorious examples which have been set before us, and the Divine Life which shows so clearly and so beautifully through Them and through all that They say to us. You are honoured to receive this new message; rise to the opportunity and go home and work. That is the best thing I can say to you : *Work*.

C. Jinarajadasa concluded:

A great deal has been said of late about the young and the old, as if somehow the elders should hide their faces. I would like to give my testimony, at least with regard to two who are twenty-eight years older than I am, and so when I was a young man would have been considered old, our brother here (C.W.L.) and our brother upstairs (Dr. Besant). I want to give my testimony: As a young man I blossomed in their sunshine and gave my perfume to the world—not their perfume, but my own. I blossomed in their sunshine; all honour and blessing to them.

Question and answer period in the Shrine Room regarding: Krishnaji's Teachings

1. You and the President have been saying that Krishnaji is a Vehicle of the World-Teacher and that He gives His teachings for the present dispensation through Krishnaji. The Theosophical Society

was founded under the direct guidance of the Masters and with the approval of the Hierarchy. The Liberal Catholic Church and Co-Masonry are also said to have been started under instructions from the World-Teacher Himself. You have been also emphasising that there is an Inner Government of the World, a Spiritual Hierarchy. But Krishnaji repudiates all these and says that the leaders of these movements are exploiters and that the members are exploited. How are his denunciations, repudiations, nay, violent abuse, of these organizations consistent with his being considered as a "Vehicle of the World-Teacher"?

2. If, as stated, Krishnaji is a Vehicle of the World-Teacher, why does not the E.S. fall into line with his teachings, and disband? If he is not, should not the clauses about recognizing him as a Vehicle, and studying his teachings be removed as a requisite for membership in the E.S.?

Answer by Bishop Leadbeater

Brothers, personally I am getting a little tired of these everlasting questions about our Krishnaji and his teachings. I hardly know where to begin in the middle of all that chaos.

The E. S. was founded by Mme. Blavatsky for the studying of certain teachings. We call them Theosophy, but you know that they are practically the teachings of all the ancient religions. The Society as a whole was founded chiefly to promote Universal Brotherhood. Then we had another question about studying comparative religions, and that very soon led to our receiving from the real Inner Heads of the Society a great deal of definite teachings; and that definite teaching is now called Theosophy. All religions have been efforts to state it, some emphasising one characteristic, some another. The Society was founded for that.

As to disbanding the E.S., first of all, our Outer Head took it over from Mme. Blavatsky, and owes obedience to Those who founded it. That has nothing to do with somebody coming along and saying it is useless.

Then you say we ought to remove certain clauses. Suppose they happen to be true; shall we remove them? I do not mind admitting that I should have been inclined to omit that one particular clause; but I do wish you would keep your feelings out of the question, and use plain common sense. Their feelings! People *feel* that their leaders have been attacked! Well, well, everybody is always being attacked by somebody else. It is the way of the world. Every teacher there ever was has been attacked. What can you do? Use your common sense.

The Outer Head is still with us, and I am sure she would not consent to dissolving the School. Besides, why on earth should she? It has done a great deal of good to vast numbers of people, and some have been brought to the feet of the Masters, thereby learning much, but even that is subsidiary. It has as an object, not so much to teach, as to do. We have learned to do a vast amount of very useful work, and we are going to continue doing it, whatever anybody may say.

So far as I remember, the clause to which objection is taken is that we recognise Krishnaji as A Vehicle of the World-Teacher, and that his books should be studied. I know very well that one more enthusiastic than wise wanted the word "only" added, his teachings *only*. The Outer Head never meant that, for he is *one* of the Teachers whose works you may study—that is all. There have been many teachers, and They were sent forth by, inspired by, and in some cases dominated by, the World-Teacher Himself. *You* here (India) follow one of These, the Lord Vyasa. That was certainly a manifestation, not of this World-Teacher but of His Predecessor. There was the Buddha, there was Zoroaster, there was Jesus, there was Muhammad. All These were sent forth to do Their work, and Krishnaji is sent forth to do his. I do not hear you making a fuss because we do not mention all these other Teachers.

Use your common sense. Read, study, try if it appeals to you. Remember it does appeal to some people very much. I went each morning to hear our Krishnaji's talks because, for one thing, I have a very strong personal affection for him, having known him from childhood and helped in his training. Our instructions were so to train him that he could go forth and do his work, and he is doing it. You must try to realize that in doing that he is carrying out the Will of the Being who sent him. He may, of course, sometimes exaggerate; we know he does, for example, when he accused us of being hypocrites. I felt that was rather a hard judgment. But don't you remember how careful he was to say: "This is only my opinion." Can't you leave it at that? It is his opinion that we do not face things. Well, we have been trying to face them, and we are not consciously hypocrites. Do you feel that you are a hypocrite? I do not. I felt at the time I wished the word were not used, because I know so many students who are not. As applied to the outer work, there may be something in it, but I do not like bandying abuse.

I have never heard that any of the great Teachers were hypocrites, because They weren't! They may have stated things we do not believe; Krishnaji does, but we do not therefore believe he is a hypocrite. He is stating his convictions, but he is talking from the point of view he desires to emphasize. Again and again he says: "From my point of view." "To me." He is carried away sometimes perhaps by the tremendous force that flows through him, but don't you see that any reformer must put his teaching with great vigour, that he must be certain? If he saw too much on the other side, he could not put his own side strongly enough. If he is to emphasize one thing, well then, he will have rather to ignore the other things. It has been done by all the Teachers. Most of Them have said that Their way was "the only way". Certainly Jesus is admitted to have said—I do not guarantee it, "I am the way, the truth and the life; no man cometh to the Father but by me." He may have meant that the Christ within is the only way to the Father; but He has been taken by those who now follow Him to mean that only those who believe in Him can obtain salvation, which is nonsense.

The same is true now: to say that any one way is the only way is nonsense. There are so many kinds of people in the world that on the face of it, this is not reasonable. The *Bhagavad Gita* says: "However men approach ME, even so do I welcome them." That seems to admit of the existence of several paths, and that is put into the mouth of a very high manifestation, an Avatara. It goes on to say: "For the path men take from every side is Mine. And we ourselves have heard the World-Teacher, not through a manifestation but Himself speak of "My many Faiths". We know that He stands at the back of them all, and wherever there is an impetus for good or for reform in any religion, it is always by His inspiration. It is something far bigger and greater than this idea that there is only one way. There may be only one way for an individual man. Krishnaji says, "So and so is the only way"; it may be for him, but it does not follow that it is for you or for me. Take your choice and follow that to which you are most attracted, but do not attack people who happen to be travelling by another path. It is the old story of ascending a mountain; which is the easier way up? It depends upon where you happen to be. Why squabble about it? St. Paul said: "let every man be fully persuaded in his own mind". But also he said: "I am made all things to all men, that I might by all means save some". He would put the thing this way or that, whichever men could take.

Mr. Jinarajadasa asked Bishop Leadbeater

I think the cause of the difficulty is not that, but, as the questioner said, certain definite proclamations were made that Krishnaji would represent the World-Teacher. Well, as the members see it, they cannot harmonize their conception of the World-Teacher as Head of all the Faiths with this particular representation which is denouncing all others except the one new line. The members want to know, is Krishnaji still the Vehicle, or what has happened?

Bishop Leadbeater answers

Nothing has happened, so far as I know. I have heard, and so have you, the World-Teacher speaks through our Krishnaji. One knows when that influence does come through; not always of course. No one person could ever express that Consciousness—a thousand men could not express it. Certainly He has spoken through Krishnaji; but I have heard Him speak through our Outer Head and—one must not be personal—other people. He speaks through whomsoever He can inspire, to give any truth He wishes to give. No one has ever said that Krishnaji is the *only* Vehicle for the World-Teacher, but that he was being trained so that a special outpouring could be sent through him, that special outpouring is taking place.

That word "hypocrite" was hurled frequently by Jesus; I dare say some of them were hypocrites, and some religious teachers may be now but not all. I am quite sure there were some good souls among those old scribes, and so it is now. I know perfectly well that your Outer Head is not a hypocrite in any way. She has stated what has been given to her, what she believes, what she knows to be true.

Our Krishnaji has never said that there were no Masters, but he has been credited with that. If he did, I can only say: "I have known Them for over fifty years now; and if it is a delusion it is a remarkably consistent delusion."

One knows what he has to do; it is to break down the attitude of blind acceptance of authority. He is always saying: "Don't accept authority". The Lord Buddha, you know went one step further and said: "Do not accept My authority unless it agrees with your reason and commonsense." I think Krishnaji has said that too. Can't you take him at his word? He is intended to start a new religion, and we are not trying to do that. We are teaching the knowledge given to us fifty years ago. Krishnaji now rises, and in his tremendous energy to do his work, I admit he sometimes goes a little too far. I would never say: "My way is the only way", I have seen many people called "good" follow other ways. From my point of view it would be a ridiculous statement to make.

So do not worry yourselves about these things, my friends. Why should you be worried? That is an attitude of mind which I find is a little difficult to understand. People worry about their beliefs. Can you not rise sufficiently above that to see that your beliefs and my beliefs do not matter a bit? Theosophy, for example, is a statement of certain *facts*. Whether you hear it or believe it does not make any difference to the facts. The only thing of importance is the facts. If you cannot believe them, your mind does not happen to see the truth. You will see it some day. Why worry? We shall have to try to put our personalities out of the thing and look at it impersonally; and above all things use your commonsense. Nothing is occult teaching which is in contradiction to commonsense, even though Krishnaji may say it.

Can't you imagine the World-Teacher looking down tolerantly on it all with a smile, and saying: "A very energetic representative; he is gong forth and doing what I meant him to do, though sometimes he goes a little further perhaps than is quite desirable, but that will tone down in time." Don't make the mistake of confounding any earthly body or mind with that of the World-Teacher. It is inspired, no doubt, by Him. A long time ago now I wrote an article about that, saying what that particular training—very terribly hard training, about which most of you know nothing—through which Krishnaji had to pass, had done on higher plains, how it had welded the two consciousnesses into one, making it possible for a tremendous influence to flow down. If you watch, you will see instances in the speeches he made here, sometimes very beautiful things were said, these might well come through directly. Imagine it as a funnel, the lower part of which is Krishnaji, the higher, the Bodhisattva. Remember you may have force coming from any of the higher or lower levels of the funnel; and the lower part is just Krishnaji, and he might or might not be conditioned by early training. He might give an answer to a question from that part and not from the higher. If you could only see a little clairvoyantly, it would help a great deal.

You say: 'How can the manifestation of the World-Teacher say such things? How can he be the manifestation of the World-Teacher when he tells us things which in our experience are not true? They are true to him; he has given you his best. He believes them. He would never utter a sentence—I know him well enough for that—which he did not thoroughly feel. He may be misled on certain points. He is human, you know, just as the rest of us are. Cannot we settle down and cease squabbling?

Some of you have said that Krishnaji is the World-Teacher. His representative, His messenger, yes; but it does not follow that all a messenger says necessarily represents that mighty Consciousness. If you will only realize the work that the World-Teacher is really doing; how He is the Teacher of Gods and men—that is, of Angels and Devas as well as humanity—you will see how very small a fragment of His consciousness is concerned with this evolution. We think it enormous because we happen to believe in it, but there are other evolutions than ours in the control of that World-Teacher, and you may be sure that "He who doeth all things, doeth all things well". He is perfect Wisdom. Down here we do not possess perfect Wisdom, and therefore we squabble. The perfect Wisdom is glorious and gives forth harmony; and you will derive much more from Krishnaji if you can listen quietly to him, and not argue in your own minds about it, but let the influence flow over you.

I sat there every day and watched, and I was rather sorry to see the way that many people reacted to it all. You know we had had a Convention just before. The feeling there was beautifully fraternal, unanimously enthusiastic. They were all keyed up toward the forming of a "Flaming Centre" here. But then when these other lectures came on, there were some among our brethren who pounced upon much with which they did not agree, and allowed themselves to feel hurt and offended. It is natural, but the fact was that instead of the splendid cloud of enthusiasm raised at the Convention, it was all broken up into fragments because the members were disputing points all the time instead of following the talk. Can't you hear a person stating his case without becoming annoyed? You didn't see any signs of excitement on the part of any of us, even when we were called all sorts of things. Hard words break no bones. I feel sure myself if you privately ask him: "Do you think so and so is exploiting you?" he is likely to say: "Oh, no; it is the general idea of the things."

I would say: Do not worry about these things. There is a magnificent and glorious heritage of Theosophical teaching to study. You go ahead and read some of the books, and try to understand what they mean. That will pay you a great deal better than disputing. I do not know how better to put it than that. Take it all calmly, and use your own commonsense. It has been given to us —and mind, it is a great privilege—to help in spreading this Theosophical teaching, and putting it into practice—a more important thing. You are all the time teaching by the Theosophical life you lead, and the kindly thoughts you send out.

We have made the facts about this Liberation known; that is a good work to do, is it not? Is it unnecessary? Well, I don't know. It is helpful to us to help other people. Maybe we are making a mistake in doing that. I do not know all about Krishnaji's special teaching; but the theory of that school of thought seems to be: "You are all feeble human beings, and therefore any effort you may make is sure to contain more or less of inaccuracy." Their theory would be: "Attain Adeptship first, and then you can teach with confidence." Mme. Blavatsky had not attained Adeptship—has not yet, if you come to that. If she had waited till she was an Adept, where would you and I be, where would the Theosophical Society be? There could be no *Secret Doctrine*, nothing to go upon at all. Another point of view is: "Time does not exist." But we have to live as though it did. There is no kind of question that the Society has done an enormous work; it is a fact publicly known, the change from the materialism that I can remember. If it be said that all this work is useless, I can only say I do not agree. Are there any other points?

Mr. Jinarajadasa answers Bishop Leadbeater

I do not think you can do much more by answering questions, because each individual has his own particular difficulty raised up by him day by day, and he must solve the thing himself. You can only give general guidance; but personally I would like once again to draw attention to your statement in January 1928, when you asked the members to listen to Krishnaji, but not to pay attention to the mind's challenging, but to listen, listen all the time. You said: "Take whatever part of the teaching that you can understand; leave alone what you want to question. But do not permit the mind to miss the greatest thing of all, the outpouring of influence from the Bodhisattva that is taking place."

There are certain teachings which our Outer Head presumes must be for the Sixth Subrace. She has told me that since evidently Krishnaji's teachings do not seem to fit in with our present work, it must be intended for the Sixth Subrace. Very well, we have our work to do now. We will co-operate with him in so far as we can.

I can say this much with reference to that clause in which she asks you to accept him as the Vehicle: She does not want to define in the E.S. what kind of a Vehicle he is, when he is that, how often, etc. I remember saying to her that many members had found that clause somewhat difficult because of the trend of Krishnaji's teaching, and that they would be more easy if the clause did not exist. What she replied is this: that a time may come in the future when it will be only those in the E.S. who will stand by him and be ready to do his work; and for the sake of that contingency she desires the members not to forget that he is the Vehicle of that great Personality to whose service we are all pledged; and for the sake of that fact she wants the members, in spite of the intellectual difficulties created for them, to remember that they are in the School to do whatever work the Hierarchy wants done. I think if, whenever we read his *Bulletin* or listen to him we would take what we can, and leave aside what seems irrational to us, we should find matters easier.

Let us assimilate what we can, but must make up our minds what service we desire to give. For us who are in the School, the goal is to be better servers to suffering humanity. If that goal is kept clear, then we had best take from whatever religion or teacher the teachings which inspire us to be better servers.

Once again, this is an intensely personal problem, and you must solve it. But I can say this: Do not leave aside the helpful work which you are dong for the world. There is need of work. If you desire to be in the School, then each problem must be solved by you at the same time that you are trying to give something of your heart to those who require your help. Little by little, as one enters into the spirit of this wonderful work of the Masters, all problems become solved, one by one. There is plenty of time to solve problems, but not plenty of time to refrain from helping.

Krishnamurti accepted the President's offer to use the conveniences of The Theosophical Headquarters for the Camp on December 24-27. Krishnamurti's talks would be organized by the Rishi Valley Trust, the organization which represented in India the International Star Publishing Trust.

Krishnamurti is seen everywhere on the estate—members see him walking, white-clad, in long swift strides to the sea, visiting with groups, chatting, laughing, or silently walking alone in the moonlit, jasmine scented air.

So many of the members are sorely puzzled by the teachings of Krishnamurti at this point, that C. Jinarajadasa has to make a public statement.

> I should like to share with you as to the difficulties in Krishnaji's teachings one factor which has strongly impressed me. It is, that we are not quite certain what is the exact significance in Krishnaji's mind of the terms which he uses. For instance, he used the term "liberation" a technical term in Theosophical literature, coming to it from Hinduism and Buddhism—in a new way. When he stated that any man, even a savage, could attain "liberation," he naturally seemed to challenge the whole principle of evolutionary unfoldment which is a Theosophical maxim.

> But after about two years, in the course of which he spoke on liberation, we realized that he used it not only for the Moksha or Nirvana Liberation, but also for other types of "liberation" or freedom from craving. I well remember Dr. Besant saying to me some years ago when we were all confused: "He doesn't mean by

liberation what we mean;" what she said explained at once many things to me.

So too when he used the term "organization," and proclaimed each organization a hindrance. A hindrance to what? To all effective *work*? Many accepted at once such an interpretation and left the Theosophical Society. But after a couple of years his thought began to be expressed more fully, and it was then seen that he did not denounce all organizations of every kind, *as such*.

A signal instance of this new use of old terms is his use of the word "exploiter". It has, in ordinary parlance, a sinister significance, implying that the one who "exploits" is consciously and purposely doing what he knows is wrong, and for an utterly selfish purpose. Naturally therefore he who is "exploited" is either deficient in character or a child. But it was evident during the Adyar Camp talks, when the words "exploiter" and "exploited" were so constantly on his lips, that he had not all the time in his mind the significance of something vicious. It did often, but not always; for on several occasions, as when he said that people wanted to be exploited, it was obvious that he was grappling with a deeply psychological situation, and used the word "exploit" because he was at a loss for another. There were some occasions when his philosophic thought seemed to me to describe by the phrase "wanting to be exploited" a state of negativity, following upon certain beliefs, which made the individual turn to another for help. That help came—or seemed to come—from another, the "exploiter," who appeared to play a role created for him. It did not necessarily follow that the exploiter was consciously grasping for power, or that the exploited was blindly seeking to rely upon another. Both might be sincere, but both were, to Krishnaji, fundamentally in error. Probably in a year's time we shall understand better what really underlies the phrase to "exploit" in his mind. So too we shall understand better what he means when he calls us "hypocritical" because we Theosophists react with enthusiasm to one part of his teachings, but refuse to go with him in his declaration, "there is no other way but mine". One thing is certain; Krishnaji is intensely friendly to all, desiring to give to each his liberty to go his own way, and would never dream of consciously hurting anyone.

This new colouring given to recognized words is very prevalent in Krishnaji's talks. As one of his friends once said to him three years ago: "Krishnaji, we know a man as Mr. Brown and you call him Mr. Green;" many words with stabilized meanings are used by him in new ways, sometimes to our confusion, but also sometimes to our great delight. It seems that a similar confusion arose in the Lord Buddha's time, when terms of Hindu philosophy were used with novel meanings; the word Dharma is a case in point. The Jews, too, were probably similarly confounded by the Christ, by the use of their sacred terms in new and unauthorized ways.

The difficulty, on both sides, on Krishnaji's and ours, seems inevitable. He is trying to describe his realizations, directly for himself and not quoting past teachers, but there are no new words. We know only the old words, and on occasion they do not release the real significance of his thought at all.

I feel sometimes that I would like to hear him in French, which he speaks well. For one thing, the language is more precise and "lucid"; and then both of us would be in a completely new sphere, he speaking a language which is not the usual medium of his thought, and I listening similarly to a medium which is foreign to my normal thought. Sometimes we might both need a dictionary; but then it would be the *same* dictionary. It is that we lack now, when he speaks in English, a language whose vocabulary is vast and often ill-defined—an excellent medium for poetry, but not one sufficiently precise for philosophy.[6]

It was around 1964, there was another investigation of Mercury, Venus, and Mars done by Melanie Van Gelder in Ojai, CA. Geoffrey Hodson wrote a letter regarding those investigations to Herbert Staggs around 1967, calling it "Occult Research". This material has never been published. Maybe one day the family will make it available, and compare it to C.W.L. investigations. Meanwhile, a copy of the documents are in the Ross Collection. Around December, 1933, *The Times* was making passages in their publications to contradict the statement made in *The Inner Life* by C.W. Leadbeater regarding life

---

[6]Jinarajadasa, C., *The Theosophist*, "Krishnaji at Adyar", February 1933, pp.583-584

on Mars. George Hall remarks that "any statement labeled scientific appearing in print seems to be accepted without question although science is constantly replacing old theories with new ones." Bishop Leadbeater was often requested to write his comments upon these articles, but he never got around to doing it before his death.

Betty Warrington seems to be the "Lady Bountiful" at Adyar. She has organized her home as a real American kitchen, an unheard of thing at Adyar. It can not have been an easy job to train a couple of Indian cooks to American kitchen methods for there can hardly be two things more unlike, and sends around to those new arrivals who are a bit under the weather most of the time baskets of life-saving sustenance. It is not only that Indian foods are different but the climate evidently has much to do with being ill most of the time. Betty keeps an alert eye on the Adyar sick list.

Among the Krotonians in 1932 were Mr. and Mrs. Tom Gibson. Mrs. Gibson related how she had first met H.P.B. when she was about sixteen, living in Philadelphia, and when she stepped on the porch the door opened and there was Madame Blavatasky.[7]

The International Fellowship of Arts and Crafts secretary was C. Jinarajadasa. Due to the changes at Adyar he appointed Miss Irene Prest to take his place. The Fellowship began its work in London in 1913 among a group of theosophists, having then for its name "The Brotherhood of Arts." As the work began to develop, its name was changed to the present one. They decided also to simplify their objects to one. "To work to develop the sense of beauty in all activities in life, and to study and realize the spirit of unity underlying the arts." There was no entrance fee or subscription.

---

[7] Forsyth, Dr. James G., *The American Theosophist*, "News and Notes", July/August 1989, Vol.77, n4, p.118.

The following was an answer to a question submitted to Dr. Arundale at a meeting of the Federation of Southern California Theosophical Lodges. Dr. Arundale reminded his audience do not take anything he says as final, even though, he tells them that he travels about the world in the service of the Elder Brethren, and that does not mean what he says constitutes the will of the Elder Brethren. Take it just as George Arundale's words. Here is the question:

Does the work of the T.S. conflict with that of Krishnaji? What are T.S. members to do about it?

Well, now that is a very useful question. I think I should like to be quite frank. It is very dangerous to be quite frank. The more frank you are, the more apt you are to be misunderstood, misquoted, and misreported.

We are in the presence today of a Great Mystery, namely of the overshadowing by a great teacher of a vehicle. I am taking that for granted. Of course, some may dispute that. They may dispute the existence of the Great Teacher, they may dispute the overshadowing by the Great Teacher of the vehicle. Now the heralding of that is seen in the light of later wisdom to be a very intricate matter. Personally, in 1908 and 1909, before Krishnaji came out in the world at all, before anybody knew anything about the Coming, I remember very well it was not at all clear as to how the Great Teacher would use the vehicle which He had selected. It was not at all clear whether there would be a complete entry, or whether, as in the case of the Christ of Jesus two thousand years ago, there would be an intermittent occupation, and the inclination was in the direction of the idea of an intermittent occupation. I think both Dr. Besant and Bishop Leadbeater were agreed on that point. Then things developed themselves and the President seemed on the whole to be inclined, especially in the light of the experience afterwards, to come to the conclusion that probably there might be something in the nature of consistent occupation of the vehicle. Not necessarily of the nature which they had been led to anticipate in the beginning of their investigations, but of a somewhat less concentrated nature, and yet definite and probably not intermittent. Bishop Leadbeater was on the whole inclined to keep to the intermittent theory which he expressed in another way in that "funnel" idea which I think was published in *The Theosophist* some years ago. The idea was of a kind of funnel, a channel coming right down with the higher regions, practically interpenetrated with the consciousness of the Lord, and the lower regions becoming increasingly less so penetrated, although there was but one channel. From the standpoint of that investigation, you might say the President was right and Bishop Leadbeater was right. It is so very complicated, one cannot say. Looked at from one standpoint, there was the channel and then from the other standpoint there are the higher reaches of consciousness, where there is the intensification of the Presence of the Lord, and the lower regions, where there is not that intensification but the personality of Krishnaji is predominant. Well, of course, there has been no conclusion actually reached with regard to that.

It is sometimes said that, after all, that is nobody's business but Krishnaji's. I do not agree with that, because he is now a world figure, so I consider it to be a public matter in one sense. That looks like an impertinence from one standpoint, but from another standpoint it is natural that people should want to know whether they are looking at the Lord, whether the Lord has, as it were, come down from His Himalayan home, and is, as it were, no longer there and is concentrated here, so that it is the Lord who speaks at every turn. it is very important to know that as a scientific fact one way or another. It is not important to know it from the standpoint of believing or not believing what He says, it is not important to know it from the standpoint of following Him or disregarding Him, because it is entirely contrary always to the policy of every great Teacher that any individual should be constrained in any wise to follow Him to believe Him, or to accept Him either in general matters or in any details. So that one thing is certain, that we must, even if we choose to discuss the question of the nature of the consciousness of Krishnaji, remember that the whole effect of the Lord's residence amongst us, or of whatever nature that residence may be, would be marred if we were to endeavor to set Him up as an authority.

I have, if I may say so, a fairly extensive acquaintance with many of the Great Teachers, and the very last thing any Great Teacher would permit would be for any chela or disciple to set Him up as an authority, to quote Him save under exceptional circumstances, or to do more than to weigh in the balance the Master's statements, and to take them or to leave them according to his best intuition.

So that the question of the actual condition of consciousness of Krishnaji is really a matter of purely technical importance. It is not a matter of ethical importance—not in the very least. It is a technical matter. So far as my own judgment goes in this regard, I have not the slightest hesitation in recognizing that it is a tremendous power sent out into the world directly from the Lord.

If you say to me, "Is there an incarnation?" and if you do not tie me down to any specific interpretation of my answer, I should unhesitatingly say, "Yes." But then I should go on to say that, so far as experience goes in these occult matters, when a Great One uses a vehicle, there is always the personal equation of the vehicle to be taken into consideration so that however much there may come down from the Lord a magnificent pure stream of life, that must inevitably be affected by the personal equation of the individual through which comes the life flow.

One knows that that is a fact in the case of Dr. Besant. I suppose there has been no more wonderful channel for another great line of force than Dr. Besant. She would seem to be eclipsed, as it were, by Krishnaji, and yet she, too, is a great vehicle for a Great Teacher. So to a very large extent is Bishop Leadbeater, and yet when one watches Dr. Besant and Bishop Leadbeater very reverently but very carefully, one realizes that from time to time inevitably the personality, the individuality of the vehicle, affects the life which is flowing through it. There is some measure of imprisonment, of constriction.

As to the extent of which there is that measure of imprisonment, I should not be competent to say. I could tell you as to the measure of the imprisonment of the life so far as the President is concerned, because she disclosed that to me. Only when I was in Adyar last April, she said to me, "You know looking back, my dear, over my life, I see where I did not quite fulfill." Of course, from our lower standpoints, she seems magnificently to have fulfilled all along the line. Yet she knows where there was from time to time a falling short. I have not known, even in going into past history, the case of any great individual where there has not been something which, as it were to a certain extent modified the nature of the inflow.

Is the Lord conscious of that? The answer, to my mind, is an unhesitating affirmative. he is a Great Master, a Great Manipulator of Power. But He knows the nature of His instruments and takes into account that nature. He has a certain piece of work to do, it has to be done within a limited time. He cannot actually do it Himself, bring His own physical body from the Himalayas down here, for that body would be immediately shattered to pieces. He has to use an instrument and to take into account the inevitable imperfections of the instrument, however few those may be, and He has to concentrate that instrument on a special line of work. He has to concentrate on a special facet of the Universal truth, on that special word in the Great Spiritual Sentence which the Great Teachers together utter for the liberation of the world.

If you will be scientific about all these things, then you will never be carried away by anyone but in an increasing measure retire upon yourselves. And so when you listen to Krishnaji, or when you listen to Dr. Besant, or when you listen to any other of the Messengers of the King at present in the outer world, if you are wise, if you have intuition, you will take great care to receive from each, profit form each, and mind your own business.

I am not myself going to be such a fool as to concentrate on one alone of the wells of life. I will drink to the full of my dear brother, Krishnaji. So will I of our President, of Bishop Leadbeater, but it is my intention to go my own way. If you say to me, "How can you reconcile your being a Bishop of the Liberal Catholic Church and a Co-Mason, and other things of the form, with what Krishnaji says?" My answer is, "I am not engaged in a policy of reconciliation, I have no time for it, I have no interest in it." I am not by profession a juggler. Nor am I one of those who can so twist words that I can easily make Krishnaji say or mean what he doesn't say or what he says he doesn't mean. Krishnaji is quite unequivocal. He says, "All these things—Theosophy, religions, ceremonials, etc.—have nothing to do with me." All right, but they have a great deal to do with me. "The Masters, karma, reincarnation, life after death," he says, "those have nothing to do with me." No? But then Krishnaji knows his own business. If I perhaps were in the position of Krishnaji, I might perhaps be saying all the things he is saying. I am in another department. I have my own work to do, and my own work lies in Theosophy and the Theosophical Society, and the other activities in which I am engaged. And then people will say, "You people said the World-Teacher is coming down into incarnation, and now He is here, He rejects all these things. What are you going to do about it?" Don't bother me about your confusions, your doubts, and your difficulties. Face your own. The question of more importance is, "What are *you* going to do about it?" If you are going to do nothing about it, well, then, you will have to wait several incarnations without getting the liberation that comes from either treading the pathway of Krishnaji, my pathway, or our own. If you are going to mean business, you are going to say, "What am *I* going to do about this?" If you are wise, you will come to Krishnaji's conclusion, which somehow or another you will find the same as mine, my friend—that each individual must go his own way. But he can go his own way very well if he will take a little bit form here and a little bit from elsewhere and use them all to his quicker movement on life's pathway.

I presume that Krishnaji knows what he is doing. I know he does. He is a magnificent person. We were all immensely proud of him, proud that the Theosophical Society gave him perhaps his original start, proud of the fact that to two Elder Brethren living in the outer world was entrusted his early education which has helped to enable him to be the splendid power he is today. If he has to break himself away from forms, ceremonies, churches, temples, organizations, so much the better. It helps the Theosophical Society enormously to know who are its stalwart adherents, who are those who mean business, and who cannot be blown about like weak straws amidst these conflicting winds which are inevitable when there is The Presence in our midst—a great storm of readjustment.

I am going my own way. Krishnaji is going his way, and there is only one way really, as perhaps he and I know, "upstairs", though down here we play about with a rainbow. up there, there is only the one white light.[8]

Among Warrington's papers, we found this unusual poem written by C.W. Leadbeater. We want to share it with you, our readers.

---

[8] Arundale, G.S., *World Theosophy*, "Timely Observations", November, 1931, pp.845-848.

Ants Came From Venus

        Ants! Ants! Ants!
What do we want with Ants?
We don't mind beetles and jungle cats,
Squirrels and crickets and snakes and bats,
Lizards and dogs and gnats and flies,
Mosquitoes and crows, and rats besides,
        But what do we want with Ants?

        Ants! Ants! Ants!
Regiments swarming in every spot,
Legions crawling on all we've got,
Myriads drowning in milk and honey,
In jam and sugar—Oh, isn't it funny
We can't get rid of—for love or money,
        The ants that came from Venus!

        Ants! Ants! Ants!
Why were you brought from Venus?
We go to the woods to concentrate,
We sit down quietly to meditate,
But not on our Higher Self, Oh, NO!
Our thoughts are fixed on the ants below,
        What do we want with Ants?

        Ants! Ants! Ants!
What had <u>we</u> done to Venus
that she sent hem here to tease us?
Can't we persuade you to leave us?
Try Mercury, Jupiter, Mars or the Moon,
We don't much care <u>where</u>—so long as its soon.
        Why Were Ants Brought From Venus?

Adyar Star bungalow, 1915

Adyar 1915, left to right: Dondekar,
Ranga Reddy, Wadia

Adyar, 1933

Front row, left to right:
Betty Warrington, A.P. Warrington, C.W. Leadbetter, unknown, C. Jinarajadasa

Back row, left to right:
unknown, unknown, George S. Arundale

Chapter II
1933

George S. Arundale, third President of the Adyar Theosophical Society, from 1934-1945, was immersed in Theosophy all his life. He was raised by his aunt, Francesca Arundale, an early theosophist who was close to H.P. Blavatsky and other early leaders of the T.S. Thus it was natural that as a young adult he dedicated his life to Theosophy, going out to India to become first a teacher then the principal of the Central Hindu College, founded in Benares by Dr. Besant.

He participated in the early training and education of J. Krishnamurti, later taking a major part in activities of the Order of the Star in the East. Always close to Dr. Besant, he was eager to serve her in any way, and through her to serve the Great Ones of the Occult Hierarchy. His intuition was highly developed, as evidenced in his books *The Lotus Fire*, *Nirvana* and later other writings.

En route from Los Angeles to India on the S.S. "Mariposa", following word of Dr. Besant's death, George Arundale had four astral "conversations" with her which he recorded in normal consciousness titled: "Conversations with Dr. Besant". George published those conversations at the T.P.H. Adyar in 1941.

> For various reasons I have so far refrained from publishing the following records of conversations I was privileged to have with our late President-Mother immediately after her passing on 20th September 1933 and during the succeeding days. I now feel they may be published exactly as I then recorded them, even with all the little precious personal touches which will ever mean so much to me. I do not say that these records are verbatim transcriptions of the conversations, but I did the best I could at the time both to listen and to take down. I have left the notes practically as I made them, with only the omission of one or two points of an obviously confidential nature.
>
> But it must be clearly understood that Dr. Besant has no responsibility whatever either for the thoughts or for the language,

though I think I have on the whole accurately reproduced the spirit of her conversations. I publish these conversations, I have had many others, because of their general interest and because they were the first clear contacts I had with her from the other side. On the first occasion there was a semi-materialization which quite overwhelmed me for a few moments until she adjusted me to her presence. G.S.A.

In 1907, the question whether members recognized Annie Besant as chosen by the Masters was questioned. Many said no, and resigned. Now the question came again in construing Krishnamurti's message as meaning: "The Masters of the Wisdom are not necessary for the world's welfare," and so the path to Them discredited.

Future of Theosophical Society

As the trend of the series of talks which Mr. J. Krishnamurti gave at Adyar for a week has been understood to mean that he was against the very principles of the Theosophical Society and that he spoke in a manner suggestive of the utter futility of the existence of a Society of that nature, our representative called on Mr. A.P. Warrington, Vice-President of the Society, to throw some light on the question.

Mr. Warrington dispelled the impression by categorically asserting that there was no truth in the rumour that Mr. Krishnamurti was out to destroy the Society and claimed on the other hand, that the spirit behind his talks was calculated to vitalise and not to weaken the Society.

The following is the text of the question put by our representative and answers given by Mr. Warrington:

Q:-What is to be the future of the Theosophical Society, of which you are the Vice-president, in view of the attacks on it by Mr. J. Krishnamurti.

A:-Mr. Krishnamurti has made no attacks on the Theosophical Society. He has said what he believes to be eternally true and anything that is erected on that kind of foundation will be helped rather than harmed by anything he may say. I therefore hope to see the interest in the Society augmented and strengthened in future as the members understand what he is teaching. The true science of Life as lived day by day no doubt has many methods. He speaks of one not yet practiced, that may become of priceless value when rightly understood. The T.S. is principally devoted to the effort of creating a brotherhood throughout the world which seeks only the welfare of humanity. It is well organized in forty-seven countries, and constitutes invaluable instrumentality for the helping of mankind in various ways, as the well known activities of our illustrious President have already made clear. I am sure if he were asked, Krishnamurti would never approve the cessation of such a Society's activities. He has emphatically said he is not out to destroy. Our motto is "There is no religion higher than Truth." We seek the truth from the living as well as the dead. Sometimes sharp truths are more valuable than smooth ones.

Q:-Will there be any change in the work and propaganda of the Society in the future?

A:-No, there is no occasion for it.

Q:-Is there going to be any counter propaganda against what Mr. Krishnamurti has been talking? If so, on what lines?

A:-Certainly not.[1]

January 12 1933
the Theosophical Society
Office of the Vice-President
Adyar, Madras, India

Dear George, (Hall)

I partially replied to your letter of Nov. 16th, by cabling my approval of your plan for introducing gas into Krotona homes etc.

---

[1] Newspaper clipping from India, no title, Thursday, January 5, 1933.

I hope you received it. The recent fire at Krotona emphasizes the need for such action, and I do hope that Mrs. Mayes will find that she can carry out the terms of her first proposition. I shall never feel safe from fires until this improvement is made, and shall be glad to carry my share of the burden whatever it may be.

On the question of money I think you had better send me an official statement of the debt due to Krotona by the President, to be presented by me to the Executor immediately upon her passing. There is no reason why this should not be done for I look on and see how her money is being needlessly wasted, and it would be much better that a legitimate amount of it should go to the payment of the debts honestly contracted by her and which she said at the time of borrowing would certainly be repaid in twelve months.

Is Australia keeping up her interest? I hope so. The radio is doing excellently there and is helping to meet many obligations. It certainly should not be saddled on America which has nothing to do with it. If any saddling is to be done it would be better we equitably to divide the obligation among a number of Sections able to carry it, the members of which would be happy to have a hand in the formation of that southern centre. This I think could be arranged after she passes if I am anywhere near the centre of power at the time. But you can see this spirit is just the same as that which animates Europe just now in public affairs, the cry everywhere being "Let America pay for it."

The future as I see it, Theosophically, is all in a tangle and therefore it is very important that the Krotona property should be held firmly to the original standard of being a corporation owned by trustees or certain objects mentioned in the Charter and regulated by certain by-laws which the Trustees have the right to make and break. There is one by-law for which I am entirely responsible and which did not meet with the approval of at least one level-headed person at the time I proposed it. And that is the one indicating the head of the E.S., a non-resident, for our President. I proposed this on purely sentimental grounds and am alone responsible for it. We could have done the same thing without tying our hands with a by-law. However what we can make we can break. The sentiment that actuated was purely personal and had to do with the person of Dr. Annie Besant and nobody else. When she passes my sentiment will pass with her, and as I happen to know who the next O.H. is to be I can say here and now my sentiment will entirely cease with her death and will not pass to her successor. I think therefore we ought to be set free from this by-law and left to act upon our best business judgement in future. We have a fine property there, one that can become very useful to our cause in more ways than one, as I can now see at this distance. But let it slip under a certain control, or under any number of certain controls I can see in my mind's eye, and you had just as well kiss the property goody-by. I understand that in other countries the properties are held and controlled locally and locally only. This is just a little bit of plain talk I am passing on to you George, for there are stormy days ahead in which you may not find your board feeling as a unit. Here and now I can say no more.

If you and Miss Poutz can find a suitable tenant for my house at a good reasonable rent, whatever you derive in this way could be credited to my monthly check which to me is a god-send. It is this that is helping me to accumulate enough to take me back home and to meet some of the expenses here. I do hope therefore something along the rental line can be developed to help matters out. There is a lot of acreage going to waste at Krotona and sooner or later you are going to find a use for it that will bring in some income. To this end we shall have to be guided in future more by our business brains than by our monastic feeling, especially as to the outlying portions of the property.

When I get back, and God only knows when that will be, I shall want to take hold if I am free to do so, and make something of the Krotona centre of real value to the theosophical world. If you were here with me now looking on as I am doing and studying people and things and looking towards the future, you would agree with me that to make anything of Krotona it must be utterly free from that which is active here at this time, and this I say after a very careful and mature survey of the situation.

The President is lingering feebly. Her brother hung on this way for years. It may be in the family. But so far as I can see the real person is gone and has been for many months not to say years. Those awful years of 1925-1929, well I will say no more about them here, nor other years that I might mention since 1925. Just remember that I am writing to you.

We had an interesting Convention. I have sent a page proof of my report to Miss Poutz. The Camp was very delightful. Krishnaji was splendid. We may go up to the Benares Camp.

I hope you and Mrs. Hall have entirely recovered. We are both very well. Many thanks for the Christmas card.
Sincerely,
A.P. Warrington

A Message from the King

The Message which follows should appear as the first article of *Shishya*, but I found it among the papers of O.H. only today (February 11th, 1933). During the last Convention, I showed certain lantern slides, which were reproductions of memoranda in her handwriting of Messages received from the Great Ones. Two of them appear in the February and March issues of *The Theosophist*.

After I had shown the reproductions, some friends assured me that a particular Message about Krishnaji, from The King, instructing the O.H. to "follow" him, had been omitted by me. I replied that I had never seen it, and Bishop Arundale assured me that it was not among the Messages in her handwriting which she had handed over to him for safe keeping. Nor had Bishop Leadbeater seen it, nor heard of it. But those who mentioned the matter to me were positive that there was such a Message, and so we searched in her safe and in the usual places where she kept her most private papers. But nothing was found. There was no such Message in the typed memorandum book which transcribed all the Messages received by her, which always travelled with her.

When searching today for another paper, I discovered in a disused drawer a second copy of the memorandum book, and in that the Message appears, in a very blurred type copy, but clear enough for transcription. It is as follows:

The Message

"Let My Peace and My Power abide in your hearts during the strain and stress of the struggle. You are preparing the world for the rule of the Wisdom which shall be the world's salvation from the evils that now oppress it. My Messenger, the Lord of Love, is with you, shattering the outworn ideals, that the God in each man may be liberated and seated on His Throne. Fear not the purging of fire that burns away all dross and purifies the gold. The gold is Eternal and cannot be destroyed. Stand round Him. Protect Him. Follow Him.

Let the Life shatter every form that binds. New Forms will be created to express the new Life."

Bro. N. Sri Ram, who recollects the O.H. reading this Message to the Pupils one morning in the Shrine Room, thinks it was immediately after the Chaitra full moon of 1928, on April 5th. Both Bishop Leadbeater and I had left Adyar on January 26th previous, and were in Sydney when she read the Message. He saw the Message for the first time, when I showed it to him on the day of my finding it.

The O.H. has spoken to me many many times about the difficulty of "following" Krishnaji in all things. She could not deny her Master, who was as her life and soul, and "follow" Krishnaji in that aspect of his teaching. She was her Master's agent to do His Work, and nothing any one could say could make her doubt the reality which she knew concerning Him.

It was because Krishnaji continually harped on the uselessness of Gurus and Masters, that they could not but become barriers in the long run to a soul seeking Liberation, and no qualification was made by him as to Gurus and Masters who might help and not hinder—that I too voiced my dissent on the matter from Krishnaji, and ventured to publish some poems on my Master, in the small book called *The Master*. I gave a copy to the O.H. She is a poet herself, and knows the best poetry from the mediocre; she understood at once my intention and gave me a short letter with these words: "Adyar, April 2, 1931. Raja dear, Thank you. I do not think you can ever do a braver and more helpful piece of work. A.B."

On May 11, 1932, she dictated to me a cable to be sent to Krishnaji on his birthday, as follows: "We send you our deepest love on your thirty-seventh birthday and are eagerly watching your work in the outer world." After dictation she said to me: "I don't think we can do anything much. We can try to co-operate with him so far as he wishes it. In some ways, there may be difficulties which we can clear out of his way; but we cannot do much. It is a strange business altogether." The next day she referred to the same matter, and said that she was "disappointed"—that was her very word—at certain aspects of his teaching. She said to me on several occasions thereafter that she presumed his teachings were particularly for the Sixth Subrace and for the work which it had to do.

On his birthday there was a discussion on the point that the "new" teaching of Krishnamurti had never been called into question except on the ground that it did not go on the old lines. It was asserted that Krishnamurti, in giving his teaching the character he had given, was only trying to rid the teaching, obtaining today in the Theosophical Society, of its mysticism and bring it back to the old lines laid down by H.P. Blavatsky. It is perfectly clear that Krishnamurti wanted all members of The Society to seek knowledge and enlightenment for themselves, for as he has said, each must find his own way. Krishnamurti's interpretations were new, his methods of employing the truth were new, his favor of freedom of thought in the T.S., which, applied to the teaching of Krishnamurti, meant that it should be welcomed, that it was the duty of the T.S. to welcome it, as all teaching conducive to Brotherhood should be welcomed.

> Two things are perfectly clear to myself; they may seem to others contradictory; they are not so to me. The first is that the work of the Esoteric School, in trying to bring disciples to the Masters to become volunteers in Their army of workers, is the strict fulfilment of the Orders given to us by The King. The second is: that the work of Krishnaji is a part of His Plan.
>
> It is for each of us to find out for ourselves under which part of the Plan of The King we are enrolled as workers. All intellectual difficulties will vanish one by one if only we will continue forgetting ourselves in order to help the world—the world which He rules with His Will, and blesses with His Love. C.J.[2]

---

[2] Jinarajadasa, C., *Shishya*, "A Message from the King", Vol. I, January 1933, n4, pp.44-46.

Statement by the O.H.

(Night of January 23, 1933)
(Written by C. Jinarajadasa, Jan. 24, 1933)

Last night at 11:30 the Outer Head called to her bedside Bishop Leadbeater and myself, George and Rukmini Arundale, and said things which, though special instructions to us four. We have a message to others also. And so, for that reason, I pass on what she said. But first I should explain how it all happened.

For several days her strength had been small, as there has been much difficulty in her taking adequate nourishment, owing to complete want of appetite. Now and then she has, however, taken a little food, and she seems to be able to live upon very little just now. Yesterday afternoon she said that she was rather tired of being all the time in her room with its two beds—we have two there so that she can move from one to the other for a change. So arrangement was made for her to lie on a sofa on the front verandah, and at three in the afternoon she went there.

She lay on the sofa, looking down the mile-long stretch of the Adyar River flowing to the sea, with the sea like a broad line of blue ribbon at the end—one of the loveliest views at Adyar which she saw in the old days every morning when she had coffee seated just there on the verandah where her sofa was. After she was settled, George, Miss Willson, Sri Ram and I had tea, sitting round her. She read quietly till a quarter to six when, as it was turning cool, George conducted her back to her bedroom.

Again she read, but went to sleep at 8. At 10:45 I saw Miss Willson, who told me that the President was sleeping; and I helped myself to some biscuits from Dr. Besant's biscuit-box, and went back to my sitting room, as I usually do not go to bed before midnight. At 11:30 Miss Willson came for me. She said that the President was calling for George; but that, as he had not been very fit and had badly wanted a complete night's rest, she wondered if my coming would be enough. She had, however, rung for George, but did not know whether she ought to have done so.

I went to Dr. Besant's room and knelt by her bedside. She was very glad to see me, as she had been feeling lonely. She wanted to know if she could see "Charles" C.W.L. I told her that it was 11:30 at night, and that he would be sleeping. As he has not a great amount of strength, I wanted to save him as much as possible. She still spoke about him, and I said I would take down any message which she had to give and hand it to him in the morning. Then she said that she was troubled because of a great danger, and she wanted the advice of Charles on the matter. When she said that, I felt that I must go and call him; but I could not leave her then and there, because there was no one else with her. However, almost immediately George came and I went to C.W.L.'s room. He happened just then to be awake after a short sleep, and I told him that the President wanted him. He put on a dressing-gown, and walked with me slowly to her room.

What she said to us was said in a rather striking setting. C.W.L., in a wine-coloured dressing-gown, sat on a low stool by her bedside, holding her right hand; George in a dark blue gown was at the foot of the bed, which is a low one and has no board at the bottom, and sitting at the foot, he reached over and held her left hand; I was in a white sleeping suit, with my purple cap and flap, and with a pad of paper and pencil in my hand, part of the time standing and part of the time kneeling with my hand just coming over the Master's Picture, which is always by her bedside facing her—the Picture which was H.P.B.'s own personal one. After a little Rukmini came, in a dark cerise kimono, and sat on the ground by C.W.L. Dr. Besant could see us all; and speaking purely artistically, it was a very striking looking group whom she addressed. She spoke very slowly, slowly enough for me to take down in longhand her sentences. She spoke very solemnly, clearly and emphatically. Often after a sentence, she kept silent for a period of from half a minute to two or three minutes. There was no hesitation about her words, the only hesitation being when she desired to remember a person's name and could not . Over and over again she came back to the same thought. It seemed clear to me that though what she had to say might have been said briefly, had she not been so worn out, yet she felt its extreme importance, and so her mind was on it all the time. Therefore she spoke again and again going over the same ground. To us who listened it was most impressive. It was not any kind of a delirious repetition, but a statement said so solemnly and so often as never to be forgotten.

There is a determined effort to break up the Society. It is a very difficult time. I hardly know what to do.

[To C.W.L.] You know I trust you; you are my Twin. I trust you as I trust no one else except the Master.

Charles, George and Raja must hold together; we must do our utmost to keep the Society together.

I can trust Charles thoroughly. Raja is here too, also Rukmini.

Charles is so wise; I want him to advise.

Raja is so intuitive. There is George. Rukmini is very pure.

Charles, Raja, Rukmini and George—all people we can trust, if we can hold together—and I am sure we can—we shall pull the Society through. Nothing must make us separate from each other.

I should like to stay here and not go away. If we can have Raja and George and Charles—we hold together firmly and trust each other. Rukmini is very pure and good.

If we stand absolutely faithful to the Masters, we shall pull the Society through. Nothing must tear us apart from each other. That is important—trust through everything—not break away, no matter what happens, against all slander, untruth and deception.

We shall pull the Society through; nothing must make us distrust each other.

You can trust Raja, Charles, George thoroughly; I think you can trust me too.

If we hold together, nothing can break up the Society.

I trust Raja completely, I trust Charles completely; George I can trust completely.

If we hold together, no matter what happens. Nothing must make us distrust each other, no matter what happens. Hold together.

The salvation of the Society is in our holding together as one body faithful to the Masters.

If we don't believe anything against each other, we shall win. Just a few of us strong enough to hold together. Charles is Masters' most faithful servant. We can trust him utterly. [Here C.W.L. made a remark depreciating his abilities.] No matter what he says, we know him.

George is not so wise as Charles, but he is brave and very true, so is Raja. We must trust each other, no matter what happens.

I am saying as it comes into my heart.

I know if we hold together we shall win; nothing must make us distrust each other.

Raja has suffered a great deal, and his suffering has made him strong.

[C.W.L.: That is supposed to be its purpose.]

It is necessary we should suffer. We must trust each other. We have been sent down to Adyar for this.

An attempt will be made to break us asunder.

We may make mistakes; we are not all wise. It is one thing to make a mistake, another to lose trust in your brother.

Jai, Manave, Jai!

If we are faithful, nothing can break us.

Charles knows more than any of us do.

[To C.W.L.] You and I will always be together, Charles. We can't be separated. We trust each other thoroughly.

Better stay at Adyar near the sea.

We have George, Raja, Charles; we have me. If we all stand together no matter what happens, if we believe in each other's good faith.

Adyar by the sea is the safest place till the present trouble is over.

We must be true to each other, never mind what it is.

I love and trust Charles absolutely, he is very wise and very brave.

We must take care of Rukmini. It think we had better stay as near the sea as we can.

We love each other very much, that is our safety.

Love and trust—the two great qualities. They will carry us through.

We must not distrust each other, stay as near together as we can, until the present strain and special attack is over. We are bound together.

[Rukmini here came, at 12:05 a.m.]

Rukmini is so intuitive; Charles is so wise. We have George and Charles; and little me too. [Here all smiled, nearly laughed] What are you all laughing about? [I explained that it was about the phrase "little me."]

[C.W.L. was holding her right hand, and George her left.] When George and I are holding hands as we are now, the Master can speak through us.

We trust each other completely. It seems to me that Charles has some anxiety on his mind.

[C.W.L: We have the Society to think of.] That's *everything*. We must hold together. It does not matter what happens to *us*.

George is always faithful.

H.P.B. won't come back; I don't know why. We want her so.

Charles must take care of his health; it is very important now.

There is going to be a great attempt to separate us. We must not allow it, no matter what happens.

They will circulate all kinds of lies [trying to set us] against each other. We have each to show that we are faithful to the Master; that is all that matters.

I wonder if Rukmini will look after Charles [about the special diet because of his diabetes]. I don't like to turn her into a cook, but that is very important. I would like to cook, but I don't know how. I can fight, but I don't think I can cook!

I am very anxious about . . . I am trying to think . . .can't remember his name.

[George here was seeking to feel her pulse, unknown to her. But she knew.]

George is studying the pulse.

[George whispered to us that it was strong.]

[To C.W.L.] Are you older than I?

[C.W.L. replied: Older in body, not as a soul.]

Charles is so humble—though he is so wise.

[Rukmini quoted: "Why the Most Wise? Because the most humble."]

There is going to be a great effort made by the enemy to make us distrust each other. We must be on the look out to have complete trust.

We have worked together so long.

I think the enemy is trying to make us distrust each other.

Charles is the oldest of us, oldest and wisest of us.

[The conversation then passed on to other things., She had some coffee, raising herself up to take it. C.W.L. and I left at 12:30 a.m., George and Rukmini a little later.]

C.W. Leadbeater
Rukmini Arundale
G.S. Arundale[3]

---

[3] Jinarajadasa, C., *Shishya*, "Statement by the O.H.", Vol.I, January 1933, n4, pp.36-43.

The Warning of the O.H.

Several members have written to me regretting greatly that I published in full the statement of the O.H. made on the night of January 23rd, and published in the last issue of *Shishya*, on pages 36-43. It is to them very painful reading, as showing the physical debility of the O.H. They think that if I had merely summarized what she said it would have served the purpose.

My reply is: When the Outer Head gives us a Message of such supreme importance as, "There is a determined effort to break up the Society," it is my duty to state everything in her own words. Certainly I could have summarized and quoted from her, but then I should have come between her and the members. My desire was to bring as near to her as possible such members as showed understanding, even though the signs of age and weakness made for them painful reading. All the more was the message of supreme importance, since she overrode the weakness of the body and struggled to give such a significant warning. Reporting every word which she said will be helpful, I think, to the majority of members, in understanding her thought more clearly than they would by getting that thought through my mind.[4]

—❧❧—

Published in *The Disciple* for May, 1934, we read a little more insight regarding what is written above by C. Jinarajadasa.

On Guard!

On the night of January 23, 1933, Brother Annie Besant called four of us to her bedside—C.W. Leadbeater, G.S. Arundale, Rukmini Arundale, and myself—and gave us a most solemn warning that a strong attack would be launched against the Society by the Dark Powers, but that the Society would be saved if we four held together after her passing. During the visit of the Inner Head to Brother C.W. Leadbeater last September, He drew attention to this warning given through her. Only three of us now remain. We shall hold together.

---

[4]Jinarajadasa, C., *Shishya*, "The Warning of the O.H.", Vol. II, July 1933, n1, p.15.

But because we do hold together, and the Society cannot be wrecked, the attack is passing to other departments of the one Work.

Brethren, be on your guard. Many will tell you what is "the will of the Masters". Accept no one's statement, not even mine, because it claims to originate from occult sources. Examine each statement, quietly, in meditation, in the light of your Intuition. You who aspire, if you also work to help, have already within you lit the lamp whose light shall guide your footsteps. Watch that light, and do not act on mere belief. O.H.[5]

To A.P. Warrington from George Hall:—

February 7 1933

Dear Mr. Warrington:

So far we have been unable to hold the annual meeting of the Krotona board of trustees for lack of a quorum. However, all of the trustees with whom I have discussed the financial situation feel very strongly that something should be done to avoid so large a deficit next year if possible.

With business conditions the way they have been the past few years, even those who have been able to retain their positions have had to accept substantial reductions of salary. People in business have, of course, suffered drastic reductions in income and in many cases lost their business and property entirely. Under these conditions, and with no certainty as to the future, we consider it highly important for the welfare of Krotona that the budget be balanced if possible.

As you know, the corporation has only three employees, all of whom are working on minimum salaries. Vernon has had to move into a more expensive apartment and pay higher rent, and Mr. Munson will have to earn less also, as the budget will provide a smaller allowance for repairs this coming year. Mrs. Goldy, who works very hard and long hours, already gets a minimum living allowance, and it therefore seems impossible to reduce the budget to any material extent in any of these items.

---

[5] Jinarajadasa, C., *The Disciple*, "On Guard!", May, 1934, n2, p.57-58.

As you have been absent a considerable time, and your return is uncertain, we would like to ask permission to rent your house and get some income from it for Krotona rather than let it stand idle. Of course there may be no opportunity for this, and if one should develop the tenants would, of course, have to be approved by Miss Poutz. Also the trustees feel that you might perhaps be willing to forego your salary from Krotona until conditions improve. It is quite out of the question that the income should be increased to take care of this by raising the rent at such a time.

Please let me hear from you with regard to this at your early convenience, and on receipt of your reply I will present it to the board of trustees.

Very sincerely yours,
George Hall

The reason for not holding the Krotona board meeting was that Henry Hotchener was absence from the city. A copy of the above letter was sent to C.F. Holland, Henry Hotchener and Max Wardall for their approval.

In spite of the depression and other stormy times, since the world events and the well known break up of the economic structure is now so apparent to everyone that even fixed obligations based on mortgages are being voluntarily readjusted to meet the great changes which have taken place.

February 11 1933
Louis Zalk
6605 Hollywood Boulevard
Los Angeles, California

Dear George:

I have very carefully read your letter of the 7th together with the first draft of the copy of your letter to Mr. Warrington.

May I say that I do not feel you are justified in believing that it would be better if Max or Henry Hotchener or Mr. Holland wrote the letter. Let us begin by giving Mr. Warrington the benefit of supposing that he will thoroughly understand our position and will have no resentment against an action that is obviously sincere and well taken. I am assuming that he will understand. If it so happened that Mr. Warrington could show resentment, it would not matter

who wrote the letter, since if he were disposed to blame you, it would be all the same. And so, dear George, it is my earnest advice to you to write to Mr. Warrington in the friendliest possible way an explain the situation. As to the members of the Board, you can tell him that this letter is written with the approval and knowledge of the members. After you have sent each a copy and received their OK.
As ever, Louis

P.S. You might also suggest that not all but only a portion of the Krotona allowances is involved as it would be rather too drastic that all of it be withdrawn.

Louis Zalk has also drafted for the Ojai Star Institute an Appeal which is to go out on March 1st. Mr. Rajagopal suggested that it be printed and distributed from the Star Office.

February 26 1933
Adyra, Madras, India

My dear Warringrton,

I suppose sometime I shall have to make public her actual words about K. I have not wanted to do so just now. I have shown them only to J. K. himself, & C.W.L., not to George even. I am telling them to you, because you are V.P., but I shall be glad if you will keep them to yourself.

Her illness that day indeed influenced her judgment. She was standing looking at the pictures on her bench, & I by her side. Looking at C.P.'s she spoke much, but that I can't tell others; then at Wedgwood's & said a few words of sympathy. Then she looked at K's big picture as a boy & said these words (they were so few & so striking I could remember to write them down half an hour later): "I suppose one ought not be disappointed, but I thought he would do bigger things,.."

Were she releasing THE MESSAGE of the KING now, I feel sure she would "footnote".
Yours ever
C. Jinarajadasa

C. Jinarajadasa made the following statement, "I made notes of several such observations of Dr. Besant concerning many things." Where these notes are today, we do not know. Most likely they are under lock and key at Adyar in the Esoteric Archives.

Why I Stood for Election

I should like now to share with my friends the record of an incident that took place on February 26, 1933. From 3:00 in the afternoon I was with Dr. Besant on her veranda, and at 3:45 Miss Willson left. At 5:50 the sun was setting. Miss Willson returned. The President got up to go inside, then stood looking over the river and said what a beautiful place it was. Of course I agreed.

Then suddenly, with no preliminary, she said to me: "I hope you will be President after me." I said: "Why?" She replied: "Because you are the fittest person." I said: "Some think George should be President." She replied: "Of course members must do the electing." Miss Willson heard the conversation, as she was behind me, but I told her not to speak or write of this. As Dr. Besant seemed to have no further need of me, and since Miss Willson was back on duty, I returned immediately to my office and made a memorandum of the above.

Dr. Besant left us on September 20, 1933. I decided not to stand for President, and three days after, I sent to be printed a statement, to be distributed, "Why I do not stand for President." On September 26th, using my right as a member of the General Council, I nominated Dr. Arundale for the post of President.

I took it as certain then that Dr. Arundale would surely come to a third term of office. But as all know he did not complete his second term of office, and passed away on August 12, 1945. When the time came for nominations for the next President, I remembered the words of Dr. Besant, and therefore intimated that I was willing to stand.
C. Jinarajadasa

March 2 1933

Dear George,

Your financial report for the past year has come and shows you to be somewhat of a prophet. But if we can make all of our assets yield their proper income I am sure we shall sail along comfortably in spite of the depression and other stormy times.

As to the Sydney loan I suggest that you notify the proper person that if they will pay their interest regularly Krotona will absorb the difference in exchange. I think it will pay us to lose this difference rather than to lose the whole of the interest. Sydney has the money judging from reports that I have seen. Moreover sometime ago Catharine Gardner promised me to contribute the amount of this interest to Sydney for some years. Whether she has stopped paying it or not I do not know. But if she is still doing so, all question of exchange could be avoided if she will make the contribution to Krotona direct. Please do not say anything to her about this, however, without first consulting Miss Poutz. And don't say anything to Billy about it in any case.

I find myself embarrassed by the whole situation, and being so far away and so uncertain of my movements thee is very little that I can do to help. Even out here one has one's expenses and must accumulate enough for the return trip home. If the president continues to live throughout the whole of the term, then we may be expected back in Ojai probably late in 1935 or early in 1936. Then I shall hope to join hands in earnest and see what we can do to make that fine property of ours bring in more income. Meanwhile, as I have written, if my house can be rented with Miss Poutz's approval that will help some in this emergency.

I don't seem to remember anything about the James D. Moore note. As to Dr. Besant's, that will be paid in time, I think, if we move rightly and at the right time.

I hope your own affairs are not suffering during this strange depression that is gripping the world. Perhaps India is suffering less than other countries, because she had already gone down about as far as she could do and keep alive. So it is all the same to her so far as the masses of the people are concerned.

With greetings to you both from us both,
Sincerely,
A.P. Warrington

James D. Moore and his wife, took a lease or note at the time when they were building their home at Krotona, and did not have enough money to complete it; they borrowed $2,000 for one year. This they were not able to pay back, but Krotona could be compelled to take over their property to cover the principal and interest.

Because of the inevitable signs of old age, terrible handicap of a body and brain that is dying, it is interesting to read the conflicting reports given out during Dr. Besant's illness on what she said. Such as the word "disappointed" with regard to Krishnamurti. Some believed that this must be not from her real self but from her lower self only due to ill health.

March 10 1933
Headquarters of the American TS
Wheaton, Illinois

Dear Mr. Warrington:

Just a note about the "tropical foliage" on the cover of the *American Theosophist*. I can give you several reasons for the particular design selected:

1. I have understood that it was the original design of *The Theosophist* in H.P.B.'s time and I read somewhere that after departing from that design and returning to it a year or two ago, H.P.B. in her present body expressed her pleasure.

2. I have been told that when the *Australian Theosophist* was considering a change from their present cover that includes the tropical design, Bishop Leadbeater made some remark to the effect that it would be all right if they wished to spoil the magazine.

3. The above two incidents confirm what I have somehow otherwise learned, namely, that on account of association the magazine design has some occult significance and link with the Great Ones.

4. And as the Theosophical Society is worldwide, it seems to me rather a nice idea that all of the national magazines should incorporate the one design.

5. It does seem to me that the Adyar design used on our magazine is an indication of our sense of attachment to Adyar

and of our recognition of the fact that we are but a unit in an international scheme.

6. Tropical (Eastern) foliage, because Theosophy is the wisdom of the East, and in our cover design there is an indication of its blending with the practical ideas of the West.

7. It at last makes a decorative boarder for the rather fine half-tone of our building.

There may be other reasons, the last one in itself is rather weak, but these are those that happen to occur to me, and I did want to get some color around the half-tone.

Tonight they are counting votes. I think it is safe to say from the appearance of the piles of ballots in the counting room, that your humble servant has been reelected for a term of three years with Mr. Holland as Vice-President.

So interested in your battalion of masseurs and what you tell us about the treatment. I do hope it will accomplish all that you desire of it. I am perfectly sure that if you survive it, you will have earned eternal life.

With kindest good wishes and affection,
Cordially yours,
Sidney A. Cook

Marie Poutz writes as the Corresponding Secretary for the Esoteric School at Krotona, "that it is difficult to imagine any E.S. member who fails to be vitally and tremendously interested in President Roosevelt's gigantic effort to settle the problems which confront the country. What are we to think of any member who says, for instance, Oh, this will not work! How do we know?"

Even George Arundale, as the International President of the Theosophical Society sends a telegram to President Roosevelt offering his respectful homage, being a temporary guest in the land over which he presides. George Arundale reminds the members of The Esoteric School that they all belong to the royal family, they belong to the kingship, if not in the human kingdom, certainly in the sub-human kingdoms.

A.P. Warrington writes the following letter to Franklin Delano Roosevelt. We do not know if the President answered his letter.

March 21 1933
To His Excellency, Franklin D. Roosevelt
the President of the United States
White House, Washington, D.C.

Dear Mr. President:

There is perhaps nothing that I desire more eagerly than to see you win the momentous historic privilege which now confronts you of bringing about the affective change in civilization which, in this day of rapid movement, will soon be overdue unless some great world figure like yourself quickly "puts it over." I feel sure that if you should fall through a temporizing timidity, or a sincere desire to go slowly in a presumably more secure experimentation of trial and error, the high privilege which is now yours will pass to some other world figure and no doubt with less happy results. That the World Plan <u>must</u> be carried out by some world power I have no doubt, the game being to the most inspired and courageous.

The fact is, our decaying civilization was doomed from its very inception, for it was based on the law of the jungle, the survival of the fittest, rather than the supreme law for man, the unity of all and the survival of the whole; for no matter what multiplicity of differences may appear in the great human family, there is a principle within each man that links him with every other in a bond of union and identity of purpose and destiny which is ultimately indefeasible, and makes the welfare of "the very least of these" an inescapable condition precedent to the welfare of the whole. Under our traditional groping <u>the race has been to the swift and the devil take the hindrest</u>; but under the fundamental law of man which is now coming to its blossom time, the goal must be passed, not merely by a favored few for themselves alone as against the whole, but by the group itself as a whole, and that means that there must be an immediate effort made, toward definitely reorganizing civilization so that the needs of the weakest are constructively provided for as also all those others onward up to the very strongest, so that the struggle for life shall not be thrown upon the infants of the race, so to say, any more than it has ever been upon the infants of the individual family, but upon the elders and the strong.

That is the need of the hour, a need that no people may any longer trifle with or ignore. Civilization is ready for the change as it never has been before and the very forces of cosmos are standing "to order" to help the turning of the tide. Plato saw the need and gave us his *New Republic*; so did Sir Thomas Moore in his *Utopia*; and Sir Bulwer Lytton in his *Coming Race*. Even in our own time we have had our Henry George, Edward Bellamy, and others, all appealing for a practical recognition, in the organized daily life of humanity, of the truth that all are one, as cells in one vast, living organism.

"Well," you may say, "What's to be done about it that promises success?"

Make a beginning! A beginning that starts at the very root of the problem and aims at a gradual growth toward a well-defined goal to be reached fully in the years to come. That goal should be reached by means that are radical, but not radical; extreme yet not extreme; revolutionary, still not revolutionary, certainly by none of the jungle methods prostituting civilization today. What the principles are I have ventured to suggest; but what the methods shall be to bring these principles into being I cannot say. That's the job of the man of destiny who shall transmute the New Deal into a New Day, the dawn of that civilization for which the world is now longing. The treats of war, the murmurings of millions of workless citizens, and the far greater impending danger of seeing the seats of power seized by the venal modern "carpet-bagger," ignorant, loud-voiced, and powerful before a prostrate, hypnotized public, are these not enough to arouse the great into a realization that there must be action that is fundamental and no longer superficial? The old order cannot be patched up. A new garment is needed. What will you do with your age-resounding opportunity, Mr. President?

May I venture to make just one suggestion as a line of thought? Mrs. Prestonia Mann Martin has advanced the most intelligent thought in the present babble of impracticable schemes that I have yet seen. (Vide her *Prohibiting Poverty*, Farrar & Rinehart.) If her suggested plan could only be given a trial, there are those who believe it would constitute the first true step in the direction of solving life's problem for all the people here and now. I do urge that you read her entrancing little book and give it deep thought. We are told our First Lady has read it and is impressed. Do let me ask, in the name of the invisible powers that be (if such be possible to a sincere citizen who loves the service of the entire race of man), that you will try to catch the inspired purpose behind that plan and resolve to pledge all your power and influence to the effective purpose of inaugurating the first steps therein called for. You would be sure to realize what a profound relief you would have in the pursuit of a plan that not only was definite and simple, but was one that carried within it the solution of a whole litter of problems which are today approached one by one by a complication of futile remedies.

Finally, Mr. President, the salvage of civilization is a gentleman's problem, and this is a gentleman's hour. In France it was a gentleman's problem and hour a century and a half ago. But there was conservatism and delay, until the resulting fever and suffering produced the Huey Longs of that age, and you know the rest. Let not history repeat itself; but reflect deeply, resolve high and nobly and act magnificently, for all the public alarms warn us that time presses.

This letter, Sir, goes to you personally as man to man, and will certainly remain private, at least until I can, in an abundantly reasonable time, have a chance to hear from you.

Most sincerely,
A.P. Warrington

March 30 1933

Dear Mr. Warrington:

I am sorry to have been so long in answering your letter of January 12. Miss Crowe has been away for about a month, and as I am quite out of the habit of using a machine I find it very difficult to do my own typing. Also there were many things in your letter which I did not know just how to answer, and I have finally concluded that I had best let them go until you come back when we can talk them over more conveniently.

I am sorry you bothered to cable about the gas, as a letter would have been quite sufficient. With your consent to use gas in your own home, I now have the approval of all the residents at Krotona but I do not think the installation will be possible because of the financial difficulties. The gas company is willing to spend $3000 for the main line, but it would still cost Krotona nearly $2000 for service lines, plumbing and fixtures. Of this amount Mrs. Mayes has so far only offered $250. So far I have been unable to arrange for a board meeting, but when it is arranged this matter will be presented.

You have undoubtedly received my annual report, a copy of which was sent to every trustee, and from that you will have learned the answer to your question about Dr. Besant's note to Krotona. I haven't the report with me but I think the amount is $6700.

Also I think that report mentioned the matter of The Manor interest. When England went off the gold standard, Mr. Houstone wrote that they could no longer afford the exchange rate on the Interest and would deposit it in a Sydney bank until such time as it could be forwarded without serious loss.

I will not reply to your fifth paragraph until I have heard from you in reply to the letter I wrote you on this same subject. Shortly after submitting my annual report to the trustees I was in Hollywood for the annual meeting, which could not be held for lack of a quorum, and so had opportunity to discuss the situation with Mr. Zalk and Mr. Holland. I had already talked with Max before leaving for Hollywood. As a result of these discussions it was suggested that I write you as I did. I sent a copy of the letter to the trustees for their approval before mailing it but had no reply from Mr. Hotchener. After waiting a week I mailed the letter anyway on account of its urgency. Sometime later Mr. Hotchener phoned me, stating that he had been out of town, and said that he would write you himself, for while he agreed with the suggestion itself he did not wholly agree with the form of expression used.

There does not seem to be any opportunity for more rentals at Krotona at present. Business conditions here at the present time seem very critical. I do not know of anything that can be done with the surplus acreage at Krotona to make it produce any kind of income, aside from leasing it as we did to Mrs. Moore. By the way, Mr. Moore has given us a year's notion of the termination of the lease, stating that he is unable to repay the loan from Krotona or to meet the interest and taxes. I wrote, offering to carry the property for them as far as necessary until their circumstances changed, and asking them to reconsider. They replied that they might possibly do so at the end of the year but wished the notice to stand.

I should be glad to hear from you, confidentially if necessary, as to the inside of what is going on at Adyar. We hear all kinds of rumors, plausible and otherwise. I cannot understand what seems to be the attitude of certain of our leaders toward Krishnaji. For the last twenty years the chief purpose of the T.S., and especially the E.S., seemed to be a preparation for his coming, and I do not see how anyone can fail to see the utter inconsistency of anything but full cooperation with him. The whole fabric of the Theosophical structure stands upon belief and confidence in the teachings and revelations of our leaders, principally Dr. Besant and C.W.L., and

Krishnaji is inseparably an important part of this structure. How can anyone remove the foundation and expect the house of cards to still remain erect?

Mrs. Hall and I are fairly well and as cheerful as could be expected with so much suffering and disaster all around us. I am still caring for all my responsibilities as formerly but am planning to relieve myself of some of them as rapidly as it can be conveniently done. Mrs. Hall has just completed her two year term of office in the local clubs and has recently been elected president of the Ventura County Federation. Mrs. Porter has not returned to this country this winter as usual. Mr. and Mrs. Logan are expected here the 10th of April for a short stay. We have had only one good rain this winter.

With cordial good wishes to both you and Mrs. Warrington I remain as ever,
G.H. Hall

Misunderstandings so easily arise between correspondents, whereas in a discussion, misunderstandings are apparent and can be corrected. But, with Mr. Reginald Bennett, of The Manor Committee, and Mr. F.W. Houstone, signing for "Trustees of The Manor" correspondence was always late or never sent. It was to the fact that the unfavorable rate of exchange at that time worked a great hardship upon them in the payment of the interest due to Krotona on the mortgage from The Manor.

Started in 1879, with H.P.B. as Editor. *The Theosophist*, a monthly magazine for all serious students of Theosophy to keep in touch with current thinking in the field of Theosophy, contained articles representing the views of leading theosophists worldwide. Within the magazine, the President's column titled *On the Wacth-Tower* draws attention to important trends in the world scene from a theosophical point of view.

We publish only the paragraphs that refer to this time period regarding Krotona, Warrington and Krishnamurti. The following was published by C. Jinarajadasa for the "On The Watch-Tower" April 1933 he says:

Dr. Besant's health is certainly feeble, but in spite of slight ups and downs there is no great change to record. Press correspondents are anxious for news, but at the moment the only reply is: "No change." "Reuter" is always ready to report news of her health, and the Reuter agency at Madras and the Associated Press of India are in telephonic touch with Adyar.

Dr. Besant does not read any newspapers, and is not trying to follow the world's developments. She has her eyes fixed on the future, particularly on a swift rebirth in an Indian body. Her preference is for a Kshattriya body, of course, a male one, for she says that in her inmost nature she is a Warrior. Not a few have been the times when she has spoken of the need to train the Youth of India to be proud of the name "Indian". She is anxious that they should know the past glorious history of her Motherland, and what doughty deeds Indians wrought in ancient days. She has not the slightest anxiety as to the welfare of the Theosophical Society after her departure, since she knows that the Society's true Founders, the two Masters who guided H.P.B. and Colonel Olcott, and guide her now, are still the Society's Guardians. On one occasion lately, when there happened to be gathered round her sofa Bishop Leadbeater, Bishop Arundale, and myself, she alluded to the prophecy about the Society recorded by the Master of H.P.B., Colonel Olcott and herself in these words:

> "You have still to learn that so long as there are three men worthy of our Lord's blessing (The Lord Buddha) in the Theosophical Society, it can never be destroyed."

Then beginning with herself, she counted one, two, three, four, and said in triumph: "There's one over!" When later Miss Willson came, Dr. Besant remarked that there were "two over."

The theosophists—at least the members of it who are in the E.S.—have made no secret of their faith that the world which has been in travail during the last half-century is in such a pitiable condition because all the nations are being rapidly moulded towards a World Reconstruction under the guidance of the Adept Brothers. To the theosophist who has had even a slight glimpse of the "Great Plan," the various political and economic upheavals have been signs not of irreparable disaster, but of quick reconstruction. Little as one would think it at the moment, the full achievement of World Reconstruction has been brought nearer during the last few days by the lead given by the Prime Minster of England in the matter of Disarmament, by the President of the United States in throwing in his weight in the World Economic Conference, by Signor Mussolini's proposed "Four Power Pact,'" and by the British Cabinet's outline in the "White Paper" describing the next stage of the "reforms" towards making India a self-governing Dominion in the British Commonwealth. In each of these, and in other departments of Reconstruction, there are many unsatisfactory elements; it requires little perspicacity to point them out at once.

And today, once again the "doubters" are raising their voice. One aspect of Krishnaji's teachings is being misconstrued to mean that the Masters of the Wisdom are not necessary for the world's welfare; the value of the Path to Them is being discredited; and grave doubts are being mooted regarding the Society's progress after Dr. Besant leaves us. To those who have joined the Society because of its ideals, and who love to give their best to mankind through it, but do not believe in the Masters, it little matters who will be the President so long as the Society works for the helping of men. For others, who do believe in the Masters, if doubts come, how shall they be answered?

One thing is sure: Not one doubt will be resolved by leaving the work undone. A thousand doubts have less value for the soul than one certainty. Whether the Masters exist or not, whether They are using a particular person as channel or not, may or may not be doubtful; but never doubtful that the world needs a Universal Brotherhood of Humanity, and that among the world's organizations for the work, the Theosophical Society is the most idealistic, as the most effective in the long run. He who does the Society's work will always be "for" the Masters,. *Tat Karma, Tad asmi*—*That Work, That am I* is the touchstone both of Truth and of the Path to that Arhatship towards which the Master is always planning to bring "My People."[6]

---

[6]Jinarajadasa, C., *The Theosophist*, "On The Watch-Tower", April 1933, pp. 1-8.

It was also a time of another great problem when the members in Australia started a movement to transfer the Section Headquarters from Sydney to Melbourne. The whole project was reported to Dr. Besant, and she returned in her own handwriting the following message.

> April 12
> Dear Brethren,
>
> Our loved Brother George is leaving Adyar shortly, to tell you that I strongly disapprove of the proposal to change the Headquarters of the Society from the place chosen by the Masters as the Headquarters of the Society in Australia.
> The place chosen by Them is final.
> Your faithful Brother
> Annie Besant, *Warrior*

Jinarajadasa reminds the members they must put their emphasis on the youth, and not on themselves, emphasizing life and unity. All depends upon their bigness of view and heart.

> I should like here to add how constantly, during the last three years, our President has stressed the need in the Society to cherish the young members—those young in age—and to train them in our ranks to fill the gaps which are being left by the passing of the older members. Her message to Australia in 1933, "Guard the younger brethren" is a reutterance of the Orders of THE KING given to her in 1922: "See how best they can be equipped and utilised, for on them much will depend."

Along with the Financial Statement for April, Krotona ran an ad that the E.S. Headquarters at Krotona has some rooms and apartments available for E.S. members at present. There are several one-room apartments with kitchenette, bath and garage; and one five-room apartment. The rent varies from $15 to $30 per month. Full information can be furnished on request. Applications should be addressed to Miss Poutz, as all residence at Krotona is subject to her approval.

The Trustees have now arranged for the leasing of building sites to E.S. members who wish to build their own homes at Krotona, and are approved by the Corresponding Secretary. One such lease has already been consummated. The details of this lease have been very carefully worked out and full information can be had from the Trustees by application through Miss Poutz,.

The yearly banquet for the Junior-Senior Nordroff high school was held in the Krotona Hall as well as the tennis dance was held at the Krotona Hall on April 27.

Krishnaji at Adyar

Krishnaji came on a very brief visit to Adyar to see Dr. Besant before he left India. He arrived on the morning of the 4th of May and left on the morning of the 6th.

During his stay at Benares he had suffered from fever, and in the course of three weeks of fever and convalescence had been somewhat pulled down. He had not shaved during this period, and he had a short beard when he arrived at Adyar. Needless to say, Dr. Besant welcomed him with intense affection, and alluding to his beard told him he was now "quite a man". When he saw her to say good-bye, she again dwelt on his appearance, this time particularly how beautiful he looked. After he had said good-bye to her, I was seated by her on the sofa, and she went on speaking about him. After a few sentences, I asked Miss Willson to bring me a pad of paper, and put down hurriedly what Dr. Besant said. The sentences were naturally separated by pauses. They are as follows, as nearly correctly as I could write them down hurriedly. I had alluded to Krishnaji's change in appearance owing to his beard, and how he reminded one of certain pictures of the Christ:

He is like what He is; he is more like that I expected.

I see the likeness, but then I expected to see.

He grows like Him every day; will it last?

She asked me if others had noted the resemblance, and I replied that many had.

Don't suggest it to other people; let us leave it to them.

The more suggestive it is, the more it will impress people.

Will every one recognize the likeness. I suppose people will hardly see it. They will see it only as they are able to see Him.

It was quite startling to me.

I bless him.

As his beard grows it will be more striking.

I feel that must be so. Don't be surprised if when he gets very like Him, we shall be startled. You can't hide it; it's wonderful.

Here I left for a moment, to bring to her a large picture of the Lord Maitreya, the picture which many E.S. members have seen. I showed her also a large reproduction of the Copenhagen Christ statue. Naturally she liked better the E.S. picture, whose original is at Benares.

I am inclined to think that people must have something of His nature in them to see Him.

She instructed me to ask Krishnaji if he would mind being painted by the best Italian painter of South Italy; she said that there "the natural colouring can be shown." I did not think it wise to interfere with the flow of her thought with any question; this much, however, is true, that in South Italy, in Palermo, and Cefalu in Sicily, there exist reproductions of the Christ face after the Byzantine tradition, where His Face is a *strong* face, though a sad one, different from the usual Christ face of pictures, which is made tender but also somewhat effeminate.

They may think it's a kind of deification; people are so tiresome and silly.

Just think what it would be now if we had a likeness of Him as he was in Palestine.

Immediately after Krishnaji had said Good-Bye and left her, she sent me to ask him if he had "plenty of money". As I went out to ask Krishnaji the above question, I told him what she had just then said: "He is like what He is." He replied with a laugh: "Tell your E.S. people that, and not 'disappointment'."

Yet *both* statements were made by her, and I have reported *both* statements accurately. C.J.[7]

Regarding Krishnamurti's statement above, one can also read what the Master Morya said about Himself once in one of those Mahatma Letters written in 1881 and 1882. Actually, He wrote very few letters, particularly when the Master Koothumi was in Samadhi. The Master tried to explain that in His directness there was no personality—as an Adept He said, describing Himself:

"I am as I was; and as I was and am, so am I likely always to be."

In the Ross Collection, under the Liberal Catholic Church documents, there is a letter dated May 4, 1933, from C.W. Leadbeater to George Arundale which deals with the L.C.C., and the problems at The Manor. The first paragraph in the letter, refers to Krishnamurti

> "Krishna duly arrived this morning, but will depart again on Saturday. He came only to see the President once more. He has had a bad attack of chicken-pax up at Darjeeling, and is consequently very weak and rather heavily marked. So he will give no addresses here, and will see no one. He is as kind and friendly as ever in personal relations. Will leave for Europe in a few days, but intends to spend a short time in Egypt and Greece on his way to Holland. He expects to be in India again in December, and thinks of paying

---

[7] Jinarajadasa, C., *Shishya*, "Krishnaji at Adyar", Vol. II, July 1933, n1, p.10-12.

the long-postponed visit to Australia and Java next year. I wonder how much harm he will do there!"

Then we read in the fourth paragraph, C.W. Leadbeater reports:

"If it be true that we have lost 600 members during the last few years, we ought to enquire into the reasons for such a failure. The commercial depression is a principal feature, but I believe the rot set in before that. I should think that the principal reason is Krishna, who is quite the severest test the Society has ever had; and possibly a secondary reason may be the reaction from the extravagant declarations made at Ommen and Huizen in 1925. But I wonder why the fine work done in Australia by Rogers and Miss Codd has not largely increased our membership. Also there should be some obvious result from the daily Theosophical Broadcasting, and from the news service. The enemy has perhaps a certain justification for asking questions about these points, and it might look well to take notice of them, even though the grumblers do not deserve our attention."

Miss Clara Codd, 1930

May 5 1933

Dear Mr. Warrington:

I was glad to get your kind letter of March 18, which I shall show to Louis and Holland when I go down to Hollywood next week, as I know they will also be glad to read it. I do not know so far of any prospective tenant for your house, but I am going to make a special effort to see Miss Poutz about this on my return next week.

As to the Krotona finances, we fortunately have a few hundred dollars cash in the savings account, which we hope will be sufficient to make up any deficits we have to suffer this year. I am in no position to judge, and I am certainly not a prophet, but all indications are that conditions are going to improve in this country from now on.

I note your suggestion about the Sydney interest. As the loss would be considerable, I think that as long as we still have the savings account to draw on we should wait a bit and see if the improved conditions do not make it possible for them to forward the full amount due us. It is almost certain now that some action will be taken in this country to deflate the American dollar, as other countries have done with their currency, and thus put foreign exchange again on a more normal basis. I do not think that Mrs. Gardener is involved in this interest any more. Quite some time ago we ceased getting her checks and were paid by Herbert Staggs from Cleveland, and then finally that was discontinued and the interest came again from Sydney. They are depositing the money regularly in a bank to our credit, and it is to be forwarded to us as soon as the exchange rate is more favorable.

You mention not remembering about the Moore note. Then they built their house at Krotona, we had plenty of money and loaned them $2000. for one year. This they have never been able to pay, but of course it is quite safe as both principal and interest will ether be paid eventually or adjusted on the payment to them if Krotona is compelled to take over their property.

It seems a long time for you to be away if you do not come back until 1936, but by that time conditions in this country will certainly have changed one way or the other. Until then Krotona will do well if it can maintain itself without serious loss financially.

Answering your personal question, I can say that I do not think anyone in this country who had anything to lose has escaped losing a least a part of it. Personally I was very fortunately situated in that the bulk of the little property I have was tied up in real estate, and so far none of that has blown away. In fact, I was even able to sell a little piece last month and thus trade in my old car for a new Ford Eight. This was quite necessary if Mrs. Hall and I are to drive east this summer as we have been expecting we would have to do. Of course, I do not know anything about Louis' personal affairs, but just general knowledge guarantees that he has had some serious losses along with the rest of us, but I think that he was probably in a position to stand them.

With kindest regards to both Mrs. Warrington and yourself, and hoping that we may hear from you often, I remain ever,
Very sincerely yours
G.H.

May 7 1933

My dear George,

I must apologize for my typewriting, for I don't know any too well how to handle this animal in front of me. Sometimes he does things that I don't at all intend he shall do.

I have read over the second time yours of March 30th which has just come, and I believe there is nothing to answer that has not been already referred to in letters that by this time must have reached you. Except the following—

Strange as it may seem you are almost as well posted as I am about things here within the Circle that is pushing the wagon just now. If you are not in that Circle you had just as well be in China. I am known to be a Krishna sympathizer and that in a very subtle way finishes me. Under the Constitution there is no power given to the Vice-President except to act as Chairman, in the absence of the President. That I do and it is about all I can do. Beyond that I am in China.

Now why it is that there was a tremendous propaganda for Krishnaji until he "Came" and than after he came very little but cold water, has not been revealed unto us, beyond certain outer things like K's condemnation of Societies etc. But we were told all along that we should not like some of the things he would say. So I am as much in the dark as you. We shall sit tight here until something happens, for that clearly is my duty. If only the President of 1915 were here! Things would be very different. Well, you can see my further views in my latest Annual Report which was not liked a bit by the Circle.

Please congratulate Mrs. Hall on the fine recognition she has received in the Valley. We both wish you both all that is good and full of blessings.
Sincerely
A.P.W.

P.S. You won't fail to see, I am sure, what it means to the Vice-President of the Society to be cut off in a land half way round the earth with no income. On our Krotona Board are men of fine business abilities. Of course I know some of the difficulties. But then you all have greater practical talents than I. There is absolutely not a pie to be expected here, nor even after SHE goes. So you see my fix. Did you write to Australia that you would absorb some of the difference in exchange? That by the way has taken a turn in A's favor. Better to do that than to get nothing, which may be the case if the thing drags on, for they may use the fund for some pressing thing, salving their conscience with the thought that it is all for the great cause. I find there are some who think that sort of thing is all right. They are not raised in our School of Business.

Why not advertise the little apartments at the entrance? It matters little whether those tenants are theosophists or not just so they are respectable people.

To reinforce some of Krishnamurti's teachings, C.W. Leadbeater gave some remarks at the Wesak Festival to his young group of E.S. Pupils at Adyar on May 10, 1933:

A Message from the Inner Head

The world is at a crisis in its history; it is a tie when its progress or failure or the next century depends upon a wise, unselfish choice on the part of those who guide it. And such a choice is possible only if a wide, brotherly, farseeing attitude can be attained. You of our Society should speak for us with no uncertain voice. But before you can do that, you yourselves must open your hearts to a world-wide view. You must put aside your petty personal prejudices, your insignificant local interests, your countless little unconscious selfishnesses, and learn to think for the world; for only so can you rise to the emergency, and quit yourselves like men.

Remember, each of you, that you are an ego, a spark of the Divine 'whose growth and splendour has no limit,' as you were told long ago. therefore refuse to be deceived by the contemptible little false 'I', which tries so persistently to dominate you, crying: ' I want freedom to express myself by rebellion against Nature's laws, by wallowing in all kinds of filth, by drinking, by smoking, by sexual excesses.' It is not you, but an uncontrolled elemental; why will you be so easily deceived?

We thank those who have come bravely forward in answer to our call, to supply us with the instrument we needed. Never forget that you, our workers, must exercise the greatest care; there must be unceasing vigilance, and no moment of slackness, for the enemy is eagerly waiting to take advantage of any weakness. We want no half-hearted service, but full trust and untiring energy.[8]

Why does the question of sex always comes up? Why has sex become a problem in our lives? Why are there so many distortions, perversions, inhibitions, suppressions? Within the Esoteric School, one learns that sexual orientation is one of the great mysteries of the human mind. For decades, researchers have tired to figure out what makes someone attracted to a particular sex. There have always been questions regarding sex for thousands of years; it is not something new.

It is obvious that the matter is a difficult one to approach due to our conditioning. Why is it so difficult? We observe that the difficulty is based on the prejudices in our minds, plus our particular point of view is necessarily the right one because we ourselves live and act in accordance with it.

Sexual passion, therefore, while a necessary and instinctive part of our nature, is a physical (and animal) characteristic, and expresses itself solely on the physical plane.

It is always a painful task for any so-called spiritual organization to have to make public statements dealing with sexual morality:

---

[8]Leadbeater, C.W., *Shishya*, "A Message from the Inner Head", Vol. II, July 1933, n1, pp.12-13.

regardless of whether it refers to heterosexuality, homosexuality, and bisexuality. Why has humanity and the church given throughout the ages such importance to general sexuality? It is a fact of life. Maybe we should give more attention to austerity. Why has sex preference been given such a place in life? It's a part of life.

The student within the Esoteric School is told to cease to drift through life, at the mercy of surrounding circumstances and of his own body, emotions and thoughts. The student must take himself definitely in hand in his daily life, sexual desires and actions, and must be moved to action by deliberate awareness, not by impulse.

Here Krishnamurti answers questions regarding sex during his Adyar talks.

> *Question*: Do you consider it a sin for a man or a woman to enjoy illegitimate sexual intercourse? A young man wants to get rid of such illegitimate happiness which he considers wrong. He tries continually to control his mind but does not succeed. Can you show him any practical way to be happy?
>
> *Krishnamurti*: In such things there is no "practical way." But let us consider the question; let us try to understand it, though not from the point of view of whether a certain act is a sin or not a sin. To me there is no such thing as sin.
>
> Why has sex become a problem in our life? Why are there so many distortions, perversions, inhibitions, suppressions? Is it not because we are starving mentally and emotionally, we are incomplete in ourselves, we have but become imitative machines, and the only creative expression left to us, the only thing in which we can find happiness, is the thing which we call sex? As individuals we have mentally and emotionally ceased to be. We are mere machines in society, in politics, in religion. We as individuals have been utterly, ruthlessly destroyed through fear, through imitation, through authority. We have not released our creative intelligence through social, political and religious channels. Therefore the only creative expression left to us as individuals is sex, and to that we naturally assign tremendous importance, on that we place tremendous emphasis. That is why sex has become a problem, isn't it?
>
> If you can release creative thought, creative emotion, then sex will not longer be a problem. To release that creative intelligence

completely, wholly, you must question the very habit of thought, you must question the very tradition in which you are living, those very beliefs that have become automatic, spontaneous, instinctive. Through questioning you come into conflict, and that conflict and the understanding of it will awaken creative intelligence; in that questioning you will gradually release creative thought from imitation from authority, from fear...."[9]

A letter written on May 17th, 1933, to George Arundale in Huizen from C.W. Leadbeater in Adyar dealt mostly with the L.C.C. history, but one paragraph is of interest.

> "When Krishnaji was here a few days ago to say good-bye to the President, he had allowed his whiskers and beard to grow, in order to conceal the traces of his illness up in the north, and she was immensely impressed with his likeness to the portrait of Jesus according to the Mount Athos tradition—which, as you probably know, differs much from the usual rather effeminate Christ-face, and is as a matter of fact much more like what He really was. I did not think the resemblance very striking myself, but she spoke of it frequently. The Mount Athos portrait was reproduced by Count Roger of Sicily in the churches which he built at Céfalu, Palermo and Monreale, so you are fairly sure to find it in any illustrated book on Sicily."

If you are interested to see the mentioned photos above, one can find them in an article "Portraits of the Christ" by Annie Besant with photos in *The Theosophist* for February 1933.

---

[9] Krishnamurti, J., *The Collected Works of J. Krishnamurti*, Volume I, 1933-1934, Dubuque, Iowa, 1991, Kendall/Hunt Publishing Co., "Third Talk at Adyar", India, December 31, 1933, p.166.

May 19 1933
The Pro-Cathedral of St. Alban
Liberal Catholic
2041 Argyle Avenue
Los Angeles, California

To The Members and Clergy of St. Alban's Pro-Cathedral:

This letter is packed with information of the greatest interest to you. It is not an appeal for funds, but a statement of impending changes which have resulted from the swift events of the last few days.

A special meeting of the Vestry was called last Wednesday evening to discuss two urgent matters. The first was the resignation of Dr. Sanford Bell from the office of Provost, from the Priesthood, from the Church; the second, a letter from the Bank drawing attention to the fact that six months' interest ($540.76) on the mortgage was due and asking that we work out some program whereby the loan might be placed in a satisfactory condition. By request I was present at this meeting.

Inasmuch as Dr. Bell's resignation was final there was nothing to do but accept it. We owe much to Dr. and Mrs. Bell. They have given freely of private funds for the improvement of St. Alban's; Dr. Bell has served the Church for years with devotion and marked ability. Our gratitude and good wishes go with them.

From the Treasurer's report, it was evident that the Rector's salary and the interest on the mortgage could not both be paid out of the at present limited income of the Church. Either one or the other would have to stop. With customary unselfishness, the present Rector, the Rev. Frank Passmore, made it possible for the Vestry to stop immediately his salary of $100 a month. He was also finely generous in the matter of past salary due him. He will not be able to carry on as Rector, but will continue active among the Clergy associated with St. Alban's. Our out-going Rector deserves the warmest praise for work well-done and for many personal sacrifices unknown to most of the members.

Because of regained health and the urgency of the need, I shall take up once more the headship of the Pro-Cathedral, motoring regularly to Hollywood early each Sunday morning, returning to Ojai Monday morning. My first public appearance will be on Sunday, June 4th, when I shall conduct the morning Eucharist and speak in the evening.

The Rev. Thomas H. Talbot has promised to take the early morning Eucharist on week-days and to be available daily for baptisms, weddings, funerals.

Dr. John Ingelman will continue to officiate at the Monthly Healing Service. I have asked him to take charge of this department of the Church' activities.

These new arrangements make it possible for Bishop Hampton to follow the desire of his heart, that of being free to tour the Province where the need is great.

The Treasurer and I had an interview with one of the high officials of the Bank. It was satisfactory and we hope to have good news shortly to report.

In closing, I ask all of you to join with us in a renewed drive forward. I hope to see all of my old friends and many new ones on June 4th.

Regionary Bishop—Bishop Irving S. Cooper
Priest in-Charge—the Rev. Thomas H. Talbot

June 8 1933

Dear Mr. Warrington,

Mrs. Hall and I are leaving Monday to drive east to see her sister and my father. Incidentally we shall take advantage of being there to drop in at Wheaton, which we have never seen, and to spend a day or two at the Fair in Chicago. In spite of the fact that we have been preparing for this trip for several weeks, I find a multitude of things to do at the last minute and so will not attempt to write you at length as I should like to do.

The headquarters at Adyar must be in a bad way if it cannot furnish a secretary to our Vice-President. Also there is the subject of Krishnaji and the attitude of the theosophical leaders towards him, which is so vital and important and complicated that one hardly dares attempt its discussion in writing.

Mrs. Hall thanks you for your kind remarks about her activities, which she very much appreciated.

Miss Poutz and Gene and Mrs. Goldy are taking every possible effort to keep the different buildings at Krotona rented, and as we can see our way to survive the current year there is no reason for present worry.

As to your personal finances, I think you should not be concerned about the cost of your return home. If you are short of the necessary amount at that time, you have only to let me know, and we can raise the money for you somehow very quickly.

I have already explained to you in a previous letter that we did not consider it advisable to absorb too large a loss in exchange on the remittance of the interest from Sydney, but I am glad you mentioned the possibility of their not keeping strictly to the arrangement as they have agreed. Perhaps it would be best to do something about this when I get back if they have not sent any interest by that time. I had Mrs. Goldy prepare a statement of the Besant loan from the Krotona books, which I enclosed herewith. I infer that it is your intention to collect both principal and interest, if possible, from her estate. As this loan was negotiated by you personally, I think any effort along the above line should also be made by you personally rather than by the Krotona Board officially. Perhaps if we knew all of the circumstances as you do, we should be inclined to take the same action. I should not want to express a personal opinion or advise a course of action in this matter without knowing the facts, and so I am glad to leave it to you.

With cordial good wishes to Mrs. Warrington and yourself from us both, I remain ever,
Very sincerely yours,
G.H.

By the end of June 1933 the joint highway between Ventura and Santa Barbara counties was complete. Elizabeth Chase reports, "The road is of great importance to the Ojai community for it will connect the Ojai with the great interior valley of California and will make the Ojai the main thoroughfare for traffic from the San Joaquin Valley to the tide-water." The highway was completed in October 1933. David Mason of Ojai reported: "At the south end of the Maricopa Highway, the state built another maintenance station in Meiners Oaks, on the highway just south of the Deer Lodge. By the late 1940's, it became known as Highway 33, the Maricopa Highway."

Death of Dr. Weller van Hook, June 30th, 1933, after long continued ill-health. A noted Chicago surgeon, he was general secretary of the American Section, T.S. (Adyar) following Alexander Fullerton and preceding A.P. Warrington.

After retirement from the general secretaryship he became somewhat of a free-lance, founding the Rajput Press in Chicago, which published a number of books by C.W.L. Also founded the Akbar Lodge, T.S., of Chicago and was its leading spirit. Further, he founded the Karma and Reincarnation Legion.

Warrington felt uneasy about the Sydney interest payments because the whole matter was put on a strictly business basis. Having come into contact with people at The Manor from time to time from Sydney, they have indicated to him, and records to prove it, that the Sydney people at The Manor have the reputation of not paying for anything to America, as they are feeling their curious right to be excused from further payment if they can get out of it. But, he felt that being E.S. at both ends presents a similar temptation, and possibly a problem. Australia is also having much financial trouble, and the pound exchange is changing daily. He was hoping that George Arundale would make a quick settlement on a give and take basis, or rather on the basis of sharing with one another, the present financial misfortunes. It seems that the exchange will never be more favorable than it is now. The mortgage Warrington took was a second mortgage on The Manor. Since then he understood that the first mortgage has been paid off which would give Krotona the first lien. Warrington also made J.J. van der Leeuw endorse both as to principle and interest, and John MacKay guarantors.

Meanwhile the indebtedness of $6,700 to Krotona from Dr. Besant was another issue. Raja needed all the papers dealing with this transaction to be given to Dr. Besant's Executors after her death. The Executors of her Estate were David Graham Pole of London and Sri N. Ram of Adyar with Sri Ram really doing the whole work, as Pole had given him Power of Attorney to act. For the courts will require a sworn statement from George Hall before it will be regarded as a true liability against her estate.

F.C. Pragnell bought the Ojai Valley Nursery stock at Krotona, and removed them to his extensive grounds at the head of Blanche Street. He has taken over both stock and equipment and even took the lath house apart to set it up again on his own property to be used in conjunction with his numerous other structures of this kind. Thirty thousand plants of various kinds were included in the deal and these added to what Mr. Pragnell has will give him about 60,000 plants.

Krishnamurti was at the Star Camp, Ommen, giving his first talk July 27, 1933. Van der Stok makes his report of that talk to C.W. Leadbeater. The paragraph below is a comment taken from that letter dated August 19, 1933, giving van der Stok's view on the L.C.C. and the Camp regarding Krishnamurti.

> "He says that the Camp seems much as usual, and about 1700 persons have registered, with a very high percentage of foreigners. He reports that Krishnaji is "'still going strong in his way, singing his own mystical song with the usual fervour, keeping aloof as much as he possibly can from the Theosophical systems (though not a word of antagonism has been uttered by him), and therefore inevitably steering his ship more and more apart from the Theosophical movement; non-Theosophical people gradually taking the place of the pledged theosophists who did all the pioneer work for him, but are stepping aside now that their cooperation seems no longer to be appreciated.'"

August 27 1933
Siete Robles
"Hall-Tuttle Tracts"
Ojai

Dear Henry, (Hotchener)

I am sorry that I could not get this in the mail yesterday. I hear very poorly over the phone and it is hard to remember a letter read that way, but I think this is the information you want.

Dr. Besant borrowed $25000. from Krotona in 1927, "confidentially" and returned $15000 within a few months. In 1928 or 29 Mr. Warrington sent out the "Besant Indebtedness Fund" appeal, which reduced the note to $6700. If you were a member of the "Eighty Years Young Fund" Committee, you will remember this, as they violently opposed the sending out of A.P.W.'s appeal.

At a meeting of the Krotona Board in 1930, I offered a resolution cancelling this note. Mr. Warrington opposed the adoption of this resolution and you agreed with him, so I did not press the matter.

As for the Ojai Publishing Company, it has no connection with Krotona whatever, and was sold last May to avoid problem bankruptcy. We hope to receive enough money from the sale to pay the debts owed by the corporation.

Our present plans are to leave for Los Angeles early Thursday morning, Aug. 31st, and I will be in Hollywood that afternoon. I will not phone Wednesday night as you suggested, as it will be better for you to phone me, if you find that you will have to see me while I am in the city. Or you can find me at Louis' office, 6805 Hollywood Boulevard Thursday afternoon. My phone number is 7791, and I will be home every evening after 6:00. You can get me after 8:30 on "station to station call" at lower rate. We often take advantage of that.

I hear that Dr. Arundale will be in Ojai for one meeting when I shall of course hope to see him, and it may be possible for us to arrange to drive down to Hollywood once during his stay, when we see the program of his activities. If I do not see you this week, I shall look forward to surely seeing you later.

Both Mrs. Hall and I send Mrs. Hotchener and you our most cordial greetings.
Ever sincerely yours,
G. & G. Hall

At the International Headquarters of the Theosophical Society under the far-seeing leadership of Dr. Besant, and the dynamic organizing stewardship of Dr. Arundale, they established an International Youth Service with a new magazine for youth entitled *The Young Citizen* with herself as Editor-in Chief and Dr. Arundale as Associate Editor. It first appeared in 1914 as a magazine for Theosophical Education. It was one of the finest magazines of youth for all times. The second incarnation of *The Young Citizen* came to an end in 1926, and then the third incarnation of *The Young Citizen* came into existence in 1939 with Shrimati Rukmini Devi as its Editor-in Chief and Rohit Mehta as its Assistant Editor. It continued for a few years as the organ of the Young Theosophists' Movement.

The result of a steady growth of the Young Theosophists' Movement brought into existence an organization called Youth Lodges comprising Young Theosophists in different lands. A small magazine entitled *The Young Theosophists* was brought out with L. Tristram and V.K. Krishna Menon as the first editors. This kept young Theosophists in touch with one another through its new publication. The first National Organization of Young Theosophists was formed in 1923 at Varanasi during the International Convention of the Theosophical Society held there. This was known as the All-India Federation of Young Theosophists with Shrimati Rukmini Devi as its President. The first Secretary of this Federation of Young Theosophists was K.S. Shelvenkar who later became India's Ambassador to Soviet Russia when India became independent. The Young Theosophists' Movement was founded in 1923 at the Vienna Congress when Sydney Cook was National President of the American Section, and C.F. Holland as his Vice-President. An outstanding event "Youth Week" on August 9th, of the 1933 Summer School at Olcott, Wheaton, Illinois was the organizing of "The Young Theosophists of America" unanimously elected Rukmini Devi the first President of the Federation, since she was also president of the magazine *The Young Theosophists* organizations in India and Holland. In 1934 the name was changed to "The Theosophical Society in America." The Young Theosophists Movement widened itself out with the formation of The World Federation of Young Theosophists inaugurated at the Diamond Jubilee Convention of the Theosophical Society in December, 1935, with Shrimati Rukmini Devi as its President, and John B.S. Coats and Rohit Mehta as its first General Secretaries with headquarters at Adyar. In 1961 John Coats was elected as Rukmini Devi his successor. For many years The World Federation of Young Theosophists had a representation in the International General Council of the Theosophical Society.

It was due to the inspiration and guidance given by Dr. Arundale that young people were brought into the work of the Theosophical Society and were recognized as an active group influencing the work of the International Body. Small though this publication of *The Young Theosophists* was issued monthly. Under the inspiring and helpful guidance of Rukmini, they discovered their motto and objectives which seemed best to express the ideals of the group. The motto "Be Happy and Face the World" expresses the feelings of courage and joyous action so necessary for the young practical idealist.

Chairman at the time was Felix Layton, Secretary; Norma Mackey, Treasurer; Margaret Barsi, International Correspondent; Mignon Reed, Editor of *The Young Theosophists*; Ellen McConnell, Assistant Editor; Egmont Reed. The European Federation of Young Theosophists came into being on July 24, 1935, the third to be organized. Shrimati Rukmini Devi was elected President, with Alex Elmore and Felix Layton as Joint General Secretaries.

Warrington reported to George Hall that Dr. Besant may leave at any moment now. They are making all preparations for the event so that they may be set in motion like pushing a button. He said: "This has never been done before."

Dr. Besant confined to her bed, passed on at 4:00p.m., September 20th giving forty years of accomplishment by a woman in a world at this time built for men.

Mr. Warrington assumed presidential responsibilities until the election of a new President. He appointed Dr. Arundale as Vice-President.

The following letter was published by C. Jinarajadasa in 1937 in *The Disciple*.

> September 18 1933
> Adyar
>
> > [I published now a letter which I wrote over three years ago to one of my oldest friends. I had forgotten it till I came across it when rearranging my papers after my return to Adyar in November. What I wrote then to a trusted friend can now, I think, be shared with the whole School. C.J.]

You said in one of your letters that if I were not so much with C.W.L. I should be more likely to follow K. I do not think this is at all likely, and I will tell you why. It is quite true that I have much in common with C.W.L. On all matters that have to be dealt with from the standpoint of the intellect, he and I nearly always see eye to eye; and even if I am at the other end of the world, I can tell fairly well how he will look upon a matter. But this is purely so far as the mind is concerned; but where the emotions come in, the reactions are different; we should be apt not to see alike.

I know that I have been a disappointment to some of K.'s friends and perhaps to K. himself, in not going with him "all the way". But the reason for not going is exactly the same as that given by her [Brother Besant]. You will remember how when he developed his teaching to the effect that the Masters were of no use in the scheme of Liberation, she instantly and definitely held back on that matter from accepting his teaching. It is exactly the same with me, and for the same reason. To me, as to her, the Master is not merely "reality" in the philosophical sense; He is absolutely inseparable from the highest ideal I have placed before myself. Ever since I was a boy of fourteen, He had been a part of my life; though, as I explained in my book of verses, He has not prevented me from making mistakes. To a person who, night and day, communes with the Master, and not merely sporadically, as seems to be the case with some people, it is utterly impossible to accept K.'s standpoint, that following the Master is incompatible with Truth or with a realisation of Liberation. I have the greatest admiration for certain aspects of his teaching, because I realise they are necessary to free the world in many ways. But, while for a certain number of souls it may be necessary to preach the doctrine of treading the Path for themselves and ignoring the idea of the Masters, it is not the way for all mankind; and on this matter, whatever he may preach, I stand by what I know.

There is also a further reason. In K.'s teaching, the conception of the Divine is the general philosophical one which all will accept; but it so verges on non-theism as to be practically like the non-theism or "atheism" of Buddhist teaching. From one aspect of philosophy, what he says is perfectly true; but so far as I am concerned, the concept of a personal God is a tremendous reality. You will recall how, ever since you knew me, from the days of college [1896-1900], I have often talked of the Logos. All those references were not mere artistic imaginations, but were centred round a great reality. While the Divine is in all things and in all men, so that every man is God;

yet the experience of my inmost soul has taught me that there is the Logos as a Deity separate from the Universe which He has created. The link between Him and me is a direct one, and I need no Master or ritual to travel along that road. But He is not a vague abstraction, but distinctly a personal God, concerning whom K.'s teachings are hostile in the main. I know of course why, because round the idea of a personal God priest-craft has woven itself and crushed mankind; but all the same, to me, there is the reality of the Logos.

Furthermore, I have perhaps done a thing which he would hardly credit, or most people; and that is, to come downwards from the conception of the Logos to see His Light in frail humanity here below. All that has happened since 1920 has been a range of realisation which has taught me that there are other ways than any so far proclaimed by past Teachers and now by K. himself. As an Irish poet once said to another poet, "I am the makings of a poet myself," so "I am the makings of a World-Teacher myself." These things of the far future have a habit of popping up in the present, so that one realises even now the work that will be done long ahead. A good deal of this new phase I have put down in some sixty or seventy poems, which I do not mean to publish as they are far too intimate and self-revealing. But some day, after I am gone, when they get published, some at least will realise the indication of another way of bringing the Highest down here below.

It is not a matter of being influenced by her or C.W.L., but a matter of standing by myself and by my own dreams and realisations. I can easily go with K. along certain lines, such as those where he is trying to free mankind from barriers, and particularly to teach each man "to blaze his trail" to realisation. That is exactly what I am trying to teach too, but my realisations have included perhaps types of realisation not intimately sensed by him to the same extent. C.J.[10]

September 21 1933

Dear Mr. Warrington:

We heard of Dr. Besant's death early yesterday morning and of course were not surprised after all we have heard of her condition

---

[10] Jinarajadasa, C., *The Disciple*, "Krishnaji and C.J.", January, 1937, n8, pp.127-129.

lately. I hope the next time you write you can tell us all the inside news connected with this momentous event. There is a very nice article in this morning's "Times" and an interview with Dr. Arundale just as he was about to sail for Australia. I will try to see that these clippings get to you.

Miss Poutz is away, but I have talked with Mrs. Couch and Gene and arranged to hold a memorial meeting on her 87th birthday at the Krotona Hall. None of the details for the program have yet been arranged. I regret very much that you are not here to handle this matter yourself, as I think something very nice and dignified should be done at Ojai because of her interests here and her wide acquaintance.

On my return from my trip east I wrote The Manor people at Sydney that we would have to ask them to forward the interest accumulated at the Sydney bank, as we were relying upon its receipt for the payment of our taxes. I have not yet heard from them. There was a definite, clear-cut, business agreement as to this matter, and I do not see how they can avoid sending the money when we ask for it.

Did I tell you in any former letter that I sold the Publishing Company to Kilbourne in May? Now that he has the strongest possible personal reasons for making a success of it, I am hoping that he will be able to complete his payments on the purchase price and thus eventually relieve me of one of the most troublesome responsibilities I ever undertook.

Financial affairs at Krotona are running very much parallel with last year. Miss Moore has finally been induced to take my old apartment in No.7 and Vernon will temporarily have to occupy one of the apartments. Mrs. Sanford has rented the vacant side of the cubicle at he Library, although she expects to use it only periodically. After long drawn negotiations with Miss Poutz, Mr. Netland and his family have removed to the Krotona apartments from their home in Berkeley. These changes will improve the Krotona income to some extent.

I do not know of any other local news of importance that would interest you just now. I think you will be interested to read the enclosed clipping regarding a California Colony.

Mrs. Hall is very busy with her club work this fall, and the Ventura County Annual Convention is to be held at Krotona on the 29, when all of the club women of the county will have an opportunity to enjoy the beauty of the Krotona Library and grounds.

I am very glad to hear that you are in excellent health and hope that you can stay that way.

With kindest regards from Mrs. Hall and myself to you and Mrs. Warrington, I remain ever,
Very sincerely yours,
G. Hall

Annie Besant

A Tribute

By

A.P. Warrington

Vice-president of the Theosophical Society

The slow fading away has reached its end. The great body that held on to life by the merest thread for so many months has now released its hold. No longer will the hand of that renowned form guide a pen in tracing words that will live as long as printing. No longer will the voice bring forth words of musical depths that shall move men by thousands to noble action. No longer will crowds gather to do honour to an elderly lady with a crown of snow white hair as she passes by. All now is still—gone into the realm of imperishable memory.

For one of those whom humanity never forgets has just passed this way, tarrying awhile to bestow blessing after blessing upon Earth's people and then vanishing into the darkness, who knows where? But she knew. And told us. Over and over again has she come and gone. Each time she has left behind some knowledge that others too might know as she has known. Wherefore has she come and gone from age to age.

It has been said that ere long the darkness will once again give up its priceless treasure and some shall see her again walking with the children of earth as of old, leading, teaching, uplifting.

Therefore, who would grieve? Such lives recognise no grief save that which they come to assuage. What then would she say at this moment were we to forget and fall into grief? Would it not be something like this? "*Turn your grief into power. Heal the sick, visit the imprisoned, raise the poor, educate all.*" That substitute would she counsel in fullest measure.

She taught that life is one, life is all. Then let us live life to the full till its cup brims over in love and service and understanding of all. And so shall we help to the end that the blessing of her beautiful life shall more widely fill the world whose needs are so great today, this afflicted world to which she gave her all in a life of noblest service.

Shanti, Shanti, Shanti

The following letter from C.W.L., has this glyph (-----) typed in it because the letter has been torn in these areas, and could not be read. The bottom of the letter regarding receiving a telegram from the Viceroy has also been torn off. George is on the Atlantic at this time heading for the U.S. so the letter was sent to the Hotcheners in Hollywood.

Adyar
September 21 1933

My dear George, (Arundale)

The long, long strain is over at last; our dear President has relinquished her physical body. Since it had to go, I think it came as quietly and gently as it could. I have mentioned again and again during the last few months that her body was growing weaker and weaker, and that her mind also was withdrawing into itself, so that she seemed no longer to take any interest in external affairs. Two or three months ago she used to lie reading almost the whole day long, but sometimes became a little more active and walked down here to my room, though even then the conversation when she arrived was somewhat monotonous and trivial. She took but little nourishment even then, but she drank two or three cups of milk and would sometimes go so far as to eat half a slice of toast. But now, for the last few weeks, she gave up reading altogether, and used to lie all day in a sort of contemplation, taking steadily less and less in the way of food. For a week or two she lived upon lemonade only, but for this last fortnight she has refused even that, and seemed unable to take a sip of water. Naturally, under this regime the body grew weaker and weaker, and the heart-beats became slow, though fairly regular.

Early yesterday morning (about 3 a.m.) a kind of crisis seems to have arisen. Her pulse went up to 104, and the heart-beats became irregular. We sent for the Doctor at that time, and he declared at once that her condition was dangerous. Nevertheless a slight improvement set in, and things quieted down temporarily; but by the middle of the day yesterday she was again in a most critical condition, the pulse being even higher. She seemed to feel no pain or inconvenience whatever, but the heart-beats became fainter, and the breathing quicker and shorter. Raja remained with her the whole time, holding her hand and counting the pulse beats. The Doctor came again and again, and I myself was in and out of the room at frequent intervals. A little before four, I went into the next room (her office) for some tea, but almost immediately Raja called me back saying that a crisis was approaching. He and I sat on her bed, with Miss Willson hovering about somewhere in the background, until gradually and peacefully the heart and the breathing stopped, and the etheric double, with what remained of the astral and mental bodies, slowly withdrew. And so she passed. The Doctor was not actually in the room at the moment of death, having been called away to some other business, but he returned only a few minutes afterwards and could only confirm what we already knew—that the life had left the body.

In fulfilment of his promise, Raja immediately telephoned to the Associated Press, and the news was very quickly spread all over the town, and apparently all over the world, for quite a full account of what had happened appeared in the evening papers here, and the first leading article of that evening's *Madras Mail* was devoted to her; and they also published a very fair biographical account of her. Today telegrams have been pouring in from all parts of the world, some of them very beautifully expressed.

I led our Ritual as usual at 7:20 this morning, and immediately after that we went down into the great Hall and recited the Universal Prayers ending for once by special request with the First Ray Benediction, which is usually omitted on these occasions. In this case, the Hall was crowded to excess, for a huge crowd had come out from Madras to attend the cremation. The body was laid upon a bier which stood on the platform directly in front of the statues, and it was entirely hidden by a huge pile of flowers, only the face being visible. For weeks that face had been pitiably wizened and shrunken, even the very eyes seeming to sink back into the head; but now after death she looked strangely younger again, and somehow very much more normal.

As soon as the Prayers were over, two or three of us stepped into our car and drove down to the Masonic Temple. We had to walk among the immense crowd, and the bier itself was carried as part of an immense procession. I believe it had been planned that some of the gardeners should carry it, but it seemed to me that a number of Indian gentlemen took that matter into their own hands. The procession went by way of the Founders' Avenue, and the whole thing was rendered very picturesque because in front of each tree of that avenue stood a Boy Scout holding the flag of his country. The body was draped in her own red and green flag, and on the breast was laid a very beautifully embroidered seal of the Theosophical Society; but all that was almost entirely concealed by the great mound of flowers. Flags bearing the names of our two Founders were carried close behind her.

The bier was placed in the centre of the Temple, the Altar being advanced a little towards the East to make room for it. The instructions were that the Masonic function must on no account exceed 15 minutes, so you may imagine that it had to be curtailed in various ways. As the only 33^0 present, I had to take the Chair, Raja being my I.P.M. We sent all the brethren in to take their places, and the Grand Officers only entered in procession. I then opened an Occasional Grand Lodge by declaration, immediately after which we sang the psalm "I Was Glad". Then I told the brethren what of course they all knew very well already, the object of our meeting, and asked them to join with me in the grateful farewell to the physical body, the triumphant declaration that nevertheless "She lives! she lives! she lives!" Then I immediately closed, also by declaration, and we filed straight out into the midst of that huge crowd in full Masonic regalia, which seemed to create a certain amount of sensation, at any rate among the horde of small boys who were well to the front.

The procession then wended its way to the place appointed for the cremation, which was that curious platform near the Sevashrama which she herself, I understand, had especially blessed and dedicated—I think it was to the use of the Brothers of Service; but as that organization collapsed about that period, it comes in handy now for the memorial of this greatest of our Presidents. Here we found a pyre of sandalwood, which seemed to me somewhat exiguous, though I was told that it really was rather larger than ordinary. The body was placed upon this, and Warrington was called upon to make a short speech; I thought that what he said was really fairly good for him, but apparently some others considered the speech as shallow. I had to follow him with a few remarks, and then Ranganathan spoke rather longer, I think, than he should have done on the debt which India owed to her. We all had to shout as loudly as we could, for the huge crowd round us kept up a stream of conversation at its outer fringes, so that it was very difficult to make ourselves heard at all. When this was over, Raja advanced and covered the face with the Theosophical flag; they laid more logs of sandalwood over the body and scattered lumps of camphor and some ghee on the whole pile. Then four of us simultaneously lit it at the four corners. Raja, Sri Ram, Dr. Srinivasamurti and I were selected for this honour, which I suppose really ought to have fallen to Digby Besant if he had been present. The crowd seemed to have a distinct predilection towards a kind of inverted form of *sati*, for they pressed forward into distinctly dangerous proximity; in fact we had to form a ring and hold hands to keep them back. I was faintly amused, even at that moment, to find myself holding the hand of Radha, who was the next link in the chain, and looked very determined about it. Very soon the conditions in that inner ring became too torrid for comfort, and as the wind was rather changeable it seemed desirable to enlarge the circle very considerably. We finally retired to our place from which it was possible to watch the proceedings at the centre only by standing on the seats. Soon the flames were leaping high in the air, and presently we slipped off quietly and went home to rest. Personally, I feel that I should like to lie in bed for a week, but the sense of relief from the intolerable tension overpowers everything else.

So ends the physical part of a very wonderful life (-----) dear President followed Madame Blavasky's example of being present at her own cremation, but took a distinctly different attitude towards the proceedings, I think we may say a more kindly one, for India (------) was rather by way of ridiculing the whole thing, and being very (-----) annoyed with those who were rash enough to show one outwards (----) grief: whereas the President felt only pity for them. And to comfort them.
I am ever
Yours most affectionately,
C.W. Leadbeater

Dr. Besant's tireless career for the Theosophical Society will not be forgotten; we should also mention her great love for her adopted land, India, giving untiring devotion to India's right to Home Rule within the Empire. Here is what one of the leading newspapers of India, *The Times of India* of Bombay wrote on September 22, 1933. It is one of many, and a most accurate description of her life work in India.

Dr. Besant's Work in India

By the death of Mrs. Annie Besant after a lingering illness, India has lost one of its greatest champions in the cause of political freedom, the Empire, a notable figure, and Theosophy, one of its greatest exponents. There are many facets to Mrs. Besant's career, but the one of widest interest to this country was her tireless advocacy of India's right to Home Rule within the Empire. To the realisation of that object within a measurable distance of time she subordinated everything else, unmindful alike of what her associates in the world of Theosophy felt about her incursion into controversial politics, or of what a section of Indians themselves thought of a foreign born woman trying to lay down their ideal for them. We are too near events to judge in the correct perspective the extent to which Mrs. Besant's whirlwind campaign really helped the country's cause, but there can be no denying the greatness and constructive nature of her work. Her claim that India was her adopted land made an excellent appeal to the imagination of thousands of Indians. Her powers of organisation and oratory, her skill as a journalist and her knowledge of the correct methods of agitation learnt in England at the feet of Bradlaugh, accomplished the rest and gave her a hold on the intellectual section of the community far more powerful in its ultimate effect than the one which Mr. Gandhi has been trying to establish over the masses.

Mrs. Besant succeeded to the extent she did because her ideals and theories left no room for doubt. The Home Rule she contemplated was Dominion Status within the Empire. She had no use for people who indulged in talk of independence. Her political programme had a social as well as a religious background, and she insisted on the preservation of India's ancient traditions and culture, seeking only to adapt the western democratic system to modern Indian conditions. She would not hear of dispossessing the Princes or abolishing their order, and actually walked out from a convocation of Benares Hindu University as a protest against certain observations derogatory of the Princes made by Mr. Gandhi. Her Home Rule movement did far more to consolidate the forces of nationalism in this country than the Congress had achieved in the preceding thirty years. The Great War was her opportunity. Side by side with day-to-day insistence on the righteousness of the British cause and on the obligations which rested on this country to give of its best in seeing the struggle through, she organised the Home Rule movement. In a misguided moment the Madras Government interned her and this "martyrdom" brought her at one bound to the forefront, and compelled the late Mr. Montagu to order her unconditional release in order to ensure a peaceful atmosphere during this visit to India for the preliminary inquiry which preceded the Reforms Act of 1919.

Mrs. Besant repaid that gesture of goodwill by supporting the Montagu-Chelmsford scheme through thick and thin as the first step in the transfer of power to Indian hands. But she was unable to control the forces which she had let loose. Militant Indian nationalism had no more use for her; her power and influence gradually began to wane. But with rare courage she kept up, at times almost single-handed, the fight with Mr. Gandhi's doctrines of non-co-operation and mass lawlessness. On the morrow of a particularly ferocious outbreak of mob fury, directly traceable to non-co-operation, she did not hesitate to declare in the columns of *New India* that "brickbats must be answered with bullets". Left wing nationalists never forgave her for this advocacy of strong action on the part of Government, but subsequent events proved that she was right in her appreciation of the terrible dangers of mass lawlessness. Mrs. Besant tried hard to prevent the national movement from flowing into wrong channels, and her failure in that direction must be regarded as the greatest tragedy of her amazingly varied life.

By September 24, C. Jinarajadasa announced Bishop Leadbeater's appointment by Dr. Besant as her successor in office as the Outer Head of the Esoteric School.

A letter dated October 5, 1933 details Dr. Besant's wishes regarding her ashes.

October 5 1933
Adyar

My dear George Arundale,

Our late President expressed a wish that her ashes should be thrown into the Ganges according to Indian custom, so after the cremation they were carefully collected and put into a silver vase for that purpose. A memorial of some sort, probably a statue, will be erected on the spot where the body was cremated, and a spoonful of the ashes was reserved to be buried there. A similar spoonful will be placed under the memorial to be erected in Benares, where she lived during most of her earlier years in India; but all the rest will be cast into the Ganges as she directed.

On Thursday morning the vase containing the ashes was exhibited on the platform before the statues in the Hall, and a large number of people came from Madras to throw flowers before it. Then Mr. Dwarkanath Telang, the General Secretary of the Indian Section, carried it off with him to Benares, and on her birthday he scattered the ashes as requested.

I sent to you last week a copy of the message to her Indian members, but I enclose a printed account of it, because that gives a little more information. I see that it has been published in *The Madras Mail* and in *The Hindu*, and it seems to be creating a sort of mild sensation, though I don't quite see why it should.

A telegram has come from Paula from Greenwich announcing that she has arrived and is quite well, which is a great relief to us, as we were naturally anxious about the possibility of rough weather crossing the Indian Ocean, but fortunately Paula seems to have escaped accident.

I notice in the newspaper this week the announcement of the death of two old members whom some of us knew very well—though I suppose they were rather before your time—G.R.S. Mead, who was for a long time General Secretary of the British Section, and G.E. Sutcliffe, who used to write a good deal for us on scientific and astrological subjects. It seems strange, all these friends so much younger than me passing away, and I still left! Mead was just 70, and Sutcliffe 71—but the latter was killed in a motor accident, which might happen to a man at any age, if it were in his karma.

On Sunday morning, being her birthday (she would have been 86 if the body had lasted 11 days longer) a very large portrait of her was placed on the platform before the statues, and all day long

people streamed in and threw flowers before it. Our regular Sunday morning meeting was naturally devoted to her and her message, and in the evening another meeting was held at which some of us gave personal reminiscences of her. It is only a fortnight since she "died", but it is difficult to realize it, for she is here so much more vividly and actively at frequent intervals all day long.
With very much love
I am ever
Yours most affectionately
C.W. Leadbeater

George R.S. Mead died at his residence in London on September 30. He was a coworker with H.P.B., revising her manuscripts and doing much of the work of revision on the second printing of *The Secret Doctrine*.

The following letter is very important, although it was never sent to Warrington; it was kept for valuable information that it contained. It was kept in George Hall's personal records. This large collection of correspondence from George Hall can be found at The Huntington Museum Library in San Marino, California. As President, Dr. Besant, while she was in Chicago in August 1929, requested that the Board of Trustees at Krotona be reduced from fifteen to seven members. She named the seven members she wished elected to the new Board, asking these trustees to carry out her wishes with regard to the future policy of Krotona and defined that policy as the safe financial maintenance of the property of the Corporation at Ojai exclusively as the Headquarters of the Esoteric School in America.

September 26 1933

Dear Mr. Warrington:

Your cablegram came this morning and I am sending Dr. Besant's note by registered mail this afternoon, as you request. All payments of interest and principal are properly endorsed upon the back of the note.

I am sure that any action you may contemplate with regard to this matter is probably the right thing to do, and I am sure you will not misunderstand me when I remind you that the final disposition of this note will have to be approved by an official action of the Board. I remember that you and Louis and Henry disapproved of its cancelation when I proposed that procedure. Without knowing any of the present conditions, we cannot have an opinion in the matter, but I am sure that most of us at least would not care to take any action that would seriously offend or antagonize any who will succeed to positions of authority and power in Dr. Besant's place. Such persons could do injury to the Krotona Institute far more serious than the financial loss of this $6,700. I merely voice this sentiment because of my natural caution, whereas if I knew the circumstances as you know them I might be heartily in favor of any action you contemplate.

Because of the fourth paragraph in your letter to me of January 12, 1933, and because your opinion thus expressed may have a bearing on this other business, I am reminding you of some very important official matters that may have temporarily slipped your mind.

When Dr. Besant was in Chicago in 1929, she took such action as she thought was necessary to finalize her wishes regarding her interests in the Ojai. Therefore the ownership and control of Happy Valley and the Publishing Company are not affected by her death. But with regard to Krotona it is different in one respect. As a California Corporation controlled by its trustees, no single trustee, even though he be the Outer Head of the E.S., can dissipate or mismanage the property. The reorganization of the Board and the appointment of the present members of it was specifically done by Dr. Besant to avoid such a disaster. Therefore I do not agree with the fear that you express with regard to that particular point, but I am concerned with what goes before.

It is true that in the beginning Krotona was not an E.S. project and did not belong to the E.S., and that the requirement in the By-Laws that the Outer Head should be president might be open to the interpretations you claim. This condition was wholly changed when the controversy over the ownership, purpose and policy of Krotona arose in 1919 and continued until the matter was submitted to Dr. Besant for arbitration. Her decision changed this whole situation. All controversies, claims, misunderstandings and confusion that could have possibly attached to the project before her decision were washed off the board by that decision and the payment to the T.S. of over $50,000 cash. In that decision and in its reaffirmation upon nonacceptance by Mr. Rogers of her first decision, she stated that that part of Krotona remaining in possession of the corporation was set aside as an exclusively E.S. center and announced that its policy would not be changed except by her. This decision was not only made final and accepted and incorporated in the minutes of the Krotona Institute Corporation, but it was published in both E.S. and T.S. documents and magazines throughout the world. I therefore see no point in changing our By-Laws with regard to the E.S. Head being president, since the physical and financial control of the property still remains with the Board of Trustees appointed by Dr. Besant.

However, this is the danger point: If the new Outer Head should feel that the attitude of the Trustees or any of them was such as to unfit Krotona as a home for the E.S. Headquarters in America, he might very well remove the E.S. Headquarters elsewhere, in which case the damage to Krotona would be irreparable.

Also we must consider Happy Valley, although it has nothing to do with Krotona. Dr. Besant committed herself to this project with widely published announcements throughout the world, and a very large number of theosophists, principally in America, have been and still are interested in the success of this project. Over $100,000 in cash has already been expended; $43,000 is still owed on the mortgage, and until this mortgage is paid there is danger of loss of the whole property. T.S. and E.S. officials at Adyar, or either of them, could seriously injure if not destroy the Happy Valley idea by public announcement, although it is my personal opinion that the Happy Valley Board of Trustees is quite determined to carry out Dr. Besant's wishes as to Happy Valley.

I am sorry that your letters since you have gone to Adyar have not been more specific as to the conditions there and as to your personal relationship with the other Theosophical Leaders. If I had such information it might not have been necessary to write this letter. In any case it can do no harm that you should know my views, which perhaps contain some points you might not have thought of yourself.

I hope you will find time to answer this rather fully, and also to give me in confidence such information about the situation at Adyar as you know I will be glad to have.

With kindest regards always, I remain,
Very sincerely yours,
G. Hall

P.S. Max is the only Trustee I am able to contact immediately, and he states that he understands Dr. Besant left a considerable estate, in which case it is obviously more fair that this note should be paid than that the money should go to other persons as heirs. I do not think there is any doubt but that all of the other Trustees will agree with this opinion, including myself, provided that it is really true that she did leave an estate which would otherwise go to personal bequest.

Dr. Besant's will stated that: "My property at Ojai, California, shall be made over to the Theosophical Society, incorporated at Madras, India, in the hope that it may be retrained for the future Sub and Root-Races."

George Hall did not know what Dr. Besant meant by her "Ojai property". She had no property personally in the Ojai Valley since 1929, at which time she transferred everything she owned to California Corporations governed by trustees appointed by herself, as George Hall tried to explain to Sri Ram who had been in correspondence with him regarding this issue.

There was a great deal of astral communication from Dr. Besant after her death to Dr. Arundale. It would not be until 1941 that George Arundale published only a few of them in a small booklet *Conversations with Dr. Besant—September 20th thru October 1st, 1933, on the high seas between Los Angeles and Suva*. The unpublished conversations are not available for research as they are kept in the Esoteric Archives at Adyar.

For various reasons Dr. Arundale refrained from publishing the conversations that he had with the late (President-Mother) after her passing on September 20, and during the succeeding days until 1941, when he then felt that they should be published exactly as he recorded them. They are not verbatim transcriptions of the conversations, but he did the best he could at the time both to listen and to take down the messages. He said that on the first occasion there was a semi-materialization which quite overwhelmed him for a few moments until she adjusted him to her presence.

A Message from Dr. Annie Besant from Beyond the Gates of Death.

On September 27th, Mr. D.K. Telang, the General Secretary of the Indian Section of the Theosophical Society, asked Bishop C.W. Leadbeater for a message for his people from Dr. Annie Besant who died on September 20th. She said:

You ask for a message from me; what message can I send you but that which I have always given—that of brotherhood, goodwill and earnest work for our Masters? The Jews thought of themselves as a chosen people; no doubt they were; but so are *you*, for *every* Nation is a chosen people, chosen by our Lord the Manu to exemplify some virtue, to emphasize some quality which He sees that the world needs. India—my India which I love so deeply, my true Motherland and that of my Master—is she not also a Nation, are not her people a chosen people? Chosen, yes; but for what? Chosen to lead the world to spirituality, chosen to emphasize always the higher, the nobler, the less material aspect of life. Are they doing this glorious duty? There are still many who are but feeble and half-hearted in their pursuit of it—many who are trying honestly but wrong-headedly, who seem to seek unity through disunion, brotherhood through hatred of their brethren. Assassination is not progress; senseless obstinacy is not progress. The true path to progress lies straight before you, and it is open to all; but it lies not through the morass of silly squabbling nor over the precipice of barbarous outrage, but through the smiling fields of tolerance, conciliation, goodwill and brotherly love. On *that* path you should every one of you be shining lights to clear away the mists of ignorance, bigotry and prejudice; on *that* path I say to you all, my comrades, press forward more strongly than ever, bearing aloft the radiant banner of Theosophy under which we have fought side by side so long; forward ever forward; onward to victory; Jai Manave Jai!

How it Happened

Mr. C. Jinarajadasa states:

On the 27th September Mr. D.K. Telang, General Secretary of the Indian Section of the Theosophical Society, arrived in Madras in order to take back the Ashes of Dr. Besant to be scattered in the

Ganges. He went to see Bishop C.W. Leadbeater, her colleague, and now her successor in her Occult School. Mr. Telang asked Bishop Leadbeater for a message. Bishop Leadbeater, in spite of his immense learning and his occult knowledge, never imagined that anyone wanted a message from him for India, and so thought that because of the close association which had existed between Dr. Besant and Mr. Telang, and the fact that Mr. Telang was the head of the Indian Theosophists, the latter wanted a message from Dr. Besant.

Since 1884 Bishop Leadbeater through his clairvoyant faculties has not had any division in his consciousness between the world of the living and that of the dead, as the world of the dead is as much visible to him as that of the living. Naturally, therefore, there has been no separation whatsoever between him and Dr. Besant after her death, and he has been all the time in close communication with her since her death as before. There was therefore no more difficulty for him to ask her to give a message to Mr. Telang and the Indian Theosophists than it was before her passing to walk from his room to hers for the same purpose. He interviewed her and wrote down what she said.

The three Sanskrit words at the end meaning "Victory to the Manu, Victory" were what Dr. Besant often said when she went on some difficult piece of work. She remembered them as her battle-cry when she was a warrior among the invading Aryans who came from beyond the Himalayas. She said them each day when she went to the Madras Law Court during her case for the custody of Krishnamurti. They were her last words as her train steamed out to Ootacamund when she went into internment.

Dr. Besant would have been eighty-six on October 1st, and on that day, a public memorial service was held in the Krotona auditorium of the Krotona Library at 2:30pm so that her friends and members of the Theosophical Society could pay their respects to her. George Hall, Secretary of Krotona Institute, presided, reading first a telegram from Miss Marie Poutz, the Resident Head of Krotona, sent from the East Coast to Mrs. Maud N. Couch, her deputy, expressing regret at not being able to attend the memorial. Elizabeth

Price Coffey accompanied Monica Ros, violinist, and Rebecca Schuyler Eichbaum, soprano, in musical tributes. George Hall called upon Max Wardall, another of the Krotona Trustees, and he told a delightful series of anecdotes illustrating the sense of humour, the courage both physical and moral of the woman who so often was designated as one of the greatest orators of the present age. Eugene Munson read a short selection from Dr. Besant's translation of the Bhagavad Gita. Henry Hotchener of Hollywood, a third Krotona Trustee, directed his talk to explaining the causes which made Dr. Besant the resolute and yet gentle being she was. He described her finding of her spiritual Teacher and how the course of her days then became plain. Mrs. Hotchener (Marie Russak Hotchener) was the final speaker being called upon by Mr. Hall to close the program. With deep sincerity of feeling she spoke expressing gratitude to the one she referred to as her "spiritual mother." The body, reported Mrs. Hotchener, was laid on a flower-strewn litter in the great hall at Adyar to allow the thousands of loving friends from all the nearby county to pass by the bier dropping a few blossom petals with a murmured blessing. Later the body was carried down Founders' Avenue between rows of Boy Scouts, Dr. Besant having been a great sponsor of Boy Scout work in India. Among them the boys carried flags of 56 countries, representing the nations in which her work is active. A private ceremony at he Co-Masonic temple was held after which the cortege proceeded through groves of fern-like casuarina trees to a spot near the Adyar River where a great stone has been laid as part of the foundation of a temple to the Lord Maitreya (the Christ). A pyre of sandalwood had been prepared on the stone and here was laid the out-worn body with her head to the north, according to the Indian tradition of Sanyasins. The Rt. Reverend C.W. Leadbeater Outer Head of the E.S., delivered the eulogy, and lit the fragrant boughs followed by C. Jinarajadasa and others. Mr. Warrington also contributed to the commemoration. At Dr. Besant's request the ashes later were scattered on the Benares River.

During the time of the election for the new president, correspondences were published in all the periodicals around the world regarding the election. We do not publish all of these, but recommend that if you are interested, you should try to locate them for future research. There is an eight page circular called "The Presidentship of the Theosophical Society" containing letters of protest against the use of the two Dr. Besant letters of 1926 concerning Bishop Arundale's succession to Dr. Besant. Most of the letters that had appeared in *Theosophy in India* in November and December 1933 are from Mr. B. Siva Rao, Rao Sahib G. Subbiah Chetty, Mr. D.K. Telang, and Mrs. Dorothy Jinarajadasa.

C. Jinarajadasa thought it his duty to The Society to publish the two letters given him by Dr. Arundale in the April issue, 1932. The below is only an excerpt from the two letters printed by Mrs. Ransom.

> One dated September 1926 (America), Dr. Besant said to Dr. Arundale: "As you are to succeed me as President, I think you should come over here. This is our most numerous Section, and you must win its affection, before the election of 1928…" In the other, 12 October (America), she wrote: "Mater said that you were to become President, and I took if for granted that it would be in 1928…" Dr. Arundale had cabled to her that as long as she was alive the question of any other President did not arise.[11]

Mrs. Josephine Ransom is author of *A Short History of the Theosophical Society* from 1875-1937, published in 1938. Her second book has the continuation of the history of The Society from 1926 to 1950.

October 3 1933
Adyar

> For many years past, Bishop Arundale has periodically handed over to me, to be kept among the archives of the E.S., various personal papers of his. Thus I have all the letters which he received from Dr. Besant, from the first reply of hers to his offer to come

---

[11] Ransom, Josephine., *A Short History of the Theosophical Society,* Theosophical Publishing House Adyar, India, 1938, p.511.

out to India to work for her. He also handed over to me the letters which his aunt, the late Miss F. Arundale, had received from Colonel Olcott, and I have published them in *The Theosophist*, since they make a most valuable record in the history of our Society. Last April, when Bishop Arundale left Adyar, he handed over to me another packet of letters.

I was too fully occupied with the care of Dr. Besant, editing *The Theosophist*, and administering the affairs of our Adyar Community to have any time even to examine what the packet contained. I thrust it into one of the two special drawers in my desk where I put my private papers.

These days after her passing, I sent for printing my statement "Why I do not stand for President," on September 23rd. As soon as the pressure of work in connection with receiving cables, telegrams, letters, etc., began to lessen, I had necessarily to get busy at once in putting a great mass of correspondence into order for answering. There was one particular paper which I was seeking, as it was a memorandum of certain wishes of Dr. Besant concerning the disposal of some of her belongings, and it had been entrusted to my care. I had taken charge of it, and had put it away among my private papers. A hurried examination of them showed that the paper was not there, so last night I sat down to examine everything carefully, for the memorandum was in a small envelope and it might easily be hidden among the mass of papers. Thus it happened that **for the first time** last night I looked into the papers handed over to me by Bishop Arundale last April. I found that they consisted of letters received by him from Dr. Besant and Bishop Leadbeater.

Among them I found, to my utter surprise, the two letters of Dr. Besant to Bishop Arundale which I reproduce. Since thousands of members desire eagerly to know what she thought concerning the future of the Society, I feel I shall be remiss in my duty to them if I do not publish these two letters.

C. Jinarajadasa

I leave Adyar on October 15th for work, first in South America, and then later in Europe. I shall be away about a year.

Copies of this can be had by applying to my friend: Mr. N. Sri Ram, Adyar, Madras.

Memories or Facts?

by
George S. Arundale

EDITORIAL NOTE:—The following memorandum was received too late for the current *American Theosophist*. The letters of Dr. Besant to which reference is made are quoted in their essentials on page 5 of the January issue. Mrs. Jinarajadasa's comments and interpretations are given in the editorial "Presidential Election Views" in the February number.

I deeply regret that the present Presidential election should be besmirched by a controversy in the course of which the revered name of our late President has been recklessly used to bolster up the prejudices of some of the contestants. Advantage is inexcusably taken of Dr. Besant's inability to offer contradiction, to make assertions in the form of "memories" as to her attitude many years ago regarding the succession to the Presidentship.

Mr. Jinarajadasa thought it wise to publish a couple of letters from Dr. Besant to myself in 1926 in order to satisfy a widespread demand on the part of the members in many countries for any indication either as to her own wishes, or as to any hint available from one of the Elder Brethren. Many members regard the Masters as the heart of the Theosophical Society, and believe that Dr. Besant, like her great predecessors, was in constant touch with Them. It was natural, therefore, that these members should wish to have some indication as to what was thought best for the Society by Theosophists far wiser and far greater, far more intent upon the wellbeing of the Society, than themselves.

In these letters Dr. Besant reveals her own judgment, and in a short sentence gives her Master's view. Dr. Besant herself writes: There is no intermediary, no question of someone else's memory.

Now the origin of those letters was in an experience of my own while in Sydney, Australia, in the course of which I had a vivid memory of being told by one of the Elder Brethren that there was a possibility of my succeeding Dr. Besant in the remote future. I wrote to Dr. Besant giving a brief summary of the experience, and asking her whether she could throw any light on it. Was it only imagination? I thought not, even though, as I wrote to her, I could not conceive of ever being able to follow in *her* footsteps.

Her letters as published were part of her reply. A third letter, in my possession, makes Dr. Besant's views abundantly clear. She writes: "I like your news immensely, that you will be the P.T.S. and Raja the O.H. The work has grown too big for one person, and there could not be a better pair."

Now let us look at Mrs. Jinarajadasa's attempt, in the December issue of *Theosophy in India*, to discount Dr. Besant's statements—under the very great advantage, as I have already said, of Dr. Besant's inability to utter a single word by way of contradiction.

Mrs. Jinarajadasa's statement is as follows:

> "Those letters were written by Dr. Besant in 1926, after Bishop Arundale had told her that he had received the impression of a message from the Master Morya to himself relating to his standing for election as President in the 1928 election. As is shown in these two letters, Dr. Besant was willing to stand aside, if the Master wished. But in the bottom of her heart she was not quite happy about it. However, Bishop Leadbeater cabled to Bishop Arundale suggesting that the matter be dropped, which was done.
>
> Dr. Besant herself told me all the above facts. I repeat them now so that the background of her published letters may be 'true'."

Mrs. Jinarajadasa remembers that Dr. Besant was not quite happy about my succession, "in the bottom of her heart." If so, why did Dr. Besant write that she liked my news "immensely?" Mrs. Jinarajadasa ought to know, if she is able to probe to the bottom of Dr. Besant's heart, that Dr. Besant was at least direct and truthful in her utterances. So here is Mrs. Jinarajadasa's inaccuracy No.1. No.2 lies in her assertion that the message was from the Master Morya. I wrote nothing of the kind. No.3 is found in Mrs. Jinarajadasa's assertion that I was told I would be standing for election in 1928. I wrote nothing of the kind. On the contrary, I wrote that even if my memory were accurate I felt that the succession would be a very long way off, in the distant future. Inaccuracy No. 4 is in Mrs. Jinarajadasa's statement that Bishop Leadbeater cabled to me suggesting that the matter be dropped. He did not cable to me—there was no need since we were both living in the same house! Nor did he suggest that the matter be dropped. There was nothing to drop. May we not, therefore, take leave to doubt that Dr. Besant, as Mrs. Jinarajadasa alleges, told her "all the above facts?" Dr. Besant could not have told her all this for the simple reason that it did not exist to be told. Dr. Besant had my letters, and these are now back in my possession. They entirely contradict Mrs. Jinarajadasa's "memory." Mrs. Jinarajadasa's subsequent memories should, therefore, be taken with no less reserve than I have shown to be necessary as regards the first set of memories. It is amusing that Mrs. Jinarajadasa proposes. For what purpose then is Mrs. Jinarajadasa using Dr. Besant's name? Mr. Jinarajadasa simply issues a facsimile of Dr. Besant's own writing. Mrs. Jinarajadasa asks us to accept her authority for a memory, which I have proved inaccurate, and hopes we shall bow down before it because she labels it "real and true!"

As for Mr. Shiva Rao's and Mr. Telang's memories, I have no means of testing their accuracy. But I at least know this, that in the years subsequent to these memories others have had frequent conversations with Dr. Besant in the course of which Dr. Besant declared that she regarded me as her natural successor; Bishop Leadbeater is one of these. It would be interesting to know the reaction of Mrs. Jinarajadasa and Messrs. Shiva Rao and Telang to the clear memory of Mr. and Mrs. Henry Hotchener that Dr. Besant told them in 1930 at Ommen that the future of the Theosophical Society would be safe since George Arundale would succeed her. A tiresome memory, this, on the "wrong" side! And so we could go on, piling memory upon memory, putting one authority against another. Perhaps it might have been better had Mr. Jinarajadasa refrained from publishing the two letters which let loose the floodgates of "memories," but at least Dr. Besant speaks for herself and is her own authority, while Mrs. Jinarajadasa and her friends evidently expect us to accept their authority in the place of that of Dr. Besant, or why did they trouble to write her?

Please do not misunderstand me. I am not seeking votes, nor am I eager for office. If Mr. Jinarajadasa had offered himself for election I should not have stood, as he knows very well. But since he decided not to stand, and since I know that Dr. Besant wished and wishes me to stand, and since I know further that there are others who approve of my standing, I offer myself for the office of President, without the slightest illusion as to the enormous difference in stature between myself and the great personage who last occupied the office of President.

I stand because it is my duty to stand, and I send out this leaflet not as a piece of propaganda, but as a means of protecting my fellow members from inaccuracies which they have not the wherewithal to gauge. It is not fair to the members of the Society that they should be flooded with inaccurate statements calculated to prejudice the issue. I would venture to suggest that all these "memories" be ignored, and, if some desire, even Dr. Besant's own statements—though personally I could not ignore them. Let each member vote according to his own intuition and judgment, thinking solely of the Society and its interests.

Mr. Wood's principal nominator, Mr. Smythe of Canada, also seems unable to weigh his statements with the care one might reasonably expect from a person holding the responsible office of a General Secretary. He does no good to his nominee, for example, by asserting in a recent issue of the *Canadian Theosophist* that Bishop Leadbeater "has entered into possession of the President's quarters at Adyar without a by-your-leave to anyone." Of course the purpose behind his statement is to show that if I am elected President, Bishop Leadbeater will be the power behind the throne, and that Adyar will become a hotchpotch of Liberal Catholicism, Esoteric School and Co-Masonry. Mr. Smythe carefully constructs this childish and ridiculous bogey, and then props it up by—well, let us say inexactitudes. Bishop Leadbeater neither possesses Dr. Besant' rooms, nor does he live in them. The keys are with Dr. Besant's executor, and only once since her death has Bishop Leadbeater entered these rooms—when all the delegates to the recent Convention passed through them to offer flowers in homage and gratitude. At the late Convention the General Council ordered that the rooms should be kept closed for one year out of respect to her memory. And this particular inexactitude is only one of many. Mr. Smythe should change his Adyar correspondent, or ask some really responsible resident for facts instead of the fiction with which he seems generally to be regaled.

How unworthy of our Society all this is! I am thankful that at least *The Theosophist* has been kept free from it by Mr. Warrington, in spite of the pressure which has been constantly exercised upon him to open its pages to manifestos and memories and letters galore. One correspondent wrote to me that he thought the whole of the February *Theosophist* should be devoted to all this drum-beating!

Well, let it be forgotten as a bad and unsavory dream, and let each member, in a spirit of eagerness to give the Society the best man available, vote according to a judgment and an intuition unswayed by specious pleadings.

Above all, despite Mr. Wood's suggestion to the contrary, let each voter remember Dr. Besant's words written in 1928, on the occasion of the then election:

"To those who did not discharge the easy duty of voting once in seven years, I have nothing to say, except that to neglect that duty is a wrong inflicted on the Society."

Conscience or Authority

by
Dorothy Jinarajadasa

I am sorry that Bishop Arundale's article "Memories or Facts" calls for an answer and further explanation from me.

This article is curious reading to me as the Bishop was aware of the contents of my article "Conscience or Authority" and read the MS several days before it was published in *Theosophy in India*. He came to tea with me on December 9th and I showed him a typed copy of the MS for, believing him to be as aware as I of the implication of those two letters of Dr. Besant, I thought he might want to do something about it, so I asked him if he would write a note saying the letters were published hastily and under a misapprehension, and that he did not want Dr. Besant's name to be used to influence the vote of members. Bishop Arundale seemed to think he could not do this, I said: But my paragraph *is* the truth. Said the Bishop: "Substantially" (his word) it was true, but had some inaccuracies. He then went from the room, and though I have asked him to continue the conversation he has not spoken to me since, until now, in print.

Bishop Arundale and I are in agreement on two points. First, I also "deeply regret" that Dr. Besant' name has been used for propaganda purposes, but obviously the fault does not lie with me. I should not have dreamed of revealing recollections of a private conversation between Dr. Besant and myself if first those two letters of hers had not been widely circulated, giving a wrong impression of an incident of which I knew the truth. The mere fact that there is "a widespread demand on the part of members asking for any indication as to her (Dr. Besant's) wishes," does not justify satisfying that demand by taking words of Dr. Besant, used by her eight years ago—and which referred to an incident occurring at that distant date (1926)—and applying them to the presidential election of 1934. And it is interesting to note that in 1928, Dr. Besant did not appoint Bishop Arundale as the Vice-President, which one might naturally have expected her to do had she regarded him as her successor.

Bishop Arundale's remarks on my alleged "inaccuracies" need but small comment from me. I can only say that Dr. Besant told me, amplified, and more strongly expressed by her in speaking, exactly what I have related. Details she may have confused as two years had elapsed between the incident and her talking to me about it. Of Bishop Arundale's version of the matter I know nothing, but only what Dr. Besant told me, and what I was subsequently told which confirmed my "memories".

Minor details as to the name of the Master, whether Bishop Leadbeater remonstrated verbally or by cable, do not affect the point of my statement, which is, that Dr. Besant gave ample evidence to those of us who were in daily and intimate contact with her up to 1930, (of that privileged number were Mr. Dwarkanath Telang and myself) that she did not wish or intend to influence members as to their choice, when the time came to vote for her successor as our President. Those two letters of 1926 in her handwriting did not refer to her successor when she had finally to leave us, but to the 1928 election.

Some who have read my article have evidently been unable to see the woods for the trees, and have been so overwhelmed by one paragraph that they have missed its significance to the whole.

Bishop Arundale's insinuations that what I stated is fabrication and his manner in referring to my "inaccuracies" show that he has read and reflected an acrimony into my article which certainly is not there—I simply related what I knew, as Dr. Besant told it to me. My object in writing it is neither to oppose, nor make propaganda for either candidate for the presidential election. I merely felt I *had* to say plainly and frankly what I know to be true. And I have said it.

Happily, for the second time Bishop Arundale and I again unite in agreement when we each suggest that members think for themselves, and use their own judgment and intuition in electing their new President to the Theosophical Society.

A.P. Warrington made his announcement that he decided not to be considered in the coming election. Of course the Theosophical Society members were not in close touch with the political affairs of the Theosophical movement, but Bishop Arundale would of course be the popular choice by a huge majority. Although stepping into the office at a very difficult time, especially under the heavy handicap of succeeding Dr. Besant, George should have the sincere support of all theosophists throughout the world.

A.P. Warrington, the acting President of the Theosophical Society after Dr. Besant's passing, kindly invited Krishnamurti to give some talks and answers to questions from the audience. Krishnamurti would accept his invitation and he appreciated Warrington's friendliness, which he hoped would continue even though they differed completely in their ideas and opinions. He always throughout his talks reminded the audience that he was not attacking any of their leaders nor the Theosophical Society. Attacking anyone is a sheer waste of time. He wanted to act as a mirror, to make clear to them the perversions and deceptions that exist in society, and in religion. But he held that while organizations for the social welfare of man are necessary, societies based on religious hopes and beliefs are pernicious. Krishnamurti pointed out, "So though I may appear to speak harshly, please bear in mind that I am not attacking any particular society, but that I am against all these false organizations which, though they profess to help man, are in reality a great hindrance and are the means of constant exploitation."

October 20 1933

Dear Krishnaji,

I most cordially offer you the hospitality of this compound, the same this year as last year, not only for yourself and Rajagopal personally, but for your morning lectures as well.

Our own staff will attend to all details this time, thus relieving yours.

There can be no doubt about the greater convenience such a plan would be to the assembled delegates.

May I have an early reply?

Betty and I are very well and are looking forward to your visit with the keenest pleasure.

Ever affectionately,
A. P. Warrington

A telegram was sent from Rajagopal to Warrington from Bombay November 7, 1933:

> Krishnaji says he deeply appreciates your kind invitation personally would accept whatever arrangements most convenient to all but feels it pity become bone of contention within Society. If you and Bishop Leadbeater really desire he should speak within Society he has no objection accept your kind invitation. Rajagopal

---

The following is the letter that was sent to Sidney Cook, President of the Theosophical Society American Section from Max Wardall, Trustee of Krotona.

September 27, 1933
Theosophical Order of Service

Dear Sidney:

Thank you for your kind letter. I am glad to assure you that my reasons for attempting to get rid of my jobs were unselfish ones. Inclosed is a copy of my letter to Dr. Arundale in the matter. I wished also to be quite free to say what I felt should be said without being charged with taking advantage of an unofficial position.

The youthful vigor evident at Convention, together with the appointment of Mr. Roest and the strong support given Anita Henkel, are pleasing signals of renewed life and energy, but there is much to be done before the T.S. can get back where it belongs. Those of you who live at Headquarters and those fresh from the enthusiasm of Convention are not perhaps as able to gauge the conditions of the T.S. as some of us who see the lodges as they function. Also, residents at Olcott and members attending Convention usually represent the most enlightened and liberal of our Society, but after all they are just a handful. Your excellent statistical survey on loss of membership gives the real clue to our trouble. It is the <u>lodges</u> that need regeneration.

In the early development of our movement lodges were alive with the inspiration of the Ancient Wisdom. Every center glowed with quickening life. There was much original thinking and spiritual independence. This gradually gave way to orthodoxy and reliance upon leaders. Superstitions flourished, and teachings that were intended to be speculative and philosophical became religious dogmas and guides. For the clear, impersonal philosophy of the ancients we substituted hero-worship, and became followers after personalities. Members grew ambitious for occult recognition and advancement. These things I have myself clearly witnessed during the last twenty-five years.

Trying earnestly but vainly to grasp and assimilate the vast and ever-growing body of doctrine, our minds have become at last slothful and imitative. Filled with thoughts of our own past incarnations and projecting ourselves into the grandeur of those to come, trying feebly to envisage the vast sweep of the cosmic plan, up to our necks in chains, rounds, races and worlds without end—imbibing great draughts of conjecture on ethereal worlds, planes, nirvana, monads, angels, nature spirits, chohans, masters, initiations, rays, ceremonials, cosmic evolution, dharmas, karmas, permanent atoms, elementals, magic and the black arts—it was but natural that our minds should have suffered under the strain and lost spring, snap, originality and creative power; mental power comes, of course, from live thinking and experiencing. Teachings that we learn to believe without experiencing become so many obstacles, fencing us away from Reality and insulating us from Life.

The Educational Plan outlined is comprehensive and excellent, but can you get anywhere without a thorough housecleaning? What about those lodges peopled and offered by orthodox, moss-grown old members who are steeped in occult superstitions? At least 50% of our centers are in the grip of people who are old—not necessarily in years but in outlook—who have lost their resiliency and have ceased to doubt, think or question. They have learned to believe so much that their critical powers no longer function, and they have become blind and sometimes bigoted followers of authority. They are extraordinarily good people, deeply devoted to their leaders, but they are just "incompetent, irrelevant and immaterial" when it comes to thinking or acting for themselves and making Theosophy a force in the world. Into such lodges are ushered new, red-blooded, modern people with questing hearts and open vision. What result can be expected? That 10% remain is something of a miracle.

In the last ten years I have visited hundreds of lodges in many countries, and everywhere I found in goodly measure the conditions above described. Here, for instance, are some of the common superstitions which I have found to prevail:

1. That Theosophists are superior to the denizens of the "outer" world.

2. That Theosophists are a select and chosen group whose only function is to ray out beneficent forces on a benighted world.

3. That we know the details of God's Plan.

4. That all members leaving the Society are only "deadwood", and needed shaking out.

5. That intellectual integrity indicates disloyalty to our leaders.

6. That bad health is largely a Karmic heritage.

7. That Astrology and Numerology are exact sciences.

8. That all visiting Hindus are yogis and spiritually enlightened.

9. That to be good Theosophists we must believe everything the leaders say.

10. That all lecturers and distinguished T.S. visitors can read our auras, tell us about our past lives, and see spirits, fairies, devas, etc.

11. That all Theosophical psychics see what they think they see.

12. That abstaining from meat, ipso facto, makes one superior.

13. That the T.S., having been founded by the Masters, can take care of itself.
14. That Mr. X, who disagrees with us, is probably in the hands of the "Dark Powers."

These, Sidney, are only a <u>few</u> of the superstitions that becloud us at the present time. You may not agree with the entire list, and may think them relatively unimportant. You may say that most Theosophists have one or more of these ideas, but that they do no especial harm. Grant that if one has a fine sense of humor and a tolerant heart he can lug a goodly number of these ideas around and still be an inspiration to new members. BUT let him be rigid, humorless, self-important, dogmatic and pious, and he will dry up any center until it becomes a musty, devitalized asylum for intellectual and psychic derelicts.

Now, answering your query, I venture to criticize the trend of the Society in its effort to repair the Theosophical structure before the necessary demolition takes place. Krishnaji I believe was sent as a destroyer and regenerator. His purpose, whether conscious or not, is to strip us of orthodoxy, credulity, Babbitry and hearsay-beliefs, and to restore us to a state of spiritual and mental integrity. Observe these remarks of his, taken quite at random:

1. I would request you to examine my ideas without comparing them with what you have read or heard. I had to give up all my preconceived ideas and look at things from the point of view of their intrinsic value.
2. Religion and philosophy but superimpose the ideas of others on your mind and thereby dull and cripple your thought.
3. Conformity kills initiative.
4. I know you have patterned your life on theories, which is one of the causes of conflict.
5. The mind that projects itself into the future and tries to understand the future corrupts the present, perverts clear judgment.
6. Anyone who seeks to realize Truth by the imitation, the following, of another—through institutions, through ceremonies—is an unhealthy person.

7. You say: 'He is wise, he must know. Therefore I must be instructed by him; I will accept his words as wisdom, because he says he knows.' I say, beware of such a person, because he creates in your mind and heart the fear which destroys all understanding.

8. Spiritually you seek power, thereby creating distinctions in which there is no tenderness, no gentleness, no affection.

9. It is in the normal human life that you find Truth, happiness and completeness. To go far, you must begin near.

10. Karma is one of the excuses of the mind to postpone effort.

11. A mind burdened with belief is not adaptable.

12. Reincarnation is only a bridge to understanding; do not make a dogma of it.

13. You cannot practice what you do not understand.

14. Your life has become stultified, and the shadows of your own creation overwhelm you.

15. I would set people free from those beliefs, dogmas and creeds which condition Life.

16. A spiritual man is a cultured man; he is so balanced that he is able to laugh at himself.

17. I want to make people think for themselves.

18. Those who fear doubt will be smothered in the dust of their own traditions.

The general trend of the Society is away from these regenerative teachings. I do not imply that there is any definite, organized effort to follow Krishnaji's ideas. Indeed most T.S. members have tried earnestly to comprehend his much-heralded mission, and would have responded whole-heartedly had they been given any help. But our great lamented leader herself, weakened by the onset of age, was unable to reconcile the apparent conflicts, and others prominent in our movement, confused and disconcerted by the orthodox wails that arose everywhere, have done nothing but utter soothing words.

Through Krishnaji the T.S. had an opportunity for a cleansing death and a glorious resurrection. It did not and has not accepted the opportunity and is gong the other way.

I do not affirm for a moment that the majority of T.S. members are silly, credulous and superstitious. If I did I should not take the trouble to write this. The majority are rather splendid people, but their force will not be felt until a clean-up campaign is put through the lodges with the fiery slogan "GET OUT OF YOUR SHELL", and a pledge "I'll Do My Part" exacted from all, especially the "sot and sartin."

I think it might be well to cease cozening the members with fine phrases, assuring them that they are the elect of earth, receiving special attention from the Hierarchy. This tendency has been in a great part responsible for the smug self-complacency that young members complain of so bitterly.

Mr. Roest I know to be strong admirer of Krishnaji's philosophy. He can do much in his work about the section, but it would be a mistake to seek to overlay this petrified foundation with perishable cultural appeals. Orthodoxy MUST be dissolved if we are to face the glorious future that awaits us.

I would like to be the first to sign such a pledge as this:

"I'LL DO MY PART to dignify Theosophy that our Society may take its rightful place in the world as a body of people intellectually honest and fearless, free from superstition, tolerant and sympathetic toward other movements, and eternally pledged to the Brotherhood of Man."

Faithfully and sincerely yours,

P.S. An excellent way to test the validity of these observations would be to publish this letter. If they are untrue they may awaken the members to active and creative dissent. If true, they should be recognized and met. With the loss of A.B.'s leadership we must create our own future. Facing facts is a good way to begin. A direct challenge often acts like dynamite—it is never soporific.

If published, this note should be included to show that it is a challenge, and not just ill humor!
Max Wardall

America inaugurated its Greater American Plan under the direction of Dr. Pieter K. Roest, for the furtherance of the dissemination of Theosophy throughout the country.

October 21 1933
Theosophical Order of Service
Max Wardall International Director

Dear Parthe: (A.P. Warrington)

Enjoyed your letter very much, and assure you my resignation from T.O.S. (Theosophical Order of Service) and Adyar Day were purely in the interests of the work. My boisterous travelling days are over and the T.O.S. needs someone to journey about. It takes a heavy wallop to waken the average T.S.'er and thereafter a continual barrage is advisable to keep him from relapsing into somnolence again. So far as Adyar Day is concerned, new blood is needed. However beautiful Adyar may be, after writing ten articles on it (as I have) one uses up his adjectives in an alarming way!

I find to my dismay, however, that Bishop George was in error about Robert Logan's having accepted headship of the T.O.S. That gentleman writes me now that he never agreed to take it over and has no intention of doing so, so that's that. We are substantially where we began. I think Robert Spurrier of London would take it and is the logical person for the post. He has indeed agreed to do so if you ask him. Will you kindly see that something is done in this matter? I have promised to write for the magazine SERVICE and help keep things going.

I wrote C.J. while Amma was alive asking him (as he had appointed me at her request) to name my successor for Adyar Day, giving him some suggestions. This was months ago and I have received no answer. Perhaps this duty will also devolve upon you.

T.S. Convention this year seems to have been a period of revival. I did not go, so this is only hearsay. Many young people came and there was a general acknowledgement that the T.S. was in rather a parlous condition so far as the Life is concerned. A new educational plan was outlined and Pieter Roest and Anita Henkel were sent out into the Section as revival missionaries.

But, Parthe dear, speaking without motive and in a spirit of love and good will. I declare to you that the T.S. needs a "New Deal". I wrote to Sidney Cook after Convention saying that I was glad to hear of the Convention enthusiasm but ventured to say that the trend of the Society was still in the direction of authoritarianism and crystallization which is the way of fading power and vitality. He answered asking me for a fuller statement. I am enclosing copy of letter sent him. I have not heard from him since and do not know if he will publish it. I doubt if he has the nerve. Sidney has grown enormously and is a fine, faithful chap, but they are all under the spell of "Hierarchitis", and determined to march to orders. They fear to offend or move without sanction from All-High. Parthe dear, **this is all a mistake**. We must get back to individual thinking, initiative and daring. Even controversy is better than this yes-yes policy which destroys the vigor and uniqueness of our people.

You who are now the titular head of this Society are so far as I can recall the only person in power who has glimpsed the relationship of Krishnaji's teaching to existing conditions in the T.S. Can you not in some way inaugurate a "New Deal" which will liberate the members from the thralldom of many and divers and odious superstitions, and give them back the will to **think**?

Of course, members are not entirely to blame for their condition. They have had too many injections of occult improbabilities. You remember Mandy who went to the hospital. The doctor asked her if she had been X-Rayed. She replied, "No, but Ah's been Ultra-Violated!"

Do not think me zealous, Parthe. There is no heat in my attitude, but I am in a unique position—a life-long Theosophist released by an act of God from all duties and obligations to enable him to study and reflect upon the condition of the Society in which he has long served. Krishnaji is right, my dear. No one can evaluate, measure or assess any situation until he is free of it, in the sense of motive, attachment, desire, etc. Being in that happy condition I think I see clearly our need, and that need is urgent. However, my letter to Cook indicates in general my point of view and I refrain from pressing it.

Lilian and I are well and divinely happy. We have established a new set of interests, drama being one of them. Perhaps some day we can be of help to the Society through this channel. Tonight we are presenting a play at Krotona under the sponsorship of the local lodge, inviting all the Valley to attend. This inaugurates a new policy of public activity, the open lodge meetings to be held at Krotona in future.

We would love to be with you there. I have always enjoyed your stimulating and courageous leadership. I should like to think that we shall always work together. But whether I shall actively work again with the T.S. depends entirely upon the trend, and whether we get a "New Deal". Life is too precious to spend fumbling among the relics for an age that is gone.

With love to you both from us two, I am always
Faithfully and affectionately yours,
Max Wardall

October 30 1933
The Manor

Very dear Friend, (A.P.Warrington)

I have just received your telegram informing me that Mr. Wood is proposing to issue an election manifesto in *The Theosophist*. I presume this means that he intends to stand as a Candidate for election.

I myself had no intention of issuing any election Manifesto, and I must frankly confess that I dislike very much the idea of one. Apart, however, from this, even if I had a Manifesto ready it could not possibly have reached you by the date specified in your telegram, November 15th.

If Mr. Wood wishes to publish his Manifesto in *The Theosophist* I have, of course, no objection. As for a Manifesto from myself it would naturally take some time to prepare, should I consider it desirable to send one out to our members. I do not, therefore, think I could be expected to push one through for the December number even could it have reached you in time which is impossible. But if, on reflection, I decide to make a statement perhaps you will be so good as to allow me some space in the January issue of *The Theosophist* for the purpose. It would presumably be in time if I handed it to you when we reach Adyar.

It was very considerate of you to send me the telegram and I am grateful to you for it.
Affectionately to you both,
George (Arundale)

Krishnamurti and Rajagopal arrived in Madras a month after Dr. Besant's death and stayed for the first time at Vasanta Vihar. At the end of his third talk on December 31, 1933, Krishanji again answered questions from the audience.

> *Question*: The one regret of Dr. Besant is said to have been the fact that you failed to rise to her expectations of you as the World-Teacher. Some of us frankly share that regret and that sense of disappointment, and feel that it is not altogether without some justification. Have you anything to say?

Krishnamurti: Nothing, sirs. (Laughter) When I say "Nothing," I mean nothing to relieve your disappointment or Dr. Besant's disappointment—if she were disappointed, for she often expressed to me the contrary. I am not here to justify myself; I am not interested in justifying myself. The question is, why are you disappointed, if you are? You had thought to put me in a certain cage, and since I did not fit into that cage, naturally you were disappointed. You had a preconceived idea of what I should do, what I should say, what I should think.

I say that there is immortality, an eternal becoming. The point is not that I know, but that it is. Beware of the man who says, "I know." Ever-becoming life exists, but to realize that, your mind must be free of all preconceived ideas of what it is. You have preconceived ideas of God, of immortality, of life. "This is written in books," you say, or, "Someone has told me this." Thus you have built an image of truth, you have pictured God and immortality. You want to hold to that image, that picture, and you are disappointed in anyone whose idea differs from yours, anyone whose ideas do not conform to yours. In other words, if he does not become your tool, you are disappointed in him. If he does not exploit you—and you create the exploiter in your desire for security—then you are disappointed in him. Your disappointment is based not on thought, not on intelligence, not on deep affection, but on some image of your own making, however false it may be.

You will find people who will tell you that I have disappointed them, and they will create a body of opinions holding that I have failed. But in a hundred years' time I don't think it will matter much whether you are disappointed or not. Truth, of which I speak, will remain—not your fantasies or your disappointments.[12]

It has been repeated again and again in the E.S., that the E.S. does not in any way control the policies of The Society. Each E.S. member is a member of The Society, and retains his right as a member to guide The Society according to his ability and judgment.

E.S. members have the duty of voting; it is told to them that it is a duty which they should religiously perform. But in doing so

---

[12] *Ibid.*, pp.165-166.

they must exercise their own judgment, and not look to any E.S. member, Corresponding Secretary, or any other, for guidance in the matter of voting. C. Jinarajadasa at this time of crises, hopes no E.S. member will proclaim to others what he believes are the wishes of the Masters; nor should E.S. members allow themselves to be swayed by any such statement to vote against their mature judgment.

Mrs. Hotchener makes an important announcement that with the December 1933 issue of *World Theosophy*, she will cease publication, the completion of its third year. This will make way for the larger circulation of Adyar *The Theosophist*, the magazine established by H.P.B. for the theosophical world.

A year before, rumors reached Dr. Besant from Adyar that some considered *World Theosophy* competitive to *The Theosophist*. C. Jinarajadasa, then acting editor of *The Theosophist*, stated definitely that he and Dr. Arundale considered *World Theosophy* competitive. Finally Warrington, Vice President, laments the small number of its subscribers, and makes a strong plea for the members to aid *The Theosophist*. Mrs. Hotchener not only ceased publication of her magazine, *World Theosophy*, but mailed a special appeal to her entire list of nearly three thousand persons urging them to subscribe to *The Theosophist* and thus help to put it on a satisfactory basis.

Reported in the *Shishya* General Notes for use in the Esoteric School only, we find this statement by C. Jinarajadasa.

> Members will note the reference to *The Theosophist* by the two Chohans M. and K.H. They should, therefore, make an effort to help the magazine in all ways, particularly by procuring subscribers. E.S. members who can afford to do so should subscribe, though I know that there are many calls upon them for various kinds of work. But as we at Adyar are trying to make *The Theosophist* a channel of occult influences, and as *Shishya* and similar bulletins of the E.S. can only appear rarely, owing to the adverse financial conditions everywhere, each E.S. group should make a point of: (1) either sending a subscription to *The Theosophist*, or (2) procuring it from some member who subscribes, and reading the Watch-Tower notes and any articles of note.[13]

---

[13] Jinarajadasa, C., *Shishya*, "General Notes", Vol.I, n2, September 1931, p.32.

Time has come now for the members of the General Council of The Society, the international governing body whose membership is composed of the general secretaries of the forty-odd Sections and some few additional members elected by the General Council itself. The members of that body have the right and the responsibility of nominating international presidents, and the Society's members all over the world have a similar right and responsibility of voting and thus selecting a president from among those so nominated as successor to Dr. Besant in the presidency of the Society.

After long years of faithful service to The Society as its Treasurer, Mr. Albert Schwarz died in Switzerland of heart failure, where he had gone for a rest.

In the correspondence box of A. P. Warrington, we discovered a typed paragraph with no date, reporting that Sidney Cook wrote a letter to A.P. Warrington in 1933 stating that Gutzon Borglum, noted sculptor, was for some years intimately connected with the Theosophical Society, and knew H.P. Blavatsky. It also reported that Borglum was the first president of the young group in Omaha. Gutzon Borglum was the father and creator of the stupendous sculpture of four U.S. Presidents at Mt. Rushmore (S.D.) in the Black Hills. No sculpture on such a scale has been previously attempted anywhere, any time.

Borglum has asked every President since Theodore Roosevelt to work for establishment of a Ministry of Fine Arts. Coolidge was the first one to be sympathetic to the idea, he says, and he has strong hopes the present administration will make it reality.

After Dr. Besant dissolved into the invisible, Warrington could never forget that life. He writes in his *Recollections of Annie Besant*:

> "Can I fail to recognize its influence on my life? At the thought of her, or the mention of her name, there would well up in me a surge of devotion and delight which I would not exchange for anything. She was a constant source of spiritual stimulation, and I think I can say that my whole life, after coming into touch with her, was devoted to the ideals for which she stood, and service to her could be nothing less than a joy. It must be that a link such as this will

hold for a long, long time, for its metal has been proven, and happy and highly privileged am I that it should be so".[14]

The following may be a reiteration of ideas previously expressed by George Arundale in other talks and speeches, and may even be stale, breaking no new ground, embarrassing to some, dull because of overuse, but there are members among the Theosophical Society, and of the Krishnamurti Foundations who do not understand even today what the complications were regarding Krishnamurti and his relationship to the Theosophical Society.

Dr. Arundale gave the closing talk of Summer School at Olcott, 1933 to the members that there must be some kind of neutrality of the Theosophical Society in the case of Krishnamurti.

> You and I have to realize that the Theosophical Society does not belong to us, is not to be maneuvered by us, is not to be brought down to the level of our lesser understanding, is not to be imprisoned and restrained within our own individual conception of life. The Theosophical Society is a powerful instrument in the hands of the Elder Brethren and They use it to mighty purposes.
>
> Take the case of Krishnaji. It was desired that a messenger should go forth from the Great White Lodge to do a certain most important and very difficult work; a work far more cosmic in its nature than we recognize; a work the nature of which probably not more than two or three people have the slightest comprehension. Krishnaji is a world force and although his appeal is very definitely to individuals, he is nevertheless working more on the macrocosmic planes than on the microcosmic planes. He is dealing with great and fundamental principles which the average individual must find exceedingly difficult to translate into terms of the lower consciousness. He is in fact striving to make Nirvana a living reality in the outer world, a heroic and almost impossible task, but a task which he must labor to achieve as a kind of background for new life. I am entirely at

---

[14] Warrington, A.P., *The Theosophist*, "Recollections of Annie Besant", April 1939, Vol. 1, n pp.21-23.

one with all that he says, but he has the task of tasks in his effort to make people with limited consciousness break through those restrictions and enter into a freedom which is beyond the emotions, beyond the mind, and even beyond the Buddhic consciousness.

When it was determined that Krishnaji should come as a destroyer and regenerator, it was decided that to the Theosophical Society the privilege should be given of ushering him in and standing by him in the very early days, and to its two greatest members, Dr. Besant and Bishop Leadbeater, was assigned the duty of guarding him in youth against many attacks and many difficulties. It is the splendid karma of the Theosophical Society thus to have been able to give to Krishnaji protection and the support he needed in the beginning of his great mission.

But now the time has come for the Theosophical Society to carry on its own work, even as equally Krishnaji must follow *his* own path. He is perfectly right to free himself from the Theosophical Society; his resignation from the Theosophical Society was vital to the great work he has to do. His dissociation from our teachings and our work generally was inevitable. He has his job and, whether entirely perfectly or not, he knows magnificently how to do it. He knows what he is about and I sometimes wish some of us knew as well what we are about. We may say that we have helped him. We wish him "God-speed!" If the time should ever come for the world to reject him, he knows where his friends always are. I do not attend the camps, not because I do not love him, not because I have not an intimate comradeship with him which has lasted from innumerable lives, but because he has his work to do and I have mine. I am among those, as are you also, who are chosen to guard the Theosophical Society. It is our job and we will do it, and he will do his job. In the meantime the work of the Theosophical Society goes forward as does that of Krishnaji. It is the greater service to Krishnaji and the greater duty of he Theosophical Society for each to go his own way. The individual members may, and indeed should, always have goodwill and friendliness and affection for him, and are wise to take whatever they want and whatever they can from his great teachings, as well as from all other great teachings. But the Theosophical Society will render service such as it has rendered to Krishnaji, to other people from time to time, and it must never have any exclusive or even any definite connection with any one. We must preserve the neutrality and the independence of the Theosophical Society so that it may help at all times whenever help is needed.

The same, of course, applies to the Liberal Catholic Church. The Lord Himself sent the Liberal Catholic Church into the world. The Lord is no less behind that Church than He is behind Krishnaji. The Theosophical Society gave a helping hand to the Liberal Catholic Church, but now it must stand on its own feet apart from the Theosophical Society; away from it. As Krishnaji fulfills his mission so must the Liberal Catholic Church achieve its own destiny, but neither must be allowed to color the work of the Theosophical Society.

Then we have another great movement, that of Co-Masonry, which gives the same teaching in another form and to it also we owe a similar obligation., Perhaps, in addition, the educational work should be included since it has also been ordered by the Lord Himself, but here again we have to be careful that any educational work we undertake shall never at any time compromise that independence of all movements, of all specific forms of truth, which the Theosophical Society must ever maintain. To us have been specifically committed the great principles given statement by H.P.B. Those basic teachings we must guard, those we must cherish, those we must stand for because those have been definitely charged to our care. As for all others we wish them God-speed, glad to have given aid, and perhaps in a time to come, if they should require it, we will again give assistance and send them forth.

It is evident that the dignity and worth and high purpose of the Theosophical Society demand this wonderful independence so that the Elder Brethren may have many irons in the world fire, each of which is shaped to do its own particular work without seeking to be like other irons which are in the selfsame fire. We add to our dignity and to our nobility and to our purpose, and we become increasingly true to our duty, when we stand aloof, free to all that works for truth, whether in our way or any other way, but going our appointed way with clear vision and unswerving steadfastness.[15]

---

[15] Arundale, George S., *The American Theosophist* formerly *The Theosophical Messenger*, "The Neutrality of the Theosophical Society", January, 1934, Vol. XXII, n1, p.1-2.

We do not know the exact date the following poem was written by Mary Gray, but it does reflect the Ojai Valley.

THE OJAI

Whispers of night in the moon's still light,
As the songbird hides in its nest;
Shiver of trees in the evening breeze,
Hushed sounds of a world at rest.

Then the faint soft purr of the cricket's churr,
And the chorus of frogs in the ponds,
The first high thrum—then the deep bass drum,
of the bull from the lily pool fronds.

From the slumbering dark comes the coyotes' bark,
And the long lone call of the owl;
The orange—tree scent with acacia blent,
Steals out from the mountain's cowl.

During hours of sleep when the darkness hangs deep,
An Angel broods over the nest,
And with joy contemplates the cradle that waits
For the race that the Manu has blest.

Interior of the Adyar Theosophical Society
Headquarter's Hall, 1905

Chapter III
1934

Dr. Besant's death did not sever Krishnamurti's last tie with the Theosophical Society. Although he was free from every form of spiritual organizations, and traveling his own way, he did not really dissociate himself from the Theosophical Society until after 1938. Records show that he gave his last E.S. talk to The Manor group in Sydney, Australia, 1936. We have seen how the Theosophical Society expressed its hostile attitude towards Krishnamurti, but at the same time extended its "hospitality," continuing to have a keen interest in what he had to say.

Krishnamurti gave his fourth talk at Adyar, on January 1, 1934 when his audience wished him a happy new year. He had forgotten that it was a new year, and wished his audience all a happy one, too. During the question and answer session, Krishnamurti was asked several questions:

> *Question*: During the Theosophical Convention last week several leaders and admirers of Dr. Besant spoke, paying her high tributes. What is your tribute to and your opinion of that great figure who was a mother and friend to you? What was her attitude toward you through the many years of her guardianship of you and your brother, and also subsequently? Are you not grateful to her for her guidance, training, and care?
>
> *Krishnamurti*: Mr. Warrington kindly asked me to speak about this matter, but I told him that I did not want to. Now don't condemn me by using such words as "guardianship," "gratitude," and so on. Sirs, what can I say? Dr. Besant was our mother. She looked after us, she cared for us. But one thing she did not do. She never said to me, "Do this," or "Don't do that." She left me alone. Well, in these words I have paid her the greatest tribute. (Cheers)
>
> You know, followers destroy leaders, and you have destroyed yours. In your following of a leader, you exploit that leader; in your use of Dr. Besant's name so constantly you are merely exploiting her.

You are exploiting her and other teachers. The greatest disservice you can ever do to a leader is to follow that leader. I know you wisely nod your heads in approval. Let me but quote her name and sanctify her memory, and I can exploit you because you want to be exploited; you want to be used as instruments, for that is easier than thinking for yourselves. You are all cogs, parts of machines, being used by exploiters. Religions use you in the name of God, society uses you in the name of law, politicians and educators use and exploit you. So-called religious teachers and guides exploit you in the name of ceremonies, in the name of Masters. I am merely awakening you to these facts. You can do about them what you will: with that I am not concerned, because I don't belong to any society, and I shall probably not come here again.

Comment: But we want you to come.

Krishnamurti: Please don't get sentimental about this. Probably some of you will be glad that I shall not come again.

Comment: No.

Krishnamurti: Wait a moment, please. I don't want you to ask me or not to ask me to return. That doesn't matter at all.

Sirs, These two things are wholly different: what you are thinking and doing, and what I am talking and doing. The two cannot combine. Your whole system is based on exploitation, on the following of authority, on the belief in religion and faith. Not only your system, but the systems of the entire world. I cannot help those of you who are content with this system. I want to help those who are eager to break away, to understand. Naturally you will eject me, for I am opposed to all that you hold dear, sacred and worthwhile. But your rejection will not matter to me. I am not attached to this or any place. I repeat, what you are doing and what I am doing are two totally different things that have nothing in common.

But I was answering the question about Dr. Besant. Human mind is lazy, lethargic. It has been so dulled by authority, so shaped, controlled, conditioned, that it cannot stand by itself. But to stand by oneself is the only way to understand truth. Now are you really, fundamentally interested in understanding truth? No, most of you are not. You are only interested in supporting the system that you now hold, in finding substitutes, in seeking comfort and security; and in that search you are exploiting others and being exploited yourselves. In that there is no happiness, no richness, no fullness. Because you follow this way of life you have to choose. When you base your life either on the authority of the past or the hope of the future, when you guide your actions by the past greatness or the past ideas of a leader, you are not living; you are merely imitating, acting as a cog in a machine. And woe to such a person! For him life holds no happiness, no richness, but only shallowness, emptiness. This seems so clear to me that I am surprised that the question arises again and again.

Question: You have spoken in clear terms on the subject of the existence of Masters and the value of ceremonies. May I ask you a straightforward question? Are you disclosing to us your own genuine point of view without any mental reservation? Or is the ruthless manner of the presentation of your view merely a test of our devotion to the Masters and our loyalty to the Theosophical Society to which we belong? Please state your answer frankly, even though it may be hurtful to some of us.

Krishnamurti: What do you think I am? I have not given you a momentary reaction. I have told you what I really think. If you wish to use that as a test to fortify yourselves, to entrench yourselves in your old beliefs, I cannot help it. I have told you what I think, frankly, straightly, without dissimulation. I am not trying to make you act in one way or another, I am not trying to entice you into any society or into a particular form of thought, I don't dangle a reward in front of you. I have told you frankly that Masters are unessential, that the idea of Masters is nothing more than a toy to the man who really seeks truth. I am not trying to attack your beliefs, I realize that I am a guest here; this is merely my frank opinion, as I have stated it over and over again.

I hold that where there is unrighteousness there are ceremonies, whether it be in Mylapore or in Rome or here. But why discuss this matter any longer? You know my point of view, as I have stated it repeatedly. I have given you my reasons for my opinion regarding Masters and ceremonies. But because you want Masters, because you like to perform ceremonies, because such performance gives you a certain sense of authority, of security, of exclusiveness, you continue in your practices. You continue them with blind faith, blind acceptance, without reason, without real thought or emotion behind your acts. But in that way you will never understand truth; you will never know the cessation of sorrow. You may find forgetfulness, oblivion, but you will never discover the root, the cause of sorrow and be free from it.[1]

Dr. Besant wanted Krishnamurti to be true to his own innermost perceptions and pursue what he considered to be true. This is what Dr. Besant did in her own life, and to think that she would have expected anything less than that from her son would be ignorance on our part. It was a relationship based on true love and respect for each other, neither of which has anything to do with the demand for support or fulfilment, much less obedience of any kind.

Krishnamurti had to remind his audience again at his sixth talk in Adyar, that he was not interested in attacking their society. In saying this, he again repeats that he was not going back on what he had said. "I think that all spiritual organizations are a hindrance to man. For one cannot find truth through any organization." Again, the question of ceremonies comes up. "Why did you give up the old ceremonies, and now you have taken up new ones? You gave them up because they did not satisfy you; and you have taken up new ceremonies because they are more promising, more enticing, they offer greater hope. You have never said, I am going to find out the intrinsic value of ceremonies, whether they are Hindu, Christian, or of any other creed."

Dr. Besant's only concern for Krishnamurti when he parted ways with the leaders of the Theosophical Society, was her anxiety for Krishnamurti's future, and she prevailed upon some of her best assistants and close associates, especially those who were Initiates to resign from the TS, and go with Krishnamurti in order to protect him.

As Krishnamurti was closing one of his answers to questions and talks to the Adyar members, he had this to say too them:

---

[1] Krishnamurti, J., *the Collected Works of J. Krishnamurti*, Volume I, 1933-1934, Dubuque, Iowa, 1991, Kendall/Hunt Publishing Co., "Fourth Talk at Adyar", India, January 1, 1934, pp.171-173.

... I am sorry but I must now stop answering questions. Many questions have been asked me with regard to the Theosophical Society, whether I would accept the presidency if it were offered me, and what would be my policy if I were elected; whether the Theosophical Society, which strives to educate the masses and raise the ethical standard, should be disbanded; what policy I would advocate for the Indo-British commonwealth, and so on. I do not propose to stand for the presidency of the Theosophical Society because I do not belong to that Society. That does not interest me—not that I think myself superior—for I do not believe in religious organizations, and also I don't want to guide a single man. Please believe me, sirs, when I say that I don't want to influence one single person; for the desire to guide shows inherently that one has an end, a goal, towards which he thinks all humanity must come like a band of sheep. That is what guidance implies. Now I do not want to urge any man towards a particular goal or an end; what I want to do is to help him to be intelligent, and that is quite a different thing. So I have not time to answer these innumerable questions based on such ideas.

Since it is rather late, I should like to make a résumé of what I have been saying during the last five or six days, and naturally I must be paradoxical. Truth is paradoxical. I hope that those of you who have intelligently followed what I have been saying will understand and act, but not make a standard of me for your actions. If what I have said is not true to you, you will naturally forget it. Unless you have really fathomed, unless you have thought over what I have said, you will simply repeat my phrases, learn my words by heart, and that is of no value. For understanding, the first requirement is doubt, doubt not only with regard to what I say, but primarily with regard to the ideas which you yourselves hold. But you have made an anathema of doubt, a fetter, an evil to be banished, to be put away; you have made of doubt an abominable thing, a disease. But to me, doubt is none of these; doubt is an ointment that heals.

But what do you generally doubt? You doubt what the other says. It is very easy to doubt someone else. But to doubt the very thing in which you are caught up, that you hold, to doubt the very thing that you are seeking, pursuing, that is more difficult. True doubt will not yield to substitution. When you doubt another, as when someone said during one of these talks the other day, "We doubt you," that shows you are doubting what I am giving, what I am trying to explain. Quite right. But your doubt is but the search for substitution. You say, "I have this, but I am not satisfied. Will that satisfy me, that other thing which you are offering? To find out, I must doubt you." But I am not offering you anything. I am saying, doubt the very thing that is in your hands, that is in your mind and heart; then you will no longer seek substitution.

When you seek substitution there is fear, and therefore increase of conflict. When you are afraid you seek the opposite of fear, which is courage; you proceed to acquire courage. Or, if you decide that you are unkind, you proceed to acquire kindness, which is merely substitution, a turning to the opposite. But if, instead of seeking a substitution, you really begin to inquire into that very thing in which your mind is caught—fear, unkindness, acquisitiveness—then you will discover the cause. And you can find out the cause only by continually doubting, by questioning, by a critical and intelligent attitude of mind, which is a healthy attitude, but which has been destroyed by society, by education, by religions that admonish you to banish doubt. Doubt is merely an inquiry after true values, and when you have found out true values for yourself, doubt cease. But to find out, you must be critical, you must be frank, honest.

Since most people are seeking substitution, they are merely increasing their conflict. And this increase of conflict, with its desire for escape, we call progress, spiritual progress, because to use substitution or escape is further acquisition, further achievement. So what you call the search for truth is merely the attempt to find substitutes, the pursuit of greater securities, safer shelters from conflict. When you seek shelters you are creating exploiters, and having created them, you are caught up in that machine of exploitation which says, "Don't do this, don't do that, don't doubt, don't be critical. Follow this teaching, for this is true and that is false." So when you are talking of truth, you are really wanting substitution; you want repose, tranquillity, peace, assured escapes, and in this want you create artificial and empty machines, intellectual machines, to prove this substitution, to satisfy this want. Have I made my meaning clear?

First of all, you are caught up in conflict, and because you cannot understand that conflict you want the opposite, repose, peace, which is an intellectual concept. In that want you have created an intellectual machine, and that intellectual machine is religion; it is utterly divorced from your feelings, from your daily life, and is therefore merely an artificial thing. That intellectual machine may also be society, intellectually created, a machine to which you have become slaves and by which you are ruthlessly trodden down.

You have created these machines because you are in conflict, because through fear and anxiety you are driven to the opposite of that conflict, because you are seeking repose, tranquillity. Desire for the opposite creates fear, and out of that fear arises imitation. So you invent intellectual concepts such as religions, with their beliefs and standards, their authority and disciplines, their gurus and Masters, to lead you to what you want, which is comfort, security, tranquility, escape from this constant conflict. You have created this vast machine which you call religion, this intellectual vast machine which has no validity, and you have also created the machine that is called society, for in your social as well as in your religious life you want comfort, shelter. In your social life you are held by traditions, habits, unquestioned values; public opinion acts as your authority; and unquestioned opinion, habit, and tradition eventually lead to nationalism and war.

You talk of searching for truth, but your search is merely a search for substitution, the desire for greater security and greater certainty. Therefore your search is destroying that which you are seeking, which is peace, not the peace of stagnation, but of understanding, of life, of ecstasy. You are denied that very thing because you are looking for something that will help you to escape.

So to me the whole purpose—if I may use that word without your misunderstanding me—lies in destroying this false intellectual machine by means of intelligence, that is, by true awareness. You can understand, put away tradition, which has become a hindrance; you can understand, put away Masters, ideas, beliefs. But do not destroy them merely to take up new ones; I don't mean that. You must not merely destroy, merely put away, you must be creative; and you can be creative only when you begin to understand true values. So question the significance of traditions and habits, of nationality, of discipline, of gurus and Masters. You can understand only when you are fully aware, aware with your whole being. When you say, "I am seeking God," fundamentally you mean, "I want to run away, to escape." When you say, "I am seeking truth, and an organization might help me to find it," you are merely seeking a shelter. Now I am not being harsh; I only want to emphasize and make clear what I am saying. It is for you to act.

We have created artificial hindrances. They are not real, fundamental hindrances; they are artificial. We have created them because we are seeking something, rewards, security, comfort, peace. To gain security, to help us avoid conflict, we must have many aids, many supports. And these aids, these supports, are self-discipline, gurus, beliefs.

I have gone into all this more or less fully. Now when I am speaking about these things, please don't think in terms of opposites, for then you will not understand. When I say that self-discipline is a hindrance, don't think that therefore you must not have discipline at all. I want to show you the cause of self-discipline. When you understand that, there is neither this self-imposed discipline nor its opposite, but there is true intelligence. In order to realize what we want—which is fundamentally false, because it is based on the idea of the opposite as a substitution—we have created artificial means, such as self-discipline, belief, guidance. Without such belief, without such authority, which is a hindrance, we feel lost; thus we become slaves and are exploited.

A man who lives by belief is not truly living; he is limited in his actions. But the man who, because he understands, is really free from belief and from the burden of knowledge, to him there is ecstasy, to him there is truth. Beware of the man who says, "I know," because he can know only the static, the limited, never the living, the infinite. Man can only say, "There *is*," which has nothing to do with knowledge. Truth is ever becoming; it is immortal; it is eternal life.

We have these hindrances, artificial hindrances, based on imitation, on acquisitiveness which creates nationalism, on self-discipline, gurus, Masters, ideals, beliefs. Most of us are enslaved by one of these, consciously or unconsciously. Now please follow this; otherwise you will say, "You are merely destroying and not giving us any constructive ideas."

We have created theses hindrances; and we can be free from them only by becoming aware of them, not through the process of discipline, not by substitution, not by control, not by forgetfulness, not by following another, but only by becoming aware that they are poisons. You know, when you see a poisonous snake in your room, you are fully aware of it with your whole being. But these things, disciplines, beliefs, substitutions, you do not regard as poisons. They have become mere habits, sometimes pleasurable and sometimes painful, and you put up with them as long as pleasure outweighs pain. You continue in this manner till pain overwhelms you. When you have intense bodily pain, your only thought is to get rid of that pain. You don't think of the past or the future, or past health, of the time when you are not going to have any more pain. You are only concerned with getting rid of pain.

Likewise, you have to become fully and intensely aware of all these hindrances, and you can do that only when you are in conflict, when you are no longer escaping, no longer choosing substitutes. All choice is merely substitution. If you become fully aware of one hindrance, whether it be a guru, memory, or class consciousness, that awareness will uncover the creator of all hindrances, the creator of illusions, which is self-consciousness, the ego. When mind awakens intelligently to that creator, which is self-consciousness, then in that awareness the creator of illusions dissolves itself. Try it, and you will see what happens.

I am not saying this as an enticement for you to try. Don't try with the purpose of becoming happy. You will try it only if you are in conflict. But as most of you have many shelters in which you take comfort, you have altogether ceased to be in conflict. For all your conflicts you have explanations—so much dust and ashes—and these explanations have eased your conflict. Perhaps there are one or two among you who are not satisfied with explanations, not satisfied with ashes, whether dead ashes of yesterday, or future ashes of belief, of hope.

If you are really caught up in conflict you will find the ecstasy of life, but there must be intelligent awareness. That is, if I tell you that self-discipline is a hindrance, don't immediately reject or accept my statement. Find out if your mind is caught up in imitation, if your self-discipline is based on memory, which is but an escape from the present. You say, "I must not do this," and out of that self-imposed prohibition grows imitation; so self-discipline is based on imitation, fear. Where there is imitation there cannot be the fruition of intelligence. Find out if you are imitative; experiment. And you can experiment only in action itself. These are not just so many words; if you think it over, you will see. You cannot understand after action has taken place, which would be self-analysis, but only in the moment of action itself. You can be fully aware only in action. Don't say, "I must not be class-conscious," but become aware to discover if you are class-minded. That discovery in action will create conflict, and that conflict itself will free the mind from class consciousness, without your trying to overcome it.

So action itself destroys illusions, not self-imposed discipline. I wish you would think this over and act; then you would see what it all means. It opens immense avenues to the mind and heart, so that man can live in fulfillment without seeking an end, a result he can act without a motive. But you can live completely only when you have direct perception, and direct perception is not attained through choice, through effort born of memory. It lies in the flame of awareness, which is the harmony of mind and heart in action. When your mind is freed from religions, gurus, systems, from acquisitiveness, then only can there be completeness of action, then only can mind and heart follow the swift wanderings of truth.[2]

The Adyar memorial is to have an excellent life-like bust of Dr. Besant created by Mr. Deviprasad Roy Chowdhury, principal of the Government School of Arts and Crafts, Madras. Warrington remarks that it may be that the American Section would like to see that its own Headquarters in due course have a replica for their compound. At this time in history, the American Section is trying to raise funds to build the Besant Hall due to the constantly increasing number of delegates and guests who attend the Olcott summer sessions and convention.

Published in *The Canadian Theosophist* for January, there appeared appreciative articles devoted to the memory of Dr. Annie Besant. Many beautiful and even tender things were said, but Warrington stated his disappointment in the article regarding C.W. Leadbeater.

> It is regrettable, however, that they should have destroyed the value of their expressions by taking occasion to throw stones and mud upon one whom the late President loved as a brother; for whose

---

[2]Krishnamurti, J., *the Collected Works of J. Krishnamurti*, Volume I, 1933-1934, Dubuque, Iowa, 1991, Kendall/Hunt Publishing Co., "Sixth Talk at Adyar", India, January 3, 1934, pp.190-193.

powers and abilities she entertained the highest regard, and with whom she for years worked in the closest harmony. It was indeed a poor tribute to her intelligence, as well as her character, to have assumed that she could have been deceived as to his real nature, for in the long years of her close association with him she had every opportunity to know him as he was. I can well remember hearing her say, more than once, that Bishop Leadbeater was the purest person she had ever known. And she who said this had spent the best energies of her marvelous life in the endeavor to discover and to live Truth. How strange, then, that those who had no such opportunities could sit in judgment upon one who (even had they ever seen him) was never so placed that they could personally judge of the truth or falsity of that which they now claim. [3]

Jan 24 1934

Dear George, (Hall)

Replying to yours of December 19th, I do not know why Mr. Hotchener wrote to me, hinting that neither Bishop George nor C.W.L. would like it if I were to present that account of Krotona's against A.B.'s estate; but I think he must have had a talk with George when in America. You know when Henry follows, he follows with his whole soul, and he is ready to break down the entire earth to prove to his leader that he is on the job. Just now George is high in his firmament, and the incident grew perhaps from this psychology; anyway, I had already presented the account at the original sum given to me by you, namely $6,700; and I shall make no claim for interest, although this has not yet been mentioned except verbally to the Executor.

There were two reasons why I thought it proper to present this account: one was that A.B., as you will remember, definitely, deliberately and categorically promised to pay back the full sum in one year, explaining that she had funds from which she could draw the repayment at that time. Now, she was a stickler for keeping her word; and as she is not here to keep it herself, she would expect us to do it for her; for it will relieve her of any karmic complications in the matter hereafter.

---

[3]Warrington, A.P., *The American Theosophist*, "C.W. Leadbeater", Vol. XXII, February 1934, n2, p.27.

My second reason was more pragmatical; and if you knew just what it was, you would agree with me; but I had rather not put it down in writing, though I may tell you when I see you. I have never liked the way some people have in robbing Peter to pay Paul, with the result that both Peter and Paul fall into a state of collapse. That is another reason why I have been strong on this point of seeing that Sydney realised its obligation to Krotona. If we cannot be honest in our Society, and specially in its esoteric side, we had just as well give up. Therefore, I say: Let us be honest first, and generous afterward.

What you wrote to Sydney was right in every way, and I could have made no suggestion to you that would have improved your approach.

The clipping from *The Times* is interesting and I will see whether the Bishop would care to discuss this subject in *The Theosophist* or make it the subject of a Friday evening Question Meeting. I fear, however, it comes too late for immediate action, because he will be leaving in a week for Australia, to be gone three months.

The election of Bishop Leadbeater as President of Krotona Institute is, of course, in order because of the by-law indicating the O.H. of the E.S. as the regular President. I think I can see complications ahead of Krotona, in my lack of foresight in drawing the by-laws originally in certain respects; but this I will reserve for discussion with you when I return. Just when that return will be I cannot say, but probably sometime during the present calendar year or the early part of the next.

I wish I had you here to dig into all these various departments on the compound and to bring out all the facts showing the waste going on and the things we need to do in order to put everything on a smooth-moving basis. This is my job here at this time; and I have not the assistance that ought to be at my right hand every day, to carry the thing through quickly and successfully. It is a big job because it is now like an in-growing nail—painful but hard to straighten out, and so few people to help. One thing I am doing—I am drawing George into the work as far as possible, putting all this compound investigation and management on his shoulders; but, of course, he is a scholar and not a business man. Yet he soon will be President, and it is just as well that he should get familiar with every detail while the going is good, and I am giving him his chance.

With cordial greetings from Betty and myself to you and your wife, I am ever,
Heartily yours,
A.P. Warrington

Much work was needed to get the compound back in some working order. Certain improvements had to be made in the main library as the books were housed in three separate places: (1) The main library building; (2) the dispensary, a furlong away; and (3) the one-time Star Building, nearly half a mile away.

As to the upkeep of the compound, Warrington appointed as garden superintendent, a practical, successful business man, an Indian, who is both a theosophist and a Mason. His hope was to make this compound self-sustaining believing that they are headed in the right direction and have the proper management.

Warrington reminded George Arundale that an Initiate once wrote of Adyar: "It is essential for the individual member and for The Society that Adyar, as a great spiritual center, should be maintained, worthy and dignified."

February 19 1934
Hotel Esplanade, Perth

My dear Bishop George, (Arundale)

I am sending a letter which Brother dictated before we reached Fremantle; the information is mainly quite out-of-date by now, but he has been unable to write anything since then, so perhaps it is best to send it.

A couple of days before we reached Fremantle he grew much worse—had a bad coughing fit which left him very exhausted, so with much difficulty I persuaded him to see the ship's doctor. The doctor said his condition was very serious, and he thought he wouldn't live more than a week or two. The swollen legs in Adyar, and the hydrocele on board are both developments of dropsy. This doctor said there is already a good deal of fluid in the abdomen, and one lung is absolutely water-logged (that is what caused the coughing), and that any strain or movement might send this fluid to his heart. He recommended that I should take Brother to hospital here, because he thought he wouldn't live through the night if there chanced to be rough weather; and he thought also that he would develop bed sores, which would get poisoned and complicate matters. I spent the last two nights on board with

Brother, but he didn't sleep, and neither did I, and I could see that he needed treatment and constant trained attention, so we came to hospital here. The doctor who came on board to examine the passenger before landing agreed that his condition was very serious and that probably he would live only a couple of weeks.

The doctor who is treating him at the hospital here was much more cheerful—he said the dropsy was not the most serious factor, but that his heart was just petering out, and that he had fluid in his lung. However, in spite of heart stimulants and whatnot he hasn't improved at all since we have been here. Yesterday yet another doctor saw him, and he rather agrees with the two ship's doctors. And the nurse says that since yesterday the fluid in his abdomen has considerably increased, and they can't get him to take the pills and things to help it to pass away.

Brother mentioned several times on board that if he had to land here he would like Harold (Morton) to come; so I telephoned to him and he came over and arrived yesterday. Brother has been terribly difficult to deal with—wants me to get him out of here at once, to take him back to Adyar at once, and so on. Obviously he cannot be moved in his present condition, and Harold can help to pacify him; also if he does die here I should be glad of his moral support. Today I have sent a telegram to you and Raja giving his condition in more detail, and if there is any change of course I shall let you know.

A rather worrying development during the last three days or so is that his mind is somewhat weak. I don't know whether it is a result of any of the drugs or not, but the hospital is of opinion that it is all a result of the failing heart. But he loses all count of time and gets all sort of stupid ideas into his head and abuses us accordingly. I think also that he has been dreaming, because he insists that on a couple of nights he found himself several times walking round the room, without knowing how he got there, while the nurse insists that he wasn't out of bed at all. He knows that he has been weak mentally, and I think he is rather frightened of going the way of the President. Yesterday and this morning that has been better, though he talks on indefinitely about nothing in particular, and slurs his words in a way very unlike him. But until Harold arrived I have not been able to talk to him in an ordinary conversational way at all for days. Yesterday he wrote out an authorization of you as Grand Master of the E.R.; but it is very badly written , and has a couple of mistakes in it, and it costs him an almighty effort to do it at all, and he was quite prostrate afterwards.

Personally I don't think the situation very hopeful, and neither does Harold. He will insist on climbing out of bed dozens of times and climbing back again, and that is likely either to overstrain the heart, or to send the liquid to it. Also if the weakening of the brain continues, one can only hope that the end will come soon. All the doctors and nurses see very little hope of recovery, so I hope he slips off quietly before it becomes painful or more difficult. Of course I have said nothing to anyone about the mental part; it is surely better that that should not be known. But I suppose the people must know the condition so far as the physical plane is concerned. I'm afraid this isn't a very orderly or coherent account of it all; but I'm in a great hurry, as the mail closes very shortly and I may have to tear away to the hospital again at any moment. But at any rate I think it gives you most of the facts in a very jumbled way. I shall keep you fully posted of course.
With very much love,
Most affectionately,
Heather (Miss Kellet,—C.W.L.'s private secretary)

Feb 28 1934

Dear George, (Hall)

Some days ago I received a note from Bishop Arundale, evidently written after he had received some communication from Australia, enquiring about The Manor debt to Krotona. My reply to him and a copy of his note are enclosed herewith for your information.

I hope you received my letter intimating that I had consulted Bishop Leadbeater, and that he and I requested the Board of Trustees of Krotona Institute to elect Miss Poutz as a trustee in place of Max Wardall. Information has come to me that it was your desire and Louis's to have Mrs. Hall elected instead of Miss Poutz. I regret that I cannot agree with either of you, for the special reason that the Bishop wants his E.S. representative in America to be represented on the board, as is natural and logical and practical, and for the further reason that it would be great mistake to give the Board the appearance of being *strictly a family affair*, as would be the case if three members of the same family were on it. You will pardon me for putting it this way. Our beloved Louis is so intimately associated with both of you in the mind of your friends and acquaintances that it would look quite the same as if three members of the same family were sitting on the Board. So far as

Mrs. Hall is concerned, I regard her as a woman of unusual, and I may say rare, ability, having both the practical masculine mind as well as the keen intuitive perception of woman; but her advice can always be given you, my dear George, in any matter where you may be puzzled, so that even if she be not on the Board you still have access to her counsel. If hereafter Krotona should be subjected to another attack by the Dark Forces and you three were on the Board, the arrangement would be open to grave criticism, which can be so easily avoided by following better counsels.

I hope you will pardon me for being so very frank. I am afraid the older I get, the blunter I become, because of my increasing reverence for the truth of things, as disclosed in an open frankness of view and opinion. With all affection for yourself and Mrs. Hall and Louis, I am,
Ever yours sincerely,
A.P.W.

No member of the Esoteric School shall pretend to the possession of psychic powers that he has not, nor boast of those which he may have developed. Envy, jealousy and vanity are insidious and powerful foes to those in search of Truth, and it is known from long experience that, among beginners especially, the boasting of, or calling attention to their psychic powers almost invariably causes the development of these faults and increases them when present. Questions regarding joining other mystic schools keep coming up within the E.S.T. American Division, that Marie Poutz, an Initiate and Corresponding Secretary has to remind the Candidates that the conditions for membership within the E.S. is that psychic development and occult arts are not taught in this School, nor are its members allowed to belong to any other association, organization or class for the purpose of mystic study or occult training, Masonry excepted, as it is dangerous to follow two lines of training at the same time.

She reminds the members of the School that they should brood over each statement, and in the silence try to make their studies as a living thing, not a mere classification of statements. But every sentence in the book *Thought Power* by Annie Besant should be the subject of earnest thinking and observation, so to pass beyond the mind to the world of the Spirit where the Unity of Life is contacted, not merely grasped intellectually. Realization should therefore be the aim.

Bishop Leadbeater left Adyar on January 31st, 1934 for a three months visit to The Manor with a frail body, and now close on 87 years old. February 29th, Thursday morning Charles W. Leadbeater lapsed into unconsciousness and passed away at 4:15 p.m. March 1.

There seems to be some question regarding why Leadbeater, who was in such feeble health would start suddenly on the long trip from Adyar, via Bombay, for Sydney, Australia. It seemed that the Bishop had celebrated the Easter Service at his Cathedral Church in Sydney each year since its foundation in 1916, and he very much wanted to carry on that tradition this year. Reaching Fremantle on February 13th, the Bishop completed his 87th year four days after reaching Perth. He dictated a message to be read to the Perth group of the Esoteric School, which was published in the E.S. pamphlet. Although there are many written reports on the passing of Bishop Leadbeater, he was cremated at the North Shore Crematorium on March 17, 1934. We publish here the report given by Rev. S. Fisher of the Liberal Catholic Church.

Bishop Leadbeater
The Passing

By The Rev. S. Fisher

Priest-in-charge of the Liberal Catholic Church of St. John The Divine, Perth, W. Australia

On the 13th February, 1934, a party of members of the Liberal Catholic Church, Theosophical Society, and the Co-Masonic Brotherhood met the R.M.S. "Mooltan" at Fremantle, Western Australia, to welcome Bishop Leadbeater, who was to stay a week in the State. The party learnt from Miss H. Kellett that the Bishop, on account of the state of his health, would have continued the journey straight to Sydney, but the ship's doctor stated he would never be able to cross the Bight alive. He had been confined to his bed on ship for a good part of the voyage. The Bishop was removed in an ambulance to St. Omer's Hospital in Perth. He was attended by Dr. Nelson. At first the Doctor considered he would be fit to travel to Sydney in about three weeks. He was suffering from dropsy, his heart was in a bad state and there was some fluid on the right lung. The weather was very much against him, being exceedingly hot with much humidity. For some days there was a cool change and his condition improved and there was hope that he would recover sufficiently to travel. The weather, however, again became trying and his condition from Sunday, the 25th February, became weaker. He retained the full use of his faculties up to the last day of his illness. Mr. Harold Morton came from Sydney at the Bishop's request, arriving on Sunday, the 18th February, coming by air from Adelaide. Miss Kellett and Mr. Morton were in constant attendance upon the Bishop. Mr. Morton took down much that he said and will no doubt pass this information on in due course.

Everything possible was done. He had a special Day Nurse and a special Night Nurse. Dr. Nelson had a consultation with another doctor, but all was in vain.

About Monday, the 26th February, the doctor and nurse abandoned hope of his recovery and, as already mentioned, he gradually became weaker. Miss Kellett and Mr. Morton saw him on the 28th February and he spoke to them for about three-quarters of an hour. As they were leaving his room, he waved his hand and said: "*Well, if I do not see you again in this body—carry on!*" These were his last words to them and are a fitting message to us all.

On Thursday morning he lapsed into unconsciousness and passed away at 4:15p.m. [March 1, 1934]

With the exception of Miss Kellett and Mr. Morton, none of us saw him alive. We knew he would indicate when he felt able to see any of us.

I viewed his body at 5 p.m. on the day of his death and again at 8:30p.m., when a party, consisting of Mesdames Fisher, Chase, Van der Hell, Poignant and Parkes, Misses Kellett and King, and Messrs. Fisher, Poignant, and Morton, attended at the Hospital. He was robed in his alb and white stole and looked majestic.

The body has been embalmed and will be sent to Sydney for cremation by inter-state steamer on Thursday, 8th March. It was not possible to cremate the body in this State because there is no crematorium, although a Cremation Act was recently passed by the legislature.

Today, Sunday, 4th March, a Requiem Eucharist was held at the Church of St. John the Divine, Perth. The casket containing the Bishop's remains was brought to the Church and placed in the Sanctuary, *in plano*, on the Gospel Side with the head facing the altar. The Bishop's white cope and stole were placed near the casket. The mitre stood on the head of casket and a cross of flowers on the foot. The Bishop's 33^0 Regalia of the Co-Masonic Order was laid out on a table, also near the casket. The Church was full. I deputed the Rev. Harold Morton to act as Celebrant and Preacher, on account of his close association with the Bishop. The whole ceremony was most impressive and declared by all to be a majestic triumph. After the recessional hymn, which was sung with the Celebrant and his assistants and the priest and servers in their respective positions in the Sanctuary, we processed out in silence round the Church during the playing of Chopin's Funeral March. Various photos have been taken of the casket, regalia and altar, and I have already seen proofs of some, which are quite successful. Copies will be sent to you as soon as possible, probably next mail.

I have received a cable request from the President of the Theosophical Society, Adyar, for some of the ashes of the Bishop for Adyar. I am sending this cable to Bishop Tweedie, Sydney, for the necessary action.

I forward the above for your information, as Priest-in-Charge of the work in Western Australia.
Rev. S. Fisher,
4-3-1934

P.S. The Bishop did not suffer any pain, only discomfort.[4]

---

[4]Fisher, The Rev. S., *The Liberal Catholic*, "Bishop Leadbeater, The Passing", Vol. XIV, May 1934, n8, pp.310-311.

March 5 1934
My dear Bishop George,

I sent you a telegram telling you of Brother's passing, but I want to give you some details. During last week, since my last letter to you, he really went gradually downhill. The intense heat and heaviness of the week-end was too much for him I think. Up till then his doctor had been consistently optimistic, but even he admitted that he thought the end was near. However on Tuesday afternoon he was more cheerful and somewhat stronger, but only for a short while. On Wednesday when we were leaving he remarked: *If I do not see you again in this body, carry on!* That was the last time he spoke to us; on Thursday morning he looked up but made no attempt to speak. His nurse said that she thought he would sink quietly and not recover from that condition, which is just what happened. He did not make any attempt to speak or eat during the day, and there was no change until a little after four, when a hemorrhage started. Even then he was not conscious of it, and died after about ten minutes. We were not actually with him when he died, but we saw him a very short while afterwards, and again in the evening, when several of our people here went to see him. They dressed him in an alb and stole, and he really looked very peaceful and serene.

There is no crematorium here in West Australia, so we are sending his body to Sydney. It's an expensive business, but I don't think he would like to be buried! They had a Requiem Eucharist here yesterday, and had the coffin in the Church with his white vestments near it; Axel took some photographs of it and will no doubt send you prints next week. Last night at the T.S. five people spoke for ten minutes each about different aspect of his life, and there was a full hall. We have suggested that they delay the Requiem in Sydney until the coffin arrives so that we can have it in Church there also.

Mrs. van der Hell and I are leaving by tomorrow's steamer for Sydney.

During the first days when Brother was here he wrote out the enclosed document. He asked me to give it to you when I saw you next, but I think I should send it this way. You will see something of his condition from it. Harold got one signature from him later than this which was quite all right.

With very much love,
Heather (Miss Kellett,—C.W.L.'s private secretary)

Krishnamurti was in Sydney when C.W. Leadbeater's funeral service was held, but stayed outside the Chapel.

March 13 1934

Dear Mr. Warrington: (from George Hall)

I finally received replies from Mr. MacKay and Mr. Houstone at Sydney, copies of which I enclose, together with a copy of my reply to Mr. Houstone. I do not understand how Mr. Houstone could hold up payment of this money in the face of our agreement regarding it, and of course I have no inkling of the nature of the interview he refers to. If the Sydney people are negotiating with you as to whether or not his interest should be paid, I think you can be quite sure that the trustees will insist upon its payment. However, I am also sure that they will approve any reasonable concession that you might have made or wish to make in order to facilitate the payment.

Personally I was very much surprised at the sudden death of Bishop Leadbeater. I had been told that his health was excellent. I do not see the necessity for trying to hold another Krotona Board meeting before we receive a reply from you to my letter of February 7. I think most of the trustees will want to elect C.J. to the vacancies caused by the death of C.W.L. I asked Miss Poutz her opinion on that point, and she was very emphatic in saying we "must" do it. In this connection I should like to inquire if the sentiment expressed by you in your letter of January 13, 1933, applied only to C.W.L., or does it apply equally to C.J.? **You will remember that you said you regretted the Krotona By-Law requiring us to elect the O.H. as Trustee and President of the Board, which was done formerly as a matter of sentiment and which sentiment would pass with the death of Dr. Besant.**

I was surprised at your reference to your return as being possibly delayed until next year. We have been expecting that you would come back immediately after the election and probably arrive here by August.

I can easily imagine what a strenuous time you must have had and must still be having at Adyar, and I am rather glad that I have not had such a task fall on my shoulders. I must be getting old because I do not welcome such things any longer. In fact, I would gladly shift some of my present burdens if I saw an opportunity and try "living in the present" for a little while.

I enclose the program of the Ventura County Federation of Women's Clubs, as you and Mrs. Warrington may be interested in seeing it.

With cordial good wishes to you both from Mrs. Hall and myself, I remain ever,
Very sincerely yours,
G. Hall

March 13 1934

Dear George, (Hall)

Thank you very much for the Annual Reports. I am very sorry to see that we are running behind. Perhaps this year you will be able to reverse this. I think that Bishop Arundale has written rather positive directions to Sydney to take care of the indebtedness to you. The exchange is in their favour, and their claim that it is otherwise is absurd, and only a very poor excuse for not paying their debts. I repeat to you that Australia never pays her debts if she can avoid it; but this is only for your ears and to stimulate you to pursue your rights.

Now that Bishop Leadbeater has passed over, it will be in order to elect Mr. Jinarajadasa the President, as he is now the O.H. of the E.S. That By-Law of ours which indicates that the O.H. of the E.S. shall be the President of Krotona was deliberately put in by myself; but I will be frank to say that when I did so I had my mind on Dr. Besant and no one else. Even so, I had an intuitive feeling that I ought not to do it but ought to have created a special advisory office to be held by the O.H. for the time being. The reason for this is purely business. Our organization should have no non-resident officer, especially it should not have a non-resident President; but I need not go into all the details of this—the By-Law is there and will have to be obeyed.

I know of nobody's desire to make any change in the management of Krotona—the question has never come up from any angle. The only point made is that the E.S. Representative in America is a logical person always to be on the Board. For some time this officer has not been on the Board, but was rejected from it in 1929 by the Council of Advisors, who can tell better than I what their reason was.

> I am very happy to learn that Miss Poutz is much improved. She must get well and go on serving us in her own splendid way for years yet to come, for we cannot spare her. I am sending her my proxy to represent me at Krotona Board meetings.
>
> Thank you for the clipping from *The Times*. How unfortunate it is that Bishop Leadbeater is gone and cannot be consulted with a view to getting a categorical answer to the points raised in the clipping! I like the spirit of the scientist who expressed his views. He apparently is very balanced and liberal. Some day these men will come still closer to our view, I hope.
>
> Mrs. Warrington joins me in sending most cordial good wishes to Mrs. Hall and yourself always.
> Yours fraternally,
> A. P. Warrington

Miss Poutz had an accident some weeks ago, requesting that no notice of her fall appear in publication, because she did not wish that any of her many friends should feel any distress on her account. Her injury, which caused some lameness and made the use of her right hand impossible for a time, has now so completely disappeared that she is out again and taking walks, and answering her own letters.

A letter dated March 19, 1934 to Bishop George Arundale from Miss Kay Maddox stated that Krishnamurti spoke to huge audiences outside of The Manor, but was not allowed to talk over the air because he was considered antireligious. While he was in Sydney, Krishnamurti stayed with Mr. & Mrs. John Mackay in the suburb of Mosman.

> Mrs. Mackay telephoned to us last week and said that Krishnaji would appreciate it if we asked him to speak to The Manor Household. So accordingly we arranged an evening and duly assembled in the sitting-room. But Krishnaji did not wish to address us, he wanted us to ask questions and to have a discussion meeting. It was a futile waste of time and I think we were all very bored. However, the next day I received a message from him asking me to lunch and to have a private talk with him. He asked specially that I should not come unless I wanted to do so and to assure me that he would not try to convert me. I had a long talk with him, and he was wonderfully patient and kind in explaining what he meant—

but, I find him quite incomprehensible. He is passionately sincere and honest, and really believes that all religions and organizations such as our own are adding to the limitations and the confusion of the world. But I am really beginning to wonder whether he is quite sane—he looked almost pathological when we were at lunch. While he was talking to me he seemed brilliantly logical, but all his logic is based on false premises—at least so it seems to me. It is a huge structure built on wrong foundations—as far as I can see all his teaching undermines everything that makes for sanity and real progress. It is extraordinary—because in himself he is very charming and courteous, and there are times when he seems quite brilliant, and yet it is all wrong-headed and flies in the face of all experience and all commonsense. He told me that he cannot now remember what his brother looked like, except when he has his photograph in front of him, and that he is forgetting Mrs. Besant's physical appearance. He has asked to address the combined Theosophical Lodges—we all think it is good policy to grant his request. Mrs. Mackay is longing to have a grievance against us—she is terribly aggressive and hostile on his behalf. She began raging to me about the way we had all treated Krishnaji, and she quoted from the bible: "He came to his own and his own received him not." But I was able to reply that we had called off every possible meeting in order to give him a clear field and that all his meetings had been splendidly attended. So she has no _real_ grievance, but she is angry because no one so far has resigned from anything. Of course it is early days yet, but we are hoping that everyone who matters will stand firm. It is much better to let Krishnaji have a clear field—the least opposition would create a very unfortunate situation. Mr. Mackay said to me quite angrily: "Why did you people at The Manor not ask Krishnaji his opinion about ceremonial? You are all immersed in ceremonies and you ought to know what he thinks about them." I replied quite calmly that those questions had been asked at other meetings, and Krishnaji himself broke in very courteously: "But Mr. Mackay, they all know quite well my opinion." Twice he would not let Mrs. Mackay tackle me when she wanted to. Once she began and I said very firmly: "Mrs. Mackay, I absolutely refuse to discuss that subject." Krishnaji said once: "Please please, Mrs. Mackay, do not let us have anything contentious." He was so utterly well-bred and determined not to let them embarrass me, I thought it was dear of him. I like Krishnaji and Rajagopal immensely as individuals, I think they are the two most courteous young men I have ever met, but I could never be even interested in their present teaching or message or whatever it is supposed to be, and I think we all feel the same—there are a few who are very interested and think they understand him, but they are all coming steadily to all the meetings, which have been reestablished. We called off Monday nights and E.S. and Egyptian Rite for a fortnight, while Krishnaji was holding meetings every night. But as soon as he went to Melbourne we reestablished them again, and now that he is back he is not holding meetings, but he sees a good many people privately. Kay

P.S. Krishnaji and Rajagopal attended Brother's funeral and Krishnaji looked very sad when he spoke of his passing to me—he feels it deeply.

The annoying questions regarding the Theosophical Society and its relationship to Krishnamurti kept coming up during his answers to questions period. Krishnamurti gave a talk to theosophists on March 31, 1934 in New Zealand. Again he repeated that Truth, that reality, is not to be found by running after it, because when we seek something, it indicates that our mind is trying to escape from that conflict in which mind and heart are caught up.

> *Question*: Do you consider that the Theosophical Society has finished its work in the world, and ought to retire into solitary confinement?
>
> *Krishnamurti*: What do you think, you who are its members? Is that not a much more apt question, than yours to me? Sirs, may I put it this way? Why do you belong to any Society? Why are you Christians, Theosophists, Christian Scientists, and God knows what? Why do you exclude and seclude yourselves? "Because," you say, "This particular form of belief, this particular form of expression, of ideas, appeals to me; therefore I am going to subscribe myself to it." Or you belong to it because you hope to get something out of it: happiness, wisdom, office, position. So instead of asking me if the Society should retire, ask yourselves why you belong to it. Why do you belong to anything? There is this horrible idea that we want to be exclusive—the Western Club, the Eastern Golf Course, and all the rest of it. Exclusive hotels—you know. So likewise, we say we have something special, so do the Hindus, so do Roman Catholics. Every person in the world talks about having something special, so they exclude themselves, and become the owners of that

special thing, and so thereby create more divisions, more conflicts, more heartaches. Besides, who am I to tell you if the Society should retire into confinement? I wonder how many of you have really asked why you belong to it. If you are really a social body, not a religious body, not an ethical body, then there is some hope for it in the world. If you are really a body of people who are discovering, not who have found, if you are a body of people who are giving information, not giving spiritual distinctions, if you are a body of people that have a really open platform not for me or for someone special, if you are a body of people among whom there are neither leaders nor followers, then there is some hope. But I am afraid you are followers, and therefore you all have leaders. And such a society, whether it is this or another, is useless. You are merely followers or merely leaders. In true spirituality there is no distinction of the teachers and the pupil, of the man who has knowledge and the man who has not. It is you that are creating it, because it is this that you are seeking—continually to be distinctive. You cannot all of you be Sir Richard Something-or-other, so you want to be somebody in this Society, or in another society, or in heaven. Don't you see, if you really thought about these things and were honest, you could be an extraordinarily useful body in the world. You could then really work for the intrinsic merit of its ideas—not for some fantasy and emotionalism of your leaders. Then you would examine any idea, and find out its true significance and work it out, and not depend on the honors conferred for your services, on the enticement to work. That way leads to narrowness, bigotry, to more divisions and cruelties and ultimately to utter chaos of thought.

Question: What is your attitude to the early teachings of Theosophy, the Blavatsky type? Do you consider we have deteriorated or advanced?

Krishnamurti: I am afraid I do not know, because I do not know what Madame Blavatsky's teachings are. Why should I? Why should you know of someone else's teachings? You know, there is only one truth, and therefore there is only one way, which is not distant from that truth; there is only one method to that truth, because the means are not distinct from the end.

Now you who have studied Madame Blavatsky's and the latest Theosophy, or whatever it is, why do you want to be students of books instead of students of life? Why do you set up leaders and ask whose teachings are better? Don't you see? Please, I am not being harsh, or anything of that kind. Don't you see? You are Christians; find out what is true and false in Christianity—and you will then find out what is true. Find out what is true and false in your environment with all its oppressions and cruelties, and then you will find out what is true. Why do you want philosophies? Because life is an ugly thing, and you hope to run away from it through philosophy. Life is so empty, dull, stupid, ignominious, and you want something to bring romanticism into your world, some hope, some lingering, haunting feeling; whereas, if you really faced the world as it is, and tackled it, you would find it something much more, infinitely greater than any philosophy, greater than any book in the world, greater than any teaching or greater than any teacher.

We have really lost all sense of feeling, feeling for the oppressed and feeling for the oppressor. You only feel when you are oppressed. So gradually we have intellectually explained away all our feelings, our sensitiveness, our delicate perceptions, until we are absolutely shallow; and to fill that shallowness, to enrich ourselves, we study books. I read all kinds of books, but never philosophies, thank goodness. You know, I have a kind of shrinking feeling—please, I put it mildly—when you say, "I am a student of philosophy," a student of this, or that; never of everyday action, never really understanding things as they are. I assure you. for your happiness, for your own understanding, for the discovery of that eternal thing, you must really live; then you will find something which no words, no picture, no philosophy, no teacher can give.

Question: Are the teachings which Theosophy gives concerning evolution of any consequence for the purpose of the growth of the soul?

Krishnamurti: What do you mean by evolution, sirs? As far as I can make out, growing from the unessential to the essential. Is it? Growing from ignorance to wisdom. Is that not so? Nobody shakes his head. All right. What do you mean by evolution? Gaining more and more experience, more and more wisdom, more and more knowledge, more and more and more; infinitely more and more. That is, you go from the unessential to the essential; and that essential becomes the unessential the moment you have attained, you have reached it. Is that not so?

> Are you too tired? Is it too late? Please, you have to think with me. This is my second talk during the day; but if you do not think with me, it will be rather difficult for me. I have to push against a wall.
>
> You consider something as essential today, and go after it, and get it; and tomorrow that thing becomes unessential, and you say, "I have learnt that." That which you had thought essential has become the unessential, so you go on and on and on, and you call that growth, evolution; getting more and more, discerning more and more between the essential and the unessential—and yet there is no such thing as the essential and the unessential. Is there? Because that which you think is the essential today becomes the unessential tomorrow, for you want something else.
>
> Let me put it differently. You see some pleasurable object you think you want to possess, and you posses it; then satisfied, you move to another thing. It may be some emotional craving, desire, and you get that. You want an idea, and you pursue that, and get it. And ultimately you want to reach God, truth, happiness, and the man who wants happiness, God, truth, you consider spiritual, and the man who wants a hat or a tie, or whatever it is, you call mundane, materialistic. The unessential is the hat, and the essential is the God or truth. What have we done? We have merely changed the object of our desires. We have said, "Well, I have had enough hats, enough cars, enough houses, and I want something else." And you go after that and get that, and then you finish with it and want something else; so you proceed gradually until you ultimately want something which you call God, and then you think you have reached the ultimate. All you have done is played with your desires, and this process of continual choosing you call evolution. Is it so or not?[5]

Theosophists have tried over and over to catch Krishnamurti saying that he was the Messiah. They were persisting in attributing to him an authority that he has not claimed. Krishnamurti has always waived any assertion that he is the manifestation of the Messiah or

---

[5] Krishnamurti, J., *the Collected Works of J. Krishnamurti*, Volume II, 1934-1935, Dubuque, Iowa, 1991, Kendall/Hunt Publishing Co., "Talk to Theosophist", Auckland, New Zealand, March 31, 1934, pp. 26-28.

any higher Being. Until we get rid of that illusion the mystification will undoubtedly continue.

Question: Are you the Messiah?

Krishnamurti: Does it matter greatly? You know, this is one of the questions I have been asked everywhere I go: by newspaper reporters for a story; by the audience because they want to know, as they think that authority shall convince them. Now, I have never denied or asserted that I am the Messiah, that I am the Christ returned; that does not matter. No one can tell you. Even if I did tell you it would be utterly valueless, and so I am not going to tell you, because, to me, it is so irrelevant, so unimportant, futile. After all, when you see a marvellous piece of sculpture, or a marvellous painting, there is a rejoicing; but I am afraid most of you are interested in who has done the picture, most of you are interested in who the sculptor is. You are not really interested in the purity of action, whether in a picture or a stature, or in thought; you are interested to know who is speaking. So it indicates that you have not the capacity to find out the intrinsic merit of an idea, but are rather concerned with who speaks. And I am afraid a snobbery is being cultivated more and more, a spiritual snobbery, just as there is a mundane snobbery, but all snobbery is the same.

So, friends, don't bother, but try to find out if what I am saying is true; and in trying to find out if what I am saying is true, you will be rid of all authority, a pernicious thing. For really creative, intelligent human beings, there cannot be authority. To discover if what I am saying is true, you cannot approach it by mere opposition, or by saying, "We have been told so," "It has been said," "Certain books have said this and that," "Our spirit-guides have said." You know that is the latest thing. "Our spirit-guides have said this." I do not know why you give more importance to those spirits who are dead than to the living. You know the living can always contradict you, therefore you do not pay much attention to them, whereas, the spirits you know, they can always deceive.

We have trained our minds, not to appreciate a thing for itself, but rather for who has created it, who has painted, who has spoken. So our minds and hearts become more and more shallow, empty, and in that there is neither affection nor real, reasonable thought, but merely masses of prejudices.[6]

———

April 18 1934

Dear George, (Hall)

I am pleased to receive yours of March 13th, with enclosures. Your letter to Mr. Houstone was excellent. I could not possibly have advised you to write more strongly or expertly. You said the right thing in the right way, and showed that you meant it, which was good. The reference to myself turned out to mean only this: Bishop Arundale approached me several weeks ago and asked me my opinion on the situation existing between Sydney and Ojai. I stated my opinion very firmly and insistently, and expected him to take some action then and there. However, it is apparent he did not act, and so I have taken the matter up with him again and he promises to instruct Sydney to begin the payment of all the arrangements at once. I agree with you that this is a business proposition and should be treated as such. When the time comes, if it ever should come, when the Krotona Board wants to indulge in generous contributions to Theosophical centres or this important one in particular, that should be done, if it ever could be done, under an entirely different head. I want to see the Sydney Centre prosper, and it would be greatly to the credit of the American members if we could go the limit in ensuring this result; but under the circumstances of our own local economics, and the fact that we are not organized to dispense funds for foreign purposes, there is nothing that we can do but that which I have distinctly outlined from the first. In a way, therefore, it seems to me that America has already done her bit, and that includes South America to some extent, whose members contributed somewhat to the curtailment which I raised many years ago.

Yes, what I said in January as applying to C.W.L. applies likewise to C.J.—perhaps a little more so. Yet as long as that By-

---

[6]Krishnamurti, J., *the Collected Works of J. Krishnamurti*, Volume II, 1934-1935, Dubuque, Iowa, 1991, Kendall/Hunt Publishing Co., "Second Talk in Town Hall", Auckland, New Zealand, April 1, 1934, pp.36-37.

Law remains in force, to which I had reference, the Outer Head of the E.S. must be Krotona's President. Krotona, as chartered, if financially stable all the while, could go on for a hundred years or more. It is not, however, certain that the E.S. will always continue as at present. There have been times when it has been suspended altogether. Moreover, it is not at all certain but that some day the American Corresponding Secretary may be forced to live in the East. So the E.S. aspect of our connection has always been regarded by me as not dominant in the legal sense at Krotona except in this, that the members of the Board must be E.S. members.

Therefore some time in the future I expect to propose to the Board that they rescind that By-Law and substitute in its place one declaring that in any case of a lack of agreement on the part of the Board upon any major question, the Outer Head must be called upon to adjudicate the matter. Also the Outer Head shall have the power to nominate members of the Board when vacancies occur. Something of this kind will reserve a connection with the E.S., and a useful one, but will enable us to have our local President, as we should do, and really should have done all along.

With the heartiest greetings to you and to Mrs. Hall from Betty and myself, and thanks for the program enclosed.

I am,
Sincerely yours,
A.P. Warrington

May 11, 1934 may have meant that a home for aged Theosophists might be established somewhere in the United States before long according to Mrs. M. V. Garnsey who after taking up a tentative scheme for such an institution, had aroused the interest of Sidney W. Cook, National T.S. President. Cook had asked her to go into the matter very thoroughly, to outline a plan in detail and to send it to him for presentation at the annual convention to be held in Wheaton, Illinois, in the summer of 1934. Mrs. Garnsey's idea arose out of gratitude to numerous Theosophic lecturers and teachers who gave all their time and often all their funds to public work which carried no financial reward. She felt that some place should be provided for their old age where the Society could repay in some measure its debt of gratitude for services so freely given. We shall see that another attempt was made in the late 1970's by Ruth Wilson in the Ojai Valley, California. One day the factual history of the Taormina Community in the Ojai Valley must be written.

Among the Warrington's papers, we came across this poem written by Catharine Gardner Mayes.

Golden Wedding—June 11, 1934

By Catharine Gardner Mayes

Gold is the king of metals, it shines undimmed and bright

Though over it the ages pass in their relentless flight.

And therefore man has made of it symbol of changeless worth

And from it lovingly has wrought the holy things of earth.

It makes the chalice for the Mass, the fair bride's wedding band,

The mighty monarch's shining crown, the scepter in his hand.

In ancient times it symbolized the flaming Sun-God's might,

The vivifier of the earth by His life-giving Light.

Later in time 'twas offered to the Sun of Righteousness

Who shone incarnate on this earth to quicken and to bless.

Therefore, this sacred metal men in reverence bestow

On those dear lovers who have kept the fire of love aglow,

Undimmed by time, steadfast through change, a beacon bright to guide

Across the perilous seas of life the hearts of groom and bride.

Lovers can do no nobler thing than by their lives to show

That time is powerless to dim true love's eternal glow.

We bring in joyous gratitude this golden gift to you

Offering to a love that is steadfast, devoted, true.

And with it comes more love than tongue or pen can ever say,

From your devoted children on this Golden Wedding day.

On the evening of June 20th, 1934, Dr. George Sydney Arundale was duly elected by a large majority as the President of the Society for the ensuing seven years. He gave thanks to Albert and Betty Warrington, who have so finely borne the flag of Theosophy during the period which has to elapse between the passing of one President and the assumption of office by his successor. "The Theosophical Society will not forget them, Adyar will not forget them."

Dr. Arundale states:

> It is well we should dream, it is well we should have visions, but of what avail these if they do not take upon themselves physical shape for the upliftment of the world? The world needs Theosophy and the Theosophical Society. Are we who are today's members capable of giving that which we ourselves have received? It is good to receive, but the consummation of receiving is in the sharing. We do not know our Theosophy, we do not fulfill our membership save as we share both with those who need then no less than ourselves.[7]

It was on the evening of June 20th, that the Recording Secretary of the Theosophical Society called a session of the Executive Committee, viz., Miss Heather Kellett and Dr. Srinivasamurti, and later reported that Dr. Arundale had received 15,604 votes for the Presidency of the Society, and Mr. Wood 4,825.

---

[7] Arundale, G.S., "Adyar News", *The Theosophist*, Vol, XXII, November 1934, n11, p.254.

By June 21st, Warrington acting as President Pro tem held its final meeting, accepting the terms which Mr. Wood offered to sell to the Society the bungalow that he had built upon Headquarters property. Later in the day, Dr. Arundale as the newly elected President confirms the election, and on his death in 1945, he was succeeded by C. Jinarajadasa, who held the position until a few months before his death in 1953.

The Inaugural Ceremony took place in Headquarters Hall the next morning at eight o'clock, and was very simple. Warrington still acting as the President pro tem, rose and announced that the President of the Society, Dr. George Sydney Arundale, had been duly elected for the ensuing seven years from June 21st, 1934. He then presented the seal-ring believed to be worn by H.P. Blavatsky, which at her passing came to Colonel H.S. Olcott, Dr. Annie Besant, and now to Dr. George Arundale.

It seems that Betty and Albert are expected to leave Adyar about the 9th of July, and will go to Kalimpong for two months or so, with a view of Kanchenjunga. Warrington said: "It is wonderful to have the feeling that one up here is living almost within the very atmosphere of the Masters". After several months they will then go on to Darjeeling, staying in Benares for some time, then to Delhi, Agra and Calcutta. Due to their low financial funds, they will sail on a cargo boat "The Silva-Java Line," or sometimes called "The Silver Line" from Calcutta, which will require about two months to make the journey from Calcutta to Los Angeles, and disembark at San Pedro Port, then to their home at Krotona. Stopping at Rangoon, Singapore, Batavia, Samaring, Sourabhaya, Macassar, Manila, hoping to meet theosophists at each stopping place. It is also reported in another report, that they left on the S.S. Mapia line for Los Angeles.

—⋞⋟—

After the Adyar Convention, Krishnamurti and Rajagopal were to sail for Australia. Although the Australian Press was very friendly towards Krishnamurti upon his arrival, not so the Theosophical Society members. Constant traveling for more than two years left

Krishnamurti exhausted. Rest would come only at the end of April 1934, on his return to Ojai, California, his home at Arya Vihara.

Education has been one of Krishnamurti's most passionate concerns. The question is, can children be educated without racial prejudices, which divide man from man? Unless there are enough unconditioned adults to show them, it is obviously harder for an adult to uncondition himself than for a child to remain unconditioned.

> Now, to me, life is not meant to be a school. Life is not a thing from which you learn, it is meant to be lived—to be lived supremely, intelligently, divinely. Whereas, if you make it into a constant battle, struggle, continual effort, then life becomes hideous; and you have made it so because your whole thought is self-growth, self-expansion, self-aggrandizement, and as long as that exists, life becomes a hideous struggle.[8]

The Vasanta Garden School, was established near Auckland, over ten years ago, by the New Zealand Section of the Theosophical Society, and where the practical application of Theosophy to education could be seen.

> So, gradually, in this process of liberating the mind from the false, there is not the replacement of the false by the true, but only the true. Then you are no longer seeking a substitution, but in the processes of discovering the false, you liberate the mind to move, to live eternally, and then action becomes a spontaneous, natural thing, and therefore life becomes, not a school in which to learn to compete, to fight, life becomes a thing to be lived intelligently, supremely, happily. And such a life is the life of a consummate human being.[9]

---

[8] Krishnamurti, J., *the Collected Works of J. Krishnamurti*, Volume II, 1934-1935, Dubuque, Iowa, 1991, Kendall/Hunt Publishing Co., "First Talk Vasanta School Gardens", Auckland, New Zealand, March 30, 1934, p.11.

[9] Krishnamurti, J., *the Collected Works of J. Krishnamurti*, Volume II, 1934-1935, Dubuque, Iowa, 1991, Kendall/Hunt Publishing Co., "Third Talk Vasanta School Gardens", Auckland, New Zealand, April 2, 1934, pp.45-46.

The beginning of The Besant Cultural Centre was in the founding of the Theosophical High School opened on June 27, 1934, one year after the death of Dr. Besant, who had so constantly urged its inauguration. The headmaster, Mr. Sankara Menon, M.A., was a young and very brilliant graduate of Madras University as well as an earnest member of the Theosophical Society. The School is located in Besant Gardens, an eighty-acre section of the Society's property temporally rented for that purpose, and has over fifty young students on its rolls. In Dr. Besant's name, as a living memorial to her, Dr. Arundale started this school. This started the intention, not only the Besant Theosophical School, but also the Krotona Institute that, as the school developed, a college could be added, and eventually a university, all embodying the spirit of one whose wise and practical love for the world was surpassed by none.

Krishnamurti arrived in Ojai, California, for his Oak Grove talks, and on the morning of June 28, 1934, wanted to deal with the idea of values. But, he discovered that his talks seemed to have created some confusion, because people are caught up in the words themselves and do not go deeply into their meaning or use them as a means of comprehension. From the question put to him, we discover that sex is still an issue.

> *Question*: What suggestion or advice could you give to one who is hindered by strong sexual desire?
>
> *Krishnamurti*: After all, where there is no creative expression of life, we give undue importance to sex, which becomes an acute problem. So the question is not what advice or suggestion I would give, or how one can overcome passion, sexual desire, but how to release that creative living, and not merely tackle one part of it, which is sex; that is, how to understand the wholeness, the completeness of life.
>
> Now, through modern education, through circumstances and environment, you are driven to do something which you hate. You are repelled, but you are forced to do it because of your lack of proper equipment, proper training. In your work you are being

prevented by circumstances, by conditions, from expressing your self fundamentally, creatively, and so there must be an outlet; and this outlet becomes the sex problem or the drink problem or some idiotic, inane problem. All these outlets become problems.

Or you are artistically inclined. There are very few artists, but you may be inclined, and that inclination is continually being perverted, twisted, thwarted, so that you have no means of real self-expression, and thus undue importance comes to be given either to sex or to some religious mania. Or your ambitions are thwarted, curtailed, hindered, and so again undue importances is given to those things that should be normal. So, until you understand comprehensively your religious, political, economic and social desires, and their hindrances, the natural functions of life will take an immense importance, and the first place in your life. Hence all the innumerable problems of greed, of possessiveness, of sex, of social and racial distinctions have their false measure and false value. But if you were to deal with life, not in parts but as a whole, comprehensively, creatively, with intelligence, then you would see that these problems, which are enervating the mind and destroying creative living, disappear, and then intelligence functions normally, and in that there is an ecstasy.[10]

Muriel Lauder Lewis, Director-Editor, from Ojai, California, calls attention to parents in many parts of the world of the material published by the Mothers' Research Group, which began in Ojai, California, as an advisory group under the Greater American Plan of the Theosophical Society sponsored by the Theosophical Society at the Headquarters in Wheaton, Illinois, founded by Dr. Pieter K. Roest.

Their aim is to gather together the mothers of the Society into one large group to prepare them to be fit channels for children of the New Race, and to train themselves to rear these children properly.

---

[10]Krishnamurti, J., *the Collected Works of J. Krishnamurti*, Volume II, 1934-1935, Dubuque, Iowa, 1991, Kendall/Hunt Publishing Co., "Tenth Talk in the Oak Grove", Ojai, California, June 29, 1934, p.97.

Its objects are:

> 1. To promote a realization of the spiritual aspect of motherhood and family life.

> 2. To gather together for mutual study, in neighbourhood groups or through correspondence, those who are interested in work for children and youth.

> 3. To bring to parents the light shed by the Ancient Wisdom on all problems in the home.

Mothers' Bulletin, the group's quarterly organ, was begun in April, 1935, as a means of communication between its subscribers scattered throughout the United States and abroad. They state that they are unique in that it attempts to study child problems cooperatively from the view point of the esoteric philosophy underlying all the great religions of the world.

It was during this year that Krishnamurti began to learn Spanish from a Linguaphone course in preparation for his tour of South and Central America coming up in 1935.

June, 1934 Krishnamurti spoke at the Ojai Star Camp in Ojai, California. The Star Camp this year was very successful in every way; and immediately this brings up many matters in connection with Krishnamurti and the T.S., which George Hall will have to discuss with A.P. Warrington when they get back.

Capt. George Ragan and Capt. Devereux Myers both theosophists, have been elected to the Happy Valley Board of Trustees to fill the vacancies caused by the death of Dr. Besant and Max Wardall.

The death of Max Wardall removes from the Theosophical Society one of its truly outstanding figures. It was told that he united the masculine strength of a splendid man with the delicate sympathy and tenderness of a woman. For thirty years of his Theosophical activity, he made Theosophy a living presence, not a text book hypothesis; he lived it wholly yet simply and helped others to make it vital and genuine in themselves.

Since the reopening of the E.S., a new Pledge was written for those who were rejoining, and for the members of degrees II & III had fewer changes.

By this time, *The Theosophist* was to become more a magazine relieved of the personal and family business of the Society.

Once upon a time there was a little boy named George Arundale, who was like any other little six-year-old in that he liked chocolates. But that this six-year-old was different, we have on no less authority than H.P. Blavatsky, the Founder of the Theosophical Society, who wrote to him:

> To George Chela, Esq.
>
> Happy New Year to the most honourable George, Esq.
>
> A box of sweets is forthcoming from Russia, a cold and pious country, where the undersigned is supposed to have evolved from. When it arrives—you shall have it, and when you understand what your loving old friend means—you shall indeed be a *chela*.
> Yours respectfully,
> H.P. Blavaatsky

Miss Anita Henkel, was attached to the Wheaton headquarters of the American Theosophical Society as National Field Representative. She was invited by President Hoover in 1931 to the White House Conference for Child Health and Protection. By December 1939, Miss Henkel, published a short article after George Arundale became President of the Adyar Theosophical Society "The Little Boy Who Became President" published in the *Theosophical Worker* for December 1939, pages 296-297.

Ojai Valley Oaks Lodge of the Theosophical Society meets on Poli Street, Meiners' Oaks, California.

The September gathering met with an open-air sunset meeting at Krotona. Seated on the lawn overlooking the lovely Ojai Valley with its tiers of encircling mountains, the members were prepared for an inspiring meeting. Soft violin music by Mrs. Monica Ros opened the program. followed by the president, Mr. E.T. Lewis, who introduced the main speaker, Mrs. Catharine Mayes. On September 30th the lodge honored Dr. Besant's birthday with a soprano solo by Miss Rebecca Eichbaum, accompanied by Mrs. Elizabeth Price Coffey.

The October program met on Poli Street in Meiners' Oaks consisted of a public lecture by A. F. Knudsen, piano solo by Mortimer Markoff, and other lecturers were: Catharine Mayes, William Kent, Mrs. Mary Gerard, Mrs. Muriel Lewis.

Another group appearing on the horizon within the Krotona history is the Universal Temple of Divine Wisdom, a non-profit Corporation governed by an Essene Council of Bishops for sustaining a standard of Ecclesiastical specification with a Board of Trustees managing all of its business affairs. The Temple's Priestly Order, The Order of the Invincible Light, received its Ordinational authorization from The Essene Order of the Golden Grail, founded by the Apostle John in 38 A.D. within the first Apostolic Episkopoi of the Antiochian Church. Dr. Frederick Werth was a member according to correspondence from Mrs. Theron (Alice) Winston of Ojai, California. By 1985, we shall see many members of the Liberal Catholic Church interested in this organization as well.

An organization known as the Lions prepare for their big party at the Krotona Hall inviting other clubs in the Ojai valley to bring their ladies to the big dance to be given on Saturday night of November 17.

We found the file among Warrington's papers that contained a translation by Mr. Theo Lilliefelt of a reading of the horoscope of Dr. George S. Arundale by the French astrologer, M. Anthony Gauteri. There are many biographies and books written about Dr. Arundale over the years. Briefly we note:

Dr. George Sydney Arundale came to America as a world personality. In 1934 he was elected President of the Theosophical Society, and with Shrimati Rukmini became the head of the beautiful center, St. Michael's, Huizen, Holland. Since that year he has fulfilled many plans, first as to the spread of Theosophy, and secondly in the improvement and beautification of Adyar, the world headquarters near Madras, now taken the name Chennai.

For over thirty years he had the good fortune to work with Dr. Annie Besant, so that he had a thorough grounding in Theosophy, in statecraft and in education. He was educated in Europe, and later at Cambridge, where he graduated in arts and law, and subsequently engaged in historical research work in the Archives Nationales, Paris, which brought him into the Fellowship of the Royal Historical Society of London.

At the invitation of Dr. Besant he went out to India at twenty-four years of age, to help her at the Central Hindu College, Benares, ascending from professor to principal. During this period the Central Hindu College became one of the most famous educational institutions in India. In 1917 he was appointed Principal of the National University of Madras, of which Rabindranath Tagore was Chancellor, and which bestowed on him *honoris causa*, the degree of Doctor of Letters.

His ideals of education for Kingship are embodied in his book, *Gods in the Becoming*. These principles were being practically realized in the Besant Memorial School established at Adyar in March 1934. The school was a flourishing experiment, and from this nucleus was hoped, a College and University of the future.

In every country he visited he identified himself with India's soul and its destiny.

Dr. Arundale spent 1937 at Adyar revising the administration of the headquarters estate, writing books and articles for the press, developing the Theosophical publications, and attending to public affairs. In the year 1938 he is guiding Theosophical activities in a new cycle in which Adyar shall become more closely and reciprocally linked with the Sections.

After his experiences with subtler states of consciousness, he has written his research in his books *Nirvana* and *Kundalini*. In his latest book, which forms the substance of his 1938 lecture course on *Symbolic Yoga*, he deals with symbolism of Yoga stressing the fact that this is not a Yoga of Renunciation, is not confined to the individual who renounces the world, is not for the so-called ascetic, but is rather for him who lives *in* the world, shares his life with the world so that the individual makes a heaven of his earth, and lives in heaven while dwelling on earth. The lectures on *Symbolic Yoga* were taken from his book to be published in 1939, *The Lotus Fire*.

The Besant Memorial School was placed under the management of the Besant Educational Trust, with Dr. Arundale as President and Hon. Educational Adviser, Dr. Srinivasamurti as Vice-President and well-known Adyar residents as an Executive Committee. The School was to be conducted on the lines laid down by Dr. Besant in her many educational writings set forth in her pamphlet on *The Principles of Education*.

Due to the conflict between the Theosophical Society and Krishnamurti, George Arundale in his Inaugural Address of 1934, tries to bridge the two camps. The following is only an abridgement of his Address.

> Theosophy has inspiration and delight for every individual, no matter whether he be young or old. And while Theosophy thus meets to serve all on the many different roads on which they travel, yet is it but one Theosophy, just as the different roads themselves converge upon one goal.
>
> Is it not, then, worth your while to study this Theosophy for which, perhaps, so much seems to be claimed, yet which has brought happiness, peace, purpose, to countless thousands throughout the world? And will you approach it without prejudice, without preconception derived from gossip or possible misrepresentation in addresses? Theosophy comes to meet you in no spirit of dogma, or of doctrine, or of creed, not as some other religion or philosophy or science, not as a setting forth of the imaginative vagaries of Blavatsky or Besant or Leadbeater; but as an age-old science of Life rich in detailed application to Life's circumstances and, if approached with a mind not cribbed, cabined or confined by the orthodoxies and

conventionalists of the present age, almost uncannily effective in its simple method of rendering the intelligible clear and the apparently useless clearly purposeful making life worth living.

Theosophy asks you to examine, to study. It does not ask you to believe or to accept on authority. But it does ask you not to make up your mind in a hurry, nor to assume that that which your mind does not conceive nor understand cannot therefore be true. And it also asks you to make up your mind for yourself, not to allow it to be made up for you by somebody else, still less by public opinion.

He also stated in that same Inaugural Address:

> J. Krishnamurti may no longer be a member of the Theosophical Society, but I call him a Theosophist. His own individual greatness is unique and is such as the Society had not before known ... Whether a member of the Society or not, he is ever a great and beneficent power in the Masters' work and in the great Theosophical Movement.

They believed all that Krishnamurti is saying is Theosophy and yet nobody will say, within the Theosophical Society, that the Society should identify itself with his teachings. Such identification of the Society would naturally mean closing down many activities. And yet no one can say that what Krishnamurti says is not Theosophy.

In an interview with Dr. Arundale in Ceylon, it is reported as follows:

> As regards Mr. Krishnamurti, I stated that I emphatically regard him as a great channel for certain lofty spiritual forces and as a messenger from the Rishis to the world. On the other hand, there are surely other messengers and other channels, the Theosophical Society being certainly one of these; and while I had the happiness of being with Mr. Krishnamurti during some part of his early youth, he now needed no help in his great work, and I myself felt my supreme duty to be the support of Theosophy and the Theosophical Society, the background and inspiration for so many aspects and forms of life and truth offered to the world during the last twenty years and more.

> I think most members of the Theosophical Society honor and respect Mr. Krishnamurti, and for my own part I do all I can as I travel throughout the world to encourage people to listen to him gladly. I have just placed at his disposal for any talks he may like to give over the air when he visits Sydney, Australia, our Theosophical Broadcasting Station in that city, the premier non-government station in Australia.[11]

By November, the *E.S.T. Bulletin* No. 64 had a "Supplement" copy sent out to all Pledged Members of the E.S., covering the Convention Talk, August 20, 1934 by Marie Poutz. But over the years, that same "Supplement" had four different printings.

Taken from the first printing, we read that many drop from the School or are asked to leave for one reason or another. They are told when that happens, they waste their opportunity in this life, which may mean that perhaps for a number of incarnations to come they will not again come into touch with those inner realities.

One of the main issues for joining the E.S. was Krishnamurti:

> We pledge ourselves to *co-operate* with the Outer Head. That is obviously fair. But here I must say a few words about the part of the clause which has been omitted, that which implied acceptance of Krishnamurti and the work for the World-Teacher. Some have asked whether it was a sign that Krishnamurti had failed in his mission, and that the E.S. was repudiating him. I want to say most emphatically that such is not the reason for the omission. But how do you think Krishnaji himself would feel about a promise which seemed to make acceptance of him an obligatory condition of admission into the E.S.? You know very well what he would think of that! None of us are in a position to know first-hand whether he is the vehicle or not. Therefore, instead of accepting blindly what we were told, every member should now retreat within himself, study some of the priceless teachings he is giving, and find in his own heart the inner conviction that through him pours down just now a message which is tremendously needed in the world. There is now no obligation of any kind, only an inner acceptance which wells up

---

[11] Arundale, George, *Ceylon Daily News*, interview regarding Krishnamurti and his teachings.

from within the heart, instead of being imposed from without as a condition of membership.

But if you will live truly, as you have pledged yourselves to do, then even in this life it may be that some of you, perhaps all of you, may stand one day where the ONE INITIATOR is invoked, where you will see His Star shine forth!

Since the death of Bishop Leadbeater, C Jinarajadasa became Head of the E.S., according to Dr. Besant's wishes. He took charge of the Shrine Room at Adyar built for the purpose by E.S. students, first under Col. Olcott's direction in 1904 and completed in 1908 by Dr. Besant, when the General Council granted the exclusive use of them in perpetuity as long as the E.S. shall exist; should it cease to exist then the room reverts to The Society.

In November it was announced that both Dr. Arundale and Ernest Wood had accepted nomination for President.

By December, Mr. H. Frei will leave Adyar for Tasmania. He had held the posts at Adyar of Acting Treasurer and Recording Secretary. He had been for seven years Bishop Leadbeater's trusted friend and personal secretary. Before taking up work at Adyar, Frei was Manager of Volkart Bros. Agency in Colombo, one of the most responsible posts in the European business world. He was also Consul for Switzerland and Italy. Even the late Treasurer, A. Schwarz, was also once Manager of Volkart Bros.

Henry Steel Olcott, Adyar Gardens, 1905

Chapter IV
1935

Who are the true owners of the Krotona Institute? Ownership keeps coming up within the board members of Krotona. Marie Poutz goes over the By-Laws which state that the ownership is vested in the O.H. of the E.S. through a board of which the O.H. is President, and the members belong to the 3rd Degree of the E.S. Evidently as our E.S. members were called to subscribe there was a clear understanding that the property was Dr. Besant's and that she was responsible throughout for its administration. With these clear words Marie did not in the least understand Warrington's action with the best of intentions to protect the welfare of Krotona, that he should have so flatly refused to carry out her request in the matter of that loan to The Manor.

When George Hall moved at a board meeting on February 18, to cancel the debt, Warrington once again opposed the idea and the resolution was not passed.

Miss Poutz says she thinks she understands Warrington's anxiety with regard to the financial future of Krotona which made him refuse to carry out Dr. Besant's wishes. Now, in her own mind the E.S. work throughout the whole world is one, and as she represented the Greatest she expected everyone to cooperate with her to carry out His Plan. Marie Poutz reminds the Board members that particular instructions were given to them by Him (Master) to throw in as much force as they possibly could to The Manor and take nothing out.

It is a strange fact that these financial arrangements between Krotona and The Manor have occult repercussions. Could it be because certain financial adjustments like in the history between Huizen and Camberley being approved by the Masters, and in the starting of The Manor community were not approved by the Masters, that They have not been able to make of the place the Centre which

They hope to presently if this financial position is not straightened out.

From the early days of the Esoteric School, it has held that no Esotericist shall, as such, lend money to or borrow it from a fellow Esotericist, or ask for favors; or use any persuasive means by word, or deed, or otherwise, to obtain benefits of a personal nature and for selfish purposes, by using the name of Theosophy and Brotherhood in matters not directly connected with the E.S.T. or the T.S. Should any such case occur, it shall be followed by the expulsion from the E.S.T. of those who break the rule. Money may be given by the richer to the poorer, but not lent in a formal businesslike way; services may be rendered, offered, and *accepted*, but *never asked*. This is the strictest of all the occult laws.

Marie Poutz could not help thinking it was similar with Krotona, had there been such an acquiescence on the part of Krotona. She also noticed at the end of the statement the words that "No change of policy will be made without her approval or that of her successor." Marie wondered whether in the new dispensation, where she comes into Krotona by the statutes. Is she to be merely a "rubber stamp" or will Krotona definitely and wholeheartedly accept the leadership of the new O.H.?

There are many letters in A.P. Warrington's file folder from all over the globe of appreciation sent to him and Betty after nine months of difficult times, working bravely and so successful with wonderful patience, and discriminative forethought, not withstanding the various limitations of weak health, hot unfavorable climate etc. The letters conveyed sincere respect and regard for Mr. A.P. Warrington, President, pro tem, for his enthusiastic and selfless work in the cause of Theosophy and of the Theosophical Society.

February 15, 1935, Krotona Hill, which has had gasoline stoves since 1924, will soon be using natural gas. A pipe line was to be laid up the hill during the coming week.

Louis Zalk has a long talk with Krishnamurti at Arya Vihara early in the morning regarding the Order of the Star Institute leasing the portion of the pasture on the lower estate for crops instead of leaving it just for pasture by Mr. Will Clark.

A letter from George Hall to the Santa Barbara Airport on February 26, 1935, reminds them that private airplanes using the property at the base of the Krotona Institute at Ojai as a landing field should stop immediately, as they are doing damage to growing crops, and as the offender is liable to prosecution. They are facing arrest the next time they commit this offence.

Education has been one of the main issues of The Society since Krishnamurti started his mission regarding education of children from the earliest age, to be brought up without national and racial prejudices, without competitiveness and ideologies that divide man from man, so there might be peace. The theosophists in America were also concerned to establish a school that would reflect their attitudes to education by opening a school called the *School of the Open Gate*. The moving spirit behind the founding of the School was Mrs. Mary Gray. Born in Paris in 1886 of American parents, Mary became a prominent theosophist early in life, becoming a well known lecturer for the the Theosophical Society, and also becoming manager and a trustee of the Krotona Institute in 1916. Married to a wealthy Boston Lawyer, Roland Gray, meant that Mary was able to give generously to Theosophical causes as well. Mary provided for J. Krishnamurti and his brother, Nitya on their first visit to California in 1922; she took Krishnamurti and his brother on an extended tour of the state and loaned the cottage (Pine Cottage) at the east end of Ojai for his personal home. Mary Gray was well schooled in Theosophical doctrine and could well deliver the message to the public. Her article *Education for the New Race* was one of the clearest expositions of the need for Theosophical concern about education.

Reminding her readers in her fifty-two page booklet that California has been chosen as "the Cradle of the New Race", the booklet is composed of radio talks given in Los Angeles during March, April and May 1935.

After the *School of the Open Gate* closed because of financial difficulties, Mary was to found another school, *The Gateway*, on her estate in the east end of Ojai, which ran from 1935 to 1940. Theosophists were on the advisory board yet it was not so closely linked to The Society as the *School of the Open Gate* had been.

—❦—

Another part of the Krotona history is the Liberal Catholic Church Province of the United States, St. Alban's Pro-Cathedral at 2041 Argyle Avenue, Los Angeles, California, Bishop Auxiliary and Vicar General , The Rt. Rev. Charles Hampton.

It was announced that the Presiding Bishop, the Right Reverend Frank W. Pigott of London, informed its members by cable on May 17th that a majority of the Clerical Synod had confirmed the election of Bishop-Auxiliary Charles Hampton as Regionary Bishop for the United States. Bishop Hampton was elected by the General Episopal Synod (the Liberal Catholic Bishops throughout the world) on April 27. The installation took place on Whitsunday, June 9th. at the Pro-Cathedral in Los Angeles.

Edward Martin joined the then Old Catholic Church in Great Britain in the early 1900's, which later became the Liberal Catholic Church where he became a priest. Martin was retired from the English Army, after having served the British Raj in India. He lived briefly at Krotona with his wife, Rhoda, who designed the mystery house "Taj Mahal" of the Ojai Valley with the assistance of John Roine, architect and builder, well-known for his unusual architecture work. As Martin was interested in the Liberal Catholic Church, he wanted to integrate some of the Old Catholic prayers, so he called the British Consulate, at 117 West Ninth Street, Los Angeles, California to receive a copy of a form of prayer and of Thanksgiving to almighty God for the protection afforded to the King's Majesty during the twenty-five Years of his Auspicious Reign ordered by the Lords of His Majesty's Most honourable Privy Council

April 29 1935
Pleiades, Ojai, California

Dear Mr. Martin,

With reference to your telephone call today, I enclose a copy of the Form of Prayer which is to be used at the Thanksgiving Service at St. Paul's Cathedral in London on May 6th, and which will be followed as closely as possible at the Service to be held in Los Angeles on the following Sunday, May 12. I also enclose a copy of the brief outline of the life of His Majesty, which may be of interest to you in connection with the celebration which you are so loyally holding in Ojai. I enclose also a circular which has been set out by the Council of British Societies in Los Angeles, giving details of the celebrations to be held here.

I enclose also a list of British Societies in the Los Angeles Consular district. You will notice that this shows the address of the National President and the State president of the Daughters of the British Empire, about whom you enquired.

May I avail myself of this opportunity to congratulate you on holding this celebration and in offering you my sincere wishes or its success?
Yours sincerely,
F. G.
H. M. Consul.

—❦—

The following is a very brief history of the 2GB Broadcasting Station located at Adyar House, 29 Bligh Street Sydney, Australia. (A. E. Bennett; Managing Director, and R.L. Power, American Representative in Los Angeles, California).

In 1926 George Arundale initiated a most important movement to "put Theosophy over the air". With the cooperation of the members in Australia, the 2GB Broadcasting Station was organized with the radio masts in the garden of The Manor. The Station became a very great success. After a few years, Dr. Arundale, in order to keep the control of the Station in Theosophical hands, asked as many shareholders as accepted his plan to donate to him their shares. He then created a special Trust with himself and two others as directors.

After several years, the Trust was taken out of the hands of George Arundale in 1935, and as the shares were about to be sold, it was necessary for George to take legal action. On the arrival in Australia of C. Jinarajadasa, he acted as co-attorney with George in the affairs of this case.

It seems that the policy of aloofness and secrecy is running the Broadcasting Station 2GB is now in question. Many theosophists in Sydney said that the amount of straight Theosophy put on the air is close to a minute. Although there were a number of talks, such as Mr. Bennett called "applied Theosophy" on Ethics, Psychology, the League of Nations, etc., they were not really Theosophy in the accepted sense by the members. It did broadcast the Sunday Service of the L.C.C., which had a very fine paid choir. The other music seemed to be mixed with a good deal of modern jazz.

Most of the old members that put up the money felt that the huge sacrifices made by them during the first few years has been in vain. Now they were asking for their money back and politely were told to go to hell. The station was really a one man show in A. E. Bennett. Due to the debt owed to Krotona, the financial part of The Manor would need a complete makeover. The station at this time in the history of the Theosophical Society was like a canker which ate into the vitals of its members, and had a very disrupting influence on the whole Section. Since George Arundale had now become the President of the Theosophical Society, it was most essential that he regain the confidence of the Section members again, and put the station on a healthier footing in the right direction.

April 12 1935
The Manor

To the Directors
2 GB Broadcasting Station
Bligh Street, Sydney

Dear Sirs,

When I decided on February 8th to come to Australia to assume responsibilities in connection with The Manor I asked Dr. Arundale if he would not come to Australia so that in this Jubilee Year the Theosophical Movement in Australia should make a spring forward. He replied that he felt obliged to stay in India to arrange for the next Convention. He stated then: "But if you yourself go, I shall propose to give you a complete Power of Attorney as regards the Broadcasting Station, and you are already the owner of The Manor and so have complete authority there."

A few days later he wrote to me as follows:

> I am preparing the necessary Power of Attorney to enable you to act on my behalf as Chairman of the Theosophical Broadcasting Station and in connection with the shares I hold, so long as you are resident in New South Wales. I have already given a Power of Attorney to Bennett whom I am asking the Notary Public to cause to be suspended while you are over there. But, of course, that particular Power will have to be resumed when you leave, though with such modifications as may seem desirable, when you discuss the whole business with the Australian people.

On February 26th, two days before I left Adyar, Dr. Arundale gave me in writing his general ideas regarding the creation of the new Trust in the place of the existing Radio Publicity Trust which was composed, until lately of himself, Mr. Bennett and Mr. Morton. Then finally he gave me his Power of Attorney.

My lawyers who have examined the Power of Attorney instruct me that it is ineffective, and the Memorandum of Association of 2GB does not mention the post of Chairman of the Board of Directors, nor invest Dr. Arundale who now holds that position with any power to create a substitute by a Power of Attorney. Under the document I can however act in his place as a Director but no more.

When I met Mr. Bennett in Adelaide on March 15th, I enquired about the Trust. He held that it ought to be enlarged so as to give 2GB a full right over the shares of the Trust, since he claimed that as 2GB had paid the money for the shares it had a "moral right" to their control. No word, however was said by him to indicate that he had already set matters on foot to change the composition of the Trust. It was only at Melbourne that I received from Mr. Bennett a letter dated April 2, stating that the Constitution of the Trust has been enlarged. This was to me the first intimation that he had used his Power of Attorney to change the Trust. Even as early as March 8th, four days before I arrived in Fremantle he had begun the preliminaries towards this enlargement of the Trust.

Under these conditions I do not propose to act on my Power of Attorney as one of the Directors of 2GB. I certainly had various plans in mind so that the present strained situation in Australia might be ended, and I believe I could have done this work, if I could have acted as Chairman of he Board of Directors, as Dr. Arundale intended, and in my capacity under his Power of Attorney as one of the three Directors of the Trust.

Seeing that the Power of Attorney is defective and that the Trust has been changed before I arrived in Sydney and that my sole power is merely as one of several Directors of 2GB, and only then provided the Directors consent, this is to state that I do not propose to exercise this Power.

I have cabled to Dr. Arundale my decision and that I must leave to his direct action the solution of the problems.

Yours sincerely,
C. Jinarajadasa

April 23 1935

My dear Hilda, (Wood:—wife of Ernest Wood)

Last night after a broadcast on 2BL on Indian Art, as I was leaving the studio a lady entered with some others, evidently for the subsequent turn. She looked nice, dressed in green, and came up warmly to me and greeted me by saying she was your sister. It was all a surprise but it brought me back to India suddenly.

Convention is finished and there has been a great deal of uncovering of the rather questionable tactics of 2GB. My really great regret is that Dr. Arundale has got himself involved in this. I think he has trusted Mr. Bennett and his advice too much and the Directors have mostly been allies of Mr. Bennett or the others, who are not, did not exercise proper supervision.

Dr. Arundale asked the members to give up to him some 700 odd shares. The intention was that out of them in some way, he would raise money to fiance the News Service of Davidge for two years. This was done but it was not made clear that in so financing he meant to sell the shares. As there has been much talk of controlling 2GB by a majority of shares, the members who gave theirs to him, were under the impression that he still had control of them. The 700 could not make the majority, so a scheme was worked up, which now that it is known has proved startling. A Trust was created by the Directorate of three of its members, Dr. Arundale, Mr. Bennett and Morton. This Trust bought the 700 shares plus 500 more. But as they had no money, the Directorate advanced it. Now, it is the law everywhere that no company can buy back its shares. But for all practical purposes the law was got round in this particular way. However, in making the Trust, rules seem to have been drawn so that of its three members, Dr. Arundale, Bennett and Morton, Dr. Arundale should have absolute control, having the right even to dismiss Bennett of his own motion, though requiring Morton's consent. This Trust was the key situation since it controls 2GB, against which there have been many complaints, both from putting over coarse material in the way of music and entertainment and also for practically giving very little propaganda for Theosophy, and trying in various ways to shut out the Theosophical purpose for which the Station was formed. Because of the huge profits from advertisements, 2GB is recognized as the most successful of all the B class Stations, and everyone recognizes Bennett's ability in having done this.

Unfortunately Bennett found a loop-hole and before I came to Sydney transformed the Trust, so that he could have sole control of it. Morton did not realize what was the full implication of his action. Anyhow Dr. Arundale has lost complete control, which he thought he once had, over those shares. As a matter of fact, since the formation of the Trust he never did have control of the shares as an individual, because it was a Trust of three, and for all practical purposes of him and another who held control. Yet even until two days before I left he wrote to me of "my shares", and told me that the Power of Attorney is no good because none such is contemplated in the Memorandum of Association of either 2GB or the Trust. When the lawyer drew them up in Madras, he did not have these documents before him, but only took verbal instructions from Dr. Arundale. Dr. Arundale had solemnly promised that he would safeguard the interests of the Section because he was the majority controller of shares.

It has been a bad business, but the Convention has come through on the whole with excellent feeling. I should mention that as soon as I came and saw the doings of Mr. Bennett, I gave him a good slap. First by rejecting £100 which 2GB had promised to The Manor, but shilled over its payment. Then 2GB wanted to get a stranglehold on The Manor by demanding a lease for 10 years on the part of the garden where the two masts are erected and there is the broadcasting machinery. They had been paying only 30/ per week, when later it was discovered by an expert and independent valuation that the rent should have been £3/10/. Anyway I objected to those masts from the beginning, and since 2GB intended to expand the Station with more masts and machinery, I felt it was time to free The Manor from an incubus, not only on the physical plane, but one which interferes with the etheric planes through which forces are being poured out from this Centre from Shamballa to effect the southern hemisphere. So I have asked the Station to take themselves away within six months. In order to free the debt of 20,000 dollars to Krotona from The Manor, I must now tackle Warrington who is the only one of the Krotona board who is opposed to this wish of Dr. Besant, which she expressed for nearly a dozen years.

On the whole the heart has come through the heavy work and it was only last night at the end of the final meeting, there was just a symptom, but no more. Tomorrow I fly to Brisbane, but only for three days, and then sail on May 1st for New Zealand. Mr. Bennett will be on the first boat on his way to America. I have no doubt we shall shake hands, but I have nicknamed 2GB "Two things—Good and Bad".

Please do not show this letter to anyone else because I don't want people to talk about the muddle into which Dr. Arundale has got himself with the best of motives to do a big thing for Australia. Undoubtedly something of all that has happened is sure to spread in theosophical circles. if you hear anything that is contrary to the statement which I have made, then you are authorized to correct it from this statement.

Every yours,
C. Jinarajadasa

P.S. Under Dr. Arundale's instructions, 2GB offered to pay me £100 expenses. I have somewhat stiffly refused the gift. I think all the members breathed a sigh of relief that someone has come to tackle Mr. Bennett, and show 2GB "where it gets off"!

C. Jinarajadasa made a resolution at the Convention, making Dr. Arundale a Trustee of The Manor and in addition Ian Davidson and Miss Maddox. It was due to Miss V.K. Maddox, detailed knowledge of the case, and her tireless watchfulness that the victory was gained. It was her prompt action which safeguarded the interests of The Manor from serious dangers from the Dark Forces. C. Jinarajadasa reported that in six months more The Manor Centre would be completely free of all interference to its occult work.

The chief duty of C. Jinarajadasa going to Sydney was to help the Australian Section, especially to build up the Blavatsky Lodge, and to protect "The Manor", which had steadily diminished in strength and influence. As we read in the earlier history, Sydney was to be a vital centre in the work since 1922 when it became the centre of force for all the countries south of the Equator. It was reported that the Centre was established in connection with the new continent which was to rise tens of thousands of years hence to be the home of the Seventh Root Race.

C. Jinarajadasa had to emphasize that the strictest probity is obligatory on all who look to the Masters, and that some actions, though permitted by business morality, were, nevertheless, unclean in Their eyes, and that this indebtedness was interfering with the spiritual progress of The Manor, and that to relieve them of this obligation would be necessary to the well being of The Manor and its future development.

There is really a mixed-up jangle of interest in between The Manor and the 2GB station, since A.E. Bennett stated in a letter to Catharine G. Mayes, Krotona, that 2GB would pay off the debt freeing The Manor from its obligation. By reading the letters, it is so complicated that the end has forgotten the beginning, and the "Middle" would represent a hopeless mixture to outside observers. It may be that C. Jinarajadasa did not know the debt had been guaranteed by 2GB., and the agreement between George and Bennett. But how can George and Bennett feel that the profits from 2GB could pay off the debt, since it did not have any official sanction to do so. The matter was strictly between Trustees of The Manor and Krotona. Krotona had no hold whatsoever on the station or over any director legally nor did 2GB have any legal obligation whatsoever towards The Manor or to Krotona.

C. Jinarajadasa writes to Warrington that he would be responsible for his procedure of action to honor the repayment of the principal of the debt to Krotona by way of a donation. They would lose the interest for over nine years if the Trustees of Krotona accepted this offer, and let it drop. If the Trustees felt that they have not been treated fair, C. Jinarajadasa consents heartily to the reopening of the whole matter for the consideration of other proposals.

Under the proposed reconstruction plans that C. Jinarajadasa was putting into action, Arundale plans to retire from his responsibilities concerning 2GB, making the memorandum therefore more nebulous than ever.

Arundale states that he would rather let the Station perish than become a source of acrimonious contention in the Australian Section, and let the Station perish than invoking the law against the great spiritual centre in the Southern Hemisphere. The Station is worth nothing to Theosophy, nor to the Theosophical Society in Australia, still less to the Masters, so long as it is a festering sore within the Theosophical organism in Australia.

Records show that the debt from The Manor to Krotona had been fully paid on May 27, 1936.

It will be on November 27, 1935 that C. Jinarajadasa writes to all **Pledged** Members of the E.S. at The Manor.

> Dear Brothers,
>
> You are, I presume, all aware of the litigation that has begun between 2GB and The Manor. I want to state, very briefly, for your information that even before I left Adyar, I received general instructions from the Chohan M. with regard to the situation. Then later at Adelaide, He expressed further His judgment on the events that had taken place.

I felt most keenly the danger to the Sacred Centre at The Manor, which had been created by the Hierarchy in 1922. That danger was not only to the work in Australia, but to all the work of the Hierarchy south of the Line. One danger <u>among others</u> came from the fact that the etheric waves sent through the aerials at The Manor were interfering with such etheric waves as were being sent out by the Sacred Centre. It was necessary <u>at all costs</u> to ward off the many dangers, for the work of the Sacred Centre deals with the work of the Masters or the Southern Hemisphere for tens of thousands of years to come.

This is the reason why I instructed The Manor Trustees to ask 2GB to vacate The Manor.

On September 20th, 1935, I received definite instructions from the Chohan M. to bring about a <u>complete separation between The Manor and 2GB</u>. I must therefore carry out to the full the instructions received.

Do not be anxious that the work in its many aspects will suffer if money promised towards that work by the Station will not be given. Better than money is the power of the Master behind the work. With Them with us, all is well. That is what really matters.

Yours sincerely,
C. Jinarajadasa, O.H.

Unexpectedly, as we were sorting out letters dated 1935 in a folder, we came across the following to be a message received from Master Morya, believed to be written by Dr. Besant. We do not know how or why it was filed among these papers, for it is not signed nor dated. The contents of the letter indicate the time period 1922.

The Master Morya said:

The suggestion to form a special centre in the Southern Hemisphere is made because of the existence of the great band which we call the equatorial current. You are aware that strong currents, mainly etheric, run from the equator to each pole and vice versa; but you may not have learnt that similar currents run through that central line in both directions, forming a belt which extends for several degrees on each side of it. It can be arranged that high spiritual forces flowing from North to South shall overleap this belt as though it did not exist; but to those of or (on) lower levels it is an obstacle to free communication which it would be uneconomical to ignore. Since the Southern Hemisphere is destined to come into increasing prominence, partly in connection with preparations for the Seventh Race, the Brotherhood considers it desirable to have a physical centre south of the line which can be employed as a power-station charged directly from Shambala so that forces of various kinds on lower levels can radiate from it without interfering constantly with the equatorial current.

The instruction to take nothing from the strength of this newly-born centre clearly refers to the suggestion recently made to carry away from it some of those whom We have drawn together to help in its development; such as Dr. Rocke and Dr.van der Leeuw. We regret the latter especially as a man of considerable promise, and in reward for good service given to Us elsewhere we have offered him this exceptional opportunity of doing for Us a piece of work the result of which will be of incalculable value to the world. As our Lord implied, the training of our future workers is for the moment the question of paramount importance, and careful consideration should be given to it.

It was in August, 1929, while Dr. Besant was in Chicago that certain changes in the organization and policy of Krotona took place: (1) That the By-Laws of the corporation be changed so that T.S. members are eligible to serve as Trustees whether or not they are members of the E.S.; (2) That the Board of Trustees be reduced from fifteen to seven; (3)That it be the duty and obligation of the Trustees as a self-perpetuating board to conserve and maintain and properly manage the physical property of the corporation so that it might not become involved in financial difficulties.

By June 22, 1935, George Hall confirms to C.F. Holland the resolution that took place with the Krotona Board meeting with C. Jinarajadasa's idea regarding Dr. Besant's statement of policy, and also the further verbal changes made in Chicago in 1929 by her namely, that the use and control of the occupancy of Krotona is wholly within the hands of the Outer Head or his resident representative, and that just as clearly it is the duty of the Krotona Trustees to so manage the finances that the stability and safety of the corporation's property is preserved. This covers the situation, stated in the resolution that with the Resident Head representing the Board and the resident agent of the Outer Head representing the E.S.

It was Dr. Besant's purpose to relinquish the previous held authority of the Outer Head to determine the fate of Krotona as a physical property. It was her intention that it be an E.S. Center in America, and to safeguard it so that it would serve that particular purpose.

She most emphatically did not intend that her successor would have "Rights" over Krotona, as a physical property equal to the condition of outright ownership, which was the state of affairs before the adoption of the new By-Laws.

It was mentioned that it was highly important, therefore, for the present Trustees, to be exceedingly careful as to the election of new Trustees so that it never be put into jeopardy by possibilities which can be easily visualized and which might dissipate its value.

It was stated that the work at Krotona would be wholly devoted to E.S. work, and the printing and issue of its publications would be done at Krotona.

There would be a training college for Theosophical lecturers and teachers, who, when ready for their work, would offer themselves to the General Secretary of the T.S. in the U.S.A., and would work thenceforth under his or her direction.

It was hoped by the O.H. that the work carried on at Krotona would create there a centre of Peace and Strength, not only for the E.S. itself, but also for the whole T.S. in the U.S.A., and that those who live there would remember that their lives are dedicated to the Service of the Hierarchy, and through its help to the Service of Humanity. Hence they must endeavor to be worthy of their high calling.

Krotona was to be so consecrated that it would be worthy to receive the World-Teacher or the Coming Lord. Questions often arose concerning the activities of Krishnamurti in relation to The Society. Many members are convinced that he is the founder of a new civilization, a new branch of the human tree, higher than the present.

The following report is not a verbatim or authentic record of what Krishnamurti said, for it has not been read or revised by Krishnamurti. It is a typed report "revised by D. Rajagopal." While Krishnamurti was in Uruguay on July 6, 1935, he was asked by several members of the Theosophical Society why he would no longer go to the Theosophical Society in Adyar. He made it quite clear:

> I ought to say before anything else that we have already explained that a complete and fundamental divergence exists between the directors of the T.S. and us. Also we have established how this difference arose and how it has continued deepening constantly, while superficially an amiable situation appears to exist. In reality, such an amiable situation between the directors of the T.S. and us does not exist; and that is the fundamental cause for which we will not be able to return to the headquarters of the Theosophical Society in Adyar.
>
> When Dr. Besant was alive, this problem had not posed itself, we were going to Adyar on our own account without it occurring to anyone to formulate the least objection. Dr. Besant was always delighted that we were going and, to facilitate our works she bequeathed to us a few years ago a piece of land in order that we might build a Headquarters for the Order of the Star. Once Dr. Besant became ill, we were invited in her name to move to the General Quarters of the T.S. in Adyar, something that we did.
>
> Dr. Besant being very ill and ignoring everything related to this matter, the building that had been constructed for the Order of the land that she had donated was bought by the T.S.
>
> During that visit of ours to Adyar, we discovered that the theosophical directors didn't want to have anything to do with us. And having been alienated from our building, the desire arose in us to have a house for Headquarters of our activities in Adyar itself.

While I was answering some questions in the General Headquarters of the T.S. in Adyar, the majority of the theosophical directors found that these answers were too bothersome, compromising, radical; and so it seemed to them that we shouldn't have our offices in Adyar, not even for a few months. Well C. Jinarajadasa said to us that, even though he had promised us that we would stay, he asked us not to oblige him to fulfill his promise. Facing this clear insinuation, we chose to leave.

C. Jinarajadasa was really speaking in the name of the Bishops Leadbeater and of Arundale. We will not return anymore to the General Headquarters of the T.S. in Adyar; we state this only because we have been asked why we left Adyar, not because we may want to influence the attitude of any member of the T.S. We do not have any organization which someone joins, such that we do not intend to induce anyone to abandon the T.S. in order to adhere to us.

At the end of the above report was typed by Mr. Adolfo de la Peña Gil, Secretary General:

D. Rajagopal had pronounced the previous declarations and not Krishnaji who was limited to agreeing in silence, when Rajagopal finished talking and interpreted it in order to say that he had not expressed himself with truthfulness.

George Arundale issued a special number of *The Theosophist* for November 17th in commemoration of the Society's Sixtieth Anniversary. He was asking for some competent member to write a suitable message with about 200 words in length. The message was to be written in a suitable way showing the relation of the American Section to Theosophy and the Theosophical Society. Sidney A. Cook offered this job to A.P. Warrington.

Dear Mr. Warrington,

Dr. Arundale has asked me to have some competent member prepare an article which will be one of a number that will appear in *The Theosophist* under the general heading "Sixty Years of Theosophy." Each writer is asked to write along whatever line seems to him most appropriate, from any point of view. He desires that there shall be included the opinion of the writer as to the way which he feels that Theosophy and the Society are likely to take on the approach to the seventy-fifth anniversary.

Would you undertake to be one of the contributors in this Section? The length of the article is not material, provided the matter is concise. May I count on some article from you representative of an American point of view on this subject?
Cordially yours,
Sidney A. Cook
National President

The following statement is what A.P. Warrington wrote for the issue.

If I were speaking for the American theosophists, I should, first, be mindful of America's Theosophical background and recognize that this land was not only the birth place of the Society, but of its President Founder, and the second birthplace of the President's Co-Founder, H.P.B., in a naturalization sense; that it is the cradle of the new sub-race and the future Root Race; the place where H.P.B. wrote her first awakening book; where some of the Society's most crucial struggles have taken place, (not always to the credit of some who participated), and where it is hoped some of the best solutions of her many problems will be found; where nearly 40% of the membership has resided; where there are many other Theosophical Societies besides our own, born likewise here; that it is a land where, after Adyar, the first substantial community centre was established; where an important and impressive feature of Krishnamurti's preparation took place, and where he gave his first lecture under the inspiration throughout of Him by Whom he was sent.

With this background of the past sixty years in mind, I should say that the American theosophists will do their utmost, in the period until the coming of the next Messenger, to realize H.P.B.'s ideal for the Society, which was that the present attempt in the form of our Society should succeed better than its successors have done, and that it should be in existence as an organized living and healthy body when the time comes for the effort of the last quarter of the 20th Century in the person of the next agent or messenger of the Masters.

To this end we shall do our part, as H.P.B. said, to see that the general condition of men's minds and hearts shall have been improved and purified by the spread of Theosophical teachings, and that their prejudices and dogmatic illusions shall have been, to some extent at least, removed, and this in order that the next impulse will find a numerous and <u>united</u> body of people ready to welcome the new torch-bearer of Truth, working, as we shall do, so that He shall find the minds of men prepared for His message, a language ready for him in which to clothe the new truths he shall bring, and an organization awaiting his arrival, which shall remove the merely mechanical, material obstacles and difficulties from his path. Let every Theosophist be inspired to labor for this splendid ideal.
A. P. Warrington

July 31st 1935
The American Theosophical Society
Olcott, Wheaton, Illinois

Dear Betty: (Warrington)

I am sorry to disappoint you in reply to your letter of July 29th, but our Records Office files contain no data whatever prior to 1913, nor do we have a file of magazines earlier than that date. The total membership as determined for the years 1913-1935 is 25, 410.

Since you do not state whether the twenty-two years missing in your own file cover the early years of the Society, or more recent ones, I cannot help you by giving data for any determined period, but I really wonder how you secured the total of 53,510 to which you refer. I am sorry that I cannot help you, but we have almost no information regarding the early years of our Society.

I am really disappointed that you will not be with us for Convention, but fully appreciate your reasons for not coming, and know also that you are no doubt wise, although your friends will be regretful.
With love to you,
Very sincerely yours,
(Miss) Etha Snodgrass
National Secretary

The debt from The Manor to Krotona has caused C. Jinarajadasa to send out a "help" call to all the E.S. members throughout the world to donate whatever they can to help him free the Southern Centre from this burden.

The Southern Centre

An Appeal by the O.H.

In June 1922, the Great White Brotherhood established in the City of Sydney an occult Centre, charged directly from Shambala. We were told then the reasons for such a departure, and one was that plans had already been set on foot in connection with the Seventh Root Race, whose continent will arise in the far future south of the Equator. The Southern Hemisphere will henceforth steadily grow in importance, affecting the work of both the Sixth and Seventh Root Races.

As a part of the work now and in the future, it is necessary that there shall reside in Sydney a band of devoted disciples consecrated to the Great Plan, and unswerving in their loyalty to the Masters. This band is to serve as the nucleus on the physical plane for the discharge of the occult forces necessary for the Southern Hemisphere. The Centre is to continue from generation to generation, each generation of disciples recruiting from among the members of the Esoteric School successors to carry on the work of the Centre.

The creation of the Southern Centre necessitated the organization of the members selected into a compact body; their usefulness required that as many as possible should live in close proximity, if possible in one community house or property. Several Theosophical families volunteered to make the community, and a suitable property was found. It was necessary to purchase the property, and the late D. J. J. van der Leeuw came forward enthusiastically to seize a rare opportunity to serve the Great Brotherhood. He gave towards the purchase price a gift of £5,000 and Mr. John Mackay of Sydney also gave a donation of £2,500.

The house was christened by Brother Leadbeater "The Manor", it is a large house of four stories capable of accommodating from forty to fifty persons. It is situated on a lovely spot overlooking Sydney harbour; it is near enough to the city of convenience, and yet is isolated sufficiently for its occult use. It has a large room which serves as a Temple for various ritual purposes; there is also a small Oratory, and a small E.S. Shrine. Various aspects of the joint work of the residents can thus be performed daily, before the day's mundane duties begin.

The gifts of Dr. van der Leeuw and Mr. Mackay were not however sufficient to pay for the purchase of The Manor. In order therefore to assist the Centre, Brother Besant, who was President of the "Krotona Institute of Theosophy," which was inaugurated in 1924 to be an "E.S. centre," arranged for a loan at interest from Krotona of the sum of $20,000 to complete the purchase price. A mortgage was given to Krotona, with The Manor as security, and Dr. van der Leeuw and Mr. Mackay signed a deed of guarantee.

At the creation of the Southern Centre, definite orders were given from Shamballa *to take nothing away from the Centre, but on the contrary to pour into the Centre, which was bitterly attacked by the enemies of the Great Brotherhood, all that we could in order to strengthen it.*

From the day the E.S. centre at Krotona lent a sum to The Manor, and held a mortgage over it, Brother Besant felt uneasy, because of the fact that Krotona, a centre created for the E.S., which is one occult organism throughout the world, and of which she was the O.H., was holding a mortgage over another and greater Centre, created by THE KING to serve HIS plans. Even to the last year of her life, she was anxious that Krotona should make a gift outright to The Manor of the sum due to Krotona. The Krotona trustees however felt that such a gift would be a betrayal of an unwritten trust, vested in them by the American members who had donated the funds to create in Krotona an E.S. centre for the United States. Furthermore, the cancellation would have reduced Krotona's income and created difficulties in meeting its current expenses.

In February 1929, however, Mr. A. P. Warrington, then Corresponding Secretary of the E.S in the United States, sent out an appeal to E.S. members in his Division (which then included the United States, Canada, Cuba, Puerto Rico, and South and Central America) for a fund to assist Brother Besant to liquidate some part of her debts to Krotona. The members contributed a sum of $6,600, and this amount was used to pay off apart of the sum owing from The Manor to Krotona.

The debt from The Manor to Krotona has been a shadow over the Southern Centre. The Manor meets all its current expenses and there is no loss on its working, but it is with the greatest difficulty that the yearly interest on the debt has been paid, and the debt itself has loomed over the Centre like a threatening shadow. The situation became serious during the last two years, not only because of this debt, but also because of other matters which have adversely affected the work of the Masters in Sydney and in Australia.

I saw clearly that until The Manor was completely freed from the shadow over it, little advance was possible in the development of the work in all its branches in the many countries south of the Equator.

It was this situation which necessitated my departure last February to Australia and to the United States. After informing myself of the situation in Sydney, I passed on to Krotona. I had been elected President of the Krotona Board, in my capacity as O.H., for the payment of a certain sum to Krotona, spread over a period of ten years. This adjustment permitted cancelling the debt from The Manor. The Southern Centre is at last free from the encumbrance which was weighing it down.

But I have made myself responsible that Krotona does not suffer in its capital and in its annual income, which is barely sufficient for its current needs. I have promised to pay annually, for ten years, the sum of $750, which is about £155 (one hundred and fifty-five pounds sterling).

This sum is not very large, if all members of the E.S. throughout the world will help me. I am therefore creating a special fund, to be called the "Southern Centre Fund". I should like *every member to help*, with however small a sum. While large sums are of course welcome, yet small sums will serve my purpose, which is to collect each year the sum of $750. With nearly 5,000 members in the E.S. throughout the world, the task is not heavy nor the burden great. I desire that the E.S. as a whole should reap the good karma of freeing the Southern Centre of THE KING from a burden which handicapped its growth.

Please send your donation to the Corresponding Secretary of your Division. I shall arrange with each Secretary for the sums collected to be remitted to America with as little loss in exchange as possible. If donations are sent to me, they should be in the form of banker's drafts on either London or New York. An acknowledgment will be sent for each donation received
C. Jinarajadasa, O.H.[1]

Miss Neely Ann Warrington has been ill in Hollywood, and will return to Krotona around September 17 to stay with her father for a few weeks of recovery.

Krishnamurti is now on tour of South and Central America. The following is taken from stenographers notes in Spanish, transcribed into English. Remember, there may be some different meaning to the words. This transcript took place in a private meeting with members of the Theosophical Society and Krishnamurti in Mexico, October 25, 1935.

> Krishnamurti: Now that Mr. de la Peña Gil has arrived, I am going to explain why I have wanted this meeting to be exclusively for the members of the Theosophical Society. I have heard some things that can cause a misunderstanding and I want to clarify points speaking in a very frank manner.
>
> Our intention was to stay in Mexico until the 22 of November, however we will leave on the 6th of November. We know that Mr. de la Peña Gil has been working during the last four years helping Mr. Rajagopal and me in the work that we do. I know what he has done and we are not ungrateful. When we were coming to Mexico, we wrote to him that he not mix us with the Theosophical Society; but upon arriving here there was such confusion that the newspapers said that I was a theosophist. I am going to explain why I am not, since I desire to break here with that in a final way, presenting the two situations perfectly clearly. Please do not think that I attack, but you will never be able to mix water and oil. My

---

[1] Jinarajadasa, C., *The Disciple*, Vol. I, n5, August, 1935, pp.45-49.

point of view is in fundamental opposition to that of the T.S. Your idea of Evolution is diametrically different from that which I think. For me, the idea of becoming the Disciple of a Teacher is, asking that you do not misunderstand me, totally stupid. I can be mistaken but that is my final opinion. You believe in authority and I am completely opposed to that authority; you have secret organizations to which I am opposed; you want organization around a belief and I am against these organizations; you predict one thing and I another. So, well, we are fundamentally opposed. During the last ten years Mr. Rajagopal and I have worked to extricate ourselves and we are now freeing ourselves from that, but, unfortunately, our leaders insist on our staying within this context. I and my friend refuse to take part in it because we believe that the complete picture is mistaken. When we accepted to come, we believed that everything was perfectly clear and for that we are in disagreement with Mr. de la Peña Gil. You have invited me and you have spent (wasted) money; you are the ones who are losing. I do not worry about the idea that I ought to speak in Mexico; upon arriving we thought that everything had been arranged with respect to the Theaters, money, etc., and nothing had been arranged. For this reason we have said "we are leaving" and we are to go. For the same reason we have said, "Nor are we going to Tampico nor to Guadalajara", and the money ought to be returned. Well, you see from how many points of view it is not dignified for us to stay here. If someone is interested in what I say, the next time they will arrange things better; if not, it is all the same to us, we will go to another part of humanity.

There is another point to which I would like to refer: Mr. de la Peña Gil told me that the theosophists are confused by the three meetings that we had especially for them; that they arrived with the idea that I would talk and they would listen; that they wanted to argue ideas and we insisted on a political agitation against the organization of the T.S.; that I was pushing to argue political matters because Mr. Rajagopal had some created interest. In other words, that I was an instrument in the hands of Mr. Rajagopal. I heard this from the lips of Mr. de la Peña Gil, that he is sorry personally and that the members of the T.S are also sorry.

I am going to tell you what the relationships between Mr. Rajagopal and I are. I ask that you believe me, but, in reality, I don't care if you believe it or not. And if Mr. de la Peña Gil, or anyone else believes that Mr. Rajagopal dominates me, I am very sorry, but it is not the case. He and I were educated together by Dr. Besant who always asked him to help me, and we have always acted together. I assure you that he has never tried to dominate me; he has no particular interest in that; both of us do the work; he has not been named by me as an employee or Secretary that receives a salary. Since before my brother died, and after his death, we have worked together, not as superior and inferior, I do not give orders that he has to fulfill; we think together and each one does the corresponding part of the work, being the same work, not that he does the inferior part and I do the superior. Together we returned the Castle Eerde with its 5,000 hectares; together we dissolved the Order of the Star and together we have established "The Star Publishing Trust". He does not do the business side and I the spiritual side. But, often, and especially within the T.S., they make that distinction between him and me. They believe that I am the instructor of the world and he is not. I have observed this not only among the theosophists of Mexico, but also everywhere. I want you to understand that it is he, not I, who controls. And please, see that if I am who since a few days ago began to fight the T.S. about the matter of Teachers and Disciples and things connected to it, it is because he did not concern himself with this. So, well, if he had had this suspicion, that has twisted the mentality impeding the most genuine cooperation between Mr. de la Peña Gil and us. This is how the matter has been. He thinks that putting himself in direct contact with me, he would know what Krishnamurti really wants. And as a consequence he has not paid attention to that which Mr. Rajagopal says or wants. This same thing has happened in India and in other part of the earth.

We want to do certain work and we have asked you for neither money nor cooperation. If you are interested, you will help as anyone does who is interested. In these moments, it is Mr. Garza Galindo who has offered. Because I would like to break with Mr. de la Peña Gil in a definitive way, to thank him for what the has done in the past, but definitely leave him; there has been confusion and, consequently, we wish that he no longer follows us. I repeat to you that Mr. Rajagopal and I wish to do certain work all over the world, and this work, understand me well, is <u>diametrically opposed to that work of the T.S.</u>, and naturally it will have to be in conflict with the interests of the Society. This literally happened in Adyar, where I said: "Since there is authority, there must be exploitation" and naturally no organization supports such a thing, no religion, sect nor society. So what psychologically happens is the following:

You feel, Mr. de la Peña Gil feels, the leaders feel that your work has been destroyed or at least disturbed; and in place of attacking me for that, you attack Mr. Rajagopal because I am able to be the Instructor of the World and it is necessary to be very careful with me; but since Mr. Rajagopal is nothing, it matters little. Your leaders have realized and are opposed to our action; and the same has happened here; you are nothing more that a reflection of those created interests.

With this explanation I plan to clarify the points, without any acrimony in our heart because we haven't had any. If you say that there is animosity on our part, that will be your judgment, but it will be a mistaken judgment. You are not able to give poison on one side and the remedy on the other, that is to say, to give with one hand that which I call poison: Organizations, Instruction, Teachers, and with the other the remedy, the remedy against fear, against the lack of comprehension, of intelligence. On one side you say: Religions are marvelous, necessary and authority too is necessary for spiritual growth; you say you need to become disciples of he Teachers. And then you turn around and talk about Krishnamurti who is opposed to all of that. One thing is poison and the other is something real; I do not want both things to be mixed. And as the interests of Mr. de la Peña Gil are on the side of Theosophy, on the side of the Theosophical Society, and I do not reproach him for this, for his voluntary decision, he is separated from us; the connection is broken; and I said to him, from now on it will be Mr. Garza Galindo who will take care of our matters. There is nothing ominous in this; you are losing nothing. And when on another occasion I may return to Mexico if there is money, if there is organization, if my teachings have been published, the people of the Theosophical Society will not bother me. You will be able to come to me as individuals, but I will never again write to any person of the Theosophical Society in any part of the world; since within the Society exists the mental attitude of "the more elevated and the less elevated", of Teacher and Disciple; in all areas it has tried to mix these things of the poison and the remedy, for which reason I have decided not to take part any more with the Theosophical Society.

Lastly, gentlemen and Mr. de la Peña Gil, believe me that we are very grateful for your having asked us to come to Mexico on this occasion.
Recorder: M.S. de C.

Especially among the ES members, they seem not to truly understand that within his message there is a marvelous "something"; but when he speaks and says that the Masters, Karma, Reincarnation and all these things are *POISON* and that which he says is the "truth" by which it is impossible, he affirms, to be a theosophist at the same time.

It seems that at times when statements were made at the T.S. meetings with Rajagopal, Krishnamurti and Byron Casselberry being present, it was reported that Krishnamurti said this or that; but, some reports indicated that these utterances were made by Rajagopal and not Krishnamurti. Raja was using Krishnamurti as a tool in his hands to enrich himself and to attack the Theosophical Society.

The issue regarding contributions or donations for the tour did not always come forth due to the fact the members who had contributed almost $6000 were very disgusted by their political attacks upon the T.S., and were told that no more money would be given except their lodging and railway fares to California.

The following letter was written in Spanish. The author had it translated, so, it is possible that some of the translation could have a different meaning.

Byron Casselberry, C.W. Leadbeater
The Manor, Sydney, Australia
1927

November 14 1935
Secretary General of the TS in
Mexico, DF.

My esteemed colleague:

Owing to the recent visit that Mr. Krishnamurti made to Mexico, I was able to realize the following facts:

1. Mr. Rajagopal holds a profound rancor toward the President, the Vice President and, in general, toward all those who find themselves in the forefront of our Theosophical Society in Adyar, rancor based on matters of monies and properties. He is carrying out a series of well thought out attacks on the Society.

2. The formidable battering ram with which he is attacking us in Krishnaji taking advantage of his prestige and of the respect, appreciation and affection that all of the M.T.S. have always felt for him, particularly for the magnificent teaching that we receive through his mediation.

3. The basis for many of these campaigns is being provided by the members of the Theosophical Society themselves.

Without a doubt, you probably know that, because of those attacks, the Section was damaged by the violent renunciation by the Secretary General and by divisions among its members in Uruguay and Argentina something similar happened, apparently to a lesser degree here in Mexico. After the first three special meetings for the M.S.T., in the ones in which the attacks took place and those in which I acted as interpreter, Mr. Krishnamurti as well as his inspirer, Mr. Rajagopal, were able to realize, with astonishment, that their seditious labor was failing. Well, NONE of our brothers admitted that the T.S. is pure psychological and material exploitation; there were no renunciations nor have there been up to the present day. Besides the painful disillusion of those who were waiting for other teachings classes, the most impressive silence accepted such attack; and right there, upon realizing the failure, Krishnaji announced to us that he would not go to Tampico nor to Guadalajara, two other cities that he was committed to visit during his stay in Mexico. All of our plans for public work that were beginning, and it was that which interested us the most, were then all upset. If for a reduced number in this city of Mexico, the work of Krishnaji was really illuminating, for the majority of the inhabitants of the country who obtained information only through the press (sad to confess it) it was almost a failure. There was no time to counteract the insidious work of the Catholic press, work hardly spoiled in the minds of many, through the persistent propaganda of the ideas of Krishnamurti, which during the year was verified by all of the Republic.

I do not stop considering that possibly we needed such an experience for the collapse of many fantasies that sheltered our Latin mind regarding how the external conduct of our guests ought to be. I do not stop understanding that they are performing a great service to the Theosophical Society, provoking the departure of its ranks of those members who ignored even for what purpose they became a member of the same; thus as they also provoke salutary rectifications and adjustments in the thought of who stays conscientiously in it. (the society) I have not stopped realizing, with satisfaction, that all or almost all of the M.S.T. in Mexico are now capable of appreciating the incomparable teaching of Krishnaji as a true "Water of Life" without confusing it with the aqueduct nor less even with the guardian of the same. But I acknowledge a duty on my part the warning to my dear colleagues of the Spanish-speaking Sections, of the possibility of a similar attack among them. In the face of the possibility that some Secretary General, as the undersigned did, may organize a visit by Mr. Krishnamurti to his country. I permit myself to direct you to that confidential letter with the former antecedents. Of the $7000, that the advertising cost us, the three public conferences and the semi-public maintenances here for Mr. Krishnamurti, about $5000 were contributed by members of the Theosophical Society or by efforts of theirs among friends and family members. And, in these critical present times, the use of forces and monies should be carried out with the greatest possible caution.

Greetings to you with highest fraternal esteem
Adolfo de la Peña Gil
Secretary General

A letter written to Miss Marie Poutz on November 22, 1935 from D. R. Cervera, Corresponding Secretary of the E.S. says:

Krishnaji told us (I am translating His words from Spanish into English), 'Why do you, Theosophists, give to the idea of the Masters so much importance?' Do you believe that They are necessary?' Some answered that They are necessary, but I asked Krishnaji: Necessary to what? to which He replied: 'To live the Life.' Not Krishnaji, answered I, They are not necessary in this way, but Their Teachings are useful to understand. Rajagopal told them that "necessary" and "useful" are the same thing and Krishnaji too, but I explained to them that in Spanish there is a great difference between these two words; the first (necessary) means that of which we can not perceive and the second one (useful) means something we can take if wanted or perceived of it if we desire so. We could not go to the end because some others spoke, but Krishnaji told us that the idea of the Masters, pupils, discipleship, is stupid.

Speaking of the T.S. Krishnaji told us that there is authority and consequently exploitation. I told Him that the expression of authority is the dogma and that in Theosophical Society there are not dogmas of any kind. "It is not necessary, I told, to believe in Karma or Reincarnation, even in the Masters to be a F.T.S.".

Then Rajagopal told, that I was speaking of an ideal T.S., and that the facts demonstrated that all over the world, not in Mexico probably, the F.T.S. voted in favor of Dr. Arundale because Bro. Jinarajadasa gave to publicity those two letters of Dr. Besant. I did not follow discussing this point because the solution to me, is very simple. It may be that some F.T.S. voted because they believe in the letters of our beloved Mother, or in the words of C.W.L., but it is not truth that this was the only reason for all voters.

Regarding authority, I spoke with Krishnaji in this way: Krishnaji, a man finds certain facts about the cellular constitution of the human body; those facts are necessary to physicians in order that they can give therapeutic applications; but they accept those facts which they do not know from first hand information; is this authority? Krishnaji answered: 'NO'. Then, he established some difference in the authority of the facts and the physiological authority. I did not continue discussing this, because it was very clear in my mind that authority of the facts and the physiological authority is necessary; the one imposing authority and the one who accepts it; and this is an individual business and not of collectivity of the T.S.

In another meeting Krishnaji told us that they, he and Rajagopal, shall not go back to Adyar and all that you know about the Adyar estate is not true. We love Adyar, he told, but we never will go back to Adyar. I broke completely with the T.S. Discipleship, Pupils, Masters, evolution etc., are poisons, and that of which I am speaking, are the remedy. You cannot mix them. He repeated many times that they do not have any relation with the T.S. though our leaders so pretend. He told me, he and Rajagopal do not want to form part of the T.S. picture, because all in this picture are BAD.

His teachings are wonderful; they are Theosophy, but Theosophy in relation to intelligence and conduct. There are some things he said that I do not understand, and in this case I take them away for awhile. I am sure that all is well in the T.S.

Regarding Krishnaji's and Rajagopal's attitude to Mr. Peña Gil I know he has already informed you or he is going to do so very soon. It is a long while since I have not received any E.S. papers.

Fraternally yours in THEIR service,
D.R. Cervera

Krishnamurti and his secretary Desikachar Rajagopal, and Byron Casselberry, Rajagopal's secretary was requested to travel with them, because he spoke fluent Spanish, and could translate the talks for Krishnamurti into Spanish for publication.

C. Jinarajadasa had travelled in 1934 to South America, where a Congress was held in Rio de Janeiro. He created in Rio a centre for the Southern Hemisphere, in liaison with the head centre already established in Sydney. He was sowing seeds which would germinate in that far off future for the Seventh Race.

Sailing from New York around March 3rd to Rio de Janeiro was the beginning of an eight month tour. They made a brief stopover at the Bahamas, but Krishnamurti was too shy to get off the boat. Desikachar Rajagopal left the tour in Buenos Aires because the weather was too cold, and moved to a five star hotel, and Krishnamurti and Byron Casselberry crossed the Andes to Chile in a TWA propeller driven Douglas aircraft. Rajagopal returned to America via New York City to California, and rejoined the tour in at Mazatlan and went with them to Mexico City.

On April 6, 2002 in the Krishnamurti Archives, Ojai, California, R.E. Mark Lee gave a running commentary for the silent film "Krishnamurti's Tour of South and Central America—1935". These 8 mm films shot seventy-six years ago, were a gift given to Joseph Ross from Byron Casselberry's family. It is worth viewing. Mark Lee gave the narrative with some background information, quotes from letters and press reports, and brief quotes from the Krishnamurti talks given in each country. There were not audiotapes of the talks at the time, only transcripts from stenographers notes.

Records show that Krishnamurti gave seven talks in Rio de Janeiro, Brazil in April/May; four talks in Montevideo, Uruguay in June and July; nine talks in Buenos Aires, Argentina in July and August; four talks in Santiago and Valparaiso, Chile in September; and four talks in Mexico City in October and November 1935.

Mark Lee reported that in the Foundation archives they have a complete record of this South American trip: letters, telegrams, cash accounts, the silent film, and the transcripts of the talks Krishnamurti gave.

The following circular letter to all Central-American "Sapientia" and tour Agents is sent out by D. Rajagopal.

> December 13 1935
> The Star Publishing Trust
> 2123 North Beachwood Drive
> Hollywood, Calif.
>
> During our recent visit to Mexico, we found it necessary to request Sr. A. de la Peña Gil to give up his work as the Agent in that country of The Star Publishing Trust, the "Fundación Hispano-Americana "Sapientia" and the Ommen Star Camp Foundation; and to appoint a new Agent. I need merely state that we were obliged to make this change because it is essential to keep Krishnaji's work free from confusion in the public mind, and in our own, with the work of The Theosophical Society, in which Mr. de la Peña Gil is principally interested. Our new Agent in Mexico is Sr. Agustin Garza Galindo, Apartado postal 1475, Mexico City. As you have doubtless been in touch with Sr. de la Peña Gil in connection with our work for Krishnaji I feel it advisable to inform you of this change of Agents in Mexico.
>
> Krishnaji's work is simple and direct, and those of us who help him in this work must try to make his teachings available to all without introducing our own particular interests and interpretations. The seeker has a right to know directly what Krishnaji says, and it is essential that we do not confuse the minds of people by setting Krishnaji's ideas in any special mould to which we may have become attached, or by giving them a background in which we may fervently believe. It is not our concern what our Agents and helpers individually believe; but it <u>is</u> our concern that, as Agents, they co-operate with us wholeheartedly in our work. Surely this is a natural

and a reasonable attitude to expect; and if for any reason this policy is not pleasing to some, then the right course for them to adopt would be frankly to give up their work as the Agents of The Star Publishing Trust.

If anything is not clear in this letter, I hope you will kindly write to me and I shall be very happy to explain again to you our point of view about the work.

May I request you to help the work of the Fondación Hispano-Americana "Sapientia" in Madrid by promptly settling all your accounts with them. It is obvious that we cannot continue the work of publishing Krishnaji's writings in Spanish without funds. Though donations are always welcome, I am merely asking you to pay for the books which you have ordered and received. I sincerely hope that this urgent request will receive your immediate attention.
With best wishes,
Yours cordially,
D. Rajagopal

There was a great deal of conflict with Krishnamurti's tour of South and Central America. They all felt that he willingly acted as the weapon Rajagopal was using for his attacks on the Theosophical Society. However, records show that the Mexican Section resisted firmly and was not disturbed by the attack. It seems that none of the members resigned, and on the contrary, some members who never attended the Lodges are now coming to Headquarters.

George S. Arundale, 1932

Chapter V
1936

The Krotona Library from the first day of its founding in Old Hollywood, had the desire to build up the Library as an occult, mystic, psychological, philosophical, religious and scientific source of books of real excellence, so that students might find it as a sufficiently attractive Library to draw them here for research and study.

As there is no fund for the enlargement of the considerable stock of books and magazines that have already been accumulated, it has been suggested that an application be made to E.S. members to remember the Krotona Library in their wills and when making final disposition of the books they own. Today, one questions whatever happened to that dream? For the Krotona Library today is not a true research library. It has become an ordinary second hand study room.

―⋘⋙―

Records show that Byron W. Casselberry, reported that he had a personal acquaintance with Krishnamurti during the years 1935 1936, and through that association with Krishnamurti's work, offered to give lectures to the public on the ideas of Krishnamurti throughout the state of California. Some of his lectures were held at the Masonic Lodge in Long Beach, California, Chamber of Commerce in San Diego, California, and the Odd Fellows Hall in Santa Monica.

―⋘⋙―

C. Jinarajadasa shares with the E.S. members what the difference is between their work and Krishnamurti's.

Our Work and Krishnaji

Since Krishnaji's visit to South America and Mexico last year, letters from E.S. members have been coming to me from those countries, and three Correspondence Secretaries have resigned. These letters narrate what Krishnaji and Mr. Rajagopal are supposed to have said concerning various events at Adyar in which Dr. Besant, Bishop Leadbeater, Dr. Arundale and myself were concerned. I have this day sent to them the following letter. C.J.

January 30th, 1936

Regarding the various matters which have caused you and others to resign, I have not cared to go into all the details, for it simply means arguments between myself, Mr. Rajagopal and Krishnaji. To put matters briefly I do not accept their version of events. I am aware myself of the facts, but I read them differently.

It is certainly true that Dr. Besant closed the E.S. with the permission of the Master M. She wrote me at the moment—her letter is among a mass of papers and I am sorry I cannot quote *verbatim*—that she was doing this to ease the pressure on members who felt a divergence between the teachings of the E.S. and those of Krishnaji—a divergence which she said did *not* exist. Then, she told me, when she found that closing the E.S. had devitalized the Society—an event which she did not expect—she re-opened it. The re-opening was also with her Master's consent. This will make you ask: "Did not the Master know what would happen to the Society with the closing of the E.S.?" Of course He knew, but He does not countermand the experiments of His agents, unless of course they totally upset His plan. Another instance of His not interfering was when Dr. Besant transferred *The Theosophist* to U.S.A. He certainly foresaw the re-opening. You must remember, as They have explained often, that They do not interfere in the development of events, but watch to see what is the outcome of them. The Society has, among other types of work, that of selecting such Egos as are going to work with Them in the colony of the Sixth Root Race. Therefore They permit the Society to be shaken again and again without interfering. In every case They have foreseen.

Certainly Krishnaji is a representative of the Great Teacher. But I do not admit, nor were we ever expected to, that every statement of Krishnaji's is direct from the Lord. Also we have known that, in connection with the Lord's work, while the plan was that Krishnaji was His representative in a special way for teachings, yet other parts of the Great Plan would have the Lord's agents in other departments. Various contradictions which are noted are inevitable, as now many types of force to develop many movements are being given to the world, simultaneously.

There is no desire on the part of the Masters to order aspirants to work in one way rather than in another. But what is expected is that they will not denounce or interfere with each other, which most unfortunately has been the case with a number of those who have enrolled under Krishnaji's banner. They have attacked the Society, and it has been necessary to defend the Society against their attacks.

There are all kinds of details about happenings at Adyar which are unessential in the history of events, and it is a waste of time to narrate the true story about them. I do not propose to go into them except to say that we on our side have not been intolerant, and have tried in various ways to assist Krishnaji's work. It was a part of the plan of the Lord that Theosophical teachings and the willing work of Theosophists should be the background of the new movement to be initiated by His disciple. This was the case for many years. As all now know, this has not been the case of the last few years. We have carried out the instructions received by us from the year 1910 onwards, not only from our two Masters, but also from the Lord Himself. If we have refused to lay aside our work, it is because we are true and obedient to the Lord Himself. C.J.[1]

In 1934 when the Kalakshetra School was established it was understood that it would remain on the present T.S. grounds temporarily. During Dr. Arundale's time Rukmini Devi's institutions were given concessions in rent and it was under C. Jinarajadasa's regime that no such concessions in rent were given to them. By 1936 much distress over Rukmini Devi and her institutions was causing much bitterness and litigation over what the T.S. calls "cross-currents". Kalakshetra was therefore Theosophical in the sense of

---

[1] Jinarajadasa, C., *The Disciple*, "Our Work and Krishnaji", January 1936, n6, (New Series), pp.90-92.

its being *in* the Theosophical Movement, but it cannot be called Theosophical in the sense of being *of* the Theosophical Society. By 1947 she was told to move Kalakshetra off the estate. Here is another story to be told regarding the "Disassociation Policy of the President, C. Jinarajadasa", and its relationship to the Theosophical Society.

January 6, 1936, Rukmini Devi was the catalyst in reviving the Bharatnatyam, and set up the International Academy of Arts, or Kalakshetra, as it is known today. Rukmini gave her first performance at the age of thirty-one at the Theosophical Society in Adyar, (Chennai) giving another interpretation of Theosophy, this time through "Beauty". She learnt Bharatnatyam from Mylapore Gowri Amma and Guru Menakshisundaram Pillai of Pandanallur, which is in the Thanjavur district in the south Indian state of Tamil Nadu. Kalakshetra means the *Sacred Abode of the Arts*, it was a school set up with the aim of reviving artistic traditions and inculcating among the youth the spirit of art devoid of vulgarity and commercialism. Shrimati Rukmini Devi dedicated her life to this cause. Braving the waves of modernist pseudo-artistic movements, she held to classical traditions in Indian art and with the devoted service of a band of disciples she cut away the cankers that were eating at the roots of a glorious culture.

March 26, 1936, Krotona announced that it would give auditions at the Krotona auditorium for the cast of the tuneful comic opera by W.S. Gilbert and Arthur Sullivan's "Ruddigore". The performance would be on May 1 & 2. This satire on Victorian Melodrama had a high esteem among dedicated lovers of Operas. The subtitle is "The Witch's Curse", played in two acts. It had first been performed by the D'Oyly Carte Opera Company at the Savoy Theatre in London on January 22, 1887.

On April, 7, Shrimati Rukmini laid the foundation stone at Adyar of the International Headquarters of Young Theosophists.

Miss Neely Ann Warrington had been at Krotona visiting her father for a week after a year of work in a melodrama theatre in New York City.

In 1920 the Roerichs formed the first groups devoted to the study of Agni Yoga in March of 1924 when he wrote to the President of the Theosophical Society, Dr. Besant, from Darjeeling offering to give the painting "The Messenger" to open the Blavatsky Museum, a sketch of which he had made while in America. The Canvas is at Adyar today. A small pamphlet shows reference to two great theosophical painters by James H. Cousins, written for the T.S. Jubilee Convention 1925. Nicholas Roerich's wide diversity of talents would have made him a unique individual in any area. Trained not only as an artist but he also wrote prolifically on subjects of Eastern Philosophy. A Russian branch of the Theosophical Society was founded in 1908, and Nicholas and Helena, his wife apparently joined it prior to World War II.

Because of Nicholas Roerich's books on ancient teachings of Agni Yoga, or the Yoga of Fire, C. Jinarajadasa writes the following letter to E.S. members as a warning.

> August 20, 1936
> E.S.T.
> Private
>
> I have received the following letter from one of the Corresponding Secretaries regarding the teachings of Professor Roerich:
>
>> "Prof. N. Roerich is publishing in Russian many books and pamphlets, in which he affirms he is giving a new message to the world, especially to Russians. Many of his writings are beautiful, especially when he speaks of art and beauty. His call to a spiritual life is also very fine. But his main teachings on what he calls 'Agni-Yoga', which he proclaims as being the new *Message of the White Brotherhood* and which must replace the Raja Yoga, Jñana and Bhakti Yoga, makes me very doubtful as to his wisdom. His main teaching is expansion of consciousness through the exercise of 'psychical energy'. He invites to awake the chakras, the Kundalini fire and psychic faculties without giving any ethical and physical discipline. People can eat flesh and live as before, but they must be one-pointed in their devotion to the Master and in their will to achieve. He speaks in terms of high authority. 'We',

(meaning the Elder Brethren) and many Russians think he is a great disciple or even a Master. On his books he puts a seal with a Sanskrit inscription, 'Maitreya's message'. As I have to answer many questions arising from reading those books, I will be very grateful to you, if you can throw some light on his occult position."

From another Corresponding Secretary in Europe, I received the following last January:

"The Nicholas Roerich movement has not only aimed at spreading art and protecting monuments during the war, but has propagated, through Mrs. Roerich, a great deal of occult literature wherever Russian is spoken and understood. It is asserted that his literature is directly inspired and even written by the Masters specially the Master M. A very subtle propaganda is being done through books during the last five years, stating that Dr. Besant had gone on to the left hand path, from the moment she recognised the World-Teacher in Krishnaji and to the end of her life."

There are just now in the world many types of teachings given by persons who claim to have occult guidance. Some of the teaching is harmless enough, but other teachings are distinctly harmful in dealing with occult forces, especially Kundalini. There are many persons in the astral world who are using the fact of the door between that world and this world being more open than usual to send all kinds of communications. They all claim high authority, mentioning the various Masters, and even the Bodhisattva.

The Great Brotherhood have not changed Their immemorial principles regarding occult teachings. As the Master M. stated, the E.S. is Their "normal gateway to Discipleship", and except in rare individual cases, is the only road to Them. Of course it is to be expected that slowly the world should be flooded with ideas concerning occult forces and their manipulations, but so far as I am aware, none of the Masters have any part in this propaganda. C. Jinarajadasa[2]

---

[2]Jinarajadasa, C., E.S.T., Private Paper, August 20, 1936, pp.1-2.

Deacon Henry W. Dawn was born on May 12, 1892 in Elgin, Tennessee and moved to the county of Ventura in 1936, settling in Live Oak Acres. Henry had been involved in California political campaigns since 1934, and was a member of the Ventura County Democratic Central Committee. He once registered 8,000 voters in one year. In 1964, he was chairman of the Johnson-Humphrey presidential campaign in the Ojai Valley. He ran unsuccessfully for the Democratic nomination for Congress in 1966. He served with the U.S. Army Corps of Engineers in the South Pacific during World War II, and was a member of Ventura American Legion Post No.339, the Oak View Lions Club and the Theosophical Society, Ojai.

It is reported that Henry was very active in the Ventura County Democratic Central Committee, that he was able to arrange an interview with the then Californian Governor Edmund G. Brown, pleading for a mutual arrangement of tax exemption for religious and nonprofit corporations in the State of California and the State of Maryland where the Liberal Catholic Church was incorporated. This saved the Liberal Catholic Church of Our Lady and All Angels in Ojai a large sum of money at the time that Sarah Peacock Rogers left them her fifty acres of property on Grand Avenue and Main for the development of an educational center for the clergy in the future. Early in the 1930's, the Coopers and Sarah Rogers together began buying land in Ojai, starting out with some four to five acres in the heart of the Ojai Valley (a mile and a half from the post office) which they intended to develop as a modest ranch-home, which they did.

Mr. Dawn was also responsible for signing his friend and contractor Mr. Thones for the building of the Liberal Catholic Church of Our Lady and All Angels Pro-Cathedral where it stands today in Ojai. He passed away at the age of eighty-nine in a Los Angeles veteran's facility after a brief illness.

A small twenty one page pamphlet was published by The Theosophical Publishing House, Adyar in 2003 titled "The Art of Meditation" by Marie Poutz from a talk delivered at Olcott, Wheaton, Ilinois, in the summer of 1935. It was in 1936 that "The Krotona Meditation" was started by Miss Marie Poutz. She was for a long time the Corresponding Secretary of the E.S.T. in America until her death in July 1951. The fifteen-minute meditation has continued every Monday throughout the year, holidays included. Its present form took shape around the beginning of the Second World War in answer to queries from members. "What can we do to help our world during this terrible crisis?" Marie replied—"We can think!" and built up the meditation based on a passage from an E.S. talk delivered by the late Outer Head, C. Jinarajadasa, who said:

> Every one of you, when you first came into the School as a Candidate, was put under observation by the Inner Head Master Morya and the Master associated with Him, the Master Kuthumi. You should understand why it is that They desire that you should form a unit in such an occult School as this—that is, if you are willing to train yourself to be an efficient member of it.
>
> The Inner Head, as part of His service to the world is building an invisible body on a high plane through which He desires to bring about certain realization of the Plan of the Logos. If He can build this invisible body, He will be able to influence the world's affairs in a new way through the cooperation of the many who come as its helpers.
>
> He will be the motive power of that new organism. All members of the Esoteric School will be units, cells of that body. Each of us will retain his individuality—each his temperament—each will go on his own road to deification.
>
> Yet at the same time, we can be utilized jointly as units of that invisible organization *if* we understand how to be members of it. Since the spirit of our Masters is in that body, obviously, *if* we are to be members of it, we *must share* something of Their spirit—Their nature—Their ideals.
>
> Our E.S. membership makes us "cells" in the Buddhic Body of the Esoteric School and its power constantly vivifies everything we think, feel and do! Each time we rise above our weaknesses and

reflect something of the glory of that high plane of spiritual Bliss, we bring our humanity a little nearer to its goal. [3]

It would be in 1986, that Robert and Sarah Jordan marked their 50th anniversary on November 3 at the Krotona Institute, where they have lived for forty years. The Jordans were married by the Rev. Edward Martin, who built the Ojai Taj Mahal in Siete Robles Estates. Before Robert's retirement, Robert worked for twenty-eight years as an electronic technician at Point Mugu. Sarah was very active in the Art Center, appearing in such plays as "The Cradle Song" and "The Farmer's Daughter." She was the Chief Knight for the Order of the Round Table at Krotona, a non-sectarian ceremony for children, based on the ideals of the Knights of the Round Table.

Sarah and Robert Jordan, wedding, November 3, 1936
Liberal Catholic Church, Berkely, California

---

[3] Jinarajadasa, C., *The American E.S.T. Bulletin*, "The Krotona Meditation", November, 1961, n118, p.12-13.

November 24 1936

To All E.S. Wardens
Share with your Groups

Dear Co-Workers,

Realizing that we are in the E.S. not only to grow individually in the spiritual life, but also to form a band of trained servers strongly united by bonds of fellowship in the service of the world, some of us at Krotona have from time to time formed a special Meditation Group for the purpose of furthering the spirit of unity and mutual affection in the school.

You remember that we are told a few years ago that the Buddhic body of the E.S. is already formed, though it is still imperfect and rudimentary, every activity, mental and expressional as well as physical, along lines of unity, helps to perfect that Body through which the forces of Brotherhood, of which the world is in such dire need, can be poured out.

I will therefore ask you to share this letter with the members of your Group. If even one or two in every Group, especially those who want to serve and have few opportunities for active work, will join us, we may in time build a golden life-web which will spread ever all the countries forming our E.S. Division and units of our various people in bonds of good fellowship and brotherhood. And you may be sure that such influence will not be limited to our hemisphere, for the human race is one, and what affects one affects all.

Marie Poutz
Corresponding Secretary

The following long statement by C. Jinarajadasa, Outer Head at the time of the Esoteric Section is very informative even for today.

Confidential
December 4 1936
Adyar

This paper is personal to you only. If you desire to show it to another please inform me and I will reply.

I fail to understand the following words in a letter from a distinguished brother. He states that last October, "Krishnaji told me himself that he would be willing to take the Society's proffered hand provided there would be no trace in it of the 1925 mistake". For, only last August at Ommen, Krishnaji stated his complete inability to co-operate in any manner with "the present leaders of the Theosophical Society". He stated categorically: "I will frankly say that there is no common ground on which we can meet".

Surely, therefore, there must be some misunderstanding of Krishnaji's thought and expression by our brother, for in this matter Krishnaji has been consistent for several years. In his visit to Mexico, in an address to members, he stated (I quote from a stenographic report in Spanish which I translated): "You cannot give a poison from one side and the remedy from the other, that is to say give with one hand what I call poison—organizations, discipleship, Masters; and with the other the remedy—the remedy against fear, against lack of understanding and intelligence. On the one hand you say: Religions are marvellous, necessary; and authority also is necessary for spiritual growth; you say that it is necessary that you should become disciples of the Masters. And then you turn round and speak of Krishnamurti who is opposed to all that. One thing is a poison and the other is something that is real. I do not wish that the two things should be mixed." Here in Madras, in this month of December 1936, in his discussions at Vasanta Vihar on the other side of the river, he has declared most emphatically that if any Theosophists after reading him for several years does not cast off his belief in Masters, ceremonies, etc., it is utterly useless to come to the discussion meetings.

After these very categorical statements, especially that of Ommen of last August which has been widely distributed, I really do not see how we can ask Krishnaji to modify his attitude. It is no longer "up to us" to move in the matter of any concordat. It seems to me that Krishnaji has definitely broken all bridges that existed between our work and his.

This division, which has become more and more pronounced, is fundamental, in my judgment. I do not mean to imply that Krishnaji is wrong, for that is a matter which concerns him; but I do emphatically assert that *we* are *not* wrong in carrying out to the best of our ability the work that is given to us. Undoubtedly we have made mistakes, but they are not mistakes *in principle*; if we have failed to achieve to full completion that part of the Plan entrusted to us, it is not due to a want of devotion or a lack of earnest work, but to the simple fact that we have human limitations. Knowing those limitations, the Masters nevertheless have asked us to do our best, and that we have done.

I have watched with very deep regret this division, which has been due in part to Krishnaji's attitude, but more particularly due to the action of several of his immediate circle. He denies that he has disciples, yet as a matter of fact his immediate circle play that role; they have already given the tone, often with their own commentaries, to the development of his work. It is one thing for Krishnaji to insist that each must completely stand on his own feet apart from Masters, organizations, etc. This of course is the teaching of the Lord Buddha in the Kâlâma Sutta, as it is also the teaching of *Light on the Path*; but it is quite another matter when his immediate circle trample under foot things that are held sacred by others.

I know instances of this supreme want of manners—this, I think, is the most charitable way that I can express myself—which came under my own notice. But I will not relate them, as they are incredibly shocking.

It is incredible to me that those who have been of us, whom we have ranked as having good taste, should ever descend to such behaviour. But it is to me an example of the way that the immediate circle have taken the bit in their teeth, and got out of hand, and made a definite attack on the whole idea of the Masters and Discipleship.

It is a long history to describe in detail all that has happened, but I was at Ommen in 1927 and noted then the rebellion—I can scarcely call it differently—against the teachings of Theosophy started by Mme. de Manziarly, Mr. Suarez, and others of the immediate circle. The cry then was: "Amma (Dr. Besant) is standing in the way of Krishnaji; he cannot express himself freely." This was during the house meetings before the camp.

This divergence between Krishnaji's teachings and Theosophy has been sometimes very crudely put, as the other day in Australia. The representative of the Star Publishing Trust in New Zealand was passing through Perth, and in answer to a question, "What is the relation between Theosophy and Krishnaji's ideas," he stated, "It is like cat and dog." I narrated this to Krishnaji and Rajagopal the other day (November 25). Krishnaji quietly said: "*That's about it.*" Rajagopal disclaimed any responsibility for the statements of his agents.

Krishnaji has stated publicly that the education that was given to him by the Chief and C.W.L. has been to him a handicap, and that he has had to break away from his past in order to get at the truth he desired. Since all his training was outlined in general principles by the Masters, the implication, which has been eagerly seized upon by his immediate circle, is that there are no Masters, and if there are, the Chief and C.W.L. did certainly not correctly report Their wishes. This is a very fundamental issue; it is the pivot upon which turns the whole question of the value of the T.S. and of the Esoteric School to the world.

Now, to my mind it is not possible to accept only one part of the facts and then reject the others. The part that must be accepted is that the discovery and removal of Krishnaji from an obscure environment was due to the instructions of the Masters. As was well known, he was seemingly dull in mind and there was not the faintest reason to suppose that he would amount to anything. And yet on September 2, 1909, C.W.L. reports to the Chief about him as follows:

September 2nd, 1909

Naraniah's children are very well behaved, and would cause us no trouble; van Manen and I have taught some of them to swim, and have also helped the elder with English composition and reading, so we have come to know a little of them. Also (but this is not generally known) I have used one as a case to investigate for past lives, and have found him to have a past of very great importance, indicating far greater advancement than his father, or indeed than any of the people at present at Headquarters—a better set of lives even than Hubert's, though I think not so sensational. I am sure that he is not in this compound by accident, but for the sake of its influences. I should not be at all surprised to find that the father had been brought here chiefly on account of that boy, and that was another reason why I was shocked to see the family so vilely housed, for it seems to me that if we are to have the karma of assisting even indirectly at the bringing-up of one whom the Master has used in the past and is waiting to use again, we may as well as least give him the chance to grow up decently!

October 6th, 1909

Alcyone is at present a boy of 13½, named Krishnamurti, the son of your E.S. Assistant Secretary Naraniah.... With the assistance of Mr. Clarke I am trying to teach him to speak English, and hope to have made some progress by the time you come.

Soon afterwards came one instruction after another regarding his training. Instructions were received from both Masters M. and K.H. and sometimes from the Lord Himself. At any rate this part of the Masters' orders was correct, that he should be selected and everything possible done to surround him with loving kindness, because he, though a boy seemingly dull in mind, was yet to have a very great future. Towards that future our two leaders gave their utmost, calling upon a very devoted band who stood round Krishnaji and tried to serve him. To reject all this that was done as having been obstacles in his way is scarcely justified. We on our side, in spite of many mistakes, have done our best to co-operate with the plan given to us by the Masters. Anything that has "slipped" in the great plan cannot be attributed to *our* mistakes only. I must reiterate that our two late leaders and Brother George and myself and others have done our best both to serve Krishnaji and the Masters.

I am thoroughly in accord with Professor Marcault that we are on the eve of the new year of intuition. I have been speaking on this matter often, particularly last year at Wheaton and this year in Australia. I have specially referred to Bergson. It is in connection with this new era that is dawning that we have (or should have) the special influence of Krishnaji, though he calls it "intelligence," the pretentiousness of which Bergson has so thoroughly exposed. I mentioned that to him the other day, and added that frankly those who would understand him required to have the creative spirit of art. No amount of mere mental analysis will supply that aeroplane view of his which characterizes the Buddhi. It is for this reason that though I encourage E.S. members to read his writings individually, I do not permit the Groups to study him collectively. Mental discussion does not reveal what each must discover alone for himself by his intuition of the new aspect of Truth. Naturally the view of Buddhi is not a variance with that presented by the higher mind as represented by science and philosophy, nor that of the pure emotions as represented by mysticism in religion. It supplements the gaps which exist in them. And then we must not forget that there is a higher vision still, that of the Atman. It is one thing to describe the vision of the intuition, but quite another to decry all value in Theosophy. But Krishnaji insists that a man must drop *everything* to understand Truth as he (Krishnaji) presents it.

I must here speak as the O.H. My task is a very special one of trying to bring workers for the Masters. The helping of the world is to me very much like Red Cross work during a battle. It is certainly desirable that all stretcher bearers and nurses should be experts in medicine and surgery, but that is not practicable. If, wanting that ideal state of things, no Red Cross should be organized, much preventable suffering would continue. Similarly, physicians, surgeons, stretcher bearers and nurses of another sort must be gathered for the great task of "helping to lift a little of the heavy karma of the world."

This is the fundamental task of Occultism—the calling towards Discipleship of those who are willing to work for mankind. That task was begun in the modern world by H.P.B. and was continued by Brothers Besant and Leadbeater. It is now my task, as it is too the task of Brother George and others. I certainly shall not give up this task with which I am identified heart and soul. I fear I must smile at Krishnaji's words implying that I am exercising authority through fear and that I am exploiting a band of mental slaves through promise of rewards. The only axe which I have to grind—I use Krishnaji's phrase in Ojai applied to us the friends of his youth—is to rouse the inner life in all men so that they may see the problem of life for themselves. I use every quality of heart and mind which I possess so that I may appeal to their minds and intuitions to see for themselves. I think I know fairly well my defects; of some of them I am acutely conscious, for they make me not as worthy as I ought to be of the sacred task committed to my hands. But I needs must struggle on, striving to be true to my Master and His work, in spite of my failings. It would be much much easier to follow Krishnaji's advice and retire from everything. But that would be like the Red Cross worker refusing to go into the battlefield. I know I *can* help, though I am still deficient.

Regarding the connection between Krishnaji and the Lord, I have never doubted its reality. No manifestation of the Lord through any agent can of course ever be "full" since He is the embodiment to us of the Second Logos. But there have been certain occasions when He has manifested in a manner which suggested that Krishnaji had stepped aside during the occupation. One occasion was at the end of his address under the Banyan tree in 1925 when he concluded with the words: "I come," etc. Krishnaji then told me that at that time all went black—evidently the reaction on him when the Lord spoke and not Krishnaji was then present in Krishnaji.

I believe the relation between Krishnaji and the Lord was rightly described by C.W.L. I asked him about it in 1927, and he watched, and his description was as follows: "imagine," he said, " a funnel that extends from the top of Krishnaji's head far, far up. It is elongated and narrow at the lower part, but it spreads out as it goes higher. The lower part of the funnel is Krishnaji; then, as the funnel begins to expand, the next part of it is the consciousness of the Lord; then finally, as it extends higher still, it is the Second Logos. The quality of the answers of Krishnaji depend on the part where the funnel of consciousness is tapped. Send a question which can only tap the funnel in its lowest part and then the answer is from there; but when it is a question that goes higher up, then the answer is from that higher consciousness." There is no possession involving the displacement of Krishnaji; but at those times when the answer is from the higher part of the funnel, we get some indication of what the Lord thinks, though of course it has to be phrased in the language that Krishnaji knows. We have *felt* when the thought was from the Lord. It is beautiful then, impersonal, and for all time.

I certainly shall not discard the idea of the link between Krishnaji and the Lord; but this does not blind me to the fact that often Krishnaji speaks purely on his own, manifesting often a non-comprehension of the problem of life as it impinges upon ordinary mankind. I certainly do not hold that everything he says must be accepted as representing the World-Teacher, for I think I know who He is, and what He wants done for the world, and what He wants me to do.

I firmly believe that if Krishnaji would only "let himself go" and not exclude from his consciousness that of the Lord, who meant so much to him once, there will be once again an effectiveness in his work which is sadly lacking today, (I give as an Appendix what I wrote on the matter in 1932.)

Needless to say, it is obvious to us that things have not gone "according to plan." Of course this does not mean that the Masters have failed; to the eyes of the Mahachohan, as the Master K.H. said, "the future lies like an open page." They always have a substitute plan, with a scheme of understudies, though naturally the second plan involves a loss of time. With regard to the great work of the Coming, very many things have happened which one wishes had not happened. Foremost of all is the fact that so many who were relied upon to be stalwarts have ceased to be that. The present occasion is a rare one, as comes perhaps once in 50,000 years or so, for upon the events of the present depends the establishment of a great civilization of World Peace. Naturally, therefore, all the batteries of the opposing Dark Powers have been turned upon us; so the "casualty list," to use the term describing the dead and sounded in a war is very heavy indeed.

As one looks over the past, I know we have not strictly followed out all the instructions given to us; our carelessness was due to pressure of local and immediate events. We have sometimes forgotten to carry out to the full the plan entrusted to us. But the main part of the plan, with regard to collecting a band of workers and training them as servants of the Hierarchy, has been carried out by the Chief and C.W.L., and by those of us who come in the second line after them. The result produced by us are not as great as the Masters have wished; but still, we have held things steady for the Plan, in spite of the terrific attacks launched upon us.

Looking back, I cannot help being impressed by certain facts, and one is the dissolution of the Order of the Star. Obviously it had certain defects; it was creating a cult. But to disband it completely was to me the throwing away of much valuable force in organization. I believe it was perfectly possible to remove the authoritative elements that Krishnaji disliked, and yet retain the splendid organization which we had created which would have served today as the distributors of his message, without coming in the way of its purity. The Star Publishing Trust cannot do as much as the Order would have done as a distributing agency. The casting aside of such a world organization, built *under orders* from 1911 onwards, and the result of the efforts of the Chief and her band, is to me a regrettable error. I cannot forget that in 1913 THE KING called it "the Order of My Star".

Nor can I forget how greatly it has been the wish of the Lord that those who were specially dedicating themselves to Him and to His message should get to know Theosophy well. When in 1914, certain children, after being put on probation by the Master K.H., were presented to the Lord, He said to them: "Learn as much as you can of Theosophy, for the more you know the more useful you will be to Me". Similarly, too, later in 1931, when so much was being said in depreciation and denunciation of the work of the Society, the Lord addressed some of His hearers at the Asala festival, beginning: "You who are members of our Theosophical Society." It was never intended that the great Theosophical philosophy should be denounced as leading to exploitation and as causing fear. I quote two other occasions when the Lord spoke of the Society and its work. Brother C.W.L. wrote to the Chief as follows:

Sydney, August 8th, 1916

Some very interesting points emerged in a recent conversation with the Bodhisattva. He explained that the work of the Theosophical Society is definitely part of the preparation for His Coming, and that it is His wish that it should in various ways show the world how things should be done—that it should along several lines establish a form and set an example. [Here follow the instructions as to the activities—Education, L.C.C., Co-Masonry, Mystic Star.]

Sydney, August 22nd, 1916

In continuation of what I wrote last week, it would be well for me to mention a further remark made by the Lord Maitreya. Having another opportunity of approaching Him, I asked whether He wished those activities of which He had spoken to take to some extent the place of our present Theosophical meetings. he replied: "No" for all these forty years Theosophy has been establishing itself, making its way intellectually; it should continue at its ordinary meetings to set an example of what a lecture should be, and with what subjects it (the lecture) may most usefully concern itself; but Theosophy should also lead the way in those other lines of which I have spoken to you."

To sum up, Krishnaji's immediate circle still think that if our late Chief were living everything would be different, and that she would throw in all her weight with his work as he is doing it now. She certainly never modified her belief that he was the messenger, but she held that his message in its entirety was not necessarily for the actual present, but far more for the future. She had explained how each Teacher came to lay the foundation for the building of the civilization of the sub-race to come. I remember vividly in 1927, when our Theosophical ideals were being denounced by Krishnaji's immediate circle at Ommen, that the Chief in one of her addresses pointed out that the ideal of Liberation was very beautiful, but there was something to her more beautiful still, and that was to renounce Liberation to order to help mankind. Her Master had done that, and she would follow Him. She refused to subscribe to the idea that ceremonials were superstition, for when rightly understood and performed, they were to her means for producing results with greater economy of force than when done without ceremonials. They were not to her necessary in any way for the spiritual life, but they were an instrument.

Her own thought concerning what had been happening up to 1932 is represented by two instances which happened in 1932. On May 11, she asked me to wire to Krishnaji the following which at my request she dictated: "We send you our deepest love on your thirty seventh birthday and are eagerly watching your work in the outer world." Immediately after dictating she said to me: "I don't think we can do anything much. We can try to co-operate with him in so-far as he wishes it. In some ways, there may be difficulties which we can clear out of the way; but we cannot do much. It is a strange business altogether." Once before, after the E.S. was reorganized in 1928, she told me that some day perhaps he might find the E.S. as the only body of people who would help him.

The next day, May 12th, she happened to look at Krishnaji's picture as a boy and said a few words, which I felt bound to communicate to him. Only to very few, perhaps to half a dozen at most, have I mentioned those words of hers. But as matters have turned out, I think it is my duty now to mention them, though I do not wish them ever made public. She said: "I suppose one ought not to be disappointed, but I thought he would do bigger things."

I should also like to point out that there are many statements on record by Krishnaji himself, of his own direct knowledge, with regard to the reality of the occult world. The most beautiful is that written out by him in Ojai in 1922. This was after those striking experiences which he went through, which have been described in detail by Nitya, and which some of us have read. At the end of them Krishnaji wrote out a statement, mentioning how in Sydney in May 1922 he received a message from the Master K.H. and how he thought over it long, and how then at Ojai he tried experiments in meditation. He then found the higher consciousness easily opening to him. He then describes the experiences that he went through, and concludes his statement with that exquisite poem which was called "The Hymn of the Initiate Triumphant". A part of this was published in *The Herald of the Star*, but not the full hymn. Were this statement of his to be made public, everyone would see that whatever may be his present reversion for the Masters, there was at least a time when he had a direct knowledge of Them, and knew the persons of the Master K.H., the Lord and the Lord Buddha also.

I would like to state once again that in the instructions received, the Lord Himself asked us to see that Krishnaji understood Theosophy, as a knowledge of the great truths were essential for the Lord's work through him. Krishnaji and Nitya, however, never cared to understand what Theosophy is as a philosophy, though of course they attended dozens of lectures of the Chief, C.W.L. and others. I must admit that right from the beginning Krishnaji evinced no desire to understand the great philosophy, so that his remarks in these days implying that Theosophy is valueless are not based on any knowledge of it. I tried to interest him in Theosophy, but somehow I never captured his imagination nor Nitya's.

I think it may be useful to add to this long statement, as an appendix, a letter which I wrote in 1932 to a few of Krishnaji's immediate circle.

Appendix I

Adyar, July 15, 1932
To Lady Emily, Rajagopal, Dwarkanath, Padmabai and Sanjiva Rao.

I know that I can write frankly to you and I do so. I have here at Adyar two accounts, by Lady Emily and Rajagopal, of the wonderful scene at Eerde a certain morning in 1926 when the Lord Maitreya was in Krishnaji's body. It was when Jadu fell at His feet. All present saw or felt the change then.

But from 1927 onwards much has happened. I was present that year at Eerde before the Camp when began that curious rebellion against Theosophy and the T.S. It was then that the statement was made that "Amma is standing in the way of Krishnaji". From then on steadily, the whole trend of the movement has been—to put matters bluntly—in marked opposition to Theosophy, and particularly to the whole conception of the Masters. Initiates have "resigned" their Initiations, and dozens of Pupils have turned their backs on the Masters and on all that once seemed vital to them. That does not matter, except to themselves; but there is something of far greater consequence.

It is the definite closing of the door against the Lord Maitreya. Krishnaji's disciples have given up as a Theosophical superstition, along with the Masters, this the most vital part about Krishnaji. Again to put things bluntly, they admire Krishnaji, believe in him, but they want to ignore the Lord. The "World-Teacher" idea has been thrown overboard, or so whittled down that the phrase "world-teacher" (no capitals now: see *Bulletin* May-June) is *anybody* "who has realised the Truth". *The Lord Maitreya is no more wanted.*

The result is that, as I see it the influence of the Lord is more and more narrowed down. It certainly is coming thro' Krishnaji. But more that could come—as when Jadu fell at His feet—is shut out. And the world loses.

So far as the Society is concerned—again I speak frankly—it has been struck at its most vital part—the recognition of the Masters. That was what happened in 1884 with the Coulombs, when the public were given to understand that They were invented by H.P.B. and so non-existent. Today, Their existence is not denied, but They are stated *as of no value* to Humanity. The Society has been shaken to its foundations, in every Section. It is recovering slowly. But our loss has been over 4,000. How much our own people—T.S. leaders, I mean—have contributed is another matter. But the world knows Krishnaji's attitude to the Society's work. Not a newspaper man who does not know that he has said that Amma started him on a road which was the wrong road, and that he had to find the right road for himself.

And the result of it all? Certainly the Society has suffered, *but the Star more.* Eerde has one; who would have dreamt of such a thing?

In India we are barely carrying on—on how long who shall say? Of course Krishnaji will go on giving more and more teachings—most valuable and inspiring.

But is it to be, that we say to the Lord Maitreya, the Saviour of the World, "Thank you, but we do not need You." That is what is happening now, in all this throwing overboard of Occultism. Is that to be the policy of those who stand nearest to Krishnaji?

There is on record what the President once day-dreamed about, when Krishnaji would begin his work—how India would be affected as the Lord trod again the ways of men. Somewhere too there is a peroration of mine of a Star lecture when I prophesy the changes brought about at the Coming in Religion, Science, Art, and how Nature responds*. (*I print it as Appendix II.) Were we but false prophets? Or is that aspect of the Coming still to come? Of this I feel sure: if that aspect of Him is barred from manifesting through Krishnaji, it will manifest through some other or others, that the world be helped. Who they be I do not know, nor care, though I shall nearly weep if it did *not* come through Krishnaji.

Is the Lord then not wanted, neither by Krishnaji, nor by those who are his "staff"? That is the problem to which I draw your attention.

Appendix II

(*Address at the close of the Post-Covention programme, Chicago, September 12, 1911, by C.J.*)

When the Great Teacher comes, perhaps we, who study the great problems, shall know more than others what shall then happen to men, for when a great Son of God moves among men it means that the divinity in each shines brighter, is more forceful. When that day shall come (and some of us will see it in the flesh), then it is that every dream that we have had in our human hearts will be brought nearer to realization; then the artist will see greater beauty in the world, the scientist will see a more magnificent synthesis than has ever come to him, and the philosopher will see pregnant before him a diviner conception; then each individual who has had to bear his cross will realize with a quickness and a power what, perhaps, he can only believe in today, that life is not a cry but a song. It is that realization of the song which is the under-current of all life that will be given to us by the Great Teacher when he comes, and it is our duty today to go into the world, where there is so much evil and suffering, to proclaim that there is that song, which we shall all hear the more clearly as we work for our fellowmen. We part today, but in a year's time we shall met again, each after a year's labour "rejoicing, bringing his sheaves with him."

Conclusion

And so I end this long statement with a question and its answer.

"Has the Lord come?"

"Yes—and No."

I have not lost all hope yet.

I still dream a dream.

Adyar, December 16, 1936

C. Jinarajadasa

By July 1938, C. Jinarajadasa publishes in *The Disciple* for members of the E.S., an article where he reprints what he translated in the above confidential statement, but with added comments.

Theosophy and Krishnaji

I have had to make the statement that follows in Brazil and Uruguay, the two countries so far visited. The visit of Krishnaji, accompanied by D. Rajagopal, to South America and Mexico in 1935, produced naturally a kind of shock to the work of the Theosophical Society. This was not due so much to his teachings, as to his emphatic declaration of the utter incompatibility of his teachings with those expounded by Theosophists. His words in Mexico were as follows (I quote from a stenographic report in Spanish, which I translate):

"You cannot give poison from one side and the remedy for the other, that is to say give with one hand what I call poison—organizations, discipleship, Masters; and with the other the remedy—the remedy against fear, against lack of understanding and intelligence. On the one hand you say: Religions are marvellous, necessary; and authority also is necessary for spiritual growth; you say that it is necessary that you should become disciples of the Masters. And then you turn round and speak of Krishnamurti who is opposed to all that. One thing is a poison and the other is something that is real; I do not wish that the two things should be mixed."

In all my Theosophical life, I have never heard the statement that "authority is also necessary for spiritual growth". Authority is necessary, *not* for spiritual growth, which is a matter of personal reactions to the events of life, but for the carrying out of definite plans of *work*, under the direction of a chief of work, under whom one enrolls oneself voluntarily, and whom one leaves when his orders are not to one's liking.

One matter that has surprised me is the creation in Rio de Janeiro of a group by Krishnaji during his stay called "The Krishnamurti Cultural Association". The group is merely to organize the work of disseminating his addresses through translations; but that he should permit his name to become a distinguishing label for any kind of an organization, even solely for printing and publishing, has surprised me. It has also created a new and unnecessary term in Brazil "Krishnamurtiano"—Krishnamurti-ites, to distinguish such a follower from the term "Tesofista"—Theosophists.

All these matters have necessitated the following statement from me "to clear the air." In Brazil especially, the Society has been seriously weakened; my task, during the ten weeks in the country, has been not only to present Theosophy to the public, but also particularly to strengthen the small band who have remained faithful, but who have to battle against many unnecessary obstacles created by the unfortunate situation.

Statement by C. Jinarajadasa

I think I may claim to know Krishnaji fairly well. During the two years, 1912-1913, Dr. Besant gave him and his brother into my charge, and I was during that period a kind of father mother, brother, tutor, nurse and guardian, and we lived in close intimacy. We traveled together, I of course being always in charge of them and their welfare. I think during such an intimacy one gets to know each other well.

Twice, during the period I was with him, I have seen that great change, when for a few moments the boy was the vehicle of Someone greater. The Great Person is called the Lord Maitreya, the Teacher of Teachers. Who is He and what is He? On the right understanding of His nature much depends.

I do not presume to lay down the law for the belief of others; but He has been known to me, at least by tradition, since boyhood, for Buddhism proclaims Him to be the successor of the Lord Gautama Buddha. In occult tradition, He was the Christ who taught for three years in the body of His Disciple Jesus. Later, in my own inner life, I claim to know Him directly for myself.

Now, it is He who has planned to bring about a great change in human affairs, by giving to the world a new embodiment of the Ancient Wisdom. As a preparation for this work, our Theosophical Society was founded by two Adepts who are His Disciples.

It was a part of His plan that His disciple Krishnamurti should be a channel of the new teachings. When occasion might arise, the disciple would temporarily step aside, and the Lord would speak directly. Such an occasion arose in 1925. I was present on the platform, on December 28, when Krishnaji spoke, and at the end came the startling words:

> I come to those who want sympathy, who want happiness, who are longing to be released. I come to reform and not to tear down. I come not to destroy, but to build.

I believe there were two wonderful occasions in 1926 when a similar event happened at Ommen, but I was not then present.

I was never told that every word that Krishnaji would speak would be spoken by the Lord. The Lord has charge of the sixty thousand millions of souls who are our humanity; His influence has to irradiate through every existing religion, and since all prayers to

God ascend through Him and the response descends through Him, it is obvious that it would be only occasionally, when a special work needed to be done, that He would manifest through the body of His disciple. Nor must we ever forget that when He so does appear, it is only a fragment of His transcendental nature that can ever be manifested on the physical plane.

It was, and is, a part of the plan of the Lord that His disciple Krishnamurti should know Theosophy well and intimately, and that he should be the greatest exponent of Theosophy; for, as the Lord Himself said, He came "to build, not to destroy".

In all that has since happened, my criterion of judgment is: Is what Krishnaji is saying and doing helping to destroy or to build? I do not ask anyone to accept my criterion of judgment. I may be completely mistaken, and I know that many are convinced that I am mistaken. All the same, I believe what I think I know.

Krishnamurti has stated—not in my presence, but others whose word is reliable have told me—that he has had no proof of the existence of the Masters, and that he knows nothing of Them. I think he must have forgotten some of his past experiences. I have, here in Rio, what he wrote in September, 1922, describing the experiences that he then went through, when clairvoyance came to him, and he knew the presences of the Lord Buddha, the Lord Maitreya and his own Master K.H. I have in Adyar letters of his to Dr. Besant which describe his knowledge of the Masters. If today he says that he knows nothing about Them, and that he has had no direct knowledge of Them, I can only presume either that he has forgotten, or that he now thinks that he was deluded when he had the experiences which he has put on record in his own handwriting. When this experience of meeting the Great Teachers happened to him, he was in California; he was then twenty-seven; Dr. Besant was in India and Bishop Leadbeater in Australia.

Krishnaji, to me, is emphasizing one aspect of the Ancient Wisdom. This Wisdom proclaims that there are two modes of arriving at Truth and Liberation. One mode is by concentrating on individual purification and perfection, leaving aside for the time the problem of opening the gates of the Kingdom of Happiness for others to enter. The second mode is by taking one's character as it is, with all its imperfections, and using it to lessen the misery and ignorance of others. through the experiences gained in such work, there arises slowly a purification of the character, and so Liberation is achieved. Krishnamurti emphasizes the first path; necessarily he ignores the second path, which is represented by the work of Theosophists, who are trying to help to build a new civilization.

I thoroughly disagree with Krishnamurti when he says that the work of the Theosophical Society is an obstacle to the helping of humanity to happiness. We, Theosophists, have many failings, and any criticisms which he makes of us must be well considered by us, for our desire is to work more efficiently in the cause of humanity. But though he criticizes us, he knows nothing of Theosophy and its magnificent outlook; he has never studied it, which is a great pity. If he had studied it, I think he would realize how a preliminary study of Theosophy helps to understand and to elucidate many aspects of his teachings, which without Theosophy remains confused in the mind.

While thoroughly disagreeing with him about what he says concerning our Theosophical work, I am a great admirer of his message. He speaks directly of his own, and does not base himself on any tradition. His imagery is marvellous and full of illumination. He is to me a brilliant exponent of one aspect of Theosophy. The Theosophical Society, however, must not limit the freedom of those who seek to find other aspects of Theosophy as well; and it should not, in my opinion, throw its weight more on the teachings of Krishnamurti however brilliant and needed they are, than on the doctrines of any other teacher.

What Krishnamurti teaches does not lessen certain facts which I know for myself; that the Masters exist; that because They exist, I am inspired in my struggles to be nobler, purer and a more effective idealist; and that the work of the Theosophical Society has been of immense benefit to millions, helping them to discover the light which is within themselves, and teaching them to work together for the cause of humanity as one whole. C.J.

There are so many Adyar E.S. documents containing sentences, and paragraphs all relating to Krishnamurti's talks, and the reactions within the inner circles of the Theosophical Society that we may never see and read. All of these E.S. documents will be invaluable for scholars who would like to recover a more realistic sense of the inner workings of Theosophy in the early years even to the present time. To date few scholars, if any, have access to Adyar E.S. material held at Adyar, (Chennai) at the Theosophical Society. Many documents may already be lost, or destroyed so as to make it easy to rewrite the Theosophical Society's history. It is particularly important that a few E.S. documents at least should survive within the Ross Collection.

Around November 23rd, 1935, C. Jinarajadasa met with Krishnamurti as he began his meetings which would continue three times a week. They were attended by invitation only. About thirty or forty from Adyar were invited. Rukmini and C.J. sat in the front row listening to the same old questions. C.J. said in a report:

> "Krishnamurti did not give an address but wanted a discussion, which finally got nowhere. I had much rather hear him for 20 minutes than these discussions trying to make people understand. I think even *our* people have not realized that he is presenting a vision which is not of the mental plane but from the Buddhic, and therefore one has to approach what he says as the creative artist and not as the scientist and philosopher."

According to the theosophical teachings, Krishnamurti lives consciously on the Atmic level. We will paraphrase from a very long London lecture given in 1907 by Annie Besant, and try to share an understanding from the theosophical point of view regarding Krishnamurti's quality of wholeness as she puts it. The verbatim lecture is kept in the Adyar Esoteric Archives, and is not available for research at this time.

"Living in full consciousness in that powerful vibration, He has no sense of bondage in any form with which He may ally Himself;" such a being has thrown away the fetters of desire for life in a form or body, or even for life without a form. He is therefore utterly free, and so wide is His awareness that His *waking* consciousness includes all five levels! You and I may have a waking consciousness confined to the physical world or physical-astral, which actually means being self-conscious on the astral level, and aware of its inhabitants. In such a case we would be able to be with our loved ones who have passed on. That would be a high state of development so far as awareness is concerned. But He, the great being is aware in His *waking consciousness* on all five levels: physical, astral, mental, buddhic, atmic!

"We may, then, define the position of the Master, (Krishnamurti) as that of a Person who has reached liberation, i.e., He is living in the Spirit consciously, in conscious relation to the Monad above the Atma, and as the result of the center of consciousness being in the Monad, the whole of the five planes become part of His waking consciousness! In regard to the bodies or vehicles, however, there is this difference: the *whole* of the five bodies of these planes of action, *act for Him as a single body, His body of action!*" Like the solids, liquids, gases and ethers act for you and me to form a single physical body which is our center of consciousness. We can therefore realize somewhat what a tremendous power of understanding He has. "But the Master, as Master, is a man, and the manhood must never be forgotten."

"These Great men stand today as the promise of what humanity shall be, the first-fruits of humanity as it is. They are specially concerned with the direct teaching, training and helping of man, in quickening his evolution; and the reason the body is retained is in order that this close personal touch may be kept, primarily with Their disciples, and then through these with comparatively large numbers of people."

"A distinguishing mark of a Master, His chief function, it seems, is to perform the greatest act of sacrifice which is known in the Occult Hierarchy, save the act of the ONE who is called the *Great Sacrifice*, the Silent Watcher.

"The particular act of sacrifice made by Those spoken of as Masters, occurs from time to time at the beginning of a new epoch in religion and civilization. It is performed by one of the Occult Body, volunteering to start a further spiritual impulse in the world, and bear the karma of the impulse that He generates. That may not appear at first glance to be such a transcendent act of sacrifice as it really is. It may seem a comparatively small thing to initiate a new epoch, and very vague ideas of what is implied in the statement 'bearing the karma' may formulate in the mind, if indeed any attention is given to it.

"The great act of sacrifice lies not only in the truth that He must wear a physical body of heavy material which hampers Him considerably, but that He *cannot lay that body aside once* He has used it for giving this great spiritual impulse, *until that impulse is entirely exhausted*, and the religion or association to which the impulse has given birth has vanished out of the physical world!

"Such a sacrifice cannot be imposed, of course, for it is always a volunteer who comes forward, a volunteer who knows what it entails, and therefore faces up to the full meaning of it. This is the central idea of the act of sacrifice, and it becomes even more a sacrificial act, in that the One who undertakes this tremendous task cannot tell how the impulse will flow in all its details, cannot even estimate the amount of difficulty, delay, even of mischief that may grow as a result!"

Free Will is a gift to every living thing and Spiritual Adept Leaders are scrupulously careful to abstain from even a whisper of interference. Furthermore, "the Master Himself is limited by the physical body and cannot continuously use the *whole* of His vast consciousness within the limits of a physical brain, since He will be restricted by the activities which must be assumed when working in the unplastic matter of the physical element. Therefore, when undertaking a work like this, of starting a great movement like the Theosophical Society, He generates causes whose effects He cannot thoroughly calculate. He takes the risk that surrounds every great undertaking. Even though His waking consciousness can be centered in the Atmic body, viewing life from that eminence, He has to limit Himself to the lower vehicles as the centre of waking consciousness when working with a new spiritual effort. He submits Himself to the conditions of this task upon which He enters, and is obliged, having once taken it, to bear it until success or failure has crowned the effort that He makes."

It is said that "the Masters who had to do with the inception of the great religions of Egypt, Chaldea and others, have long since cast away Their physical bodies, and thereby ceased to be what we call Masters, because the religion that each gave to the world had done its work, and no souls remained who could be further helped by passing through the training and teaching that they gave."

"This difference between Adepts of the same high grade and Masters Who give the impulse to a new religion or philosophy, is very illuminating, the Adept apparently Who works along other lines not involving humanity's religions, does not need to encumber Himself with the physical body. The Master *must* keep the physical body for contact in spite of its many deficiencies and burdensomeness. Those who are growing old and find the body to be obstructive and an obstacle can have some *faint* idea of the sacrifice involved in keeping one usable over long periods of time!

"When, therefore, a Master volunteers to serve as what may literally be called the scapegoat of a new spiritual movement, He takes up a karma whose whole course He is unable to foresee,"

To close this chapter, Krishnamurti on May 10, 1936, was asked the question: *Are you, or are you not, a member of the Great White Lodge of Adepts and Initiates?*

> Krishnamurti: Sir, what does it matter? I am afraid this country, and especially this coast, is inundated with this kind of mystery, which is used to exploit people through their credulity and fear. There are so many swamis, both white and brown, who tell you about these things. What does it seriously matter whether there is a White Lodge or not? And who talks or writes about these mysteries except those who, consciously or unconsciously, wish to exploit man in the name of brotherhood, love and truth? Beware of such people. They have set going incredible and harmful superstitions. Often I have heard people say that they are guided by Masters who send out forces, and so on. Don't you know, cannot you perceive for yourself that you are your own master, that you create your own ignorance, your own sorrow, that no other can by any means free you from suffering, now or ever? If you discern this fundamental fact, truth, law, that you create your own limitation and sorrow, that

you yourself help to bring about a system which exploits man ruthlessly, and that out of your own inner demands, fears, and wants, are created religious and other organizations for cunning exploitation, then you will no longer encourage or help to create these systems. Then authority ceases to have any significant position in life; then only can man come to his own true fulfilment.

This demands a tremendous self-reliance. But you say: "We are weak and must be led; we must have nurses." Thus you continue the whole process of superstition and exploitation. If you will discern deeply that ignorance is perpetuating itself through its own action, then there will be a profound change in your relationship to life. But I assure you, this demands a deep comprehension of yourself.[4]

---

[4]Krishnamurti, J., *The Collected Works of J. Krishnamurti*, Volume III, 1936-1944, Dubuque, Iowa, 1991, Kendall/Hunt Publishing Co., "Sixth Talk in the Oak Grove", Ojai, California, May 10, 1936, pp. 25-26.

1925 Adyar Convention

C. Jinarajadasa, 1935 in Ceylon
"Brother Raja"

Chapter VI
1937

George S. Arundale shares his thought: "The Truth shall make you free, for it is only Truth that can ever give freedom to anyone. So long as teaching remains teaching, so long as doctrine remains doctrine, so long as authority remains authority, so long as argument remains argument, Truth has not yet come, for the essence of Truth is individual experience. But where there is experience, there is Truth, and there alone is Freedom. Freedom which is real is Truth, and Truth which is real is Freedom. All else is at best but the way to Freedom-Truth."

Dr. Arundale, gave instructions when he gave his Yoga talks, as to how we were to listen, not with mind, or emotion, not with tenseness or strain, but quietly, easily, fully relaxed. If that could be done, something quite out of the ordinary would happen.

January 11 1937
The American Theosophical Society
Olcott, Wheaton, Illinois

Dear Mr. Warrington: (from Sidney Cook)

I have been thinking that there ought to be an authentic history of the Theosophical Society in America. There is much of the history that will be lost unless in each generation the record is made. I suppose material is available in some considerable measure and a great deal of research would discover it, but I know of no one who would properly utilize that material and write it up with understanding, except some Theosophist who has been a part of the Society's development and has seen that development with an understanding of the value of incidents and trends.

I thought you might like to undertake to write this history. I don't know that we could afford to publish it for some time to come. It is not the kind of thing that has much sale, but is the kind of thing that ought to be on record. I don't think we could afford to pay to have it done or that it would produce anything in royalties. It would be purely a gift to the Society.

I haven't consulted our Board about this idea. It may be entirely impractical. I am simply passing it along for your consideration. Many people would say probably that it was a useless undertaking, but the course of development of the Theosophical Society I think is something that the people of the future should have an opportunity to know. There must presently come a time when the beginnings of the Ancient Wisdom as a philosophy in America will be a matter of much more general interest than it is at present.

I know that you have been quite ill but hear that you are recovering, for which we all have reason to be joyful.
Cordially yours,
Sidney A. Cook
National President

In the January issue of *The Disciple*, C. Jinarajadasa stated that the last line in the Invocation, *O Hidden Life* has sometimes been recited as "Know he is also one with every other." He said: "This is an error, and that the line should be as originally written by Brother Besant: "Know he is *therefore* one with every other." In *The Disciple* for July, 1939, C. Jinarajadasa draws attention to the fact that the Invocation was written for the use of theosophists. The later form: "Know he is also one with every other," was the modified form which Dr. Besant gave for use by the Boy Scouts of India.

C. Jinarajadasa writes in the January issue of *The Disciple* for E.S. members, a clarification of what happened at Ommen last August as the result of Krishnamurti's talk. We will read how he has to repeat history of what had taken place in the early years to clarify his point of view.

The Society and Krishnaji

I REGRET greatly that Krishnaji last August, in a statement issued at Ommen, has completely barred the road towards any cooperation on our part with his work. He stated as follows:

> Then, I am constantly asked, both privately as well as at meetings, whether the relationship between the present leaders of the Theosophical Society and myself is not that of friends working together in a common cause although

along different lines. Many persons have a fixed idea that this is so, and they desire to have any misgivings on this point cleared up. I have already stated publicly a number of times, in answering questions put to me, what my attitude is towards the Theosophical Society or any religious or other organization which has a so-called spiritual basis or purpose. Such an organization, from my point of view, cannot help man to understand himself, and to understand oneself. I consider to be the true spiritual state; and this state cannot be brought about through a belief or through following any system or method.

However, since in spite of my repeated answers, the question is constantly asked me regarding my attitude towards the present leaders of the Theosophical Society and their work, I will frankly say that there is no common ground on which we can meet. There can be cooperation only when there is an intelligent common objective, which at present does not exist, although many people are asserting that it does.

This situation was foreseen by Brother Besant in 1932. On May 11th of that year, she asked me to wire to Krishnaji the following which at my request she dictated: "We send you our deepest love on your thirty-seventh birthday and are eagerly watching your work in the outer world." Immediately after dictating she said to me: "I don't think we can do anything much. We can try to cooperate with him in so far as he wishes it. In some ways, there may be difficulties which we can clear out of the way, but we cannot do much. It is a strange business altogether." Once before, after the E.S. was reorganized in 1928, she told me that some day perhaps he might find the E.S. as the only body of people who would help him.

I want to put on record what she said concerning this division between the teachings of Theosophy and those of Krishnaji. Writing to me on October 24, 1928, concerning the suspension of the School, she wrote:

> I am going to suspend it for a time, to relieve the strain on those who feel a contradiction (which is unreal) between the old teachings and the new.

There is no question whatsoever that the Lord Bodhisattva desired a close cooperation between The Society and His messenger. On several occasions He has advised young pupils of the Masters to know Theosophy well. When in 1914, certain children, after being put on Probation by the Master K.H., were presented to the Lord, He said to them: "Learn as much as you can of Theosophy, for the more you know the more useful you will be to Me". In the instructions given in 1913 by the Lord regarding Krishnaji's training, He said:

> Knowledge there must be, but first and most of all a knowledge of Theosophy. He must be an enthusiast of it, the greatest living authority upon it, and the important thing is the Theosophical attitude; to be able by means of that to pronounce unerringly with regard to worldly problems, to decide instantly between right and wrong. All other lines, whatsoever they may be, must be recongised as subsidiary to this; art, music, poetry, philosophy, science, religion, history—all these are good, but all only methods of expression and illustration, only channels or lenses through which shines forth the sun of Theosophy.

Similarly, too, later in 1931, when so much was being said in depreciation and denunciation of the work of The Society, the Lord addressed some of His hearers at the Asala festival, beginning: "You who are members of our Theosophical Society." The full address of the Lord, as reported by Brother Leadbeater, was printed in *Shishya*, September, 1931, p. 8-10.

It was never intended that The Society should be denounced as leading to exploitation and as causing fear. I quote two other occasions when the Lord spoke of The Society and its work. Brother Leadbeater wrote to Brother Besant as follows:

Sydney, August 8th, 1916

Some very interesting points emerged in a recent conversation with the Bodhisattva. He explained that the work of the Theosophical Society is definitely part of the preparation for His Coming, and that it is His wish that it should in various ways show the world how things should be done—that it should along several lines establish a form and set an example. [Here follow the instructions as to the activities—Education, L.C.C., Co-Masonry, Mystic Star.]

Sydney, August 22nd, 1916
In continuation of what I wrote last week, it would be well for me to mention a further remark made by the Lord Maitreya. Having another opportunity of approaching Him, I asked whether He wished those activities of which He had spoken to take to some extent the place of our present Theosophical meetings. He replied: "No; for all these forty years Theosophy has been establishing itself, making its way intellectually; it should continue at its ordinary meetings to set an example of what a lecture should be, and with what subjects it (the lecture) may most usefully concern itself; but Theosophy should also lead the way in those other lines of which I have spoken to you."

As to all that has happened, of course the Masters must have foreseen much, for it has been said of the Lord Mahachohan that before His eyes "the future lies like an open page." But the Masters do not warn us beforehand of possible lack of fulfilment; on the contrary They urge us to try to surmount all obstacles, even if They do not mention those obstacles.

As Brother Besant remarked: "It is a strange business altogether". Personally I have not yet lost all hope that the work as planned will be accomplished in some measure.[1]

Jan 22 1937
Prof. J. E. (Emile) Marcault
University of Paris

Private and Confidential

Dear Raja, (C. Jinarajadasa)

I have your printed letter of Dec. 4th 1936, and meant to have replied more fully to its contents, but have had too much on my

---

[1] Jinarajadasa, C., *The Disciple*, "The Society and Krishnaji", January, 1937, n8, (New Series), pp.135-138.

hands recently to do so. I therefore send you an account of my conversation with the Chief in 1927.

It seems to me, and I know that it will seem to Krishnaji also, that your comments cut across an already grown plant and do not go to the root of the problem. The root is the discrepancy between the description given in advance by our Leaders of the foundation of a new sub-race, and the actual facts as they happened within Krishnaji's experience when his mission began, and especially the occupation of the "BODY" theory; also the organizations erected in 1925 as a frame for the future coming thus described.

Now Krishnaji never accepted these organizations as anything to do with his mission (you probably have the letter he wrote to the Chief in 1925 telling her so), and from January 1927, he knew and said that the occupation of the body theory was not and would not in the future be supported by the facts.

I am assured that it is not against the T.S. as such, or against Theosophy as such, nor against the Leaders of the T.S. as such, that Krishnaji is so vehement but against their adherence to statements of facts concerning his own mission as a Race-Founder which, he says, have not been borne out in the reality of his experience. It is not "between our work and his" that Krishnaji has definitely broken all bridges, but between our description of his work and that work as it is, between our clinging to the theory, our refusal to look at the facts, and his own dedication to the present needs of men in this evolutionary phase.

As a General Secretary, I am enabled to see the danger there is in continuing in this position. Krishnaji will be active in Europe for two more years, and many are the members in whom the conflict is reflected and will be fanned into decision by his presence.

There need be no such decision, I think Theosophy and the T.S. have to do with the evolution of the whole human Race, because Theosophy, as it has been given to us by the Founders of the Sixth Root-Race is the vision of perfected Buddhi, and because Buddhi is the Life of our universe, the Buddha of the Sixth Root-Race, I mean. But the Buddha with which Krishnaji has to do is that of the sixth sub-race, the Buddha of Manas, not the Buddha of Buddhi, and it is, or ought to be, up to us, I think, to see whether his message, is even doing the work of Evolution. You seem to deny this, when you mention use of the word "intelligence". It is true that Bergson adopts that word as an equivalent for "la pensée conceptuelle", i.e., the mechanisms and categories of the higher mind, but he often identifies 'la pensée" with "l'intuition". I think Krishnaji's use is the better one. Intelligence is a better word for the life of the mind, the buddhi of manas, than either thought or intuition. Intuition is a function of intelligence when acting through the mind (either mental or affective), but Intelligence is a better word for Buddhi in view of the latter's link with Mahat.

I think K's message is a far deeper, richer, fuller description of the consciousness of man when centered in the Buddhi of Manas, than any that we could find in the world today. Can we not, then, take it at its face value and, if we cooperate with one of his precursors, Bergson, also cooperate with him, it being one of the three directions in which the T.S. has to help the evolution of mankind, to press forward the development of the sixth sub-race, as we do for all the existing races, and for the preparation of the Sixth Root-Race?

We must confess to a failure and a failure which reflects on the real Founders and Guides of our Society as well as on the memory of our departed Leaders, only if we maintain that there has been no mistake ever made in the description of how the founding of the new sub-race was to take place. Then every one has failed, most of all, in the eyes of our adversaries, the Great Ones.

But can we not look at the facts as they are, and cooperate with K. without compelling him to accept now that which he has never accepted, because he is doing to whatever extent we need not define. I think we may learn 6th sub-race Theosophy from him, the work of evolution and opening the road towards the new era? That is what K meant when he said that he would accept the extended hand of the T.S. if there were nothing in it of the 1925 mistake.

Pardon my ignorance in occult matters, I speak from a point of view. I do not wish to bring agitation again in the T.S. I shall remain silent as to this as I have been since 1927, and my letter to you, alluded in your circular was private and confidential as this one is. You are our leaders, and I am happy to follow your lead. I have done what I thought was my duty, I shall abide by your decision.
In all devoted love,
Marcault

Feb 13 1937
Adyar, Madras, India

Dear George: (Hall from Henry Hotchener)

Your letter of Jan 12th has just come, with the Krotona annual report; thank you for both. You are quite right to call my attention to the difficulties in my being absent from California for so long and therefore unable to fulfill my duties as a member of the Board, and I should have mentioned the matter myself had my plans been definitely settled before now. But they really have not been. However, within the last two months they seem to have become crystallized, especially as the President has appointed me the Society's Treasurer as well as Manager of the Theosophical Publishing House. Hence, unless there is an unexpected upheaval in my real estate interests in California, I shall remain here for at least a year or longer. I talked the matter over with C.J. today, and he agrees that it would be best to elect someone in my place, and he suggests Miss Sommer, whose name you mentioned. Of course I concur, and in withdrawing wish to express the pleasure it has been to be so long in friendly association with my fellow Board Members and to hope for every success for Krotona.

You are good enough to ask about Mrs. Hotchener and me, and I am glad to say that we are very well and entirely happy and we hope that all of you at Krotona are the same. Our love to each and all of you and to all other California friends. Excuse the brevity for there is indeed a mass of work to be done here.

Ever affectionately to you and Mrs. Hall
Henry H.
(To Warrington and Betty). Love to you and your dear wife from Helios and Henry.

Sometime around April, 14, C. Jinarajadasa writes in *The American E.S.T. Bulletin* of the American Division for November, 1937, n70, as a front page paragraph.

> I would prefer that you refer to me as 'Brother Jinarajadasa' or 'Brother Raja' or even 'Mr. Jinarajadasa'. I shall particularly be obliged if you will ask all friends to get away from the habit of calling me 'C.J.' We got into this habit with H.P.B. and she asked for it as preferable to 'Madame Blavatsky'. But I have always felt a distaste for using the initials 'A.B.' Anyway, I think alphabetical designations, though convenient, are not desirable, for they take away from the dignity of our work.
> C. Jinarajadasa

Chapter VII
1938

On Sunday, March 20, 1938, Mr. C. F. Holland, of Los Angeles, California, passed to the higher life. He was seventy-seven years old. Mr. Holland had been a devoted theosophist for more than thirty years. For many years he had been Vice-President of the Theosophical Society in America and a member of its governing Board and Judiciary Committee. He had been a member of the Board of the Krotona Institute since it founding in 1913, President of the Los Angeles Lodge for eight years, director of the Ojai Publishing Company, Board member of the Happy Valley Foundation. His vacancy on the Board was filled by William Mayes of Krotona.

A lawyer by profession, serving faithfully as attorney of the Society for thirty years, drafting all its existing By-Laws, he had taken charge of its legal affairs, appearing in court in various cases where an attorney was required, always giving his services without compensation.

A.P. Warrington paid his tribute:

> It is a valued privilege that I am given to pay my tribute to an old and cherished friend. The man whose remains lie here and who now has retired to the higher life, came into my life with the founding of Krotona (1913), and held all his connection then formed from the beginning right up to the last. During this period of twenty-five yeas he worked for Krotona as an act of service, although the most he bore was a professional character. Whenever he was needed he faithfully responded, and always with a hearty good will. He regarded all work for Theosophy in any form as work for the Master, for whom, as his life showed, he held an undeviating devotion.
>
> It is a source of gladness to his friends, now that he has withdrawn to the higher life, to realize that he is so much nearer the Master whom he here served; that he may now feel the joy that comes to such a one who has merited many rich rewards which can be paid only in heavenly joys. Can

you not imagine what it all means to him now? And may we not wish for his early return to his earthly labors, to which we can but believe he has dedicated himself for ages to come? One thing is certain, that C.F. Holland will long dwell in our memories and with warm fraternal affections.

May the Master give to him of the richness of his glorious heart!

His selfless service and his loyal devotion to the cause of Theosophy placed him in the ranks of its most valued leaders.

A small quarterly magazine published at 1218 Public Square Building, Cleveland, Ohio, called *The New Citizen*, beginning with eight pages was shortly increased to twelve pages. The first issue came out on October 1st. to celebrate the birthday of their leader, Dr. Annie Besant.

A series of booklets of some 4000 words each, was planned as a joint production called "Wake Up America" under the sponsorship and production of Mr. Perkins, printed in the summer of 1939. The booklet was the first in a series of three whose aim was to apply the principles of The New Citizen Pledge to this country's problems at this particular time in history.

The Pledge was written by George Arundale with five steps. By the end of 1939, some 60,000 copies of the Pledge were placed in the hands of all those interested in joining.

> At the Theosophical Convention of 1938 at Olcott, Headquarters of the American Section, The Better Citizenship Movement was born, under the gracious leadership of Dr. Arundale.
>
> A small committee met, as it chanced on July 4, American Independence Day, composed of members who felt that something more was needed to arouse citizens to the need for better citizenship, a breakwater of good government and the strengthening of the ideals of American Democracy.
>
> Promulgated by the Founding Fathers, Washington, Franklin, Jefferson and others, advanced by Lincoln, Theodore Roosevelt, Wilson and other statesmen and leaders of thought and culture,

these ideals and principles, despite the present enlightened leadership of President Franklin D. Roosevelt, are under severe pressure....

The Better Citizenship Association with thirteen charter members was duly formed as a non-profit incorporation. Among these members are the National President of the Theosophical Society in America, Mr. Sidney A. Cook; the National Vice-President, Mr. James S. Perkins, Jr.; the National Secretary, Miss Etha Snodgrass; and another member of the Board of Directors of the American Section, our beloved Miss Marie Poutz. As stated in the articles of incorporation, the purposes are: (a) To engage in, participate in and promote civic, patriotic, educational, charitable and benevolent purposes and activities of all kinds, particularly such activities as contribute to a better and higher type of American citizenship; (b) To advance and promote the ideals and purposes set forth in the New Citizen Pledge....[1]

Documents show that after seven years of harmonious, and fruitful work, by August 1945 The Better Citizenship Association was dissolved, and handled by Mr. Kidder, an Ojai attorney and member of the Society.

Official publication of a magazine "Youth & Culture" ended its brief existence, rounding out the year under that title with the summer issue, Vol. I, n4, 1938. It will appear again as *The American Young Theosophist*. Published at 865 Dayton Avenue, Saint Paul, Minnesota by Lillian Boxell, Editor.

January 13, 1938, Harold Kirk moves to Krotona to occupy the house which Dr. and Mrs. Pieter Roest had.

On May 1st, the Southern California Federation held its gathering at Krotona.

> October 3 1938
> Dear Lenore,
> I promised to write you something about Sarobia and something about the Sarobia Country Theatre.
> Sarobia is the name (made out of Mrs. Logan's name, Sara, and mine, Robert) of a country place 20 miles out of Philadelphia

---

[1] Staggs, Herbert A., *The Theosophist*, President, "The Better Citizenship Association", July 1940, pp.313-316.

which Mrs. Logan's father bought and presented to her in 1914. It consisted then of 46 acres of meadow field and woods on which stood a large square cupolaed mid-Victorian, 16 room house, a large barn and two small farmers houses at the two entrances. Here we lived for over ten years in the usual way with the usual succession of competent and incompetent servants and farmers.

In 1927 Dr. Besant threw out a suggestion that we try community life, so we dismissed our indoor servants (but not the 2 or 3 farm employees) and substituted theosophists at a nominal wage of $50 per month, who lived on a parity with us, and sat at the same table, with meals served in buffet or cafeteria style. This arrangement worked well enough except for the cooking, it being found impossible for those who were not too ambitious to tie up their abilities and talents that way for any length of time. So now for two or three years we have had a colored cook come in by the day and a laundress and scrub woman who comes in one day a week and the rest of the staff consists of Mabel K. Zimmers, general secretary for me and also National Head of the Animal Welfare Dept. of the T.O.S. (as you know), H.K. Campbell, former National Secy. of the American T.S. and now housekeeper and also my T.O.S. Secretary and Maud E. Randolph, a semi-invalid and deaf T.S. friend who does most of the sewing and mending while listening with earphones to radio concerts, news broadcast etc.

In addition to these and to many temporary visitors we have two permanent guests in the persons of Richard Blossom Farley, the artist who did the decorations at "Olcott" and who divides his time here between painting school murals and digging out and planting an immense rock garden now reaching part way to China, and J.G. Sommer, another artist, once upon a time art editor of Colliers, who is now doing poster work for the W.P.A.

All but one of the Krishnamurti Camps held in the East have been held at Sarobia and to accommodate them we have added a number of small buildings, two apartments over the greenhouse, 6 summer cabins, a dormitory in the barn and a cottage outside the grounds, so that we can lodge and feed cafeteria style (cafeteria under the barn) about 75 people. The acres have grown by various purchases to about 135 plus a larger sandy peninsula piled up on our river front by Government dredging of the Delaware.

What all this adds up to I don't know. Mrs. Logan (usually known as Mrs. Robbie) thinks the whole experiment has been a failure, but I think it has been a success for it has been a test of character for all of us and I think no one has lived here or even visited briefly without feeling that it has been worthwhile. The place is really quite beautiful in an old fashioned and somewhat raggedy way and even three men cannot farm it (vegetables and hay) and take care of the garden and keep it in anything like tidy shape. There are many beautiful trees, oaks, beeches, pines, cedars, tulip trees, maples, magnolias, dogwoods, etc., and much rhododendron, laurel, azaleas, and other flowering bushes. The land is flat, with only a slight drop in the quarter mile between house and river, but the river itself is always a lovely feature, now gray and stormy, now peaceful and reflecting, now over with ice, now harboring hundreds of ducks and gulls. All this summer there has been a pair of snowy white egrets stalking about our marshes and in winter we may have as many as twenty to forty ring-necked pheasants parading about the lawn and several pairs of cardinals feeding at our birds' cafeteria.

As for the theatre, it began about six years ago when someone introduced us to a boy of 19, Clyde Robinson, who wanted to try his ability in amateur theatricals with some of his friends and acquaintances. Mrs. Robbie altered our barn into a passable theatre and the young players camped out in the cabins and one of the lodge houses and cooked their own meals. They did about as well as the average amateur group and had a pleasant and profitable time and when they departed, Johnny Woodrow, the one who had cooked for them in the improvised carriage-shed kitchen, stayed on for nearly two years as cook for us. The following year he took a hand as theatre manager and got together a nice group of boys and girls from Temple University together with Prof. & Mrs. Randall, dramatic teachers, as chaperones. Following this venture the State Fire Dept. forbade our using the barn except for rehearsals as it did not meet the fire laws so the two theatre groups of 1937 and 1938 (the first under Clyde Robinson again and this year under a 20 year old girl Mary Myers who lives near us) had to give their plays out of doors or hastily dash into the big garage if it rained.

Last year's group was the best and their performance of "Death Takes a Holiday" was so good that old Daniel Frohman came down to see it and said it was as good as any Broadway show. That was because two young professionals Bill Bock and Carman Jones were really fine actors and pulled the whole company along with them. They were also with this year's group but the general level of the cast was not so good.

Of course all this is of little moment in comparison with the really important people of Sarobia, Charlie Chan, a collie-Airdale or something who came as a stray eight years ago and gradualy took over the supervision of the estate assisted by Mr. Farley, Andy, Pete and Marvin. We had always refused to have dogs, on account of the cats but Charlie said he had been given orders to settle here so after some protest we gave in. Charlie thereupon produced a wife and a week later another wife and shortly thereafter the wives produced 15 puppies so that from no dog we graduated to 18 dogs almost overnight. For some years, however, he has apparently been celibate and is now growing portly and less inclined to pester people for romps and stick throwing. He is a great watch dog though he reserves his loudest warnings for the approach of well-known friends. As for his bite, he hasn't any and wags his tail whenever addressed. His charm consists in a sort of rugged honesty allied to a pardonable pride in being one of the silliest people on the place.

As for the cats, there are departed heroes and heroines whose graves adorn the garden and whose memory is still green in our hearts. These we will not mention lest they dim the lustre of the present rulers of whom the Grand Mogul is Packie, or Pack Wack, large, portly, Maltese gentleman who turns suddenly into a penguin when he sits up and drops his forepaws like flippers at the offer of a saucer of cream. He also is proud of his silliness and it is a proverbial question whether he or Charlie takes the prize; hence they are often spoken to as Big Sill and Small Sill. Pack Wack has in the past nine years (since as a kitten he earned the name of Packie by sleeping on the top of the Packard) tested every sofa, chair, cushion, basket and nook in the house and can sleep longer and in more relaxed and abandoned positions than any cat known. His favorite spot however is Mr. Robbie's desk whenever Mr. Robbie has an unusual number of clean white sheets or freshly typed letters spread out there. He then spreads himself upon them with the protective air of a setting hen and the placid inevitability of the Sphinx. Next to this he enjoys most hanging fire in the doorway when urged to go out on cold winter nights until Mr. Robbie or his Aunt Mabel are quite frozen. He looks upon Charlie (who is not admitted to the house) as the "dweller on the threshold" or rather he considers that there are two Charlie's, one the obvious and objectionable dog who lives here and whom he avoids with a mixture of caution and disdain, and the other a perfectly strange dog whom he stares at with lashing tail as if he had never laid eyes on him before. But that is cat nature, a mystery not to be lightly inquired into!

The other feline persons consist of Tessie, Yellow Kitten Pussie and Shadow who is not only black as night but a constant shadow to Y.K.P. Tessie (originally named Thespis then Thespuss by a theatre group) graciously presents Sarobia with from 10 to 15 kittens every year and is the loudest and most annoying mewer when hungry that we have yet survived. Yellow Kitten Pussy was brought from Maine three years ago as a tiny kitten and is the most gentle and affectionate cat ever seen. Mr. Robbie says he is "not very bright" but his Aunt Mabel and Kay indignantly deny the impeachment. Several names have been tried on him but Yellow Kitten Pussy is the only one so far that will stick.

The rest of the above letter is missing. We believe the letter is written by Robert Logan.

A.P. Warrington and Betty are in Santiago de Cuba. He leaves brief notes among his papers, that Cuba was a most interesting country; reminding them both so much of India with the same palms and the Brahma cattle from India which they have imported. The people were so kind and warm hearted, that they could not do enough for the Warrington's. He commented that the province was very much alive theosophically due to the especially good work of the Duany's, father and daughter. He made a comment, that Krishnamurti tried to destroy everything when he was there, and through it all, they have rebuilt up to twelve live Lodges. They are a very affectionate group and take their work very seriously. They are staying on a hill, overlooking the bay, which he says is a beautiful and rare sight. The climate is warm, eighty-eight degrees with some nice tropical showers which they enjoyed very much, not having seen any rain for months. The tropical fruit is in abundance of so many varieties, especially the papayas, but vegetables are not so plentiful. They season with herbs much as the Indians do, but do not use curry. They also have to cook on a charcoal stove like the Indian but fortunately it is built up to a comfortable height and not on the floor. Since it is so much like India, they go in their bare feet about the house, and wear Indian sandals outside.

Most of the flowers and shrubs that they considered rare in California, grow wild in Cuba. They have so many lovely vines growing all over the hills.

He says that Cuba is an ideal spot for a Centre as it is covered on three sides with water. It has a feeling of purity and the Master Morya's influence is strong, evidently he wants a Centre here.

C. Jinarajadasa spent Christmas with the Warrington's as they were busy fixing up a nice room for him. He gave an E.S. talk to the members on Christmas day as follows:—

The Vulgarization of the Idea of the Masters

There is one aspect of Krishnaji's work which puzzles us all and confuses some. It is the definite stand which he has made against the idea of the Masters, denying that They can in any way be useful to the searcher after Truth. Obviously, if his consciousness is at all related to that of the Lord, any denial of the existence of the Great Ones and of Their work for Humanity means the very negation of that link. It has occurred to me that perhaps there is a reason for his denunciation. I cannot of course be positive on the subject, but I share with others the idea which has occurred to me.

During this long tour among the peoples of South and Central America, Mexico and Cuba, I have noted with great alarm what a number of organizations have sprung up in the wake of the Theosophical Society, proclaiming the same ideas, but *with a twist to them*. There is one organization in U.S.A., known as "Amorc," which claims to be the one and the only genuine source of Rosicrucianism, which advertises largely in U.S.A., and also here in Cuba. I am told it sends out pictures of the two Masters. I have seen their advertisement in the most popular magazine in Cuba announcing in large letters: "You can influence others with your thoughts." There is one man in Mexico who claims to be a Tartar prince and a representative of the Great Hierarchy; he declares himself to be the Master K.H., and is sending out communications with those initials. All the Masters are announced as having Their channels through this or that group or individual. Thus, the Venetian Master, the Master Hilarion, the Count de St. Germain, the "Tibetan Master" (whoever he may be) are supposed to be behind this or that organization.

Four years ago in Cochin China I found a worthy body of spiritualists who proclaimed that they were followers of the Masters. They get their communications through "basket turning," and claim to get directions not only from the Masters, but also from the Lord Maitreya, and even from, as one of their devotees assured me, "the four Sanats"—that was the phrase which he used. They all have read *The Masters and the Path* in its French translation and quote it. In some countries of South and Central America, some of these organizations are aiming to capture the young Theosophical Lodges, promising the new members teachings on how to develop powers.

When years ago Brother Leadbeater published *The Masters and the Path*, I could not help feeling a sense of repugnance, lest the wonderful and inspiring facts which he revealed about the Masters and Their work might become vulgarized. The publication of those facts, reserved once to a few trusted members of the E.S. only, has undoubtedly helped thousands of Theosophists to a more vivid and intimate realization of this most wonderfully inspiring fact in Nature—that the Masters exist and are working for Humanity. Our Brother's work has been translated into many languages and of course into Spanish.

The facts which it revealed about the Masters have had one unexpected and unfortunate result, which is to induce a blind credulity in many who now accept as truth any assertion about Occultism, provided it claims to come from the Masters. There are thousands ready to believe blindly about Occultism, as once they were ready to believe blindly the assertions of their religious leaders, especially in the countries where I have been recently. That is the unfortunate part; for their credulity is being exploited.

I fear that in this matter we Theosophists are not without blame. We have said that within The Society each is free to accept or reject any teaching; yet, in this matter of the existence of the Masters, many a Lodge almost enforces a belief in Them. I have been present in a Lodge where, with the general public present, proceedings began with an invocation to the Masters. Naturally the public present will go away with the impression that the Theosophists also have their saints, whom one must accept before becoming a member of the Society.

There are Theosophical Lodges named Maitreya, Morya, Koot Hoomi, Mahāchōhan; but also Lodges called Blavatsky, Olcott, Besant, Leadbeater, Dāmōdar, Arundale, Shrimati Rukmini,

Jinarājadāsa. Wherever I can interfere, I prevent a Lodge being named after me, for it gives a personal element to the teachings of Theosophy. For if we permitted Lodges to be named after us, and then permit Lodges to be named after the Masters, do we not bring Them down to the level of Their pupils? This is what has happened. Of course the members who name Lodges after the Masters do so to express their fervent attachment to The Society and to its unseen Leaders. All the same, there is already a kind of superstition about Them—against which They warned us long ago.

Of course in all this I refer to the work of a Lodge, where a presentation is given to the public at large of what is Theosophy, and not to Groups of the Esoteric School.

We know that for many centuries the facts as to the existence of the Masters, and the way to Them, were divulged only in the Mysteries; the door to Them was not only unknown to the world at large, it was further closely guarded. Then, in order to offset the deadening influence of scientific materialism and to prevent its triumph, the way to Them was once again proclaimed. They came out of Their retreats to tell the world of Their existence. But the pendulum has swung too far.

Perhaps it is necessary now, in order to safeguard humanity, that the pendulum should swing back again. And that perhaps is one part of Krishnaji's work. His teaching, "Away from Masters, Away from Occultism," is perhaps to restore the balance, and to prevent the terrible exploitation of the thousands who are seeking a higher life, but whose excess of blind faith will lead them to disaster.

Those who really aspire to the higher life, especially of service to suffering Humanity, will always find the door to the Mysteries. They will be guided there. The knowledge published in such a work as the Masters and the Path will always exist for the true seeker. But since so many want to come near to the Masters not for the sake of serving Humanity, but simply to gain power or instruction from Them, it is perhaps salutary that scepticism regarding Them, and the Way to Them, should once again be the orthodox creed of the men and women who represent public opinion. C.J.[2]

Tess McLean lived in a small house on South Signal Street in Ojai, California, given to her by Catharine Mayes. Tess was white-haired and lived with her younger sister. Catharine had built a large parrot cage on the corner of the house to house Catharine's parrots when she was away. One parrot used to tease dogs when they passed by, whistling to them. Tess adored Catharine as anyone can imagine who knew Catharine. Here is a poem she wrote to Catharine.

To Catharine Gardner Mayes

Orange and emerald, gold and blue,
And a gypsy heart in the soul of you.
A wild, sweet spirit with flashing wings
Caught in the vortex of modern things.
A vital spark from our Lord, the Sun,
His devotee till the day is done.
The far roads whisper, the desert sands
Are intimates, holding with golden hands
The secret of some strange, far-off clime
That links the 'now' with that ancient time
When chains were forged time cannot break,
And vows were made for the future's sake.
Down through the ages from every land,
The old loves follow and take her hand,

---

[2] Jinarajadasa, C., *The Disciple*, "The Vulgarization of the Idea of the Masters" January, 1930, n12, (New Series), pp.254-257.

> Glad for each symbol that bears her name,
> And the gypsy spirit no fate can tame.
> Orange and emerald, gold and blue,
> And the gypsy heart that is ever true.

Tess belonged to the Scribblers Club and would sit by the hour, writing poetry. The house was torn down long ago and was replaced by the Ojai Festivals building.

Right Rev. Edward M. Mathews joined the staff of St. Alban's Cathedral Church in Hollywood, Calif. and was appointed rector of that church in 1943, a position he has held for the last forty-two years.

Among Rukmini Devi's archive boxes, are several interviews on tape casettes telling the listener how the unfolding of the book *Lotus Fire* came into being. How Dr. Arundale was deeply engaged in studying Yoga, under the direction of his Teacher. The lessons were used as the basis of his Roof-Talks. These have yet to be transcribed. According to the following written notes left by Rukmini Devi, we find her telling the story or tales as yet untold by George S. Arundale himself in the writing of the book:

The Lotus Fire—Symbolic Yoga.

> The unfoldment of *The Lotus Fire* from beginning to end was an intensely interesting record of clairvoyant investigation. At our Friday Night Roof-Talks, George started telling us of these out of the body experiences when he was shown the symbolic poses of a Lord of Yoga of the Shiva line. He was as fascinated as we were. Neither he nor, of course, we, had the faintest idea of how these would develop, what were the order of the Cosmic symbols which reproduced themselves in all creation.
>
> He was very distressed when some of his symbols seemed to contradict the order in The Secret Doctrine, but what could he do about it? He had to give us what he saw. He saw the vertical line as coming before the horizontal line. Later his attention was called to a footnote by H.P.B. who said in the Trans-Himalayan system the

perpendicular line came first. Of course, he was very much relieved. The difference between what H.P.B. saw and what he saw was one therefore of points of vision, not an intrinsic difference. While the power to correlate is the buddhic nature working through mind, with direct perception, the buddhi working on the planes of buddhi, he could never be lured into making correlations. He either saw or he did not see. A most interesting case in point is his linking his symbols to every one of the chakras but the brow chakra remained unlinked and his circle-globe he had linked to the body as a whole and the head as a whole. When his attention was called to this discrepancy he refused to amend but left his charkra symbolic correlations just as they were. Actually when later he made jewelled symbols for healing the one he constructed for the Circle-Globe was highly suggestive of C.W.L.'s description of the Brow Chakra, for it was divided into halves and while some of us firmly believe these two are linked we do not have his authority for the belief.

Many correlations were made which he happily inserted into the last portion of notes and help, but ONLY if they appealed to him as true. For example he refused to have the Platonic Solids linked with his symbols, but on the other hand permitted a footnote to be put in the book in itself showing the bridge through polarities given by both C.W.L. and himself with the Rays. So one has to a certain extent G.S.A.'s own authority for considering his point symbol as in a measure linked with Ray 1, his Circle-Globe with Ray 2, his Web Womb with Ray 3, his Diamond Line with Ray 4, his Swastika with Ray 5, his Cross with Ray 6 and his Lotus Flower with Ray 7. But in studying *The Lotus Fire* one must not be led into the mistake of taking these symbols of his too literally. His point was Point-ness or the power of anything to become a nucleus of a centre round which all else could revive. Similarly his Web-Womb was that power to weave out from a Centre those fine filaments of force that would later become the ethnero-nervous system in the physical body itself. His Diamond Line was the perpendicularity that gives law to all things and makes the possibility of uprightness, symbolized by the perpendicular streak in the embryo and the North and South poles in cellular life. His Circle-Globe was the principle of Circularity through global dimensions that makes possible every organism from cell life upwards, that which become a field of evolution of evolving life. His Horizontal Line was the laterally that with the Perpendicular Line makes stable the circle itself, especially shown in such organs as the heart. His Swastika was always a moving, whirling wheel that was the principle of life itself whirling the form to its perfection in *The Lotus Fire* which was the Symbol of Flowering or perfection in any form.

That is how he showed these great symbols to us and that is how he himself saw them, always not static but dynamic.

When certain illustrations of the growth of cell life both in plant, animal, and human were shown him from *Grey's Anatomy*, they had been copied by Conrad Woldringh for block making, he was amazed and said "You are not trying to make these fit the symbols." These pictures so exactly represented what he himself had seen, they seemed almost made to his order. It was so obvious that what he was contacting were Cosmic processes that reproduced themselves in all life.

He was not so well acquainted with Theosophical nomenclature and when he is describing the Nirvanic Plane, looking upwards therefrom, he said he saw an Atmic Plane, a plane where the Self only dwelt. It was a very natural thing to consider the plane above the Nirvanic as Atmic, because Atmic means of the Self. When his attention was called to the fact that our Theosophical literature had been calling the Nirvanic, also the Atmic Plane, and had been calling the one above Nomadic, that quite contented him for it was the Monad, the One Self in its Home Plane that he had been seeing and calling to himself the Atma in the Atmic Plane. We must remember that while so many of us glibly use these terms without the slightest perception of what they mean, our great seers using every effort of the will to place the veils that mercifully shield us from these planes of glory, are constrained to tell us in words we can understand that which is ineffable and beyond description.

During this process to piercing the veils, he remarked to the person who was sitting quietly with notebook and pen to take down his words, "This must be a great strain on you, My Dear," equating what he himself was feeling with the lesser consciousness that was attempting only the part of the recorder. Actually there was no strain save that of remaining absolutely still both within and without that no thought or feeling could jar on him who was scaling the heights and bringing these heights to the levels of human consciousness.

Many a time a question was asked him, say, "What are the colours of your Symbols?" This would bring about a week or two later a very full answer, though at the time the questioner asked G.S.A. had not contacted that aspect of the Symbols.

He was a passionate lover of music and often "brought through" music from the other worlds. One such piece was his *Symbolic Yoga Music*, where the Devas are invoked and send their fairy messengers down a bridge of rippling sound. In attempting to show this coming of the Devas, G.S.A. almost danced it himself for Conrad and me, who were attempting to give it form in notation.

His *Symbolic Yoga* book from the beginning were great adventures known only to the one who gave them to us in his Friday Night Talks, as we were awakened to tread our own paths of *Symbolic Yoga*.

Conrad Woldringh, a theosophist, was also a theatre artist and dear friend of Rukmini's.

The piano score *A Yoga In Sound* was written by G.S. Arundale and published in 1938. George reported that this little piece of music was sketched for his personal convenience as a means of helping to bridge the gulf between an inner and an outer Yoga. Therefore, the experience was personal to George Arundale, like the laying of a foundation, as it were, for he believed the time has come for the invocation to the Angels or Devas, that they may help to build as they alone can build. Quoting George, "Each student of Yoga should of course build his own music bridge with the material of his own uniqueness. And there are innumerable bridges. "This Yoga of Sound is only one bridge among very many." A copy of this score is held in the Ross Collection along with a recording by Eleanor Hepburn Noall playing the score for the author at his home in Montecito, California, on December 4, 1978. Eleanor was a distinguished musician of New York City and Opera Coach at Juilard School of Music. She passed away at the age of ninety-five peacefully on January 18, 2000. She was the widow of Hugh Fraser-Noall.

In his Presidential Address in December, at Benares, Dr. Arundale spoke on the great strain, and that so much conflict and sorrow was in the world. He made a call upon each individual member to make the world conscious of the reality of its Universal

Brotherhood. Maybe the wisest choice of words came when he had come to the conclusion that it was not wise for The Society to intervene by way of special pronouncements regarding Krishnamurti.

> Krishnamurti's message was causing confusion and unrest. Leaders, Scriptures and so on are not that they may mould us into the likeness of their images, but to help us to discover our Selves and to fulfil them. Krishnamurti discloses *his* Law, not *the* Law. We must do and believe in things because it is our unfettered will to do so.

In closing he reminded the members to be in the forefront of the Masters' work.

Rev. Byron W. Casselberry, 1928
St. Michael's Huizen

Chapter VIII
1939

A.P. Warrington and Betty took an extra stay over in Cuba, he wrote to George Hall on February 8, 1939, giving his address as Ave. #17 Vista Alegre, Santiago de Cuba. He remarked that they would be staying until March 20th, returning back to Krotona about April 23, or 24th, but they did not return until March 9, 1939. His health condition was getting worse with a strong probability that he might not make it home. He was thankful for the clippings from the *Times* on Atlantis, and remarked that H.P.B. was being vindicated very rapidly these days.

One more faithful servant has gone from this world on February 5, 1939; Mrs. Grace S. Hall, wife of Mr. George H. Hall, manager of the Krotona Estate, passed on suddenly to her reward. From Old Hollywood to the Ojai Valley she was among the pioneers who helped to establish Krotona along with her husband George Hall. She was a leader in community and country club activities. President of the Ojai Valley Woman's Club and Chairman of the Nominating Committee of the State Federation of Woman's Clubs.

George Arundale would send out an open letter on March 29th, 1939, to all fellow members of the Theosophical Society, so that every Lodge would take it and read it, to see if the letter or any of the others awakens a stirring to do something within the Lodges. George was trying to find a way of giving fire to the very Lodge itself and its members as they were facing a grave responsibility to help the world out of its present distress, of war. He reminded them that if the Theosophical Society is to help the world, it must put its own world in order. It must be a Brotherhood, as is its highest purpose. Therefore must every Lodge be a real, though smaller, brotherhood within the wider Brotherhood.

Mrs. Fred (Lida) Hart, of Los Angeles, passed on February 1. She operated the Ojai Theater, and was a member of the Ojai Valley Women's Club, and also active in the Ojai Valley Oaks Lodge.

George Arundale felt that this was one of the major test periods of the Theosophical Society due to the fact that a War was coming. For some weeks he would write weekly several open letters to his fellow members of the Society explaining the difficult time it was.

Gefforey Hodson, the famous seer for the Theosophical Society, could no longer hold back his reaction to the strong remarks made by Krishnamurti denouncing the theosophical teachings as "poison" and the leaders as "exploiters", which has deeply shocked theosophists throughout the world. By June 1, 1939, Byron Casselberry wrote an open letter to Geoffrey Hodson regarding the booklet written by Geoffrey against Krishnamurti entitled *Krishnamurti and the Search for Light.*

Casselberry's letter would have been more effective had he been able to reduce it to one or at most two pages. We leave the whole letter as it was written, but italicize what we thought was important.

2123 N. Gower Street
Hollywood, California
June 1, 1939

Dear Mr. Hodson:

There has come into my hands a copy of your booklet, Krishnamurti and the Search for Light. I am not interested in defending him or in attempting to elucidate his teachings, but your views concerning Krishnamurti in relation to the Theosophical Society interest me greatly. As I find myself in complete disagreement with you, it occurs to me that you might like to know what I think. Hence this letter. I hope you will not mind my being quite frank. It is a pity that we cannot discuss this directly, as you seem interested in discussing; but, under the circumstances, correspondence is the only way open.

To begin with, I want to say that, although I am no longer a member of the Theosophical Society, I believe my devotion to Theosophy is unequivocal, there are in life certain laws which one instinctively feels to be true. There must be in every thoughtful individual a growing sense of responsibility, a realization that he cannot live for himself, that as a living unit in the human race, he has a duty to perform. The awakening perception of those laws, and the unswerving dedication to that duty, I call Theosophy.

To me, it is an absurdity to think of Theosophy as a system of ideas limited to certain books. Wisdom is never contained—is it?—in books. A book may be written by a wise man, and be the expression of wisdom. But wisdom is in the man, not in the book. Wisdom may be awakened in another by reading the book; but wisdom is still in the man, not in the book. The book is merely a symbol of something that can live only in the heart and mind of man.

The same thing exactly applies to organizations. Wisdom is never contained in any organization, though it may have existed in a man around whom or because of whom an organization has sprung up.

I dare say you will agree with this. Most members of the T.S. would, I think, quite readily agree. But I hold such agreement is only theoretical, because your practice is quite the reverse. You give enormous importance, not to Theosophy (which is wisdom in man), but to the Theosophical Society, and it has come to be a hearsay for anyone to criticize it or its leaders. Leaving the Society has become a kind of spiritual tragedy, and the Theosophical faithful sadly wag their heads over the lost sheep, precisely as do the orthodox Christians. You are chiefly concerned, not with Theosophy, as you maintain, but with the preservation of the Theosophical Society. I am not saying that the Theosophical Society should not be preserved. But the Society and its leaders have become a mental sore spot that you cannot bear to have touched by the acid of honest critical thought.

Why? What are you defending so resentfully? Not Theosophy, not wisdom surely. In order to defend, one must first possess something. A man feels resentful only when threatened with the loss of property, actual or psychological. Wisdom, Theosophy, is not the property of anyone, and is not therefore defensible. What you are defending can only be your pet prejudices—your intellectual furniture, your eminence in the reigning hierarchy, your beatific conception of the leaders and the Masters—all of which you call by the name of Theosophy.

I maintain that your so-called defense of the late leaders is but a way of justifying your own false position.

Take Krishnamurti's statement that there is exploitation in the Theosophical Society. To me this is obvious, and you yourself are contributing to it. There has sprung up in the Society a blind devotion to Masters whom the devotees do not know and have never even met, and you are—aren't you?—one of the chief priests of this amazing cult. What essential difference is there between representing a Master, and representing God; between an initiated leader and an infallible Pope? Superficially, verbally, there is a lot of difference. One can recite it endlessly: the Theosophical leaders never demand blind obedience, they never say they are infallible, they insist that each man must find truth for himself—and so on indefinitely. But actually there is no fundamental difference whatever. You have merely refined the thing and made it intellectually more appealing. The principle of coercion through authority, which is the root of exploitation, is still present. This must be obvious to any thinking mind, and the pious denials of it which one meets everywhere is simply a glossing over of the facts.

I have it in writing from C.W.L. that I am an initiate. Notwithstanding this circumstance, I know nothing whatever about the Masters, and never have, except what I have read and been told, which cannot be called knowledge. This being the case, I may perhaps be excused for wondering how much the rest of you really know about the Masters. You give the impression that you know them personally. Do you? Have any of you now living ever met any of the Masters physically? You will forgive me if I doubt it.

Now, if you base your knowledge of the Masters exclusively on clairvoyance and experiences during sleep (we need not consider so-called intuition as a means of contacting the Masters, as it can be dealt with in the same way), then one of two things must be true: either your psychic faculties are perfectly developed, and hence your knowledge of the Masters infallible: or your faculties are imperfectly developed, and there exists a serious possibility of delusion and error. If you and G.S.A. and others claim to be perfectly developed clairvoyants (thorough perfection in these matters is, on the best authority, exceedingly difficult, and is attainable only through years of arduous specialization and training), then on this point I have nothing to say. But if you *don't* claim this perfection, and consequently are by no means infallible, then what right, may I ask, have any of you to make *definite assertions* that the Masters or other invisible entities are here or there, or that they say this or that? How can you guide people towards something which may be an illusion? And yet you put forward this possible illusion, which you are pleased to call the Master, as the greatest reality, and urge the members to be inspired by it and to serve it. If there was ever a case of the blind leading the blind, surely this is it.

Exploitation is inherent in the idea that you or I can act as the mouthpiece or connecting link between Divine Beings and ordinary mortals. Whoever assumes such a position has at once a spiritual whip, however subtle and concealed, with which to keep the faithful in order. He can always withhold the message or the blessing, thereby sweetly blackmailing his devotees. However benign his intentions, the position he has assumed automatically makes of him an exploiter. People are always more impressed by a professed seer or prophet than they are by a man who merely puts forward his own ideas. Hence the extraordinary crop of seers and prophets that have sprung up all over the world. It is a mutually satisfactory business. The seers and prophets have a flock over which to pontificate, and the flock feels secure in the thought that it is being led painlessly to heaven.

The immediate point is this: in the Theosophical Society, people who would ordinarily not be interested in a given action, will do it if told the Masters want it done. And this is exactly what they are told, and have been told from the beginning. So the seed of exploitation was planted in the T.S. in the days of H.P.B., and has since sprung up and waxed strong. I am aware that this statement is a shocking example of what you call the vilification of the T.S. leaders and members, but I know that I am not vilifying anyone. I am merely stating an obvious fact, which does not at all deny the original and essential purpose of the T.S., any more than weeds deny the essential purpose of a garden. But weeds can never be made into flowers, however they may be decorated and cultivated. They can only be destroyed.

H.P.B. claimed to be in touch with invisible Teachers, and she produced handwritten communications from Them, which have been published and may be judged on their own merits. Today, similar claims are made by others, but they are unsupported by any such evidence. I do not say the present claimants are *not* in touch with the Masters, because I don't know. But I ask: Has anyone the right to undertake to lead others to an invisible Teacher if his own conscious contact with that Teacher depends solely on his imperfectly developed psychic faculties? Has the President of the Theosophical Society the right to state that certain of its members are pupils of a Master, or to pronounce them initiates?

There was exploitation in C.W.L.'s methods at The Manor. And no one need think that I am bitter toward C.W.L. I know that my affection for him and respect for his attainments are unchanged. But I'm afraid my feelings do not run to the sentimental or fanatical variety that refuse to see things as they are for fear of dimming a little the lustre of one's teacher or one's friend. I maintain that while I was at The Manor, people were quietly advised that they would not "get on" spiritually—become pupils and initiates—unless they did certain work and associated with certain people. Other kinds of work, and certain other people, were to be avoided. Dr. Arundale has seen fit to continue and extend this practice. Thus T.S. members were and are constrained by T.S. leaders. If this isn't exploitation, eating like a worm at the heart of the Society, then I don't know the meaning of that word.

One of the most deplorable and shameful things is, to me, the fact that the Masters and the late leaders of the T.S. are used to bolster the authority and the position of the current leaders. What is the psychology of this continual use of the Masters' names? Why are the names of H.P.B., C.W.L., and A.B. so continually trotted out? What has all this harping on persons to do with Theosophy, with the understanding of oneself and the study of natural laws? The answer to the last question is: nothing. To the preceding questions the answer is simply this, that it lends weight to the authority of the present leaders, which might seem a little insufficient without these bright stars in its firmament. The members might get bored or might even begin to doubt the wisdom of G.S.A. or of Hodson, so the dead luminaries are made to back them up. It is noteworthy that the dead always *do* back them up. They manage to turn up at conventions now and then and approve the proceedings. They never criticize or question. That is one of the convenient things about death—it effectively throttles all criticism. And back of this spiritual puppet show stand the Masters, ready to be dragged in as needed. Against this formidable panoply of gods, what chance has independent judgment and thought in the Theosophical Society? The moment a really independent thinker arises with the courage of his convictions, he is ostracized and branded a vilifier of the leaders and a denouncer of the Ancient Wisdom. What unmitigated rot! It would be funny if it weren't so dismally stupid. Krishnamurti has consistently attacked the principle of exploitation, whether in the T.S. or elsewhere, but I have yet to hear him attack persons. People who feel themselves or their friends attacked may well look to see where the shoe pinches. But few directly involved are likely to see the exploitation, for where would you be without it? Arhats, initiates and seers, reduced to human beings with human problems! Unthinkable. There is only one solution: get rid of Krishnamurti. And that, I grant, you have pretty successfully done. But I don't think this act will stand in years to come as a monument to the wisdom of its authors.

Though small importance seems to have been attached to its content, to me one of the most significant documents in the history of the Theosophical Society is the brief and, I believe, last letter said to be from the Master K.H. to Dr. Besant, published for the first time in the May, 1937, Theosophist. As you may remember, it says in part:

"The T.S. and its members are slowly manufacturing a creed. Says a Thibetan proverb. 'Credulity breeds credulity and ends in hypocrisy.' How few are they who can know anything about us. Are we to be propitiated and made idols of? ... No one has a right to claim authority over a pupil or his conscience. Ask him not what he believes ... We show no favours. The best corrective of error is an honest and open minded examination of all facts subjective and objective ... The cant about 'Masters' must be silently but firmly put down. Let the devotion and service be to that Supreme Spirit alone of which each one is a part. Namelessly and silently we work and the continual references to ourselves and the repetition of our names raises up a confused aura that hinders our work. ..."

Mr. Jinarajadasa says this letter refers to the situation among certain Theosophists thirty-seven years ago.

Thirty-seven years ago indeed!
Yours sincerely
Byron Casselberry

In the Introduction of the booklet to which Geoffrey says: "The principles of justice, fair play and common courtesy have been so flagrantly outraged for some seven years that at last I am moved to a reply."

George Hall mentioned that in the changes in the water lines last year, 1938, they discovered that the old two inch pipe is in very bad condition, and it was only a question of time until the rest of the line would have to be replaced. Anticipating this, George was in correspondence from time to time with a Mr. Potts in San Francisco, who owns the easternmost portion of the Old Grand Estate, with the view to getting a right of way along his east boundary line and thus avoid crossing the railroad tract twice. It seems that Mr. Potts is a very difficult person to deal with, and George began to feel that they would have little chance of making a deal with him.

But the water system was very much more improved than was anticipated. The water company proposed to enlarge their lines from two inches to four for a distance of 460 feet, and the state of California Highway Department agreed with Krotona to pay half of the expense of extending this four inch line 410 feet to the intersection with Maricopa Highway. Krotona was able to arrange with the water company to lay all the pipe, thus avoiding liability and other complications for crossing the public highway. It would be by November 3, 1939, that the Krotona water well would have thirty-seven feet of water. The well drilled at Krotona by Newton Paler of Ventura was down 165 feet and had thirty-seven feet of water in it, according to Eugene Munson, superintendent at Krotona, who was in charge of the work. Although the supply of water at the present level was not tested, it was not thought that it was of sufficient quantity to justify the stopping of drilling, so it was planned to go deeper. However, the drillers have encountered very hard rock and drilling has been slowed up considerably.

On August 19, 1939, Krotona Institute unanimously passed at a special meeting of the Board of Trustees the following:

> Whereas: the Krotona Center has suffered an irreparable loss in the passing of its Vice-President, its Founder and Guide, Mr. A.P. Warrington June 16.
>
> Be It Resolved: that the Krotona Board of Trustees hereby expresses their deepest gratitude to the inspiration he has constantly been to the Center.
>
> Be It Further Resolved: that the only way in which we can prove that gratitude is by making every effort to live according to his constant ideal of Brotherhood and Service, so that the Center he founded shall be a worthy channel of help to the world.
>
> Be It Further Resolved: that this Resolution and the minutes with a copy sent to Mrs. Warrington

Mrs Warrington's reply:

Board of Trustees Krotona Institute of Theosophy

Dear Co-workers,

Your flowers were so beautiful! Thank you for them and your loving message.
I felt it only fitting that they should have the place of honor, as Krotona always came first in Mr. Warrington's life, it being the child of his heart and brain.
Sincerely
Betty Warrington

Dr. Henry A. Smith in association with the Theosophical Society played an important role in introducing A.P. Warrington to the Liberal Catholic Church. His ordination to the Priesthood took place on November 2, 1939 in the Church of St. Francis when it was at 218 South Wabash Street, Chicago, by the Right Reverend Charles Hampton, at the age of forty-one. Funding for the present building housing the Church of St. Francis was accomplished through the efforts of Dr. Smith. He arranged for the financing of $8,000 needed for the down payment. The balance he funded from his personal account. Much of his personal money also went into furnishing the interior.

The association between Dr. Smith and the Theosophical Society was very active. In 1960, he became National President, a post he held for five years. He also served as A National Lecturer. His retirement occurred in 1973 and he took up residence n Ojai, California. On September 10, 1979, Dr. Smith completed this incarnation.

In November of 1939 Madame Doctor Maria Montessori went to India with her son, Signor Mario Montessori, on the invitation of Dr. Arundale, and were later interned until the end of the War.

Sara Logan died in 1939 and was replaced on the Board of the Happy Valley School by Erma Williams, long time assistant of Louis Zalk, and Rosalind Rajagopal's sister.

A. P. Warrington, after visiting Lodges in several countries of the Far East, was impressed with the fact that the weakest Lodges were those that would have nothing to do with Krishnamurti or his philosophy of Life, whereas those which were vital and progressive were more or less enthusiastic about him and his work. It was these latter which had the broadest understanding of Krishnamurti and his relation to the great work of Theosophy, while a few had taken a narrow sectarian view and had left the Society altogether, thus serving finally neither Krishnamurti nor The Society. His motto was "Age for Wisdom: youth for execution."

> He always had a word to share with the youth in his lectures. "O, young people! If you, and we, could only take a clear peep into the future and see some of the great and beautiful things that are in readiness to come about, you would grow at once enthusiastic and eagerly desire to equip yourselves as completely as possible to meet the rare opportunities of the meaning of a new way of Life.
>
> There are two ways, at least, that can be pursued in meeting these opportunities when they come: one in the small, conventional, conservative way, and the other in the big, free, and progressive way. *Age for wisdom: youth for execution.* Those of the conservative [path] are bondsmen to the past, bent on the preservation or perpetuation of old, crystallized, rigid, forms, since they have had no adequate vision of the future. Those of the latter will be the pioneers of the new day, of the New Race. If among these pioneers there can be a good sprinkling of theosophists, who are well-versed in the teachings and principles of Theosophy, because of the accuracy of their general vision of the plan for the future, human progress will be hastened by many centuries, much to the happiness of mankind.
>
> Where will you stand, my young friends, in that future; in the ranks of the reactionary and back numbers, or in the front ranks of those pioneers of the New Race, marching with the sunshine gleaming from their shining foreheads?"

Brief Biography of Albert Powell Warrington 1939

Albert Powell Warrington was born in Berlin, Maryland in 1866. He was the son of a planter. After leaving high school he entered the railway service, rising in a few years to the position of traffic manager at the age of twenty-six. The law, however, proved more attractive to him than railroading, and he set himself to prepare for its practice, training under Professor John B. Minor of the University of Virginia where he was admitted to the bar in 1892, and practiced law for a number of years with Hon. John Neely, joining the firm, and married John Neely's daughter Elizabeth and had one daughter, Miss Neely Ann Warrington. Strongly attracted by Theosophy in 1896, under Mr. Alexander Fullerton, then the American General Secretary, Warrington joined the Theosophical Society of Adyar, India. When he retired from active law practice in 1911 in order to give himself wholly to theosophical work, in which he soon rose to a position of leadership within The Society.

In 1905 he was employed by Colonel Olcott, the President of the Theosophical Society, to aid in obtaining the Fuente bequest in Cuba; and, incidentally, spent a month there in close personal touch with the Colonel himself.

In 1906 he attended his first Convention (in Chicago) and was one of the little handful to take a strong and successful stand there in the fight for true Brotherhood in the Society. By 1907 he had been appointed the Corresponding Secretary of the E.S. for North and South America.

In 1910 he went to California, where in 1912, he was made General Secretary of the American Section, Krotona thus becoming the American Headquarters for both the Theosophical Society and the Esoteric School. With generous assistance he founded the Theosophical center in Hollywood known as the Krotona Institute, of which he has since been the leading spirit, as well being the editor of *The Theosophic Messenger* and of *The American Theosophist*.

In 1922 returning from Australia he accompanied J. Krishnamurti and J. Nityananda to Ojai Valley in California, which formed the basis of Krishnamurti's interest in the Valley, and for later developments in making this his permanent home, and for holding periodic Star Camps. By 1924, with Dr. Besant's approval, Mr. Warrington ordered the Hollywood Krotona estates to be sold and the center removed to Ojai Valley with the view of great beauty, where it is now located on a lovely site of a mid-valley hill, or ridge, chosen by Mr. Warrington, and with the help of his friend Frank Mead, then head of the Ojai Valley Company. Warrington then became a member of the American Federation of Human Rights, and numerous other progressive organizations. He served as a member of the advisory board of the Ojai branch of the Bank of America as well as Lodge President.

Although Krotona has never grown into the scope and importance Mr. Warrington's day-dreams pictured for it, yet it has rendered valuable service and promises greatly for the future.

In 1928, upon the nomination of the President and the confirmation of the General Council, Mr. Warrington became the Vice-President of the Theosophical Society, relinquishing the Corresponding Secretaryship to Miss Marie Poutz, his able assistant.

In the autumn of 1931 he was called to Adyar because of the continuing illness of the President, Dr. Besant. There he represented her in preparing the annual reports for the years 1931 and 1932 and at her death, on September 20, 1933, there fell upon him, as Vice-President, the duty and responsibility of the Presidential Office. For the period of nine months provided in the constitution for the choosing of a new President he served in that capacity. He was also editor of *The Theosophist* writing the "Watch Tower Notes" during the many months of interregnum while the world-wide election of a new president took place. For twenty-one years he was Dr. Besant's active agent for the Western Hemisphere in the Esoteric School of the Society. His writings include chiefly magazine articles and editorials, and the article on "Theosophy and Occultism" in the *Encyclopedia Americana*, which he was commissioned to write by the publishers soon after he came into the Society in 1896. He is a thirty-second degree Co-Mason.

In his passing on June 16, 1939, at 4:50 p.m. at his residence of old man's disease, or rheumatism the Society lost a stalwart and courageous supporter, its leaders a loyal comrade and thousands of individuals throughout the world a counselor and friend.

The real record is written, however, not alone in pages of Theosophical history, but in the lives he inspired to take up some part of the work for which he gave the utmost that he had; not in executive achievement alone, but in giving and creating unwavering loyalties to the Theosophical Society.

Krotona Hall was filled with friends at 3:30 on Saturday afternoon, June 17, when funeral rites were conducted for Mr. Albert P. Warrington, age seventy-three. Masses of gladiolus in delicate shades glowed at the base of tall candles which lighted the improvised altar in the east of the Hall. At the foot of the steps rested the casket, covered with a blanket of red carnations and lavender sweet peas, the tribute of the trustees of Krotona Institute. The Rt. Rev. Charles Hampton, Regionary Bishop of the Liberal Catholic Church, and for decades a close friend, officiated at the service which was adapted for the occasion, sounding the keynote of hope and joy, and establishing an atmosphere of peace and trust and inspiration which was tremendously heart lifting. Rebecca Schuyler Eichbaum, accompanied by Elizabeth Price Coffey, sang favorite solos: "O God Our Help in Ages Past" and special words arranged to a portion of "Finlandia" by Sibelius. Miss Marie Poutz, co-worker with Mr. Warrington for over thirty years, delivered a brief eulogy, touching in its sincerity, as she described the life just closed as one that had been lived perfectly. The body was taken to Ivy Lawn crematory in Ventura, where final brief rites were performed.

The pall bearers were Eugene Munson, Dr. Pieter K. Roest, Harold Kirk, Vernon Hill, V.C. Eicher, and E.T. Lewis. The Reverend Thomas Talbot of Hollywood assisted Bishop Hampon in the service.

From 1939, owing to war conditions, and the death of A. P. Warrington, this brings to a close an era in Krotona's history.

Krishnamurti did not leave Ojai at this time because of the threat of war for the next six years.

Question: How can we solve our present political chaos and the crisis in the world? Is there anything an individual can do to stop the impending war?

Krishnamurti: War is the spectacular and bloody projection of our everyday life, is it not? War is merely an outward expression of our inward state, an enlargement of our daily action. It is more spectacular, more bloody, more destructive, but it is the collective result of our individual activities. So, you and I are responsible for war and what can we do to stop it? Obviously, the impending war cannot be stopped by you and me, because it is already in movement; it is already taking place, though still chiefly on the psychological level. It has already begun in the world of ideas, though it may take a little longer for our bodies to be destroyed. As it is already in movement, it cannot be stopped—the issues are too many, too great, and are already committed. But you and I, seeing that the house is on fire, can understand the causes of that fire, can go away from it and build in a new place with different materials that are not combustible, that will not produce other wars. That is all that we can do. You and I can see what creates wars, and if we are interested in stopping wars, then we can begin to transform ourselves, who are the causes of war.

So, what causes war—religious, political or economic? Obviously belief, either in nationalism, in an ideology, or in a particular dogma. If we had no belief, but goodwill, love and consideration between us, then there would be no wars. But we are fed on beliefs, ideas an dogmas and therefore we breed discontent. The present crisis is of an exceptional nature and we as human beings must either pursue the path of constant conflict and continuous wars, which are the result of our everyday action, or else see the causes of war and turn our back upon them.

Obviously, what causes war is the desire for power, position, prestige, money, and also the disease called nationalism, the worship of a flag; and the disease of organized religion, the worship of a dogma. All these are the causes of war, if you as an individual belong to any of the organized religions, if you are greedy for power, if you are envious, you are bound to produce a society which will result in destruction. So again, it depends upon you and not on the leaders, not on Stalin, Churchill, and all the rest of them. It depends upon you and me, but we do not seem to realize that. If once we really felt the responsibility of our own actions, how quickly we could bring to an end all these wars, this appalling misery! But you see, we are indifferent. We have three meals a day, we have our jobs, we have our bank accounts, big or little, and we say, "For God's sake, don't disturb us, leave us alone." The higher up we are, the more we want security, permanency, tranquility, the more we want to be left alone, to maintain things fixed as they are; but they cannot be maintained as they are because there is nothing to maintain. Everything is disintegrating. We do not want to face these things; we do not want to face the fact that you and I are responsible for wars. You and I may talk about peace, have conferences, sit round a table and discuss, but inwardly, psychologically, we want power, position, we are motivated by greed. We intrigue, we are nationalistic, we are bound by beliefs, by dogmas, for which we are willing to die and destroy each other. Do you think such men, you and I, can have peace in the world? To have peace, we must be peaceful; to live peacefully means not to create antagonism. Peace is not an ideal. To me, an ideal is merely an escape, an avoidance of *what is,* a contradiction of *what is.* An ideal prevents direct action upon *what is,* which we will go into presently, in another talk. But to have peace, we will have to love, we will have to begin not to live an ideal life, but to see things as they are and act upon them, transform them. As long as each one of us is seeking psychological security, the physiological security we need—food, clothing and shelter—is destroyed. We seek if, if we can, through power, through position, through titles, names—all of which is destroying physical security. This is an obvious fact, if you look at it.

So, to bring about peace in the world, to stop all wars, there must be a revolution in the individual, in you and me. Economic revolution without this inward revolution is meaningless, for hunger is the result of the maladjustment of economic conditions produced by our psychological states—greed, envy, ill will, and possessiveness. To put an end to sorrow, to hunger, to war, there must be a psychological revolution. and few of us are willing to face that. We will discuss peace, plan legislation, create new leagues, the United Nations and so on and on, but we will not win peace because we will not give up our position, our authority, our monies, our properties, our stupid lives. To rely on others is utterly futile; others cannot bring us peace.

No leader is going to give us peace, no government, no army, no country. What will bring peace in inward transformation which will lead to outward action. Inward transformation is not isolation, is not a withdrawal from outward action. On the contrary, there can be right action only when there is right thinking, and there is no right thinking when there is no self-knowledge. Without knowing yourself there is no peace.

To put an end to outward war, you must begin to put an end to war in yourself. Some of you will shake your heads and say, "I agree," and go outside and do exactly the same as you have been doing for the last ten or twenty years. Your agreement is merely verbal and has no significance, for the world's miseries and wars are not going to be stopped by your casual assent. They will be stopped only when you realize the danger, when you realize your responsibility, when you do not leave it to somebody else. if you realize the suffering, if you see the urgency of immediate action and do not postpone, then you will transform yourself; peace will come only when you yourself are peaceful, when you yourself are at peace with your neighbor. [1]

Dr. Pieter Roest

---

[1] Krishnamurti, J., *The Collected Works of J. Krishnamurti*, Volume V, 1948-1949, Kendall Hunt Publishing Co., "Second Talk, in Bangalore", India, July 11, 1948, pp. 14-16.

Chapter IX
1940

Because of the War, it was not possible to travel outside India, so the President, George Arundale and Shrimati Rukmini remained in the country. All documents, especially those which were marked "Private" such as E.S. papers, were being censored by the government of India.

Miss V.K. Maddox of Sydney, Australia, was the leading exponent of Masonry especially in its theosophical interpretation, for she was for some years Private Secretary to Bishop Leadbeater.

Yet another school appears on the horizon called "The New Age School", founded by Mrs. Ruby Pitkin from Belleville, New Jersey. It was to be on 110 acres donated by Mr. Harden, a West Coast theosophist. Instead, his wife gave the land to the Theosophical Society at Wheaton. Ruby had been working with Mr. Sidney A. Cook's approval and cooperation, for the establishment of this school at Wheaton with no cooperation in sight. It was an attempt to provide a place where new age children might live and develop in the proper atmosphere. All rooms were to be spacious and sunlit. Children of both sexes, of the ages six to fourteen inclusive were to be accepted, maintaining an ideal home atmosphere. Diet was strictly vegetarian, and was supervised by a competent dietitian. The tuition was $65 a month. Since Wheaton turned down the school project, Ruby looked at property in the hills overlooking the Pacific, Santa Monica, California. We have no other information at the present time regarding its outcome.

C. Jinarajadasa has a great deal to say regarding the War, although he says it is difficult to say it all briefly. So he published several booklets "The War—*And After*". The booklets contain his viewpoint, presented to fellow theosophists. The following letter was found within one of the booklets.

March 20 1940

Dear Fellow-Member:

When I received from Mr. Jinarajadasa a copy of this booklet, I was impressed by its splendid sweep and perspective and his own breadth of vision. He recounts for us important happenings in the Society's history and places each in true relationship so that their significance in the Great Plan becomes clear. In the light of these, present world events become more intelligible and a right position and attitude are indicated. The work of the Theosophical Society stands forth in its greatness—something so much bigger than we ordinarily think of it in our small member activities. Here is vision regarding our work. Yet by our membership we have contributed to this greater work and in that membership we are privileged.

This all seemed to me so valuable that it is sent directly to each member. You will welcome, I believe, this important clarifying statement of Mr. Jinarajadasa. Theosophists, bringing their understanding of the Ancient Wisdom to bear upon the world situation and knowing that out of it a new world will emerge, have a very definite responsibility to the future that can be fulfilled only by right thinking, feeling and action in the present. In the midst of a vastly complex world condition drawing us in many different directions, we all wish to see more clearly. That Mr. Jinarajadasa's 'The War—*And After*" enables us to do.

The booklet is sent with the hope that every member who welcomes and finds it illuminating will send a contribution towards its cost. Extra copies may be purchased from The Theosophical Press.

I trust that you will find inspiration in it, as well as encouragement and new hope for the future.

Faithfully yours,
Sidney A. Cook
National President

The following letter was written by Julia K. Sommer, regarding "Education" under the Theosophical World University in America.

It was published in the collective works by D.D. Kanga, M.A., I.E.S., as managing Editor, Physical Science Section, "Journal of the University of Bombay", *Where Theosophy and Science Meet*. The scheme of the book is in four parts; Nature, Man, God, and some practical applications.

Easter,
March 24, 1940

Dear Co-Worker,

 At last my educational monograph, which was accepted by our leaders at Adyar and included in the 4th Vol. of *Where Theosophy and Science Meet*, has arrived and the enclosed is your copy. In it I have endeavored to show that our educational ideals, as a thoro study of Theosophy reveals, are in harmony with the best and most advanced educational principles revealed by modern scientific research, or approaching a harmonious point of union.

 The monograph alone is not a complete exposition of Theosophical teachings concerning education, nor can it be regarded as a textbook on education. It lacks the practical application of the principles as outlined. I have in mind the writing of an addition to it in which I shall endeavor to show how these principles should be carried out in a school system, the home, or a private school. Extra copies may be had by members at 25 cents each, while they last. No further copies then obtainable.

Most cordially ours,
Julia K. Sommer, chairman

The following letter is a reply from C. Jinarajadasa while he was in London to a worker at Krotona in the Esoteric School, who has the privilege of addressing E.S.T. groups, and asks if he can discuss in them Krishnamurti's teachings. This is C. J.'s reply.

April 5 1940

London

The E.S.T. stands for a certain definite attitude to life which must be kept constantly before its members. The School is a body of organized WORKERS for the service of humanity. There are necessarily many requirements or those who desire to serve. The particular requirements which the E.S. emphasizes may be summed up in the phrase, "The world problem is the individual problem."

For, the individual is expected to discover his possibilities of highest service by expanding his mind and making it a mirror of the Divine Mind. Therefore, the knowledge gathered by the Masters through millennia of discovery, and stated today in the Theosophical scheme of evolution, must be carefully and urgently studied by him, if he is to be successful in service. Through such intellectual and intuitional grasp of the great scheme, the individual is inspired to see for himself how to work at his personal reorganization and purification. In order to assist him, the Great Teachers offer Themselves as ideals of the work which is to be done. For each Adept is fundamentally a mirror of an ideal of service. In addition, and under certain conditions, a Master is willing to train as apprentices those who show, by life and by pledge, that to them "the world problem is the individual problem."

There is, however, another angle to this great problem of service. It is the reflex of what I have stated, and is summed up in Krishnaji's phrase, "The individual problem is the world problem." That, too, is a correct statement of the relation between the two problems, but seen from an angle opposite to that which is represented by the E.S. Yet, if a person honestly and with true purity of heart works at his individual problem, having no resentment or criticism of others at the way they work at their problems, such an individual will presently discover his unity with all who suffer, and he will then dedicate himself to the healing of the world. It is with this thought that Krishnaji concludes his KINGDOM OF HAPPINESS:

"There you will find the Eternal Refuge, the Eternal Truth; and there you will lose the identity of your separate self; and there you will create new worlds, new kingdoms, new abodes for others."

So long as the "goal" is that vision of "for others", it does not matter in which way the idealist states the solution of the two problems—the individual and the world.

The chief duty of the E.S, member is—if he has any belief in the Masters as the Directors of Evolution, and if the idea of working under Them attracts him, and there is no other reason why he should be in the E.S.—to understand the work which the Masters are doing, and to train himself to give his contribution to that work. This does not mean that there are no other possibilities of spiritual growth, outside of this particular career within the E.S.

For instance, there are thousands of Gurus or teachers in India who gather disciples around them, offering to conduct them to Moksha or Liberation. They all stress in various terms the urgency of the individual problem as the key to Liberation. The E.S. has no quarrel with them, but it concentrates its energies to help a selected band ALONG ITS OWN SPECIAL LINE, which is to lead them to the presence of the Masters.

E.S. members are aware of my attitude to Krishnaji's teachings, how I have advised such as feel drawn to them to study them and gain what help they can from them. But I do not desire in any way that there should be an imposition on any to study his teachings. The teachings of the Lord Buddha also emphasize the individual problem, and the individual is warned of the pitfalls of ceremonies—there were no organizations in those days—and how he must rely on no one, not even his Guru. But I do not think that E.S. members will gain in the work, which they need to do for the growth of their character, by my insisting that they should study Buddhism rather than the teachings of Bhakti of the Gita. On these matters I want to leave members alone. But while they are within the E.S., their chief task is to assist in certain ACTIVITIES; and since character is essential as an instrument of action, the E.S. gives a certain training. This training, however, does not exclude every possible help which they can get from the teachings of the Lord Buddha, Sri Krishna, Jesus Christ, or any other Teacher, and today from Krishnaji himself.

It is because I have recognized the value of Krishnaji's teachings to all sincere idealists that I advise a person interested in Krishnaji NOT TO ATTEMPT TO UNDERSTAND HIM THROUGH THE MIND OF ANOTHER. There is an Italian proverb that "traduttore a traditore"—"translator is traitor", which to my mind applies to Krishnaji's teachings. For he has a very lofty standpoint which must be understood primarily by the intuition; if that standpoint is filtered through the medium of another's mind, it is difficult for the seeker to contact Krishnaji's mind directly with his intuition. Moreover, in the process of picking up Krishnaji's ideas through the mind of another, there is necessarily misunderstanding. That unfortunately is what has happened in various countries, where enthusiastic followers of Krishnaji, taking up what he has said about not being entangled in organizations, have definitely set to work to smash the Theosophical Lodge of the place in the name of Krishnaji's teachings.

I do not want members in the E.S. AS GROUPS to study his teachings, though I do advise those drawn to him to read and study them, each for himself. I have consistently in India urged Krishnaji's band of workers to flood the country with his literature, translating his teachings into the Indian vernaculars, so that the minds of hundreds of thousands of men and women who cannot read English can directly contact his thought.

I know fully how greatly his standpoint is required to supplement the other standpoints, and how thousands will be awakened to a new vision by Krishnaji. There is plenty of room within our Theosophical studies for Krishnaji's standpoint, for there is only one Wisdom of the Ages and not two. But unfortunately, as you know, he, and more particularly his followers, will not allow any room whatsoever for the Theosophical standpoint.

I think that such an exclusion of Theosophy from a new presentation of Truth is inevitable. The Buddha as He emphasized His message, excluded Hindus, though He did it in a gentle way which gave offence to none; Christ had no place in His outlook for the discovery of Reality characteristic of Greece. Each new presentation meets a definite need of the age; it is intended to push the million a few steps onwards to the higher life. But Theosophy is not the presentation for one particular age; it embodies what is needed for all ages. While there are truths in Theosophy for all, even children, yet its full inspiration is for the few, whose hearts and minds long, not for any personal fulfilment, but to know Truth IN ITS ENTIRETY and to live by that Truth for the fulfilment not of the individual alone, but of all. Theosophy is a science, philosophy and ethic of the universe as one whole; the teaching given by a great Teacher at any one time is a religion, philosophy and ethic of the individual and for the individual. There really is no contradiction to "one who knows", as is the Upanishad phrase.

It is true that no statement has been made by Krishnaji to the effect that the Masters do not exist. But what he has said concerning Them, when questions were asked, have clearly given the impression that, if They exist, They can have no value at all for an individual who is seeking true understanding. Furthermore, I think it is not incorrect to say that he has clearly given his listeners to understand, that those who pin their faith on the existence of Masters, and on the guidance to be received from Them, are utterly deluded and are going on a wrong path. And his representatives particularly—for though he states that he has no disciples, there are those who have taken upon themselves to be his mouthpiece—have pointed the finger of scorn at us, members of the E.S., because we do believe in the Masters.

To sum up, I do not want the teachings of Krishnaji to be made the point of discussion or even study within E.S. Groups. For there will inevitably be disputes, with the result first of misunderstanding his thought, and second, of creating unnecessary feeling among the students. For it is a strange fact that those who accept Krishnaji's ideas with enthusiasm are very impatient of any other standpoint.

I give my sincere wishes always to anyone who will study Krishnaji's teachings; and if the study makes him leave the E.S. I have no criticism. But as said before, it is the private and personal study, aiming directly to contact Krishnaji's thought with the intuition, which will be more fruitful, than listening to another's exposition of what Krishnaji means. In that sense it is indeed true that Krishnaji can never have any "followers". C. Jinarajadasa

Because of the War, Marie Poutz reminded the members of the Esoteric School, that each one had his duty at this solemn hour in the history of our country when at last we also are doing our share in this fighting for the cause of Light and Liberty.

But she sends a warning as well. "Let not the shadow of hate enter our hearts and minds. There are many shades of the emotion of hate, from actual hatred to ordinary ill-will, and hate binds as much as love. Any such feeling therefore binds us to those who at the present time are the agents of the forces of retrogression, and makes us co-workes with them and channels for their hate. Don't think of them, leave them to Those who guide evolution and will know how to deal with them".

Since the War, C. Jinarajadasa reminded all E.S. members how things are so uncertain just now, and he feels that he must send out definite instructions as to their duty as E.S. members at this time of crisis.

> In the war, no single member of the Esoteric School can be 'neutral'. He who is not for the Masters is AGAINST Them; there is no middle point for the waverer, who wants to suspend his judgment. He can be neutral, he can suspend his judgment, but only OUTSIDE the School, not while a member of it. This is definite, and it is a waste of time to discuss the matter.

Since this was a crisis, when the future progress of mankind for several thousand years was in the balance, the E.S. members must give all they can to those who are battling against the forces of evil.

Marie Poutz trusted that those who were either "neutral" or "against" the Plan as indicated by the Outer Head would honestly return their papers and be neutral outside the School.

The below message was given to Anita Henkel from Dr. Arundale when she left Adyar after two years work there. After returning to Los Angeles, she stopped at Lodges all over the Section and gave them this Message from Dr. Arundale.

> July 9 1940
>
> My full and affectionate comradeship with you all, brethren of mine, in these great days, unique in the new life they are unleashing for the world, unique in the opportunities they offer to each one of us of helping to steady our world on its onward and upward course when the forces of evil would shatter it into pieces.
>
> Thank God, I say, for Theosophy.
>
> Thank God, I say, for the Theosophical Society. With these there is Light abundant, without them our way would be far less bright, our duty far less clear. With them we have certainty and peace.
>
> God bless you all and strengthen you.
> George S. Arundale

A brief history of the American Section of the Esoteric School.

Before the Second World War the American Section had all of Latin America, Central America and South America.

When the Germans infiltrated with an E.S. spy in Bolivia, the American E.S. was investigated by the F.B.I. and they could no longer keep contact with South America.

Then Bro. Raja (C. Jinarajadasa) who was then the O.H. separated the American E.S. Division from South America, and gave each country a Corresponding Secretary. Colombia and Peru remained with North America.

Cuba which formerly belonged to the American E.S. was separated in 1952 or 1953 with Col. J. Cruz Bustillo as Corresponding Secretary.

By 1941 Sidney A. Cook reminds the members at Convention that "Only two things could cause the Society to fail: neglect to do its essential work in the true spirit of its purpose, or lack of management of its affairs. Either would be fatal."

A historic structure not yet a landmark in the Ojai Valley is the famous Oak Glen stagecoach daily stop from Ventura for twenty years. William and Mary McKee, builders and owners of Oak Glen from 1874 to 1885, and Benjamin and Mary Gally, owners and operators from 1885 to 1940 when it was known nationally as Gally Cottages, was the first health resort in the Ojai Valley.

It was the first place in the Valley to serve ice cream. The 240 Gridley Road property was built as a retreat for invalids who marveled at the healing benefits of Oak Glen. Later, Mr. Gally, who ran two stagecoaches a day to Ventura and one a week to Santa Barbara for his patrons refurbished it as a sanitarium.

Oak Glen is also where a tradition of golf resorts got its start in the Ojai Valley. In 1898 golf links were opened on forty acres of Oak Glen land where you could play for fifteen cents for a half day, a quarter for a whole day and $1 for a week's golf on the six-hole course.

In the late 1940's Sarah Peacock Rogers owned the property and the golf course acreage was subdivided and sold. When Sarah Rogers died in the 1960's a gift of the property created the Rogers-Cooper Memorial Fund.

> The educational work that fell to my lot to attend to some years ago keeps me as busy as if I were earning my own living still. The work it entails and the necessary housework where I live at Krotona, fill my days and often evenings so that I have very little spare time for added work. Also, my income from a small pension as a retired teacher, while it allows me to do this bit of service for the educational world, is not sufficient to pay for help in the way of secretarial work or housework. All this by way of introduction and explanation of why I shall have to cease sending Christmas cards to my friends beginning with this year 1941.
> This does not mean that I shall forget them.
> Julia K. Sommer,

From all over the globe, since the passing of Dr. Besant, and C.W. Leadbeater, members of the E.S. claim to receive directions, and instructions from them. Another warning has to go out from C. Jinarajadasa for all E.S. members.

A Warning

> Sometimes it is through some inner or psychic communion, and at other times through a spiritualistic medium. Not so long ago Brother Besant was said to be giving in London teachings through two mediums—in each case, of course, a different "Dr. Besant".
>
> Any member who attempts to communicate with them through a medium or any other form of spiritualism will lay himself open to expulsion from the School. Our teachers when living never believed in spiritualistic communications as a source of knowledge; and, since death makes little difference to them so far as their ideas are concerned, I feel sure they never communicate in any such manner, and that all such supposed communications are false. Some dead or living entity on the astral plane is giving a communication, masquerading as one of our Teachers, with the best of intentions, it may be.

> With reference to any personal inner or psychic communion with them by a member, all I can say is: Such a communion may be true, or it may be no more than a hallucination. But no member of the School may give to another person any such communication as "a message from Dr. Besant," or as "a direction from Bishop Leadbeater". Where such claims are made, they should be completely ignored. And where any attempt is made to influence any Lodge of The Society with such occult messages; the attempt must be resisted vigorously. C.J.[1]

Why does one what to waste his energy on such dangerous games? The author knows several people who claim they are receiving astral communications from J. Krishnamurti since his death. Believe me, when we say that the body has gone, "the spark has entered into the flame", you are not contacting the mind of J. Krishnamurti. When one is truly living the teachings, there is no need for communications or communion with the dead. If you should receive grandiloquent spiritualistic communications, use your commonsense, and do not be carried away by the fact that the statement happens to be a personal statement, that it is addressed to you or that it flatters you. Do not be carried away, it is a dangerous thing, and along that very line many promising people have been shipwrecked. You may think you are advanced, and cannot be led astray, but the sad case is where such communications have led to total loss of intellect. But in the ultimate every man must stand by himself, and it must be your commonsense which is your final guide in all occult matters, as it should be in all matters of the physical plane.

The following reprint of a warning given by Dr. Besant years ago is timely for today, for several people recently have come to my attention where E.S. members in spite of all warnings, have been dabbling in practices which have already done harm to some of them. On May 24, 1931, Dr. Besant told C. Jinarajadasa to remind the E.S. members who wanted to develop psychism, "They like to be clairvoyant and such things; they like to hear about the

---

[1] Jinarajadasa, C., *The Disciple*, "A Warning", July, 1939, n13, New Series), p.266.

Masters. *But they won't pay the price.*" Whether they have done so deliberately or through forgetfulness of the rules, the result is the same. Such practices, meditations, concentration on psychic centres, invocations and affirmations, automatic writing, etc., whether given by an organization, an individual teacher, in a class, in a book, by some entity on the inner plane parading as a Master, are specially prohibited in the Esoteric School.

> Instructions on Meditation are like the instructions of a professor to a student who is engaged in some practical form of science in which by doing a thing ignorantly he might do damage to himself, his professor, and other people who may be in the building. It is quite obvious that if you are dealing with certain forces of Nature of which the results are far greater than those of the physical plane, you cannot turn people loose and say, "Meditate as you like". Any one who does not like to follow out the instructions on Mediation must not belong to the E.S. at all. It causes certain pranic currents to move in a particular direction, in certain channels in the physical body, and if you leave these to rush about anywhere, you may do yourself serious physical harm, the kind of harm it is almost impossible to remedy.
>
> I have come across several people who are experiencing certain things they should not experience and would not experience if they had not followed wrong lines. There are certain books written by an American which start people along lines of meditation, often based on the Tantras. There is a good deal in the Tantras which is useful, but there are also a number of ways of meditating which are exceedingly dangerous, and if an ignorant person takes these out and makes a hash of them and then publishes them to the world, it is no wonder the public get uncomfortable results.
>
> In Raja Yoga the attempt is made to quicken the growth of consciousness by working on the cerebrospinal system of nerves— never on the sympathetic system. The sympathetic system is much easier to arouse; almost anyone who chooses to fix attention on certain parts of the body can start that working. The sympathetic system used to be the only one. On top of that the vertebrate, the cerebrospinal system developed, and it is a retrogression in evolution to arouse the sympathetic system by turning your thoughts in that direction, especially in Meditation where prana follows the thought

and flows along the nerves. By doing that you make it more active. We have finished with that at present, and we leave to it the management of all our vital machinery; the beating of the heart, for instance, and the breathing of the lungs, the working of the whole digestive system.

The centre of that system for its effective working is in the solar plexus. One of the most dangerous things you can possibly do—it is comparatively easy—is to stimulate again any organ in the body which has passed out of consciousness, of conscious control, in the great evolution which lies behind us. All these organs at one time were within the conscious life of the creature. We, having outgrown that stage, and having with the development of mind enormously increased the power of the cerebrospinal system, our way of evolution is to continue along that line with the fuller knowledge of natural laws that is ours, and with control or (awareness) of the thought that works through it and that can be turned to its more rapid development. From that area we ought not to go.

The solar plexus is peculiarly refractory in nervous diseases, to which it sometimes gives rise. There are certain symptoms which are at once recognizable as due to working on the sympathetic nervous system; that always brings about certain definite results, and it is almost impossible to stop it when once it has been set going. The trouble generally shows itself at first by some slight disorganization of the digestive regions or in a certain irritability of the nervous system generally, and is often accompanied by a great sense of fear. The person does not exactly know of what he is afraid; sometimes he is unable to sleep at night, in the dark, and has a general feeling of fear and a kind of shrinking. That is perfectly simple, and might be got over by an intellectual effort. It means that he is becoming slightly awakened on the astral plane, and can be affected by certain beings on that plane. And, as a large number of these are sub-human, and are extremely hostile to ordinary human beings because of their destructive nature, it is obvious they are trying to frighten people away from the astral plane; they do not want them there.

You may have that to some extent, if you are sensitive, without having done anything to the solar plexus. The only remedy is to think of yourself as above it all, and try to realize that the beings who cause the sense of fear cannot possibly injure you, unless you choose to let them. Say to them: "Well, you are sub-human, and I am human: the powers of the soul are much more developed in me than in you." Then put it quietly aside. But supposing it has gone farther than that, then the disorganization that has come about through entering that realm by an illegitimate way it is almost impossible to get rid of. I have come across many instances of it principally caused by following Hatha Yoga practices. When that has gone a little farther it creates a condition of general nervousness which is very distressing. That is why, in the Masters' School, They disapprove wholly of this line of evolution. That is why I ask you not to pay the smallest attention to books which speak about meditation on the solar plexus. To do that is to run the danger of very seriously injuring your bodies. And I really cannot help you if you do.[2] Annie Besant

It is not necessary to travel to India because one has heard the rumor of an Occult School can be found within the Theosophical Society. One has to be very cautious, for it is very rarely that the door to this occult relationship with a Master, which was then called Chelaship can be opened as it had been through the Esoteric School in the beginning started by H.P.B. in 1875. When H.P.B. passed away in 1891, it went through many changes quickly. By the year 1894 divisions began to appear. In 1895 the division between Mr. Judge on the one side and Dr. Besant on the other, became very marked. There is a great difference between occultism and spirituality. It is important not to give teachings on occultism, but to give practical advice and encouragement concerning little things, little acts of daily actions and reveal that beauty in hourly living. We can observe that today there is a great change taking place. This change is not due to the fact that the fundamental principles have changed with regard to secrecy in occultism, but to the unusual situation in the history of humanity. The Theosophical Society was a pioneer to break up the hard materialistic thought and make new trails. No occult school, nor the Masters are going to lift us out of our particular place of distress and give us a vicarious salvation, nor are They like the gurus in India who make us grow merely because we have come to them

---

[2]Besant, Annie., *The American E.S.T. Bulletin*, American Division E.S.T., n77, May, 1941, p.10-13.

and serve them. There may be many organizations teaching plenty of occultism, but of the wrong kind. We need to ask the question, if it appeals to the selfish element in men, saying that the occult world is a place from which you are to gain more things for yourself, and a great deal about your own unfoldment is concerned, or the reward, you can be sure that is not the *Path* on which you will find truth. There are certain qualifications required, that is an intense *unselfishness* which the Secret Science depicts, and the attitude to mankind and its problems, which are our problems.

Krishnamurti said; "if I hadn't been a speaker, I would have been a gardener."[3] Could it be, because it is reported that the Lord Maitreya is said to have a beautiful garden, and takes time talking to His gardeners while attending to His roses and plants. One first has to inquire are we capable of remaining in one of these greater magnetic auras, even for a comparatively short period of time. From the author's point of view, those great Personages are blinding as a flash of brilliant pure white Light. We cannot stand in Their presence until we are as a child, innocent and pure. We still have not understood our vices, brutality, violence, avarice, greed, selfishness and all of the other things which go with it.

What would it be like to travel and live in the presence with such a being as Krishnamurti? One record on file is from a letter Byron Casselberry wrote to his wife, Mignon, in 1935 while on tour in Mexico with Krishnamurti.

He said in one of his letters:

> I have found out that traveling with Krishnaji is no job for anyone who is looking for a peaceful life. Not that the traveling and the work in themselves amount to so much. All that is quite ordinary, as such things go. It is the inward shaking up that I mean. One must stay awake, and wide-awake, or something not very pleasant is likely to happen. There are moments of ecstasy, and of black despair. Everything inwardly in intensified. All one's moods

---
[3]Coyne, Alasdair, Pine Cottage Gardener since 1978, "Foundation Focus", Volume IX, issue 1of 2, August 2011, p.3.

are more potent to make one see this anew. One has to be careful to keep one's thoughts alert and away from silly notions of hurt feelings, pride, loneliness, sex, and innumerable things. I don't mean "away" in the sense of control, but in the sense of knowing what you are feeling and thinking in the moment of feeling and thinking it. Otherwise the blind feeling whips up into a storm in no time that can seriously affect one's physical health. The storms come even when you are awake; but then one rides on the crest of it instead of being almost shattered under the full weight and fury of a conflict in which there is no perception to give one pause. Conflicts with awakened interest are marvelously clarifying, like a thunderstorm on a hot, breathless day; but conflict that overtakes the mind when it is lost and insensible, is deadly.[4]

After sixty-six years, in September, 1946, a school was opened known as the Happy Valley School by J. Krishnamurti, Rosalind Rajagopal, Aldous Huxley, and Dr. Guido Ferrando located in Besant Meadow along the first leg of Besant Road. The only building that survives is Besant House, which was the Happy Valley School girls dormitory and is now the dormitory for Oak Grove School. The original school has been torn down and rebuilt on the original Happy Valley Foundation property in the Upper Valley. The school was recently renamed "Besant Hill School."

The two houses across the field and across Besant Road were constructed in the 1920s as part of the original Star Camps, when Krishnamurti was still the head of the Order of the Star. They were held from 1926 to 1928. Thousands attended these talks.

One has to read the history of the land in the Meiners Oaks area which once totaled several hundred acres. It extended across the entire Krotona ridge, from Tico Road on the west to the Y intersection on the east, and from central Meiners Oaks on the north to Highway 33 on the south. These lands at one time were owned by Krotona, but today these lands have been purchased by a variety of individuals and groups for the purpose of creating a center

---

[4]Mark Lee, R.E., "Krishnamurti's Tour of South and Central America-1935; KFA, Ojai, CA, April 6, 2002.

to further Krishnamurti's work, first as Theosophy's new "World-Teacher," and later as an independent philosopher and educator. Because Krishnamurti's organization in the early days was called "The Order of the Star Institute," all this land was once known as "Star Land." Today, nearly 150 acres of this land still remains, held in a trust by the Krishnamurti Foundation of America.

It is believed by the Theosophical Society, that the Masters of the Wisdom made it clear that Their object was to make The Society an instrument whereby to change conditions in the world, so that a Universal Brotherhood of all races and peoples might come into being, in spite of mankind being divided by color, creed and culture. It is reported that the Masters promised to give Their Wisdom and Their aid so long as theosophists worked for Brotherhood.

We can observe Krishnamurti emphasizing a new and constructive phase. His discussions and reasoned addresses have always ended with the statement that Love is the only way. Love of one's fellow men, in spite of mankind being divided by color, creed, and culture. Then such is the Brotherhood. Krishnamurti preaches no doctrine, sets forth no teaching, but what he said contains the Truth, and urges us to examine and question what has been accepted blindly.

If we could see that a Love that is genuinely inclusive, many other things fall into place, for the I, or the self ceases to be the object to be served. From Krishnamurti's point of view, "To give up one's prejudices is virtually to give up one's personality". He asks us to try it and see, "It is immensely difficult."

It surely can be on no other basis that Krishnamurti traveled and talked for over sixty years, but to awaken us from dependence on others, and falling to sleep with satisfactions.

According to the teachings of the Theosophical Society, when Universal Brotherhood instead of being a catchword and a slogan is a supreme fact in life, the Society would mirror the model of what the world is to be, even as the members of the Theosophical Society would mirror the model of a perfect citizen, free, abiding always in

Love, courageous in the movement of life in the light of unity and brotherhood.

Here is a gem by A.P. Warrington during 1928.

A Crowning Work

A.P. Warrington

One approaches the review of a book by Mr. Krishnamurti with a feeling of hesitation, not to speak of one's own unworthiness. His latest work, *The Immortal Friend*, has just come from the press of Boni & Liveright, New York ($2.00). In the issuance of this work Mr. Krishnamurti has bestowed upon his readers an inestimable blessing. It is the gem of his productions. Difficult it is to estimate its value, because it will mean so many different things to so many different people. As poetry, it will be measured by certain well recognized standards; these measures will undoubtedly be applied as they always are. The craftsmen have their work to do, and that is the way they do it. But the real test of all of Mr. Krishnamurti's works lies in the application of the higher measures—measures that determine the changes wrought in one's nature by the reading of his words.

Although *The Immortal Friend* is the story of how the Poet-Teacher found his Beloved, in his quest for the happiness that should be eternal, yet the poem may be read as a mystical story of race attainment—that attainment by humanity as a whole which it must ultimately achieve when its goal finally is reached.

The Immortal Friend marks a crowning top in a series of inspiring works by the author on the Path to Liberation. The first was *At the Feet of the Master*. This showed the way to the Teacher. Later, *The Kingdom of Happiness* appeared, disclosing the need for a world of happiness and the way thereto. Then came *The Search*, representing the aspirant eagerly bent upon the search for the eternal; and now we have *The Immortal Friend* revealing in the most exquisite and inspiring lines the mode of attainment; the means whereby the author poured himself out into the very life of the Eternal Companion, the Teacher of Teachers, as "the dewdrop slips into the shining sea."

The poem opens with a disclosure of how the author met his Beloved.

> I sat a-dreaming in a room of great silence,
>
> The early morning was still and breathless,
>
> . . . .
>
> Seated, cross-legged, as the world knows Him,
>
> In His yellow robes, simple and magnificent,
>
> Was the Teacher of Teachers.
>
> Looking at me,
>
> Motionless the Mighty Being sat.

Then follows a great rhapsody of delight over the union that has come.

And then a retrospect showing the stages passed through in lives gone by; the motives that inspired the pleasures that turned to pain; and—much as has been recounted in the story of the Buddha—the nature of his search for God, through many channels, in which one sees how in the answers given by the devotees of these channels, each believed his own path to be the only one. Such were the experiences which the struggling soul of the author passed through before he could say:

> My search is at an end.
>
> In Thee I behold all things.
>
> I, myself, am God.

A multitude of forms, vivified by the Beloved, are implied in the sweep from the highest to the lowest.

> Thou art the naked beggar
>
> That wanders from house to house,
>
> Wearily crying for alms.
>
> Thou art the great of the land
>
> That are rich in possessions and books,
>
> That art the priests of all temples
>
> That are learned, proud, and certain.
>
> Thou art the harlot, the sinner, the saint, and the heretic.

This immortal poem parallels that of *The Light of Asia* in spirit. Those who read it will enjoy a pure delight in the beauty of the lines, in the loveliness of the imagery. But its value lies far deeper than in the enjoyment of that greatest of arts—poetry. There is a note within it that thrills; a note that awakens something within one that plumbs deep; something that arouses an up-springing hope that promises to lead to the true wonders of life.

I am writing this with the call of the press in my ears, but let me close by relating an incident:

If my memory serves me, the opening verses of this poem were read by Mr. Krishnamurti soon after they were written, and under rather striking circumstances. It was at Krotona, in Ojai Valley, and the date was January 11, 1927. A few days before (December, 1926) he had spoken in the Music Room of the Krotona Library—as it happened, standing under the beautiful picture representing Eternal Peace. He had on this occasion shone forth the radiancy of a Presence—a Presence which we believed to be that of the World-Teacher—had shown it so clearly that at the conclusion all left the room in great silence.

Naturally, therefore, as Mr. Krishnamurti stood on the terrace on January 11th facing the valley and its impressive wall of mountains, the audience gathered at his feet were keenly expectant. He read. And, as said, I think the lines were those in the beginning of *The Immortal Friend*.

But on this occasion when all were so expectant, there were those among us who believed that the Presence we felt was not as before, but was that of another—even the Buddha Himself. And then the striking incident occurred.

While Mr. Krishnamurti was reading the closing lines, there fell a few drops of rain. Suddenly, as if out of the mountainside, a rainbow appeared. And then all was over.

When the audience had gone, and while I felt still under the spell of the occasion, a friend came to me and said that he had somewhere read, or heard the tradition, that once when the Lord Buddha had spoken, and the audience had gone, a woman came and begged of Him comfort because of the loss of a relative. Before the Lord replied, He drew her attention to a little sprinkle of rain that had begun to fall, and then to the rainbow that followed. The Lord then spoke to the woman, using this occurrence to show the transitoriness of earthly existence, and the beauty and delight that follow for those who understand.

And ever after that, it is said, that whenever the Buddha appears in person to inspire the words of true teacher, there falls a sprinkle of rain and appears a beautiful rainbow.[5]

Krishnamurti makes a point and relentlessly drives it home for over some sixty years answering the same questions over and over again. The following very few questions and answers were directed at the theosophists, and can be found in the pamphlet, *Let Understanding Be the Law,* which contains very valuable statements: These statements are alive today as they were back at the time Krishnamurti answered them.

> *Question*: Some people hold that while the World-Teacher has no concern with the founding of a new religion, yet the Bodhisattva Maitreya in His larger Cosmic consciousness is concerned with and supports all religions and creeds.

---

[5]Warrington, A.P., *The Star*, "A Crowning Work", Vol.I, n7, July 1928, pp.11-13.

Krishnamurti: Oh, what a comfortable idea! How you worship words. You are in love with labels and not with Truth. What do you mean by "Cosmic consciousness?" Life? How can you divide Life into the World-Teacher and the Bodhisattva? Oh, you people of little understanding! Do you see what is implied in this question? That which you like you will attribute to the Bodhisattva; that which you do not like to the World-Teacher—or perhaps to Krishnamurti. What do you think yourselves? Where is your understanding after all these years? How you deceive yourselves with all these words! You divide life into the World-Teacher, Bodhisattva, and that which is pleasant is the one, and that which is not pleasant is the other, and if neither suits, then it is Krishnamurti. What has Truth to do with the terms "World-Teacher," "Bodhisattva," or "Krishnamurti?" What has life to do with these names? If you are carried away by my authority now, you will be carried away by some other authority later. You will obey by authority and disobey by authority. You have no understanding in the matter. You want comfort all the time, and you find that comfort in words, in authority, in gods, and in dogmas.

Question: It has also been said that the Christ worked essentially through the Liberal Catholic Church and but a portion of His consciousness manifests through Krishnaji. May we have your opinion on both these points.

Krishnamurti: That which is pleasant you will accept and that which is not pleasant you will reject. Truth, which is life, has nothing to do with any person, with any organization. Friend, you are playing with these things. To you they are not vital but to me they are vital. I am concerned with Truth and with the awakening of the desire in each one of you so discover that Truth. You are concerned with the consciousness of Krishnamurti. How can you tell when you know neither Krishnamurti nor the Christ? I do not know who tells you these things, but how you are all caught up in the lovely designs of words! I am not concerned with organizations. I am not concerned with societies, with religions, with dogmas, but I am concerned with Life, because I am life. You do not want life and the fulfilment of life which is the Truth, but a passing shade of comfort either in this organization or in another, and sweet words and smooth ideas are sufficient for your small understanding. So, friend, by these things you are held. Because you place organizations before life, the authority of another before life, the saying so of another before life, you are caught and strangled... .[6]

Question: It is said that with your coming, evolution is quickened in all beings and that the number of Initiates in the world will be rapidly increased. But you tell us that these stages on the Path are unessential and that Liberation may be attained at any stage of evolution.

Krishnamurti: I say that liberation can be attained at any stage of evolution by a man who understands and that to worship stages, as you do, is not essential. As you have snobbery in the outside world, and pay reverence to aristocratic titles, so you have spiritual snobbery; there is not much difference between the two. So you must develop your understanding and your desire to attain and forget all the stages and the people who are at those stages. Of what value are they to you?

Because you lose sight of the goal of life, because you do not desire urgently, vitally, and strongly to attain it, these stages, with their labels, catch you up and hold you in their bondage... .[7]

Question: Are you the Christ come back?

Krishnamurti: Friend, who do you think I am? If I say I am the Christ, you will create another authority. If I say I am not, you will also create another authority. Do you think that Truth has anything to do with what you think I am? You are not concerned with the Truth, but you are concerned with the vessel that contains the Truth. you do not want to drink the waters, but you want to find out who fashioned the vessel which contains the waters. Friend, if I say to you that I am, and another says to you that I am not the Christ—where will you be? Put aside the label, for that has no value. Drink the water, if the water is clean: I say to you that I have that clean water; I have that balm that shall purify, that shall heal greatly; and you ask me: Who are you? I AM ALL THINGS, BECAUSE I AM LIFE.[8]

---

[6]Krishnamurti, J., *Let Understanding Be the Law*, The Star Publishing Trust, 1928, pp. 18-20.
[7]*Ibid.*, p.14.
[8]*Ibid.*, p.27.

Index

A

Adepts, 6, 261, 267
Adeptship, 51
Adyar Bulletin, 18
Adyar: TS Headquarters, xxvii, 2, 38, 53, 106, 110, 190, 197, 218
Agastya, Rishi, 18-19
Angels, xxiv. 50, 141, 293
Ants, 62
Amma, 146, 248, 257
Aquarius, the Age of, xxvi
Arhat, 93
Aryan, xi, 8
Astral, 65, 118, 127, 242, 264-265, 320-321, 323
Athos, Mount, 104
Atlantis, 26, 295
Atma, 265, 292
Atmic, 264-266, 292
Arnold, Dorothy, 1
Arundale, George, 65, 86, 97, 104, 108, 127, 135, 152, 169, 179 190, 195, 198, 208, 219, 280, 293, 295-296, 311
Arundale, Rukmini Devi, i, 4, 73-75, 77-79, 111, 197, 239-240 239-240, 264, 287, 290, 311,
Arya Vihara, (house, California), 10, 191, 205
Australian Theosophist, 85
Avatars, 6

B

Baba, Meher, 30
Bailey, Alice, xxvi
Bailey, Foster, 23
Banyan Tree, 251
Barsi, Margaret, 112
Bell, Dr. Sanford, 105, 115

Bellamy, Edward, 88
Bennett, A.E., 207-214
Bennett, Reginald, 91
Bergson, 250, 276-277
Besant, Annie, ix, xi, xv, xviii, xxvi, 1, 10, 18, 31, 37, 53, 65, 79, 95, 104, 110, 116, 121, 125, 128, 131, 148, 160, 172, 192, 215, 241, 264, 272, 301, 320
Besant, Digby, 120
Bhakta, xiii
Bharatnatyam, 240
Blavatsky, H.P., ix, xvi, 4, 6, 32, 45, 51, 65, 72, 151, 182, 190, 195,198, 213, 241, 278, 287
Bock, Bill, 283
Borglum, Gutzon, 151
Bose, J.C., 23
Boxell, Lillian, 281
Brain, 16, 21, 39, 85, 171, 266, 303
Brethren, Elder, 1, 37-38, 57, 61, 133, 152, 154, 242
Broadcasting, 2GB, 200, 207-209, 212
Brotherhood of Arts, the, 56
Brotherhood, Great White, 152, 222, 267
Brown, Governor Edmund G., 243
Buddha, Lord, xiii, 13-14, 46, 49, 92, 248, 256, 261-262, 315-316, 329, 331
Buddhism, xiii, 53, 261, 315
Burnier, Radha, I, 31

C

Camberley, 203
Campbell, Kay, 1, 282
Canadian Theosophist, 136, 166
Carpenter, Edward, 23
Casselberry, Byron W., 229, 233, 237, 296, 301, 325
Ceremonials, 60, 141, 255
Cervera, D.R., 231, 233

Chaitra, (full moon), 71
Chan, Charlie, 283
Charter, 68, 281
Chelaship, 17, 324
Chennai, 197, 240, 264
China, 100, 286, 282
Chowdhury, Deviprasad Roy, 166
Church, Antiochian, 196
Churchill, 309
Church, Liberal Catholic, 45, 60, 97, 154, 13, 175, 196, 206, 243, 245, 290, 303, 307, 332
Church, Roman Catholic, xiv
Christ, xiv, xxvi, 13-14, 47, 55, 57, 95-96, 104, 130, 185, 261, 315-316, 332-333
Clark, Will, 205,
Coats, John B.C., 111
Codd, Miss Clara, 98
Coffey, Elizabeth Price, 130, 196, 307
Collected Works of J. Krishnamurti the, 104, 160, 166, 184, 186, 191, 193, 268, 310
Co-Masonic, 130, 136, 154, 173, 175 254, 275, 306
Cook, Sidney A., xxvii, 24, 86, 111, 140, 146, 151, 187, 219, 271, 281, 312, 319
Cooper, Bishop Irving S., 106
Cottage, Pine, 205, 325
Consul, H.M., 207
Couch, Mrs. Maud N., 115, 129
Crematorium, 173, 175-176
Crowe, Miss, 89

D

Damodar, 287
Dawn, Henry W., 243
Demarquette, Monsieur, xv
Devas, xxiv, 50, 142, 293

Disciple, ix, x, xv, 17, 58, 226, 228, 239, 242, 261-162
Discipleship, xxiii, 17, 232, 242, 247-248, 251, 260
Disloyal, xxii
Dharma, 55

E
Eichbaum, Rebecca Schuyler, 130, 196, 307
Eicher, V.C., 307
Elmore, Alex, 112
Emily, Lady, 256
E.R., (Egyptian Rite), 181
E.S.T. Bulletin, 200, 245, 278, 324
Esoteric, i, viii, ix, 31, 83, 127, 168, 194, 246, 264

F
Farley, Richard Blossom, 282, 284
Ferrando, Dr. Guido, 326
Fisher, Rev. S., 173-175
Frei, Mr. H., 1, 201
Fremantle, 169, 173, 210
French, xv, xvii, 35, 196, 287
Forces, Dark, 172, 213
Fullerton, Alexander, 108, 305
Fund, Southern Centre, 224
Fussell, Joseph H., 4, 6, 9

G
Garnsey, Mrs. M.V., 187
Gateway, x, 206
Gandhiji, 22
Gauteri, M. Anthony, 196
Gerard, Frank, 23
Gerard, Mary, 196
Germain, Comte de St., 286
Gil, Adolfo de la Pena, 219, 225, 228, 231, 234

Gilbert, W.S., 240
Gibson, Mrs. Tom, 56
Gita, Bhagavad the, 13, 47, 130, 315
God. Xiii, xiv xvi, xviii, xxi, 2, 8, 26, 41, 50, 69-70, 113, 142, 147, 149, 153,-154, 158, 163, 181, 184,197, 207, 258, 262, 298, 300, 307, 309, 313, 318, 329, 332
Goldy, Mrs., 80, 106
Gray, Mary, 155, 205
Gray, Roland, 205
Greenwood, Donald, 22
Group, Mothers' Research, 193
Gulick, Hervey, 22
Guru, xxiv, 13, 17, 71, 163, 165, 240, 315, 324

H

Hall, George, H., 56, 109, 112, 124, 127, 129, 194, 203, 205, 216. 295, 301
Hall, Grace S., 295
Hallucination, 321
Hampton, Charles, 106, 206, 303, 307
Happy Valley, 10, 125-126, 194, 279, 304, 326
Hearers, Order of, xiv
Heather, Miss Kellet, 171, 176, 189
Helios, 278
Hemisphere, Southern, 212, 214-215, 222, 233
Henkel, Miss Anita, 141, 146, 195, 318
Hierarchy, xii, 11, 19, 45, 52, 65, 145, 215, 217, 253, 265, 286 297
Hilarion, Master, 286
Hill, Vernon, 307
Himalayas, 60, 129
Hindu, xiii, xvii, 14, 18, 53, 55, 65, 122, 142, 160, 181, 197, 316
Hodson, Geoffrey, 16, 18, 55, 296, 300
Holland, C.F., 81, 86, 90, 97, 99, 111, 216, 279-280
Hotchener, Henry, 81, 90, 117, 130, 167

Hotchener, Marie Russak, 110, 117, 130, 135, 150, 278
Huxley, Aldous, 326
Hypocrite, 47-48

I
Illinois, Wheaton, , 85, 106, 111, 187, 193, 195, 244, 250, 311
India, viii, ix, xii,
Ingelman, John, 106
Institute, Krotona, i, iii, v, ix, 10, 31, 125-126
Institute, Ojai Star, 7, 10-11, 25, 82
International Star Bulletin, xxv

J
Jesus, 13, 46-48, 57, 104, 261, 315
Jews, 26, 55, 128
Jinarajadasa, C. J., (Raja), i ix, x-xi, xv, xvii, 11, 18, 23-24, 28, 31-38, 44, 48, 52, 55-56, 72-73, 78-80, 83, 91, 93-94, 97, 112, 144, 122, 128, 130, 132-133, 150, 178, 190, 201, 208, 213-216, 219, 221, 225, 232-233, 237, 239-246, 259-260, 264, 272, 278, 286, 288, 289, 301, 311-313, 317-321
Jinarajadasa, Dorothy, 131, 133-135, 137
John, Apostle, 196
Jones, Carman, 283
Jordan, Robert, 245
Jordan, Sarah, 245

K
Kalashetra, 239-240
Kanga, D.D., 312
Kent, Wilham, 196
Kirk, Harold, 281, 307
King, the, 60, 70, 72, 82, 94, 188, 207, 223-224, 253
Knudsen, A.F., 196
Kuthumi, (Koothoomi), Master, 244
Krauss, Blanche, 22

Krishnaji, xi-xiii, xv-xviii, 7, 12-17, 25, 27, 40, 44-55, 57-61, 70-72, 90-100, 104, 106, 109, 114, 140-145, 147, 152-154, 179-181, 200, 219, 230-235, 238-239, 242, 246-262, 272-276, 286, 288, 314-317, 325, 332

Krishnamurti, J., v, vii-xi, xv, xviii-xxv, 1-2, 6, 11-12, 15-16, 23, 31, 53, 65-67, 72, 85, 91, 97, 101, 103, 105, 109, 129, 139, 148, 152, 157-160, 166, 177, 179, 181-186, 190-194, 198-200, 205, 217, 220, 225, 232-235, 237, 247, 249, 260-268, 272, 282, 285, 294, 296, 300, 304, 308, 310, 313, 321, 325-333

Kundalini, 198, 241-242

Kunz, Dora van Gelder, 22

Kunz, Fritz, 10, 22

Kunz, Miss Minna, 22

L

Layton, Felix, 112

Leadbeater, C.W., ix, xiii, xv, 1-2, 11, 20, 24, 26, 40-41, 45, 48, 52, 55-61, 70-73, 79, 85, 92, 97-98, 101-104, 109, 122, 128-130, 134-138, 140, 153, 166-168, 171-173, 178-179, 198, 201, 219, 222, 238, 251, 262, 274, 287, 311, 320

Lee, R.E. Mark, v. viii

Let Understanding be the Law, 331, 333

Lewis, Muriel Lauder, 193, 196

Liberation, xix, 1-2, 13, 51, 53-54, 60-61, 71, 113, 255

Library, the Huntington Museum, 124

Light on the Path, 248

Lilliefelt, Mr. Theo, 196

Linder, Fred, 31

Lodge, the Ojai Valley Oaks, 23, 195, 295

Logan, Robert, 91, 146, 281, 285

Logos, 39, 143, 113-114, 244, 254

Loma, Point, (Govina), 2-6

M

MacKay, Mr. John, 198, 177, 179-180, 222-223
Mackey, Norma, 112
Maddox, Miss V. Kay, 179, 213, 311
MahaChohan, 19, 39, 141, 150, 214-215, 252, 275, 287
Maitreya, Lord, (the Bodhisattva, the Christ), xii, xxiii, 96, 130, 242, 254, 258, 261-262, 275, 287, 325, 331
Marcault, Professor, J.E., 250, 275-277
Maricopa, 107, 302
Markoff, Mortimer, 196
Mars, 27, 55-56, 62
Martin, Edward, 206-207, 245
Martin, Prestonia Mann, 88
Martin, Rhoda, 245
Mason, David, 107
Masters, x, xiv, xvi-xvii, xix, xxiv, 5-6, 12-13, 15, 19, 23, 27, 34-35, 38, 40-41, 43-46, 49, 53, 60, 66, 71-72, 75, 80, 92-94, 113, 128, 133, 141, 143, 150, 158-159, 163, 190, 199, 203, 213-215, 220, 224, 229, 231, 239, 242, 244, 247-253, 256-257, 260, 262,-263, 265-267, 274-275. 286-289, 294,-297, 301, 314-318, 322, 324, 327
Matthews, Edward M., 290
Manor, The, 90-91, 97, 108, 115, 148, 157, 171
Manu, xi, 20, 26, 128,-129, 155
Manziarly, Mme. De,
Masonic, 29, 45, 60, 119, 169, 172, 237, 311
Mayes, Catharine Gardner, 28-30, 68, 89, 188, 196, 213, 289
Mayes, Sarah C., 22, 25, 30
Mayes, William, 28, 279
McConnell, Ellen, 112
McLean, Tess, 289
Mead, G.R.S., 123-124
Mehta, Rohit, 111
Menon, Krishna, 111
Menon, Sankara, 192

Menzenwerth, Fred, (Werth), 22, 196
Mequillet, Miss, 6
Mercury, 27, 55, 62
Messiah, 184-185
Minnich, Eva, 22
Moksha, 13, 53, 315
Montessori, Madame Doctor Maria, 303
Moore, James D., 84-85, 90, 99
Moore, Thomas, 88
Morton, Rev. Harold, 170, 174-175, 209, 211
Morya, Master, 97, 134, 215, 244, 286-287
Mothers' Bulletin, 193-194
Muhammad, 46
Munson, Eugene, 7, 28, 80, 130, 302, 307
Mussolini, 93
Mysteries, 18, 102, 267, 288
Myers, Capt. Devereux, 194
Myers, Mary, 283

N
Naidu, Sarogini,
Nitya, (Nityananda, Jiddu),
Nirvana, 53, 65, 141, 152, 198
Noall, Eleanor, 293
Noall-Fraser, Hugh, 293
Nordroff, 95

O
Occultism, xiv, xxii, 251, 258, 287-288, 306, 324-325
Ockenden, Nethie, 22-34
Ojai, (California), viii, 1, 6-7, 10-11, 22-23, 25, 30, 55
Olcott, Colonel Henry, xxvii, 15, 92, 132, 190, 305
Ommen, (Holland), 98, 109, 135, 234, 247-248, 255, 261, 272
On the Watch Tower, 91, 93
Ootacamund, ix, 21, 129

Order of the Round Table, 245
Order of Service, 140, 146

P

Parthe, 146
Passmore, Rev. Frank, 105
Perkins, James, S., 280-281
Pigott, Frank, W., 206
Pitkin, Ruby, 311
Plato, 87
Pole, David Graham, 108
Porter, Mrs. 91
Poutz, Marie, 9, 11, 29, 69, 81, 84, 86, 95, 99, 106, 115, 129, 171-172, 177, 179, 200, 203, 231, 244, 246, 281, 306-307, 317-318
Power, R.L., 207
Pragnell, F.C., 109
Press, Rajput, 108
Prest, Miss Irene, 56
Pupils, 17, 32, 71, 101, 182, 232, 237, 274, 288, 299, 301
Purucker, Dr. G. de, 2-6

R

Race, Aryan, xi, 8, 129
Race, Seventh Root, 213, 216, 222, 233
Ragan, Capt. George, 194
Rajagopal, (Rajagopalacharya, D.), xxv, 82, 140, 148, 180-181, 190, 218-219, 225-235, 238, 248, 256, 259, 304, 326
Ram, N. Sri, 71, 73, 108, 120, 127, 132
Ramanujacharya, Shri, xiii
Randall, Mrs., 283
Ranganathan, 120
Ransom, Josephine, iii, 131
Ray, P.C., 23
Ray, Second, xii, 27, 291

Reed, Egmont, 112
Reed, Mignon, 22, 112, 325
Regent, 18-21
Rishis, 6, 18, 199
Robinson, Clyde, 283
Robles, Siete, 109, 245
Rocke, Dr Mary, 216
Roerich, Nicholas, 241-242
Roest, Dr Pieter 141, 145-146, 193, 281, 307
Roest, Mrs. Pieter, 281
Roine, John, 206
Rogers, L.W., xxvii, 6, 24, 98, 125
Rogers, Sarah Peacock, 243, 320
Rogers, Stanley, 24-25
Roof-Talks, 25-26, 290
Roosevelt, Franklin Delano, 86-87, 281
Roosevelt, Theodore, 157, 280
Ros, Monica, 130, 196
Rule, Home, 21, 121-122
Russia, 111, 195, 241-242

S

Samsara, 1
Sanyasins, 130
Sarobia, 281-285
School of the Open gate, 205-206
School, Esoteric, i, iii, xi, xv, 32, 72, 86, 102-103, 122, 124, 136, 150, 172-173, 204. 222, 244, 249, 288, 305-306, 13, 317-318, 322, 324
Schwarz, A., 1, 151, 201
Scouts, Boy, 119, 130, 272
Service, Brothers of, 119
Sexual, 102-103, 192
Shamballa, 5, 20, 212, 216, 222-223
Shankaracharya, Shri, xiii

Shanti 117
Shelvenkar, K.S., 111
Shishya, xv, xvii, 32, 38, 70, 72, 78-79, 102, 150, 274
Shiva Rao, G.B., 135
Smith, Dr. Henry A., 303
Smythe, Mr., 136
Snodgrass, Miss Etha, 221, 281
Sommer, J., 278, 282, 312, 320
Srinivasamurti, Dr., 32, 120, 189
Staggs, Herbert, 6, 55, 99, 281
Star, xi, xx, xxv-xxvi, 7, 10-11, 25, 30, 43, 53, 65, 82, 109, 169, 194, 201, 205, 218, 227, 233, 234-235, 248, 253-258, 306, 326-327, 333
Star, Mystic, 254, 275
Stone, Dr Ernest, 23
Suarez, Mr., 248
Subrace, Sixth xi, 52, 71
Sullivan, Arthur, 240
Sutcliffe, G.E., 123
Sydney, (Australia), 20, 71, 84, 90, 94, 99, 107-108, 111, 115, 133, 157, 168, 173-179, 186, 189-190, 197, 200, 207-213, 222, 224, 233, 254, 256, 274-275, 311
Symbolic Yoga, 198, 290, 293

T

Tagore, 23, 197
Taj Mahal, 206, 245
Talbot, Rev. Thomas H., 106, 307
Telang, Dwarkanath, 123, 128-129, 131, 135, 138
Tesofista, 260
The American Theosophist, xviii, 56, 85, 154, 167, 205, 220, 305
The Disciple, xviii, 79-80, 112, 114, 225, 238, 259, 272, 275, 289, 321
The Essene Order of the Golden Grail,
The Immortal Friend, 328, 330

The Inner Life, 55
The Invincible Light Order, 196
The Lotus Fire, 65, 198, 290, 292
The Messenger, 30
The New Citizen, 280-281
The Ojai, viii, 10, 22-23, 125
Theosophical Worker, 195
The Principles of Education, 198
The Temple's Priestly Order, 196
The Theosophical Messenger, 6, 18, 22, 154
The Theosophist, 5, 9, 18, 26, 28, 30, 55, 57, 70, 85, 91, 93, 104, 132, 136, 148, 150, 152, 168, 189, 195, 219, 238, 281, 306,
The Times, (London), 55, 168, 179, 295
The Young Citizen, 110-111
Tibetan, 23, 286
Tingley, Mrs. K.A., 2, 4
Thones, Mr., 243
Thought Power, 172
Tract, Mercer, 7-8
Tweedie, Bishop, 175

V

Vaivasvata, Lord, xi
Valley, Santa Ana, 7
Van der Leeuw, Johann J., 108, 216, 222-223
Van der Hell, Mrs., 174, 176
Van der Stok, 109
Van Gelder, Melanie, 55
Van Hook, Dr Weller, 108
Vasanta Garden School,
Vasanta Vihar, 148, 247
Vedanta, Vishishtadvaita, xiii
Venetian, Master, 286
Venus, 55, 62

W

Wadia, B.P., 21
Wardall, Max, 81, 130, 140-149, 171, 194
Warrington, Betty, 8, 27, 56, 140, 168, 187, 189-190, 204, 221, 278, 285, 295, 303
Warrington, Miss Neely Ann, 225, 240, 305
Wesak Festival, 101
Williams, Erma, 304
Willson, A. J. 31-33, 73, 83, 92, 95, 118
Wilson, Ruth, 187
Winston, Mrs. Theron (Alice), 196
Woldringh, Conrad, 292-293
Wood, Ernest, 1, 201, 210
World-Teacher, viii, xi, xii-xiii, xxvi, 44-50, 60, 114, 148, 200, 217, 242, 2562, 257, 327, 330, 331-332
World Theosophy, 61, 150

Y

Yoga, Agni, 241
Yoga, Raja, xi, 241, 322

Z

Zalk, Louis, 7, 9, 11, 81-82, 90, 205, 304
Zimmers, Mabel K., 282
Zoroaster, 46

www.ingramcontent.com/pod-product-compliance
Lightning Source LLC
Chambersburg PA
CBHW071649160426
43195CB00012B/1398